Crisis Investing
for the Rest of the '90s

Also by Douglas Casey

The International Man
Crisis Investing
Strategic Investing

Crisis Investing
for the Rest of the '90s

Douglas Casey

A Birch Lane Press Book

Published by Carol Publishing Group

A Birch Lane Press Book
Published by Carol Publishing Group
Birch Lane Press is a registered trademark of Carol Communications, Inc.
Editorial Offices: 600 Madison Avenue, New York, N.Y. 10022
Sales and Distribution Offices: 120 Enterprise Avenue, Secaucus, N.J. 07094
In Canada: Canadian Manda Group, P.O. Box 920, Station U, Toronto, Ontario M8Z 5P9
Queries regarding rights and permissions should be addressed to Carol Publishing Group,
600 Madison Avenue, New York, N.Y. 10022

Carol Publishing Group books are available at special discounts for bulk purchases, for sales
promotion, fund raising, or educational purposes. Special editions can be created to specifications.
For details, contact: Special Sales Department, Carol Publishing Group, 120 Enterprise Avenue,
Secaucus, N.J. 07094

Manufactured in the United States of America
10 9 8 7 6 5 4 3 2 1

Library of Congress Cataloging-in-Publication Data

Casey, Douglas R.
    Crisis investing for the rest of the '90s / by Douglas Casey.
      p. cm.
    "A Birch Lane Press book."
    ISBN 1-55972-177-4 (cloth)
      1. Investments—United States—Handbooks, manuals, etc.
  I. Casey, Douglas R. Crisis investing. II. Title.
  HG4921.C33 1993   92-35971
  332.6'78—dc20   CIP

Contents

Acknowledgments

I'd like to thank the following for their help (in various ways) in making the publication of this book possible:

Michael Baybak, Jim Bennett, Bob Bishop, Jim Blanchard, Darrell Brookstein, Harry Browne, Maggie Carey, Betty Casey, Michael den Hertog, Robert Friedland, Mike Friedman, Bill Gary, Ken Gerbino, Frank Giustra, Bruce Greene, Frank Holmes, Gene Jewett, Ben Johnson, Ian MacAvity, Becky Mangus, Bruce Meadows, Kathy Overton, David Paxton, Chris Petersen, Keith Presnell, Jack Pugsley, Rick Rule, Peter Sepp, Mark and Joanne Skousen.

Special thanks go to Terry Coxon and Ancha Van Eeden for their heroic last-minute editing. And, of course, Hillel Black, my editor at Carol.

Introduction

Roughly once in a decade—the U.S. economy reaches a major turning point. It's possible, at such turning points, to make truly spectacular returns on the right investments and to do so with very little risk. We are again at such a juncture.

Perhaps "crisis" is a better word than "juncture." The Chinese symbol for "crisis" combines two other logograms: "danger" and "opportunity." I have no doubt that the next ten years will offer a greater measure of both danger and opportunity than any decade in the last fifty years.

My two previous investment books, *Crisis Investing* (1979) and *Strategic Investing* (1982), described how to profit from two such turning points that arrived in quick succession. Although those two books are out of print, it's not hard to find copies, since many hundreds of thousands were published. Reading them will help to put this book in perspective.

At the time those books appeared, many of the predictions I made seemed outrageous, and most of the investments I suggested to readers were unpopular. Since many suggestions in this book will sound equally radical, it will be useful if I review the results of the 1979 and 1982 recommendations.

Here is how you would have fared if you had followed the advice in *Crisis Investing*, which was published early in 1979.

- **Buy small energy stocks.** I listed twenty-three stocks selected according to the parameters spelled out in the book. If you had invested $1,000 in each issue, your position would have tripled in value to $69,000 by the end of 1980.

- **Sell bonds.** When *Crisis Investing* went to press, yields on AAA corporate bonds were approximately 9 percent. By 1982 yields had risen to 16 percent and the average bond price had fallen by about 40 percent.

- **Sell real estate.** In 1979, real estate reached one of its cyclical peaks. By 1982 most prices had fallen significantly, pushed down by mortgage rates ranging as high as 18 percent. Real estate sales were off by more than 40 percent.

- **Buy gold and gold stocks.** Gold was $270 an ounce when *Crisis Investing* was published and had reached $850 by January 1980. Gold stocks did even better. Prices of the forty South African gold stocks I listed shot up an average of 600 percent, with most returning more in dividends alone than they had originally cost.

- **Buy silver.** Silver climbed from $6.50 to nearly $50 at its peak in 1980—a profit of more than 700 percent.

- **Prepare for a wave of bank failures.** *Crisis Investing* explained exactly why banks were in trouble (thousands have failed since then), with particular emphasis on the forthcoming S & L disaster, which few anticipated at the time. The book explained why the FSLIC and the FDIC would run out of funds and need to be bailed out.

By 1982, however, it was becoming clear that the economy was embarking on a new course demanding new investment strategies. In many regards, *Strategic Investing* recommended doing exactly the opposite of what *Crisis Investing* advised, although the economic principles it was based on were identical.

Here's what *Strategic Investing* recommended:

Stocks. Nine chapters of *Strategic Investing* were devoted to the stock market. The book asserted that the "bull market of the century" would take place during the '80s. I zeroed in most strongly on Blue Chip New York Stock Exchange stocks and on utilities (which were then yielding 12 to 15 percent in dividends). What happened since is well known.

Gold. Use gold only as insurance against disaster (as a long-term store of value). Forget about it for speculation. Gold was then at $400 and is now around $330.

Gold Stocks. I said sayonara to the South Africans (which subsequently lost 75 percent of their value, and in some cases as much as 96 percent). I strongly recommended the little-known junior North American gold mining companies. These junior gold stocks have been extremely volatile, giving investors two separate 1,000 percent runs (1982–1983 and 1985–1987)—two of the most spectacular gold stock bull markets in history.

Real Estate. Still negative on property, I pegged the bottom at 1984, saying a "new class of millionaires" would be made in the subsequent boom. I was a year off, but close enough to be useful.

Strategic Investing was a better book than *Crisis Investing* because it spoke more to the "why" and "how" of things, which do not change much, rather than to the ''what,'' which changes constantly. Learning to fish is more important than being handed a fish.

Of course neither book was right in all regards. One major error in *Crisis Investing* was the expectation that inflation would go to far higher levels than it did. In *Strategic Investing* I made the same mistake with nominal interest rates. And neither book gave the economy as much credit for resilience as it deserved.

But I was not pretending to be a fortune teller, and I'm not doing so now. What I do, as you will see, is assemble the available data, look at it through the lens of free-market economics, and draw conclusions. If you disagree with the conclusions, you'll be able to pinpoint easily where our thoughts diverge, and why.

Most of the investment recommendations in the 1979 and 1982 books worked out exceedingly well for readers. Of course, my own views on the markets have changed over the last ten years, just as they did in the three years that separated those two books.

WHY THIS BOOK NOW?

The suggestions you'll find here are, almost without exception, actions I myself am now taking, or will take when the time is right. I'm a professional speculator by trade and consider writing only an avocation. The great benefit of writing a book is that it forces you to think out your premises, and the resulting plan of action, in detail. It's hard to be sure things make sense until you've spelled them out on paper. For that reason, even if this book were not intended for publication, I might still have written it much as you see it. It helped crystallize my thinking. I hope it will have a similar effect on yours.

There hasn't been a major sea change in the economy or the markets since *Strategic Investing* was written in 1982, so until now I haven't felt the need to write another book, although I do write a monthly newsletter. Plenty of things could have gone wrong in the '80s, and almost did; but things hung together. The '80s were a wonderful time to be alive, especially if you were long the stock market. But the '80s are gone like the Roaring Twenties, which they resembled. And it's a safe bet that the remainder of the '90s will be totally different.

Now, in many ways, the economic clock on America's wall reads about the same time as it did when I wrote *Crisis Investing*. Many—but not all—of the investments that looked good then again seem to promise spectacular upside potential, with very limited risk, after more than a decade in the dumps. And the problems the economy is facing are far more serious than they were in the late '70s, although, paradoxically, people seem much more complacent. They won't be for long.

HOW TO READ THIS BOOK

This book is divided into three sections. The first portion—chapters 1 through 6—explains why, notwithstanding the '80s boom, we find ourselves at the brink of the

Greater Depression. Little here agrees with the conventional wisdom emanating from Washington, the media, and other mainstream sources.

The second portion—chapters 7 through 28—deals with the various investment alternatives and how to use them as wisely and as profitably as possible. Some, like buying property in the Third World, are exotic. Some, like the use of hedges, in Chapter 8, are usually thought of—incorrectly—as the province of sophisticated professionals. Others, like short selling, gold stocks, and venture capital, can be risky but offer spectacular rewards. If you succeed in making just one of the techniques in this section part of your permanent repertoire, the time you spend with this book will pay for itself 10,000 times over.

The third portion—chapters 29 through 36—deals with the dominant, long-term trends of society itself and is, in effect, a framework in which to put the other two sections. It is somewhat abstract and futuristically oriented, and is the most speculative part of the book; it is also perhaps the most important part.

Reading this book from start to finish would be ideal, but each chapter can stand on its own. So don't be afraid to start wherever the spirit may move you.

Throughout the book I explain my own goals and my strategies for achieving them. These strategies have made me millions of dollars and helped make life fun and exciting to boot. I expect the going to be tough for us all in the years to come, despite the tremendous opportunities that will arise. But if you follow the strategies explained in the following chapters, stay alert, and keep up your courage, virtually everything you've ever wanted can be yours.

Part I

What's Going On and Why?

1

The Great Transition
and the Greater Depression

It may be observed that provinces, among the vicissitudes to which they are subject, pass from order to confusion, and afterwards pass again into a state of order. The way of the world doesn't allow things to continue on an even course; as soon as they arrive at their greatest perfection, they again start to decline. Likewise, having sunk to their utmost state of depression, unable to descend lower, they necessarily reascend. And so from good, they naturally decline to evil. Valor produces peace, and peace, repose; repose, disorder; disorder, ruin. From ruin, order again springs, and from order virtue, and from this glory, and good fortune.

Niccolò Machiavelli
Florentine Histories, 1532

What are the rest of the '90s going to be like? Will we have prosperity, depression, or something in between? Which investment markets will boom, which will crash, and which will just muddle along? What kind of world will we be living in? These are among the questions this book attempts to answer.

In *Crisis Investing* (1979) and *Strategic Investing* (1982) I argued that a depression was inevitable. This prognosis still holds, and I believe this depression will dwarf the events of 1929. That's a radical prediction, I know, so it's important to put it in context. In the next few pages, therefore, let's look at the human condition from a long-term perspective, from an eagle's point of view.

I believe Herman Kahn may have put forward the best framework in which to view the rest of the '90s. Although the near future will likely be much more problematical than he hoped, his basic perspective is so sound that it begs to be used as a starting point.

A GUARDEDLY OPTIMISTIC SCENARIO

I had the pleasure of getting to know Herman Kahn in the early '80s, shortly before his death.

Kahn is best known as the author of *On Thermonuclear War* (1960) and *Thinking About the Unthinkable* (1962), which made him a *bête noir* of the peace movement during the '60s. Those books were about war, but Kahn was far from a warmonger. To the contrary, he was, as he accurately described himself, "a reasonably realistic observer whose imagination and logic often lead to unfamiliar (sometimes apparently outrageous) conclusions and speculations."* Perhaps because he had not been trained as an economist, he had not cluttered his mind with the irrelevancies occupying the minds of most trained economists. Instead his training was in mathematics and physics, occupations that gladly bow to the demands of logic, and the facts of the real world.

Although Kahn is remembered today as a scholar who pondered the practical consequences of nuclear war, I believe tomorrow will remember him more for his several books on the economy (which are listed in the bibliography). They share a theme of optimism: Until just 200 years ago, at the start of the Industrial Revolution, human beings almost everywhere were few, poor, and at the mercy of the forces of nature; but 200 years from now they will be numerous, rich, and largely in control of the forces of nature.

Kahn believed things will turn out well. I believe his projections will prove highly conservative both in how good things will be and in how quickly they will become so.

THE GREAT TRANSITION

Approaching the year 2000, we are approximately in the middle of what Kahn called the "Great Transition." Like all periods of rapid change, this one has its dangers, discomforts, and inconveniences.

Human history in general, and the problems society now faces in particular, can be put in perspective by Figure 1-1.

Until only about 10,000 years ago, our ability to control and transform our environment, including feeding ourselves, amounted to the random use of available materials—sticks and stones, wild plants and animals. The total population of the world was probably no more than several million people, which was close to the earth's carrying capacity with then-minimal technology. But about 10,000 years ago, the agricultural revolution began. People began to abandon the ways of hunter-gatherers and started to assemble into permanent villages, which eventually grew into towns and cities. The ability to create and store a surplus of goods gave some

*Kahn, *World Economic Development* (1979).

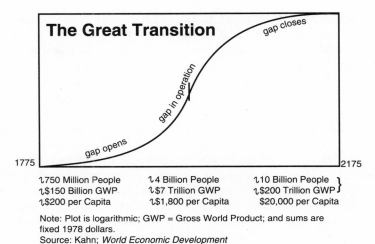

Figure 1-1

members of society the leisure to invent new technologies, such as writing, metal-working, irrigation, and architecture. But even then, technology consisted largely of modifying natural materials—turning a tree into beams and planks or piling a large number of stones atop one another to form a building.

Not until the industrial revolution, about 200 years ago, did man gain the ability not just to modify but literally to create his environment. Muscle power was replaced by mechanical energy; materials that didn't occur in nature were developed. Man's place in the physical universe of matter, energy, space, and time began a rapid transformation.

As a result, the earth could sustain infinitely more people than it could in the primeval era, and in far more comfort and safety. Excepting anomalies caused by war and politics, even the poorest primitive people today live as well and (what is far more important) with infinitely more prospect for improvement than any of their preagricultural forebears.

It is probable that we are now only halfway through the Great Transition in years and in the numbers of people affected. Soon the billions of people (in China, India, and the rest of the Third World) emerging from the last epoch will of necessity adopt the attitudes and values of those who went first. Population will level off, and then probably decline, as capitalism allows people to save for their future instead of raising many children to provide for their old age. Modern technology will allow people to create far more wealth, more efficiently, and with less input. They will stop regarding nature as an adversary and instead come to view it as a valuable asset to be conserved and used wisely.

Today the average middle-class member of an industrialized country lives better, and in general longer, than even royalty did in preindustrial times. And there is even more reason to believe that the trend will accelerate. You will recall how

Hobbes described the lot of man in his time, which was only 350 years ago, as a life that was "solitary, poor, nasty, brutish, and short."* This is no longer true, mainly because of capitalism and technology. But many people, for ideological reasons, do not like to be reminded of that truth. They are one of the few reasons the trend could change.

THE FORCES OF PROGRESS

Kahn's optimistic view of the future was based on the same factors that set the mainspring of progress in motion 200 years ago: a work ethic, political freedom, and technology. They are still in play and will remain so, notwithstanding the best efforts of people who are misinformed, ill-intentioned, or just plain stupid. (After all, those folks have been around since day one.) In the future we will endure wars, pogroms, plagues, persecutions, natural disasters, confiscations, inflations, depressions, and a whole list of other calamities that can make the world a vale of tears, just as in the past. But life is likely to get better, just as it has in the past; indeed, life most likely will improve at an accelerating rate.

The rate of technological advance is accelerating faster than ever and much faster than the economy itself. More scientists are alive today than ever before and science is breaking barriers at an unprecedented rate. And although we complain about the collectivist inclinations of politicians, the fact is that mankind has advanced from the primeval era's state of nearly 100 percent theft and slavery to a level of around 50 percent today, if we consider taxes in all forms and at all levels as a proxy for robbery. From the long-term view of centuries, the trend is clearly positive. Unless we are really unlucky, a hundred years from now our present problems will be considered teething pains.

Although the work ethic may be in decline in the United States at the moment, this is not the case elsewhere. A depression would, if nothing else, serve to restore the work ethic here. In other words, a trend has been underway since the industrial revolution and, momentum being the force it is, the trend is unlikely to wind down for at least another century. By then the amount of capital in the world will be so great, technology will be so advanced, and the average standard of living will be so high that seemingly worrisome conditions like pollution, resource depletion, and overpopulation will simply be nonproblems.

To produce a realistic assessment—a credible scenario, as it has come to be called—of the future, it is necessary to integrate and correlate data from science, demographics, military technology, politics, economics, sociology, and many other disciplines. Even so, Kahn's conclusion (with which I agree) is that, barring a perverse combination of extremely bad luck and bad management, life will probably progress much as it has in the past. Just faster.

*Thomas Hobbes, *Leviathan* (1651).

In a hundred years the descendants of today's starving will live significantly better than we do today. (If that sounds unlikely, it was equally unlikely a prediction for the descendants of the starving peasants in Ireland during the potato famines.)

In many respects the trend is already exceeding expectation. For example, Kahn predicted that the U.S.S.R. would continue to drift from totalitarianism to authoritarianism. Its breakup (notwithstanding the caveats you'll read in chapter 29) is a huge bonus. China will prove its experiment with communism to be just another blip on the 5000-year screen of Middle Kingdom history. Kahn thought Japan would continue growing more quickly than the West and also become more import-oriented. Newly industrialized countries (such as Brazil and Korea), which now have about two-fifths of the world's population, will continue growing at about 5 percent a year, more than enough to give them an interest in a stable world. Simple common sense, a desire not to be left out of a good thing, and better worldwide transportation and communication will act to replace socialist thinking with something closer to the free-market views of Milton Friedman.

Kahn was no Pollyanna; after all, he wrote the book on nuclear war. He acknowledged that much could go wrong. Perhaps a severe political backlash in the United States if the economy collapses. Maybe the Japanese will become arrogant, chauvinistic, and warlike, traits well within their tradition. Maybe remnants of the Soviet Empire will become aggressive and ideologically militant. Perhaps the Moslem world will join in a massive jihad against the West. A reaction against technology could occur, or severe trade barriers be erected. It's a long list and far from complete. For individuals, as for the world at large, it is essential to avoid being blindsided by truly disastrous surprises.

AN ERA OF MALAISE

Herman Kahn never pretended to speak *ex cathedra*, and he wasn't trying to be a fortune-teller. He did not posit a major technological revolution (not even one as probable as space colonization, much less one as seemingly improbable as nanotechnology; see chapter 35) or any change in the spiritual nature of man. He simply concluded, in light of the data he had, that continued progress was likely. In his books I find much to take issue with, but nothing unreasonable or dogmatic. And I find nothing that should be dismissed out of hand—a statement I'd find hard to make about most economic thinkers with an Establishment bias.

But how can I reconcile my conclusion that we're in for a Greater Depression with the prospect of continued economic progress? Actually there is no conflict. It is worth remembering that only 3 percent growth per year will double the Gross National Product (GNP) in the next 23 years. Since the end of the U.S. Civil War, the economies of the world's industrialized nations have grown at just about that rate. But the growth has not been steady. Like the stock market, it has moved in fits and starts.

Kahn found it convenient to divide the twentieth century into four periods, starting with the Première Belle Epoque, from 1886 to 1914, a period of unprecedented economic growth and freedom with almost no wars. It was followed by the Première Mauvaise Epoque, from 1914 to 1947, a really disastrous period comprising two world wars, the Great Depression, and the mass murder of millions in Germany, the U.S.S.R., and China, among other places. Then followed the Deuxième Belle Epoque, from 1947 to about 1973, years of generalized peace and plenty, with economic growth of about 4.9 percent per year in the advanced capitalist countries.

Since 1973, we have been in what might be described as the Epoque de Malaise. A malaise isn't really a sickness as much as a time when things are just under the weather, or noticeably suboptimal. We've had several serious recessions, declining rates of increase in the standard of living, and lots of brush-fire conflicts with some pretty ugly, small wars in the Third World; but things haven't been nearly as bad as they were from 1914 through 1947. In fact, even that generally disastrous period showed real compound growth of 1.8 percent. The question is when and how the current period is going to end.

I believe it will end soon, and that we'll again enter upon another Belle Epoque. I believe, however, it is likely to get worse—much worse—before the next Belle Epoque begins. The cyclical nature of progress Machiavelli noted 500 years ago (a notion that observers such as Spengler and Toynbee have expanded on since) still seems part of the cosmic landscape. My reasons for believing today may yet prove to be the Deuxième Mauvaise Epoque before matters improve are detailed throughout the rest of this book.

At a minimum we're headed for a financial collapse. A financial collapse does not mean that any real assets disappear. It means that assets change ownership. The buildings, factories, machines, and technology that were created during good times do not vanish just because the stocks, bonds, and bank accounts that represent them are devalued or dishonored. Nor does the desire of people to create and produce vanish when their finances go bad; instead they may become even more motivated. Still, during the last depression there were some starving in the midst of plenty, and I think the hardships are likely to be even worse this time, despite my generally strong agreement with Herman Kahn's case.

Kahn tended to underestimate the problems that accumulate during a business cycle and the pain of curing them. My belief, which is spelled out in chapter 3, is that when this business cycle peaks and the market distortions and the misallocations of capital forced by the government's intervention in the economy are finally unwound, the consequences will probably reach far beyond the economic sphere. We will find out before the end of this decade.

Kahn's frame of reference covers many decades, far longer than is meaningful to an individual investor, as opposed to an institution (or a futurist). He used to joke, when everyone was excited about some event, that "there are only two important things that have happened in history so far, and this isn't one of them."

The two things he was referring to were, of course, the start of the agricultural revolution (circa 10,000 years ago) and the beginning of the industrial revolution (circa 200 years ago).

That is an absolutely correct view. In the big scheme of things, the Greater Depression is trivial. A century from now it may merit no more notice than the Panic of 1907 does today. That's the good news. The bad news is that it's unlikely that anybody now reading this book will be around 100 years from now (though by no means out of the question, if people like Durk Pearson and Sandy Shaw, the authors of *Life Extension*, or Eric Drexler, the author of *Unbounding The Future*, are right.)

It is an interesting footnote that Kahn, of the Great Transition, and Casey, of the Greater Depression, actually ''debated'' the subject in 1980 before the Congressional Caucus for Science, Technology, and the Future. The meeting (attended by about 75 senators and congressmen) was chaired by Albert Gore, now vice president (who impressed both Kahn and me as an ingratiating Yuppie). Kahn and I each presented our viewpoints and realized that there really wasn't anything to debate about. I looked around the audience, during both our speeches, at a room of faces that were at once blank, confused, and humorless. I remarked on that to Herman after the conference (he had noted it as well) and suggested that the fact that these men were to some degree controlling the fate of the world was evidence for a gloomier scenario. He chuckled ironically.

The point bearing emphasis is that, even using a conservative projection, the future should turn out very well. There will be problems to confront and solve along the way, but they are largely the result of government intervention and would rapidly become nonproblems in a true free-market environment. If you invest wisely, your effort and attention can insulate you from the problems that may crush others, and can make the future an excellent place in which to live. The longest trend on record is, to use Jacob Bronowski's phrase, the ''ascent of man,'' and it will almost certainly continue.

In the meantime, let us return to the near-term future.

TIMING THE GREATER DEPRESSION: WHAT HAPPENED IN THE '80S

Why should a depression occur now? A depression could have materialized out of any of the credit crunches in the last three decades, including the financial squeezes of 1962, 1966, 1970, 1974, 1980, and 1982. With each episode inflation went higher, interest rates rose, unemployment increased, and the bankruptcies were bigger. Near bankruptcies (such as Lockheed, New York City, Chrysler, Continental Bank) became more numerous and dangerous and more likely to demand a government rescue. But each time we experienced just a recession that the government ended before the underlying distortions in the economy had been eliminated.

And each time the authorities succeeded in preventing a financial collapse, the system became more carelessly confident of government doing so the next time.

The economy neared the edge of a precipice in the early '80s. Fortunately it did not go over, and we've had some very good years since, for reasons that in retrospect are fairly obvious. I have listed eight below, not necessarily in order of their importance. It is unfortunate that many of them were one-time boosts that won't be repeated.

1.   The natural, self-correcting forces of the market. When interest rates went high enough, people preferred saving to borrowing. When unemployment went high enough, a large pool of eager labor made running a business easier at a critical time, since workers could be hired easily. When enough businesses went bankrupt, the reduced competition made it easier for the remaining businesses to survive and prosper.

2.   Some intelligent Reagan administration policies, starting in 1981. Regulation was reduced in certain areas, a trend that actually started under President Carter. The elimination of tax shelters and the lowering of marginal tax rates let capital be deployed more productively. And the Federal Reserve, imbued with a fear of inflation from the '70s, monetized less of the government's debt and was less reckless than it might otherwise have been, thereby restraining inflation. The Clinton administration, however, seems inclined to the kind of *dirigiste** policies that work against economic growth: more regulations, freer spending, higher taxes, and rising inflation—just the opposite of what is needed.

3.   A worldwide trend toward economic liberalization. Taxes and regulation declined almost everywhere as socialism was generally discredited. In Europe Prime Minister Thatcher was the leading figure, and even socialist politicians on the Continent followed her lead. Free-market policies were implemented widely in the Third World, if only out of desperation. Now the tenor of the times has changed in most of Europe, as in the United States, and governments are becoming more activist.

4.   The computer revolution, which made production of many goods and services more efficient. This raised living standards and counteracted the effects of inflation by creating new wealth. Of course, the same is true of any new technology, and many more are on the runway. But we cannot count on another revolutionary technology taking off at the right time to bail us out when the next economic crisis hits.

5.   The rapid increase of women in the workplace, which increased income and wealth. On the other hand, this change took away the average family's backup system if the primary breadwinner lost his job. Now, if either party becomes unemployed, the mortgage payments are in jeopardy.

6.   The large expansion of the money supply, with no corresponding rise in prices.

*Interventionist.

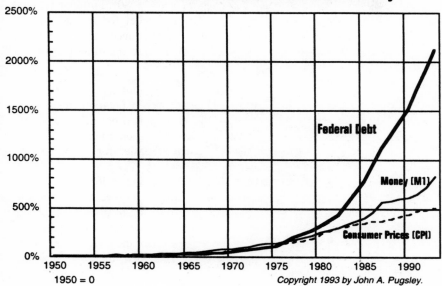

The Deadly Anomaly
% Growth of Federal Debt, Prices and Money

Figure 1-2

Figure 1-2, by John Pugsley,* shows that federal debt and the money supply have gone through the roof, while prices have risen comparatively modestly; he calls it the "Deadly Anomaly." Like all anomalies, it will come to an end; when it does, the party will be over.

7. The huge growth of debt on all levels; debt allows a country (or an individual) to party now and pay later. Total debt has risen from $4,000 billion to $15,000 billion since the beginning of the decade (see Figure 1-3). The rise was in large part responsible for the good times of the recent boom, but it's questionable how much more can be added (see chapter 5).

8. The gigantic trade deficits run by the United States, which sent hundreds of billions of dollar-denominated IOUs abroad, in exchange for goods and services. That had a substantial role in quelling the inflation that usually accompanies expansion of the money supply. We've exchanged hundreds of billions of intrinsically worthless paper dollars for the same amount of valuable goods from overseas. As a result, we've enjoyed an artificially high standard of living. When the trade deficit turns around, as it eventually must, the process will go into reverse with a vengeance, and we will be flooded with dollars that

*Author of *Common Sense Economics* (1975).

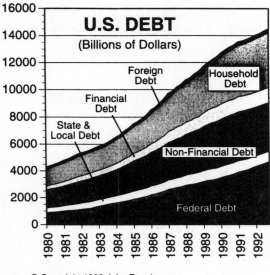

© Copyright 1993 John Pugsley

Figure 1-3

will drive prices up even as the goods they bid for will be crated up and shipped overseas.

It is important to recognize that there was no guarantee the economy would rebound in 1982. We could have seen 20 percent unemployment, wholesale bank and corporate failures, and widespread bond defaults, just for openers. The phenomenon of the business cycle, described in chapter 3, could have continued downward into a real depression. We were lucky, and the economy showed hidden reserves of strength. Now the situation is much more serious than it was in the late '70s.

The government has more power to control the economy today than it has ever had in the past. That's good in that things are still together. But it's bad when they're prolonged by extraordinary efforts. It's like doping an injured athlete so he can keep playing. He may score a few more points, but it may kill him.

WHAT WILL THE GOVERNMENT DO?

The depression of the 1930s was deepened, and was prolonged for years, by Hoover's and Roosevelt's interventionist policies.* The Work Projects Administration (WPA), the National Recovery Administration (NRA), the Tennesse Valley

---

*For a discussion of Hoover's interventionism, see Murray Rothbard, *America's Great Depression* (1972).

Authority (TVA), the Federal Deposit Insurance Corporation (FDIC), and numerous other New Deal creations not only prevented the economy from cleansing itself, they also produced new distortions in the economy. Roosevelt's "solutions" to the depression were almost identical to Hoover's, but Roosevelt's public relations was far superior, enabling him to position himself as the savior of capitalism even while he lengthened the depression.

As the going gets tougher in the 1990s, President Clinton will probably attempt to emulate Roosevelt to prevent being perceived as a "do-nothing" president in the image of Hoover. One might think that, with the collapse of socialism and the intellectual bankruptcy of its adherents, politicians would have learned that government intervention is the problem and that a free market is the cure. But instead of associating the upsurge of prosperity in the '80s with lower taxes and deregulation, they blame the problems of the '90s on those very things. Socialist ideas are therefore likely to resurface for a time, as they did during the Première Mauvaise Epoque, but under new labels.

Socialism is not a serious intellectual challenge. It persists because it expresses so well an underlying set of spiritual and psychological problems. Few reasonable people who have actually looked at the historic results of socialism honestly believe government intervention is the solution to economic problems, rather than the cause. But how someone reacts to economic ideas is much more a question of values and psychology than of intelligence and knowledge.

Most of the laws on the books today, and many more that will be enacted in the '90s, arise from envy and fear. When people are unhappy, when the pattern of their lives unravels, when they lose their job, their savings, or their house, then they want action, even if it's irrational action. They may know it's destructive, but they want to strike out anyway.

This is much more true of people when they're members of a group (such as Congress, the electorate, or a lynch mob) than it is of them as individuals. To paraphrase Kierkegaard, "Every person, taken as an individual, is tolerably intelligent, thoughtful and rational; but as soon as he's part of a group, he at once becomes a blockhead."

It's not only the fallout from the financial catastrophe we're facing that will make the going rough; it will be people's unpredictable (and destructive) reaction to the catastrophe. There is much more scope today for the economy getting completely out of hand than in the 1930s. People are much more urbanized now and much less self-sufficient. Before the last depression there was no caste of institutionalized welfare recipients. Regulation of the economy was heavy before the 1929 collapse, but far lighter than it is today.

Taxes were high, but even in 1929 the maximum rate was 23.1 percent, and then only at the $1 million level (more than $10 million in 1993 dollars). Few states levied an income tax, and there was no Social Security tax. As we approach this depression, fewer untapped resources are available than in 1929. The government has fewer reserves (although that's probably a good thing, for reasons I will make clear later). People may be forced to rely on themselves, even while they petition the government to make it better.

In any event, since the public has come to believe that the government drives the economy, they will not countenance their government deserting them. The cry will go up to "do something." They do not want to hear about letting the market sort itself out when their job, bank account, and pension promises may be among the distortions in need of liquidation. And you can bet that those in office, and the economists who advise them, will oblige with attempted bailouts. After all, it was Clinton's mandate and the promise that got him elected.

Still, it makes more sense to rely on oneself, not the government, good luck, or the Easter bunny, to ensure one's quality of life in the future. Before exploring the strategies that should make that possible, some important concepts—like who economists are, and what a depression actually is—will be clarified in the next chapter.

2

Economists and the Greater Depression

"Political economy" is in danger of dissolving into "statistics" which is much as if anecdotes of animals were substituted for the science of biology.

Walter Bagehot (1826–77)

The government are very keen on amassing statistics. They collect them, add them, raise them to the nth power, take the cube root and prepare wonderful diagrams. But you must never forget that every one of these figures comes in the first instance from the village watchman, who just puts down what he damn well pleases.

Anonymous
Quoted in Sir Josiah Stamp,
Some Economic Factors in Modern Life

There now exist whole branches of abstract economic theory which have no links with concrete facts and are almost indistinguishable from pure mathematics.

G. D. N. Worswick
"Is Progress in Economic Science Possible?"
Economic Journal, March 1972, p. 78

For at least two decades, the most widely used undergraduate economics text has been *Economics* by Nobel Prize–winner Paul Samuelson. If you have wondered about the value of taking a conventional course in economics or what being a Nobel laureate means, consider this quote from Samuelson's text: "What really counts is results, and there can be no doubt that the Soviet planning system has been a powerful engine for economic growth."* Or, again, "The Soviet economy is proof

Economics, 13th ed. (1989), p. 837.

that, contrary to what many skeptics had earlier believed, a socialist command economy can function and even thrive."*

That Samuelson is among the world's best-known economists underlines the truth of George Bernard Shaw's joke: If all the world's economists were laid end to end, they still would not reach an accurate conclusion.

But perhaps the joke is unfair to economists, because most of those who claim to be economists today are really something else. After all, if a witch doctor somehow convinced people he was a neurosurgeon, we would be hearing neurosurgeon jokes, but it would be a case of mistaken identity.

The best way to see who might qualify as an economist is to define the word. If a word is used in a nebulous, imprecise manner, the result can only be cloudy thinking.

Economic pundits often use words in loose, and frequently intentionally inaccurate, ways. The same word may be used to refer to different things, such as "capitalism" to describe the economic system of both the United States and Nazi Germany. Words with different emotional force may be used to refer to the same things (for example, "hoarding" and "saving" to describe the accumulation of wealth). Words with different meanings are used interchangeably: "currency," which is an arbitrary substitute (such as government paper) for money, is equated with "money" itself, which is a natural, universally accepted commodity, usually gold. Sometimes emotive rhetoric is used to dress up unappealing facts (such as when the phrase "get the country moving again" is used to cover the staging of an artificial, inflationary boom).

Let's look at who economists are, since everyone is relying on them to tell us how we're going to do. The best simple definition of an economist is someone who explains the workings of wealth. Some who claim to be economists do not explain things very well, if Professor Samuelson's assessment of the old Soviet Union is any indication. In fact, most "economists" turn out to be merely political apologists. They prescribe the way they would like the world to work and tailor their theories to help politicians demonstrate the virtue and necessity of their quest for more power.

Another definition of an economist is someone who studies economics. But what is economics? It can be described variously as the study of who gets what, how, why, and when; or the study of how men cooperate with, and compete against, one another to produce wealth; or the study of how men interact, voluntarily, with one another. It is unfortunate that economics is usually confused with politics, which is slightly different. Politics deals with who *decides* who gets what, how, why, and when. It deals with how men cooperate with, and compete against, one another in the process not of producing wealth, but of taking it. It also deals with how men interact with each other, but only sometimes voluntarily. Most of the economics practiced today is politics by a different name.

*Ibid.

An "economist" today is usually someone who takes polls, does complicated and irrelevant mathematical models, and acts as an overpaid political apologist for governments and large corporations. A modern soothsayer.

Partly because of their education and partly because of what their employers want to hear, most economists are conventional thinkers. Their forecasts are simply extensions of present trends, albeit tarted-up with lots of mathematical formulae. Calling for the millennium or the apocalypse is unlikely to win the favor of the Establishment, who prefer the status quo. And on the surface, it always seems much more likely that trends will continue than that they will change dramatically. The chances of being right in any year are much better if one just predicts that we will muddle through. For this reason we hear little about how bad the situation really is from conventional economists. And, of course (with some notable exceptions, like the Grace Commission),* we hear even less from the government or business, who have a vested interest in maintaining confidence.

Confidence is considered a critical commodity today, because the dollar and the economy itself rest on confidence alone. Yet confidence can vanish like a pile of feathers in a hurricane, once the extent of our problems becomes clear. Confidence in the economy is a very shaky foundation upon which to build your future. I suggest you lose that confidence now and beat the last-minute rush.

Instead, place your confidence in yourself and in your own ability as an economist. Every thinking person must be his own economist, simply because everyone needs a worldview to deal with reality. You can't delegate it to an "expert" any more than you can delegate the formulation of your personal philosophy and ethics to someone else. You need to decide whether we're to experience prosperity or a depression, and how you want to prepare. For the reasons I've just given, you're not well advised to depend on "economists" for an answer, since it is *your* money on the line. Further, very few economists have seriously confronted the probability of a depression, which would radically alter the world around us.

WHAT IS A DEPRESSION?

In 1978 Carter appointee Alfred Kahn, when he warned of a possible deep depression, suggested that we rename a "depression" a "banana" because everyone was so afraid of the word that they didn't want to talk about the subject. Kahn was absolutely right.

We'll use "depression," not "banana," even though the word used for the phenomenon has changed several times. It used to be called a "panic," and before the unpleasantness of the 1930s, a "recession," which has now acquired a milder

---

*The "President's Private Sector Survey on Cost Control" (later dubbed the Grace Commission, after its chairman) was set up by Ronald Reagan in 1982. The commission members spent $75 million of their own money to recommend potential government savings of $1.9 trillion by the year 2000. None, or a trivial number, of its recommendations has been implemented.

**DANGER +
OPPORTUNITY =
CRISIS**

Figure 2-1 Chinese Symbol for Crisis

meaning. A depression is a period when the standard of living of most people drops significantly. It is the opposite of prosperity.

The prospect of a depression terrifies most people, and they understandably do not want to confront the possibility. But refusing to confront what is fearful only adds to the danger. Better to face it squarely, and do so in the context of the Chinese symbol above. A depression is an economic crisis with both danger and opportunity. Everyone will feel the danger, but those who see the opportunity will profit from the crisis. After all, one function of a depression is to return wealth to its rightful owners.

If we look at the definition, a period of time when most people's standard of living drops significantly, we can find many possible causes of a depression, including war, flood, drought, and all types of natural and man-made disasters. All depressions are economic events, but the worst depressions, including the one to come, have economic causes as well. Disaster-caused depressions destroy wealth and make it harder to produce more. Economically caused depressions, through regulations, make it impossible, or at least unprofitable, for the average person to produce wealth.

The villain behind economically caused depressions is the government. In the next chapter we will examine the government's direct role in causing a depression—through the business cycle.

3

Cycles of Boom and Bust

Capital is most advantageously employed when no inducement whatsoever is made use of to turn it out of one employment into another. It is most advantageously employed when it follows that direction which the interest of the owners would, of its own accord, impress upon it.

John Stuart Mill
Elements of Political Economy, 1848

So far, indeed, are men in business from knowing the conditions on which future prices and profits depend, that they are often ignorant, after the event, of the causes of their own past profits and losses.

Thomas Edward Cliffe Leslie
Essays in Political and Moral Philosophy, 1879, XII, p. 187

Our analysis leads us to believe that recovery is sound only if it does come of itself. For any revival which is merely due to artificial stimulus leaves part of the work of depressions undone and adds, to an undigested remnant of maladjustment, new maladjustments of its own.

Joseph A. Schumpeter (1883–1950)
Essays, ed. Richard V. Clemence, 1951, p. 117

The physical world is unlikely to be changed much by the Greater Depression, but the way people relate to the world will change a great deal.

A real estate collapse doesn't mean buildings will tumble. But their prices will and their owners may change. A corporation's bankruptcy doesn't mean that the factories or technology it owned will vanish; they will become the property of a different corporation. A government default on its bonds doesn't mean the country (which is not at all the same thing as the government) is bankrupt. It just means that those who held the bonds are poorer and those who otherwise would have been taxed to pay the bonds are richer.

In other words, all the real wealth will still be there, but its ownership will change. And some commodities will become more (or less) valuable relative to other commodities.

The people who wind up wealthy as the Greater Depression unfolds will, predictably, be those who understand what's going on. A grasp of the business cycle is essential to that understanding.

The business cycle is the phenomenon of boom and bust caused by inflation. It has been labeled as one of capitalism's "internal contradictions" since the time of Karl Marx, but it is in fact the work of government. In a pure laissez-faire economy, the business cycle would not exist because there could be no politically driven inflation.

How does inflation cause the business cycle and, in turn, a depression? Let's perform an autopsy.

STAGE ONE: INFLATION AND BOOM

Suppose that the city of Santa Monica, California, is an independent nation. People are producing and trading to get what they want and need out of life. With no welfare, everyone is forced to work to support himself. The government concerns itself with maintaining the police and the courts and pretending that its little army keeps the rest of the world at bay. Life is mellow, and the weather is good.

Let's further suppose that the reelection campaign strategist for some local politician persuades some of the government's economic advisors that Santa Monica is not as prosperous as it ought to be. The economists opine that because there is a pool of "unemployed" (recent graduates, bored retirees, fire-ees and recent job quitters), the economy suffers from a lack of consumer demand.

Creating demand seems like a good idea, so the government credits the bank account of every Santa Monican with $10,000. (The idea isn't as outlandish, or unlikely, as it may seem. In 1972, presidential candidate George McGovern proposed crediting every American's savings account with $1,000.) The picture changes rapidly. Although there is no more wealth, there is a lot more money, say 20 percent more. Everyone feels, and starts acting, much richer. They spend more. The economy is "stimulated." We'll follow the fortunes of the swimming pool industry, although every business in Santa Monica would have a similar tale.

The first business to prosper because of the government's new monetary policy might be the telephone company, because all the phone lines are jammed with citizens trying to call the local swimming pool company to place an order. Believing that their "reach out and touch someone" marketing campaign is finally catching on, phone company executives make plans to put in more lines and hire more operators.

But the telephone company's expansion isn't nearly as dramatic as that of the swimming pool company, which is soon swamped with orders. Its owner is gratified that the market is finally rewarding his skills. It never occurs to him that the government's actions might be causing a temporary upsurge in demand. In any event, he raises prices to take advantage of the demand and then runs down to his bank to borrow some money for expansion.

The suppliers of swimming pool materials, such as concrete, copper pipe, and earthmoving equipment, also go out and borrow money to expand.

Because the banks have just taken in billions of dollars, courtesy of the government, they have plenty of money to lend, and at very low rates. "Interest" is the rental price of money, and with money in such ample supply, the price drops. Like any other businessmen with excess capacity, the bankers have a "special" on money.

All the expanded companies need new workers but have trouble getting them, since everyone willing to be is already employed. To induce workers to change jobs, the pool suppliers offer higher wages. Late-night television is filled with ads for schools who will train people to drive heavy equipment, pour cement, and lay pipe to take advantage of those great new jobs.

Meanwhile, all this activity hasn't escaped the notice of budding entrepreneurs. Soon the family leisure vans and custom surfboards are put up as collateral for loans to start new swimming pool companies. Bankers are eager to oblige, since they now have so much money on deposit and can only make profits by lending it out. Stockbrokers, seeing a new growth industry, raise millions from eager investors with an unexpected $10,000, and float new issues. Business is excellent, and many millionaires are made overnight.

A new class of swimming pool construction millionaires emerges. They, and their highly paid employees, drive Ferraris and wear Georgio Armani suits, gold chains, and silk shirts. Merchants draw down their cash reserves to stock up on inventory. Many people liquidate their savings to move into bigger houses (the banks have loads of money for mortgages), and the real estate market moves up. So does the stock market, since companies everywhere are expanding. With wages and profits up and stocks and real estate adding value daily, most people tend to work less and play more. A "new era" appears to have arrived, with universal prosperity and a higher standard of living for all. It looks like the economists were right, and a little inflation is a good thing.

So far, it's a pretty picture. But this is a game, like the "What's wrong with this picture?" puzzles we used to have in grade school. This is where it pays to have the skills of an economist. The immediate and direct effects of the government's inflation certainly seem good, but what are the delayed and indirect effects?

The folks in the government have little concern for delayed effects, even assuming some spoilsport points them out. The problems are in the future—after the next election. And since long-term effects are indirect, they are easy to blame on something or someone else. The perceived benefits of inflation, however, are not only very clear, they're in the here and now. Moreover, the "economists" say "fine tuning" may extend the boom indefinitely.

So the government will probably fail the "What's wrong with this picture?" test that a six-year-old would pass. But let's find out.

STAGE TWO: A SLOWDOWN

After a while, everyone who wants a swimming pool has placed an order, and sales taper off. Furthermore, people have started to notice a disturbing trend: prices around town have been moving up. The "economists" have neglected to mention that prices always rise when the supply of money increases without a corresponding increase in the supply of goods and services.

But what about all the new pools and other items? Aren't they the goods and services that the inflation made possible? Yes, but no new wealth has been created, just different—and more visible—types of wealth. Everyone who got into the swimming pool business was doing something else before, something that he's not doing now. Even though everyone's standard of living has gone up in some obvious ways, it's already started dropping in other ways. All those new heavy equipment drivers used to be parking cars, pumping gas, and washing dishes. Their ex-employers have found out that no one wants to work at menial jobs. Good help has become hard to find. Perhaps they can import a lot of Mexican labor.

If the government's inflationary gift to the people has increased the money supply by 20 percent, then prices in general have increased by 20 percent. The price inflation will be uneven, however; not all prices will increase by the same amount. The prices of some particularly desirable goods—like swimming pools, the water to fill them, and the big houses new millionaires can suddenly afford—now cost much more. A few things may actually drop in price, like the rice and beans that only poor people eat. The demand for them has decreased, since poor people are trading up to chicken and beef, which hit new highs.

It is impossible to get a plumber to fix a leak in a home, perhaps because his time is much more valuable subcontracting to a pool piping entrepreneur. The rare doctor who once made house calls no longer will; he has made millions investing in newly floated swimming pool company stock. Baby-sitters now start at $15 an hour, for a minimum of four hours. And interest rates are starting to head up, since people have exhausted their savings and will not save more unless they get an "inflation premium"—higher interest rates to compensate for the debasement of the currency—on their capital.

In fact, lots of subtle distortions are filtering through the economy. Some people, who spent their $10,000 to buy a swimming pools, are finding that demand has driven the price of water way up and they cannot afford to fill their pools, nor can they afford to maintain them with higher-priced labor. And since most people are consuming more and producing less, as people do when they feel wealthier, there is less wealth than there was before the magic of monetary policy transformed the way their world worked.

Santa Monicans acted in ways they wouldn't have if the government had not created all the new money. Inflation has encouraged them to produce things they would not have (like swimming pools) and not to consume things they would have before (like rice and beans). The inflation also has encouraged an overallocation of capital to inventories of luxury goods. Even though a lot of people have fine new pools, the standard of living has gone down in subtle ways.

STAGE THREE: FULL RECESSION

Soon there is a rapid decline in new orders to the many pool companies now in business. Bankers and brokers had not realized that an economy that could support only one pool company before the boom might have trouble supporting twenty a short time later. In fact, less demand exists now than before, when only one company operated, since many sales have been stolen from the future. The companies have to start laying off employees; many have trouble repaying their bank loans. The telephone, copper, and cement companies feel the ripple effect, as do the Ferrari and gold chain dealers, and the stock market collapses. Doctors fret as their swimming pool stocks plummet.

The Santa Monica economy is experiencing a recession. A recession follows an inflationary boom when the market tries to readjust to normal patterns of supply and demand. It's a painful period when the free market corrects the misallocation of resources encouraged by government inflation. People have more of some consumer products than ever, and there is more plant capacity to produce those products, but few people are as well off as they were before the inflation. They're actually less well off than if the government had only taxed them. Taxes alone would not have led people to think they were richer than they really were; there would be much less need for bankruptcy lawyers.

It is a paradox that even though the artificial boom caused many problems (however much fun it was at the time), the recession actually has many positive aspects. Consumers cut back on spending, so they are again building up savings. Businesses lower prices to induce consumers to buy. Workers, afraid of losing their jobs, work harder (that is, increase productivity). Companies (and workers) that cannot give consumers what they want, at prices they can afford, are forced to improve the way they do business. And citizens who were prudent during the boom have numerous bargains to choose among.

Whether the recession becomes a depression is largely up to the government, which should admit that its effort to stimulate the economy was a stupid idea; the government hasn't raised the general standard of living, just changed people's patterns of production and consumption. It actually reduced the overall level of prosperity.

At this point the government should exit the scene, let the swimming pool companies go bankrupt, allow the banks' shareholders to eat their loan losses, and permit the would-be tycoons to go back to parking cars and pumping gas. But doing this would make politicians immensely unpopular, and they would have to find a new line of work after the next election. Besides, if they play it right, the crisis can be turned into an opportunity to increase their power and prestige. And of course their economic advisors have plenty of "new ideas" for "change."

STAGE FOUR: RECOVERY

No politician wants to be blamed for a recession. Moreover, strong vested interests are at work to keep the swimming pool boom going. In private, businessmen make it clear that any incumbent failing to support the industry can forget about campaign contributions.

The Association of Swimming Pool Contractors declares that it would be "economically disastrous and a criminal disregard of their sacred public trust" for government officials to let the industry collapse. The Santa Monica Water Authority suggests it would be in the public interest for the government to subsidize water so people can afford to fill their pools and children can get daily exercise by swimming in them. It is clear that not just the economy but the nation's health and youth are at stake. The Silk Shirt and Gold Chain Retailers Association proclaims: "The city can never recover from the blow if the pool industry is allowed to fail." The bankers point to losses their depositors may have to take, and the Santa Monica Pool Supplies Association recommends tax credits for pool equipment as a cost-effective way to get the economy moving again. All the workers agree; they have no interest in pay cuts or unemployment.

A deflation could easily happen. Many borrowers could default on millions in bank loans, and much of the money supply could be wiped out. The stocks and bonds of failing companies would become worthless. As people scramble for money to keep the doors open, interest rates move up sharply. Even with the millions of new dollars in circulation, there's a shortage of cash.

Everyone is screaming at their elected representatives to bring back prosperity and the good old days. The screaming isn't about "theoretical" issues, like whether the government should have had the ability to manipulate the money supply, or how a gold standard (that would have prevented the boom and bust in the first place) might best be established; those issues are considered irrelevant because they won't solve the immediate problem.

What economic pundits suggest, instead, is more stimulation. Since the currency has lost 20 percent of its value, it will take $12,000 of "stimulus" per person to achieve the same effect that $10,000 achieved in the first cycle. The injection of new money drives down interest rates, reliquifies the markets, and heads off a deflation.

Seeing how close they came to the precipice, the pundits suggest a "safety net" so it won't happen again. This would include unemployment insurance, so workers won't have to worry about quickly getting new jobs at wages lower than they would like; bank deposit insurance, so no one has to worry whether his bank is prudently managed; some government agencies to help business, and some others to ensure business does not abuse that aid. Perhaps an industrial policy to coordinate the economy and make sure business and labor do not make the same mistakes they made in the last boom. All this can be financed by borrowing, which is much less painful than taxes. It will all suck a tremendous amount of wealth out of the economy, but no one really cares because investors can pad their portfolios with government bonds.

A full business cycle has been completed: stability, followed by inflationary expansion, slowdown, and deflationary contraction. The contraction will be called a recession if the government acts quickly and reinflates the money supply in time to prevent complete collapse. It will be called a depression if the government decides not to act, acts too late, or acts with too little reinflation. In other words, it will be a depression if the government allows the economy to cleanse itself of the distortions that have occurred due to earlier government intervention and inflation; it will be a recession if the government steps in before the liquidation is complete.

SUBSEQUENT CYCLES

Even if the government does act, it cannot undo the past. People have experienced inflation. They are therefore much less willing to save money and far more eager to borrow to take advantage of its loss in value. Interest rates go up, as both savers and borrowers allow for the risk of future price inflation.

Businessmen and consumers start planning for higher prices. Some businesses hire economists to second-guess the gyrations of the economy and retain lobbyists to argue for their "fair share" of further government spending.

Everyone saw the fortunes made during the inflationary boom, and also saw that the government had the power to prevent a collapse, so many people are willing to speculate on the inflationary trend continuing. Some take courses on buying real estate with "no money down." People feel richer than ever, consumer confidence hits new highs, and most investment is directed to cater to these different, and higher, levels of consumption. There are more construction companies, more big houses, more long lunches at Spago to celebrate.

The longer this goes on and the more business cycles the economy goes through, the more convinced people will become that the government not only can but should "manage" prosperity. The distortions in the economy harden and set. More and more capital is allocated to activities that would be deemed silly were it not for government policy. Where once it was inconsequential, the government eventually becomes THE major force in the economy. People plan their lives around what it will or won't do.

But the economy becomes more heavily burdened with each business cycle, as more debt is accumulated. When later recessions hit, business finds itself stuck with more spare inventory and plant capacity and has to lay off even more workers. Later recessions find both businesses and consumers deeply in debt, with no savings to rely on during hard times.

If the government had ended the game the first time around, the economy would have had only a sharp, but brief, depression, like those that occurred before World War I. The longer the process continues, the more severe the eventual outcome. After a while people start to see both inflation and recession at the same time. Despite the presence of more luxury cars, houses, and restaurants than ever, the quality of life for middle and lower income classes is fading, as are hopes for the future.

The government has put itself in the position of driving a fast car with a sticky throttle. If it stamps on the brakes to slow it down, the car will spin; if it doesn't, the car will run off the road. Of course the driver wants neither to happen, so he attempts to use moderation, stepping on the brakes but releasing them before the car spins. The ride inevitably gets wilder and crazier. First to 10 mph, then back to 5 mph. Then to 20 mph, and back to 10 mph. To 40 mph, with a disinflationary bust back to 30 mph.

In the early '70s the inflationary gas took the roadster up to 100 mph, and the 1974–1975 recession dropped it back down to 75 mph. Restimulation took it up to 120 mph by 1980, and it has been careening about the road for the last decade, to the alternating exhilaration and terror of the passengers. Now the roadster (the economy) is approaching a spin on the edge of a cliff. If it survives, the next escalation will be to 160 mph, on a mountain road.

It is unfortunate that Bill Clinton is no A. J. Foyt.

BEYOND SANTA MONICA

If the problem were limited to the People's Republic of Santa Monica, a small place, residents could easily move to surrounding areas to rebuild their lives, and there would be lots of outside capital available. But the United States is the largest economy in the world, so the solution will not be that simple. Worse, the U.S. dollar is the world's reserve currency; it constitutes most of the foreign exchange reserves of the majority of other countries. What happens to the dollar has direct bearing on what happens to other currencies. And what happens to the U.S. economy is critical to what happens to every other economy in the world. If U.S. citizens were unable to buy Japanese cars and electronics, the Japanese would have massive unemployment, along with a real collapse of their economy. They would then be unable to buy the annual $50 billion in goods they now buy from the United States, leading to even bigger problems. The situation could, and probably would, move out of control.

The situation is really much worse than the example presented in the story about Santa Monica. It would be bad enough if the government inflated only by crediting everyone's account. That would propel a business cycle, but there would not be any special beneficiaries. Instead, the government raises money by borrowing. It sells bonds to the public. The Federal Reserve honors the government's checks, used to repay the bonds, by increasing the depositors' reserve balance—like handing out poker chips. The government borrows dollars and repays the debt with poker chips, trading them for real wealth at face value. This process drains resources from the private sector, to the benefit of well-connected special-interest groups. The government doesn't distribute the money it borrowed equally, or even randomly.

Its beneficiaries receive federal grants, loans, and purchase orders. They can spend dollars at close to their old value, before the money starts filtering down through society, raising prices. They are the groups close to the government: Big Business, Big Labor, and the establishment in general. They differ on details of personality and policy, but ardently support the system as it is, with money, rhetoric, and influence.

Politics is the critical driving mechanism of this process. Considering that the U.S. groups in control of the political process have a vested interest in the status quo, it is problematical to look to politics for change.

The change we're likely to see will depend on whether the forces of inflation or deflation win out. Hence, it is a choice not between prosperity and depression, but between an inflationary and a deflationary depression.

THE DILEMMA

At some point, the economy is no longer controlled by individual citizens in the marketplace but by government "planners," who find they have only one of two alternatives: stop "stimulating" and permit a full-scale credit collapse, or continue stimulating until the dollar loses all value and society breaks down.

Depending on which they choose, we will have a depression characterized by *deflation* or by *hyperinflation*.

Deflationary Depression

This is the 1929-style depression, where huge amounts of inflationary credit are wiped out through bank failures, bond defaults, and stock and real estate crashes.

Before 1913 (the inception of both the Federal Reserve and the income tax), having the dollar pegged to gold (at $20 an ounce) inhibited the scale of monetization. When depressions of this type occurred, depositors acted quickly to collect their money; they had no illusion that the government would bolster their banks; once the banks ran out of gold, their bank accounts were worthless. Their quick response and the fact that the federal government could not monetize its deficit spending as freely as it now can forced the market to correct distortions rapidly.

Until the 1930s, depressions were sharp but brief. They were short because unemployed workers and distressed business owners were forced to lower their prices and change their business methods to avoid starvation.

The 1929 depression was deeper and more widespread than any before it since the Federal Reserve (by becoming the lender of last resort) allowed banks to maintain far smaller reserves than ever before. By backing the dollar with Reserve

Bank IOUs instead of gold, the money supply could be increased enormously, and large distortions could be built into the economy before a depression liquidated them. It was far longer than those before it, because government attempted to hold wages and prices at levels few could afford to pay, while its make-work and income redistribution schemes retarded the rebuilding of capital and the productive employment of labor. Meanwhile, the government discovered the freedom with which it could have its deficit spending monetized and proceeded to spend at an unprecedented rate to finance the New Deal's spending programs and World War II.

Since the end of the last depression, there have been numerous small recessions. Since at least the '70s, any one of them could have snowballed into another 1929-style deflation. Government has been able to forestall a deflation each time, since it has far more power than it did during the '30s. But the government's success so far has linked all the cyclical recessions since the end of World War II into a much larger "supercycle." Just as each of the past recessions had its moment of truth, so will the current one. And it could well be the turning point for the bigger supercycle as well.

Hyperinflationary Depression

This is the Weimar-style depression, like the one Germany experienced in the early '20s.* Here, rather than let a collapse of inflationary credit wipe out banks, securities, and real estate values, the government creates yet more currency and credit to prop things up. It pumps massive amounts of new purchasing power into the economy to create "demand" (even, or rather, especially among corporate and individual welfare recipients, who produce nothing in return). The government extends past misallocations of capital, when the economy instead needs to readjust to sustainable patterns of production and consumption.

Hyperinflation could result from overstimulation when the authorities try to boost the economy out of a trough. If they expand the money supply too quickly, it might encourage the hundreds of billions of U.S. dollars owned by foreigners to flood back here at once, in a bid for real wealth in competition with domestically held dollars. That would reverse, overnight, the muted inflation figures of the '80s, and prices could jump at a 20 percent to 30 percent clip.

It is hard to anticipate all the implications of that happening but, presumably, everyone would panic out of dollars and into real goods. There would be a wave of bank failures. Possible government reactions would be price controls, withdrawal restrictions, foreign exchange controls, and many other forms of "people controls."

This country is arguably unique in having a gigantic long-term debt market; bonds and mortgages are worth several times what the stock market is. If the dollars that debt is denominated in were to evaporate, it would be a world-class disaster.

---

*Under the Weimar government, people took shopping carts of paper money to the store to buy one or two grocery items.

Previous runaway inflations in other countries have been characterized by the printing of literally tons of paper money. But the U.S. economy is based largely on credit. Would credit cards be accepted if the dollar were to start losing value at a very high rate? Quite possibly not. In other hyperinflations there was usually some alternate currency to facilitate trade. Weimar Germans had substantial amounts of gold coins salted away. In South America people simply use U.S. dollars. In the ex-U.S.S.R. today, dollars (and deutsche marks) have practically become the new national currency. But what would Americans use?

All this would be an academic case, or perhaps an interesting topic for a science fiction treatment, if the U.S. government were a manageable size, and instead of a "legal tender" currency, "dollar" were just a name for a certain quantity of gold. But that is not the case, and we have to deal with things as they are.

WHICH WILL IT BE?

The Clinton administration, Congress, and the Federal Reserve are confronting a far more serious problem than ever in past business cycles. At the bottom of each past cycle, interest rates were high (bond prices were low), inflation was high, and the stock market was very low. This set up ideal conditions for recovery, as each of these situations went into reverse. But now, in 1993, stocks and bonds are already very high, and inflation is already at (what have come to be accepted as normal) very low levels. Even though the economy is staggering along, these traditional indicators are already at levels we would expect only at the best of times.

At the same time, the government has far less flexibility than in the past, despite being more powerful than ever. Most of its revenues are already spent before they come in, and it has a gigantic debt load to service. If some unexpected shock hits, it will be like watching a tightrope walker over the Grand Canyon during a windstorm.

In their efforts to quell inflation, the authorities could make the supply of credit either too small or too costly. With as much debt as there is today, the wave of bond and mortgage defaults would cascade through the economy. Loan defaults would wipe out banks, and foreclosure sales would depress prices and wipe out the net worth of individuals. A corporate bankruptcy can take down its suppliers, its workers, its community, and its lenders as well. Perhaps a scramble to pay debt would result in the wholesale liquidation of assets at distress sale prices, further reducing everyone's net worth, even while the dollars they owe gain value.

In their efforts to head off a deflation, the authorities would undoubtedly attempt to supply liquidity by creating more currency and credit. But that would just bring back the inflation scenario. And world credit and currency markets are far larger than they were during the early '80s. The financial problems the government has created have taken on a life of their own, and there is a good chance we'll have a nasty surprise when the next recovery is slated to occur.

Betting on inflation has been the winning strategy since the bottom of the last depression, but a financial accident could change all that overnight. The inflationists will almost certainly be right in the long run, but they may get wiped out in the short run. In any event, the moment of truth is approaching, and there likely will be a titanic struggle between the forces of inflation and the forces of deflation. Each will probably win, but in different areas of the economy. As a result, we're likely to see all kinds of prices going up and down like an elevator with a lunatic at the controls. It will not be a mellow experience.

The strategy I suggest in this book hedges against either eventuality and positions you for the era of eventual prosperity described in chapter 1.

4

The Destruction of the Dollar

There is no subtler, no surer means of overturning the existing basis of society than to debauch the currency. The process engages all the hidden forces of economic law on the side of destruction, and does it in a manner which not one man in a million is able to diagnose.

John Maynard Keynes
The Economic Consequences of the Peace, 1919

Among the many disadvantages arising from alteration of the coinage which affect the whole community is . . . that the prince could thus draw to himself almost all the money of the community and unduly impoverish his subjects. And as some chronic sicknesses are more dangerous than others because they are less perceptible, so such an exaction is the more dangerous the less obvious it is.

Nicholas Oresme (1320?-1382)
The Origin, Nature, Law and Alterations of Money, trans. Johnson, p. 32

To shake ourselves free of these illusions it would help greatly if, for the phrase "a general rise in prices," we should substitute the phrase, "a fall in the purchasing power of the dollar." Our attention would then be focused on the money, which is the chief controller and disturber of prices.

Irving Fisher (1867-1947)
Stabilizing the Dollar, 1920, p. xxxiv

"Inflation" occurs when the creation of currency outruns the creation of real wealth it can bid for. It isn't caused by price increases; rather, it *causes* price increases.

Inflation is not caused by the butcher, the baker, or the auto maker, although they usually get the blame. On the contrary, by producing real wealth, they fight the effects of inflation. Inflation is the work of government alone, since government alone controls the creation of dollars.

In a true free-market society, the only way a person or organization can legitimately obtain wealth is through production. "Making money" is no different from "creating wealth," and money is nothing but a certificate of production. In our world, however, the government can create dollars at trivial cost, and spend them at full value in the marketplace. If taxation is the expropriation of wealth by force, then inflation is its expropriation by fraud.

To inflate, a government needs complete control of a country's legal money. This has the widest possible implications, since money is much more than just a medium of exchange. Money is the means by which all other material goods are valued. It represents, in an objective way, the hours of one's life spent in acquiring it. And if enough money allows one to live life as one wishes, it represents freedom as well. It represents all the good things one hopes to have, do, and provide for others. Money is life concentrated.

As the state becomes more powerful and is expected to provide more resources to selected groups, its demand for funds escalates. Government naturally prefers to avoid imposing more taxes as people become less able (or willing) to pay them. It runs greater budget deficits, choosing to borrow what it needs. As the market becomes less able (or willing) to lend it money, it turns to inflation, selling ever greater amounts of its debt to its central bank, which pays for the debt by printing more money.

As the supply of currency rises, it loses value relative to other things, and prices rise. The process is vastly more destructive than taxation, which merely dissipates wealth. Inflation undermines and destroys the basis for valuing all goods relative to others and the basis for allocating resources intelligently. It creates the business cycle and causes the resulting misallocations and distortions in the economy.

WILL INFLATION EVER RETURN?

I use the question "Will inflation ever return?" colloquially as shorthand for "Will retail price increases (the result of excessive growth in the money supply) ever return?"

Many people seem to think that inflation is gone forever and a "new era" of high securities prices, steady low consumer prices, and political and financial stability has dawned. Take note of Figure 4-1, by Harry Browne.

You will notice from the graph that the money supply has gradually increased, with fits and starts, over the last thirty-odd years up to 1987. During the 1950s and early '60s, M-1 changed at a typical rate of between 0 percent and 5 percent, sometimes dropping into negative numbers. At the same time the economy was expanding rapidly. The net result was price increases ("inflation" in the popular sense of the word) in the 1 percent to 2 percent range, since the economy was growing at about 3 percent.

Later in the '60s and the '70s, monetary growth moved into the 5 percent to 9 percent range, while productivity fell. As society became more consumer-oriented, the government simultaneously mounted a very expensive war on the other side of

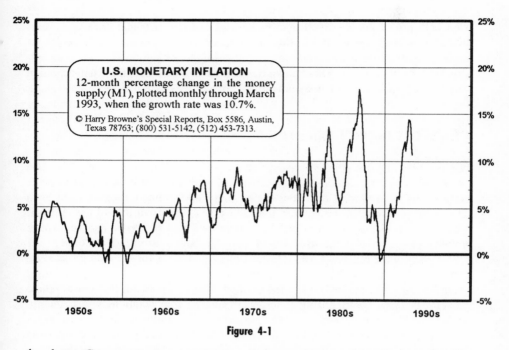

U.S. MONETARY INFLATION
12-month percentage change in the money supply (M1), plotted monthly through March 1993, when the growth rate was 10.7%.

© Harry Browne's Special Reports, Box 5586, Austin, Texas 78763; (800) 531-5142, (512) 453-7313.

Figure 4-1

the planet. Consumer prices rose by 5 percent to 10 percent annually throughout the 1970s. Pretty much what one might have expected.

Then came the '80s, which were quite anomalous, at least on the face of it. The long-term acceleration in the growth of M-1 continued, reaching 18 percent. One might have expected consumer prices to more or less reflect this growth in M-1, much as it did during the previous three decades, but it hasn't. Why not?

WHAT HAPPENED IN THE '80S?

Figure 4-1 shows that more money was created during the '80s than in any previous decade. We were fooled because the money did not flow into hard material goods, but instead into financial instruments, like stocks and bonds. As a result, the prices of financial instruments exploded, but the prices of raw materials and consumer goods stayed relatively flat. The standard of living of those holding investments rose and, since tangibles rose only moderately, the man in the street was not hurt as badly by the inflation as he might have been.

At the beginning of the '80s, stocks and bonds were at their lowest level in decades (the Dow Jones Industrial Average [DJIA] was at 800, and bonds were yielding 14 percent). Meanwhile, commodities were at an all-time high (gold touched $850, oil was at $40, the Commodity Research Bureau Futures (CRB) Index of 21 commodities went over 330). But markets adjust, and capital flows from high-priced areas (which tend to be high-risk for just that reason) to low-priced, lower-risk areas. Production of commodities ballooned, while scores of large companies were taken private and the supply of public stock contracted. Consumer prices also were held down by the near-trillion-dollar trade deficit which brought in boat-loads of merchandise paid for with IOUs.

INFLATION AS THE RICH MAN'S FRIEND

This explains to some degree why the rich got so much richer during the '80s. The "rich" already had capital in the investment markets. Their stocks and bonds exploded in value during the '80s. Poorer and middle-class people did not have substantial positions in the market and so lost out. That's also why top-end real estate (houses priced at $500,000 and more) soared, but low- and mid-range property prices were stable to lower in many areas.

We know the old saw "The rich get richer, and the poor get poorer." No one ever said life had to be fair, but usually there is no a priori reason why the rich must get richer. In a free-market society the sayings "Shirtsleeves to shirtsleeves in three generations" and "A fool and his money are soon parted" might be better descriptions of reality. We do not live in a free-market society, however.

The rich and the poor do have a tendency to draw apart as a society becomes more bureaucratic, but not because of any cosmic law. It's a consequence of any highly politicized system. Government, to paraphrase Willy Sutton,* is where the money is. The bigger government becomes, the more effort the rich, and those who want to get that way, will put into making the government do things their way.

Only the rich can afford the legal counsel it takes to weave and dodge through the laws that restrict the masses. The rich can afford the accountants to chart a path through loopholes in the tax laws. The rich have the credit to borrow and thereby profit from inflation. The rich can pay to influence how the government distorts the economy, so that the distortions are profitable to them.

The point is not that rich people are bad guys (the political hacks who cater to them are a different question). It is just that in a heavily regulated, highly taxed and inflationary society, there's a strong tendency for the rich to get richer at the expense of the poor, who are hurt by the same actions of the government.

Always, and without exception, the most socialistic, or centrally planned, economies have the most unequal distribution of wealth. In those societies the unprincipled become rich, and the rich stay that way, through political power. In free societies, the rich can get richer only by providing goods and services others want at a price they can afford. The freer the society, the easier it is for the poor to join the ranks of the rich.

---

*Probably recent history's most famous bank robber.

In her last public speech, just a few months before her death, Ayn Rand was asked: "What about the poor?" I feel Miss Rand's answer was instructive. She said: "Make sure you're not one of them."

WHAT'S NEXT?

The Federal Reserve has bought over $25 billion of government securities in the last year, accounting for the sharp upturn shown in Figure 4-2.

This process, the monetization of debt, is the actual engine of inflation. The Fed, which regulates the money supply, buys government debt and credits the government's account with dollars. The more debt the government floats, the more the Fed is likely to buy and the more dollars are created. The quick rise of Fed debt holdings during the '60s was in good part responsible for the inflation of the '70s. The relative decline in holdings at the end of the '70s helps to account for the lower levels of inflation we had during the '80s. There's always a time lag between monetary inflation and the price inflation that results from it. (Milton Friedman once made a case that the lag averaged about two years.) In fact, there are so many other influencing factors (capital movements, tax structures, fiscal policy, debt levels, and general market psychology) that the average is a very poor guide. The only certainty is that persistent high rates of monetary inflation lead to price inflation.

The recent infusion of "supermoney" accounts in good part for the stock market remaining at high levels. The effect of this credit inflation on consumer prices will not show up for "X" amount of time. But it *will* occur, and in proportion to the explosion in monetary inflation since 1989, as illustrated in Figure 4-1.

Figure 4-2

5

Is Debt a Big Deal?

We can pay off anybody by running a printing press, frankly. So it's not clear to me how bad that [the U.S. having become a net debtor] is.
Thomas Gale Moore, a member of the president's Council of Economic Advisers, when asked about the national debt in 1988

A "sound" banker, alas! is not one who foresees danger and avoids it, but one who, when he is ruined, is ruined in a conventional and orthodox way along with his fellows, so that no one can really blame him.
John Maynard Keynes (1883-1946)
The Consequences to the Banks of the Collapse of Money Values,"
in *Essays in Persuasion*, 1933, Pt. II, p. 176

The overleveraging of the U.S. government, corporations, and consumers became a matter of popular concern in the 1980s. In fact, the country's slide into debt has been in the news for so long that people are bored by the topic. If debt is a problem, it has been manageable for so long that it no longer seems like a problem. Debt has become an abstraction; it has no more meaning to the average investor than the prospect of a comet smacking into the earth sometime in the next hundred millennia.

Many commentators believe that debt doesn't matter. We still hear sound bites that trivialize the subject. Here are some of the most popular.

- "We owe it to ourselves." Actually, some people owe it to other people. There will be big transfers of wealth depending on what happens.
- "It's small relative to GNP." It is true that government debt (at 117 percent of GNP after World War II) has been much higher. But that was at a time when private-sector debt was tiny, the economy was liquid, government spending was falling, and the GNP was about to soar—just the opposite of today's conditions.
- "Other countries have even more debt and do just fine." The only major governments with more debt (relative to their GNP) are Italy and Canada,

which is small consolation. Governments with an extreme gap between income
and expenditure usually wind up with severe problems. The old Soviet bloc,
and most of the Third World, are examples.

- "We'll grow our way out of it." That's impossible unless real growth is
  greater than the interest on the debt, which is doubly impossible because the
  rate of increase in debt is starting to grow exponentially.

- "We've learned to manage debt intelligently over the last few decades." The
  authorities have indeed gained expertise in crisis management and damage
  control. They may, therefore, be able to build the debt structure even higher
  before it collapses. But in the end it must be repaid or defaulted on.

One way of putting an annual federal deficit of, say, $400 billion in perspec-
tive is to compare it to the value of all publicly traded stocks in the United States,
which are worth roughly $4 trillion as of January 1993. The government's debt of
more than $4 trillion already exceeds the stock value of all public corporations. If
the annual deficit continues at its current $400 billion rate—in fact it is likely to
accelerate—the government will further borrow the equivalent of the entire equity
capital base of the country, which has taken 200 years to accumulate, in only ten
years.

You should keep all this in the context of the nature of debt; it can be insidious.

THE NATURE OF DEBT

The only way a society (or an individual) can grow in wealth is by producing more
than it consumes; the difference is called "saving," or reserving present production
for future consumption. Conversely, "borrowing" involves consuming more than
is produced; it's the process of living out of capital and possible future production.
Saving increases one's future standard of living; debt reduces it.

If you were to borrow a million dollars today, you could enhance your standard
of living for the next decade. But, when you have to repay that money, you will
sustain a very real decline in your standard of living. Even worse, since the interest
clock continues ticking, the decline will be greater than the earlier gain. If you do
not repay your debt, your creditor (and possibly his creditors, and theirs in turn) will
suffer a similar drop. Until that moment comes, debt can look like the key to
prosperity, even though it's more commonly the forerunner of disaster.

Of course, debt is not, in itself, a bad thing. Not all debt is for consumption; it
can be used to finance capital goods, intended to produce further wealth. Nevertheless, a substantial part of the debt you'll see in the charts below (including almost all
government debt, most mortgage debt, and all consumer debt) represents pure
consumption. And much of the capital represented by corporate debt has been
malinvested, to cater to artificially high levels of consumption. That debt won't
produce enough new wealth to liquidate itself.

Suppose a peasant produces three bushels of wheat per year—one to eat, one to
give the king for taxes, and one for seed next year. Now suppose that the king

decides he would like to increase his standard of living, but he doesn't want to raise taxes, because he knows the peasant can neither eat less nor set aside less for planting. So the king decides to borrow instead. He issues the peasant an interest-bearing bond on the seed wheat, promising to pay the wheat back in a year.

Everybody is happy. The king consumes two bushels, perhaps funding a war with part of it and some popular welfare and subsidy programs with another part. The peasant probably consumes more as well, since he not only gets some of the king's new social benefits but is probably earning interest on the seed grain he lent the king. The standard of living in the kingdom has gone up, and debt seems like a good thing. That is, until next year when the wheat bonds come due. The king's bushel basket, which should be full of seed wheat to repay the peasant, is empty, and printing currency or new bonds won't fill it. What happens then? Both king and peasant starve to death.

WHERE ARE WE NOW?

Since debt is related to the prospects for the Greater Depression, it makes sense to compare present levels to those before the unpleasantness of the 1930s. You will note in Figure 5-1 that in 1929 the ratio of all debt to the GNP was similar to the ratio that existed in 1980; the ratio soared in the early '30s mainly because GNP collapsed, not because debt increased. The drop in the ratio throughout the late '30s was not due to an increase in GNP, but to massive defaults on debt.

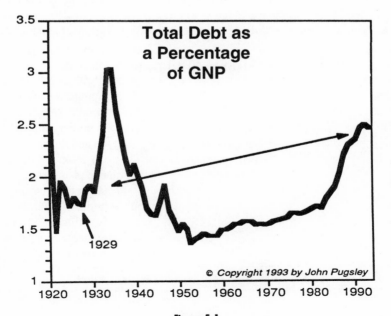

Figure 5-1

In the '80s, the ratio of debt to GNP also soared, but this time because of an absolute increase in debt. It is a reasonable conjecture that an economic collapse in the '80s was averted only by this explosion in debt. But that just moved the problem into the '90s, when the debt burden will be even harder to bear.

This chart may also help us see when a genuine recovery will be possible. You'll notice that the ratio bottomed out in the early '50s, after an enormous amount of debt from the previous generation had either been repaid or defaulted on, and individuals were awash in savings. The ratio would have been even lower were it not for the huge World War II federal deficits. Similar conditions seem many years in the future now, but only when they exist can the economy be given a clean bill of health.

What will happen to this chart in the '90s is impossible to predict. But the fact that debt is at such high levels tells me that there's going to be a major upset of some nature.

Figure 5-1 shows debt for individuals, corporations, and government. We will look at them one by one.

INDIVIDUAL DEBT

Figure 5-2 tells the story for individuals. You'll notice that total debt (consumer plus mortgage) has been in a strong uptrend, from about 65 percent of income in 1970 to more than 95 percent in 1992. This tremendous accumulation of debt has limited the individual's financial freedom and flexibility. How can he think of changing jobs (God forbid he gets fired) when he is burdened with multiple monthly payments? Rising household debt is one of the reasons disposable income has been

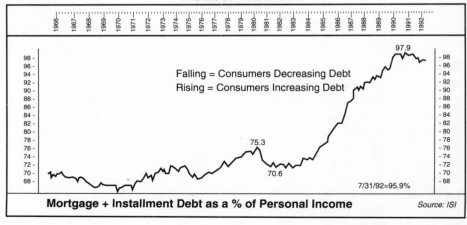

Household Debt

Falling = Consumers Decreasing Debt
Rising = Consumers Increasing Debt

97.9

75.3

70.6

7/31/92=95.9%

Mortgage + Installment Debt as a % of Personal Income   *Source: ISI*

Figure 5-2

Change in Nominal Disposable Income

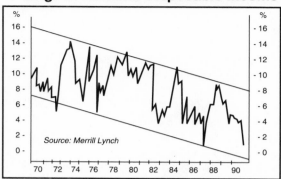

Figure 5-3

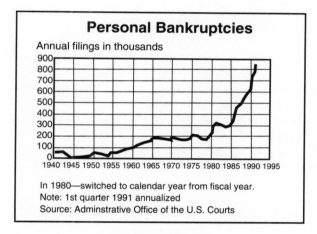

Figure 5-4

dropping for years. Although there have been fluctuations, the trend for the last two decades has been downward, as shown in Figure 5-3

The practical consequence has been a dramatic increase in personal bankruptcies. You'll notice that bankruptcy was rare when the current supercyclical boom started after WWII. Small cyclical increases in the rate of personal bankruptcy occurred during the recessions of 1970, 1975, and 1982, each spate of bankruptcy worse than the one before, but minor compared to what has been happening over the last five years. When is this trend going to level off? The U.S. courts are predicting a further 20 percent increase in annual filings by the end of 1992. A real recovery in the economy will not take place until the distortions and malinvestments represented by these bankruptcies are totally washed out and Figure 5-4 again approaches the levels of 50 years ago.

CORPORATE DEBT

The debt posture of individuals has been deteriorating for a long time, but not as drastically as that of corporations. If you doubt that the insurance companies are in just as much trouble as the banks and S&Ls, take a look at Figure 5-5. You will note that debt inside the banking system has increased about six times in the past 20 years. One reason the banks made so many stupid loans is due to their insistence on rapidly expanding their lending. They just couldn't lend that much capital prudently—any more than banks in Santa Monica could during the Great Swimming Pool Bubble of chapter 2. But debt outside the banking system—mostly insurers—grew about 900 percent in the same period, which means insurance companies are bound to have made even worse investment mistakes than the banks.

The debt in Figure 5-5 represents, in effect, the assets of U.S. financial institutions. Like all debt, it's also someone else's asset, mostly held by consumers and corporations. In the case of the latter, a good part of the debt is in the form of bonds. Until the middle of the '80s, the amount of corporate bond defaults was trivial, reaching only about a billion dollars in 1982, in the middle of a deep recession with all-time-high interest rates. Since then defaults have skyrocketed: $5 billion in 1988, $12 billion in 1989, $25 billion in 1990, and an estimated $50 billion in 1991. And all that in an environment of much lower, and declining, rates. Figure 5-6 shows business failures in relative terms; even during the "boom" years of the 1980s, with declining interest rates, failures soared.

In 1932, at the bottom of the last depression, the number of corporate bankruptcies peaked at about 30,000 (almost 160 per 10,000 businesses). By 1946, after the economy was completely washed out from the depression, there were only about a thousand bankruptcies (5 per 10,000 businesses)—a trivial number. Bankruptcies

Figure 5-5

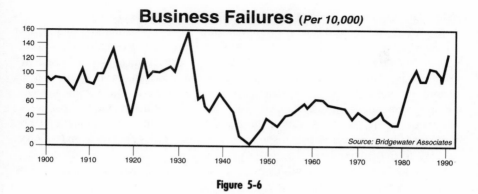

Figure 5-6

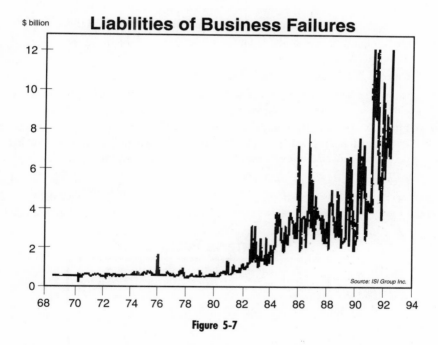

Figure 5-7

averaged 10,000 to 15,000 annually throughout the '50s, '60s, and '70s. They were running at a rate of about 90,000 annually at the end of 1992.

Figure 5-7 shows the amount of debt owed by failing businesses. It tracks the number of corporate bankruptcies. Business failures themselves are not the problem. They're part of the *creative destruction** that allows an economy to grow by putting its mistakes behind it. The problem is debt. When money is easy to borrow,

*Joseph Schumpeter's term for the workings of the market.

more marginal businesses start up, and the number of business failures increases. It is impossible to go bankrupt if you don't owe money. The number and size of business failures exploded during the '80s; if you refer back to Figure 5-1, you will note failures tracked the explosion in debt that started in the '80s. The time for optimism is when the numbers of failures are again down to trivial levels, and the distortions cranked into the system have been liquidated. The rise in business failures continues unchecked. Figure 5-8, showing number of failures *per week*, illustrates activity in the '90s more closely. During the first five months of 1992, business failures increased 14 percent from a year earlier, 74,715 up from 65,368 in January to September 1991.

Let us look at the composite balance sheet of the industrials monitored by Value Line for the last five years.

- On the asset side of the balance sheet, corporate cash and equivalents have grown, from $147.7 billion in 1986 to only $159.7 billion in 1990, but receivables (uncollected bills) have risen from $288.8 billion to $648.4 billion.

- On the liability side of the balance sheet, notes payable have risen from $61.9 billion to $231.7 billion.

- Current liabilities have gone from $508 billion to $864 billion.

- Long-term debt due in five years or less has gone from $151 billion (19% of corporate net worth) to $339 billion (31% of net worth)

- Financial ratios have deteriorated radically: The percentage of cash to current liabilities has dropped from 29 percent to 18 percent; accounts receivable as a percentage of sales have risen from 13 percent to 21 percent.

Investors do not watch balance sheets: they watch earnings per share, which have been good. That's partly due to all that debt, which has leveraged earnings per share by allowing companies to finance growth without issuing more shares.

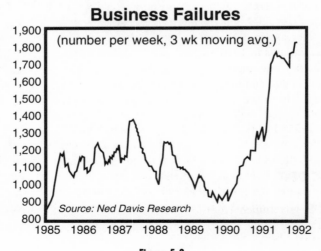

Business Failures

(number per week, 3 wk moving avg.)

Source: Ned Davis Research

1985 1986 1987 1988 1989 1990 1991 1992

Figure 5-8

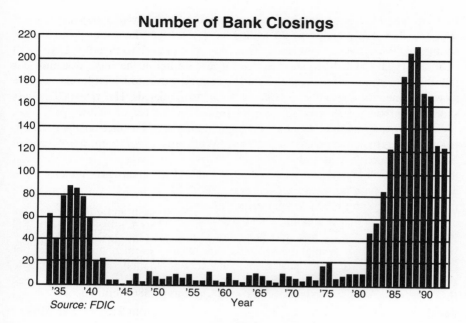

Figure 5-9

But the balance sheet—not leveraged earnings in boom times—determines whether a company can make it through tough times. Over-leveraged outfits have gone under even while their earnings were rising, just as an individual who earns a lot of money can be forced into bankruptcy. Right now net interest payments as a percentage of cash flow are running close to 30 percent. They averaged about 10 percent through the '70s. If business slows down, the cash flow could disappear, but the burden of interest payments will not.

Correlate Figure 5-9 with Figure 5-1 "Total Debt as a Percentage of GNP." The gigantic increase in debt caused, albeit with some delay, the current wave of bank failures. Failures in 1990 to 1992, while high, were not at crisis levels due to the extraordinarily low interest rates we now have. Low rates contribute to lower rates of loan defaults, and they also increase banks' margins. But when rates again go up, we're likely to see a new wave of bank failures. The Greater Depression, which has just started, will not be over until the number of failures once again approaches zero.

GOVERNMENT DEBT

It took the U.S. government from 1791 to 1916 (125 years) to accumulate $1 billion in debt. World War I took it to $24 billion in 1920; World War II raised it to $270 billion in 1946. Another 24 years were needed to add another $100 billion, for a total of $370 billion in 1970. That debt almost tripled in the following decade, with debt crossing the trillion dollar mark in October 1981. Only four and a half years later the debt had doubled to $2 trillion in April 1986, four years more added another trillion by April 1990, and then in only 34 months it reached $4.2 trillion in February 1993. Off-balance-sheet borrowing and the buildup of massive contingent liabilities are not included. And this most recent growth in federal debt occurred in an environment of unusually low interest rates. Moreover, 70 percent of the debt is short-term, financed at only 3 percent interest.

The rate of growth in debt today is high, but not nearly as high as it was (2,400 percent in less than four years) during World War I. And although the absolute level of the government's debt is also very high relative to the economy, it was higher at the end of World War II; the problem today is that both debt and its rate of growth are very high, with no war to account for it. Both are caused by chronic spending that we have come to take for granted.

The U.S. deficit is running about $400 billion per year, depending on who juggles the numbers. Do you remember in 1974–1975 when a $50 billion deficit was a major scandal, even at the bottom of a recession? Further, the current run of gigantic deficits began at the peak of the longest boom in modern history. What do you think will happen if the next downturn hits after only a brief and weak recovery? The annual deficit is going to reach $500 billion, and then a trillion dollars.

The question arises: Where will this end? Various arms of the government, notably the Congressional Budget Office (CBO) and the Office of Management and Budget (OMB) have made occasional projections since the federal deficit became an issue in the early '80s. Figure 5-10 shows how inaccurate four widely publicized projections have been (1982–1991). It is interesting that the most recent (1992) projection of the CBO doesn't assume the federal deficit will ever get back to zero. Both the CBO and the OMB projected that the deficit will go back to the $200 billion level during the 1990s, then rise to the $400 billion area around the turn of the century. There's every reason to suspect that the current projections are as unreasonably optimistic as past forecasts.

A more realistic approach was taken by Harry Figgie, founder of the $1.3 billion Figgie International Corporation and a member of the president's Private Sector Survey on Cost Control, better known as the Grace Commission. The Grace Commission was composed of 160 top business leaders, plus about 2,000 of their employees. They spent $76 million of their own money to look for ways to eliminate government waste early in the '80s.

As expected, the commission found waste on a colossal scale, but not one of its recommendations was implemented. That was especially interesting during a "conservative revolution," when Reagan's minions were saying, "If not us, who? If not now, when?" The Grace Commission projections of government debt for 1982 to 1993, based on the existing commitments, matched actual deficits almost exactly (Figure 5–11). I see no reason why their projections should not continue to be on target.

In his 1992 book *Bankruptcy 1995*, Harry Figgie pays attention only to the government's debt, focusing on the interest component. That alone is enough to

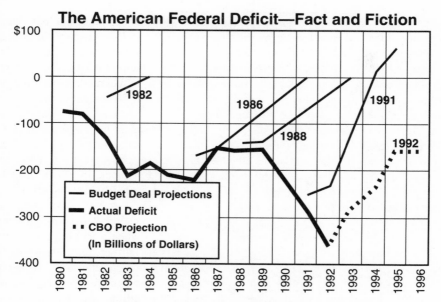

The four lines reaching toward zero on the above graph shows how the U.S. federal deficit was to be reduced to zero and eliminated within a specific timespan. For example: According to the balanced Budget Act of 1985, the U.S. federal deficit should have shrunk to zero by 1991. In reality, the federal deficit for 1992 totals $350 billion.

Figure 5-10

precipitate a catastrophe. In 1964, the year Lyndon Johnson was elected, federal debt stood at $316 billion and interest on it was $10.7 billion, which was equal to 14.8 percent of personal and corporate tax revenues. When Reagan left office in 1989, the debt stood at $3.2 trillion, and interest was $214.2 billion, taking 43 percent of tax revenues. When Bush left office in 1993, the debt stood at $4.2 trillion and interest at $293 billion, consuming 52 percent of personal and corporate income taxes, despite a drop in short-term interest rates from 14 percent to 3 percent between 1980 and 1992. Figgie realistically projects that by 1995 the debt will reach $6.56 trillion. Interest expense alone will be $619 billion per year, consuming 85 percent of all taxes.

In other words, by 1995 most taxes will be collected to pay interest alone. This will give new meaning to the old saw about how we "owe it to ourselves," as taxpayers start to really resent paying higher taxes for fewer and poorer services.

We don't know just what future deficits will be, except that they'll be much, much higher. That is because much federal debt is contingent in nature—obligations that seem to mean nothing until something goes wrong. The Federal Savings and Loan Insurance Corporation and the Federal Deposit Insurance Corporation are

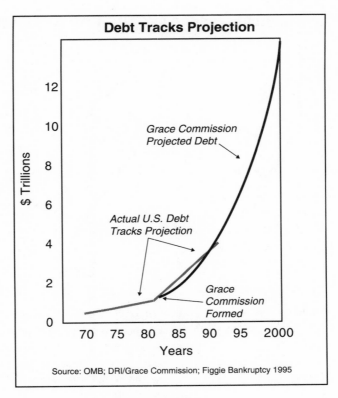

Figure 5-11

examples of programs that seemed to come out of nowhere to present taxpayers with gigantic bills when banks and savings institutions failed en masse. Other insurance programs—including that of the Pension Benefit Guarantee Corporation, which is likely to cost another $40–$100 billion before the decade is done—won't start crying for their billions until their sectors of the economy start to collapse, which they will. And the billions of government guaranteed loans, such as those linked to the Small Business Administration, Veterans Administration, Rural Electrification Administration, Federal Housing Authority, and many others, will default when things get tougher still. The invisible mountain of contingent liabilities could materialize into an expense of hundreds of billions of dollars.

Even though the Figgie book concentrates on federal government debt, a single dimension of a much larger problem, it is well worth reading. It gives little coverage to the indirect effects of taxes, government debt, inflation, and regulation, and none at all to the more serious problems of private and corporate debt and the effects of the business cycle. His conclusion, however, is quite accurate: in just a few years the government will have less income from taxes than it must spend to service the interest alone on its debt. That is without even beginning to pay for the military, for

Projected Debt Level
in the Year 2000

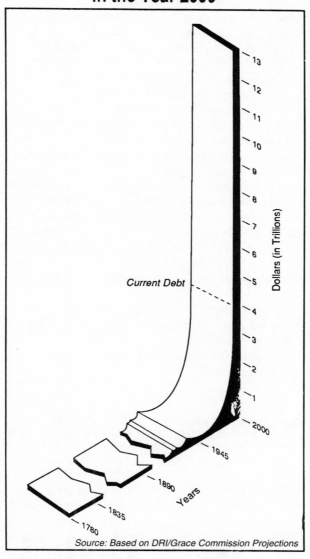

Figure 5-12

domestic programs, or for the enormous expense of the government's own administration. When the government borrows just to pay interest, it will have no flexibility at all, and that will be the end of the game.

Figgie's solution amounts to organizing political action committees, voting, staging demonstrations, petitions, speeches, writing letters to congressmen, and the like, most of which are exercises in futility at best. Protesters in the '60s were right when they said, "If you're not part of the solution, you're part of the problem." Political action is the problem.

In principle, an unsustainable amount of government debt should be a matter of concern only to the government (which is not at all the same thing as society at large) and to those who foolishly lent them money. But the government is in a position to extract tax revenues from its subjects, or to inflate the currency to keep the ball rolling. Its debt indirectly, therefore, becomes everyone's burden. And it presents some direct problems, as well.

At any given moment a fixed amount of capital in the world is available for borrowing. The government is considered the most creditworthy borrower, since it has what amounts to a 100 percent lien on all the wealth in its bailiwick, so it can borrow all it wants, and at the lowest rates. Why should anyone lend to a business, which could go bankrupt, when the government is available? The ultimate result is "crowding out." The potential for real problems first arose in the middle of the 1970s; as of 1991, the government consumed approximately 79 percent of all new credit.

Federal debt is not a new problem, but its trend points to whether we're in for prosperous or depressed times. In Figure 5-15 you will note that the overall trend relative to GNP was up through World War I, the Depression, and World War II. In the boom years following World War II up through the '60s, federal debt dropped radically. Now it is rising rapidly.

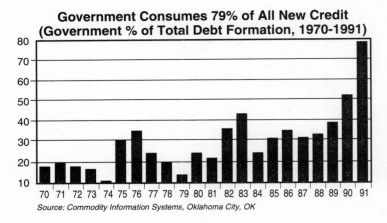

Government Consumes 79% of All New Credit
(Government % of Total Debt Formation, 1970-1991)

Source: Commodity Information Systems, Oklahoma City, OK

Figure 5-13

Total Government Outlays as a Percentage of GNP

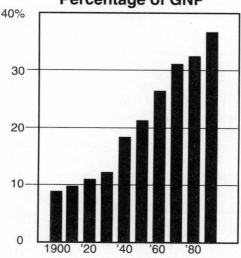

Sources: Cato Institute, Census Bureau

Figure 5-14

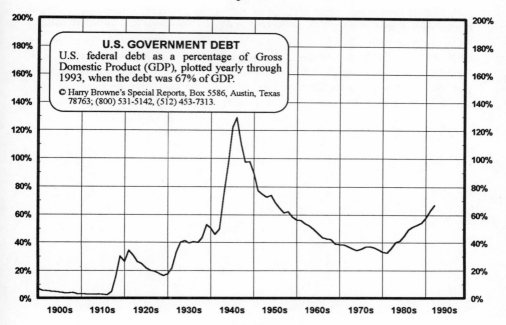

U.S. GOVERNMENT DEBT

U.S. federal debt as a percentage of Gross Domestic Product (GDP), plotted yearly through 1993, when the debt was 67% of GDP.

© Harry Browne's Special Reports, Box 5586, Austin, Texas 78763; (800) 531-5142, (512) 453-7313.

Figure 5-15

The consequences of all this are grim, but the timing is hard to predict. Perhaps the government can somehow borrow amounts that no one previously thought possible. But its creditors will look for repayment. Either the creditors are going to walk away unhappy (in the case of a default), or the holders of all dollars are going to be stuck with worthless paper (in the case of a hyperinflation), or the taxpayers' pockets will be looted (the longer things muddle along), or most likely a combination of all three will happen. This will not be a happy story for all but a few of us.

Along the way we could experience a severe deflation due to massive defaults on private debt. But, in the long run, the fate of the dollar is sealed. Its value is likely to approach that of a peso, perhaps before this decade is over. At best, the dollar's value will be much, much less than it is today. This is an argument that some major fireworks—once-in-a-lifetime-type stuff—will take place soon. The problem is that it's impossible to predict when things will start unraveling. An economic time bomb doesn't have a dial one can read.

CAN DEBT CONTINUE COMPOUNDING FOREVER?

There is no telling how high the debt will be piled or how many more cyclical recoveries can be wrenched from the economy. As of 1992, U.S. corporations were raising record amounts of equity to pay off debt incurred during the '80s, and consumers were doing likewise.

The unanswerable question is one of timing. As Milton Friedman said, "There is a lot of ruin in a country." A collapse could have happened as early as 1970, was more likely in 1974–1975, and was more likely again in 1980–1982. There may be enough stretch left in the system to avoid one this time. But it is not prudent to plan one's life around that hope. What we are looking at is big trouble, and the public is ill-prepared to deal with it. But few were prepared for the '30s after the good times of the '20s. A chicken the size of an ostrich is coming home to roost.

6

Taxes and the Greater Depression

Taxes are not levied for the benefit of the taxed.

R. Heinlein

The tendency of taxation is to create a class of persons who do not labor, to take from those who do labor the produce of that labor, and to give it to those who do not labor.

Wm. Cobbett, 1811

Taxes are the number-two factor in economic life after earning an income. If you pay the taxes, they directly reduce your standard of living. If you don't pay them, you run the risk of having your assets forcibly removed and of serving serious jail time. Taxes are worth looking at, but not in the way most investors do. You can get innumerable tips on how to cut your tax bill, but they are not nearly as important as the effect taxes have on the economy and investments.

TAXES AND THE ECONOMY

Income taxes reduce nearly everyone's income by 20 percent to 50 percent. That leaves much less for you to save or consume, and it decreases the income of those you do business with.

And taxes substantially increase the cost of everything you consume, again reducing your standard of living. These include not only obvious levies, like a sales tax, which reduces purchasing power from 3 percent to 8 percent in most jurisdictions, but the income tax everyone pays, which must be reflected in what they get for their products to net a given return on capital. Further, there are the hundreds of license fees, transfer taxes, stamp duties, property and inventory taxes, excise taxes, import duties, and innumerable layers of government-mandated expense.

This creates a "multiplier effect." Take a car, for example. An iron ore mining company pays X percent of its revenue in taxes, so the ore costs the buyer X percent more. The railroad that transports the ore pays R percent of its revenue in taxes, so it must charge R percent more. The steel producer, the auto manufacturer, and the auto dealer each pay S percent, A percent, and D percent. So by the time the consumer buys the car, he's paying X + R + S + A + D multiplied scores of times, as each intermediary contributes to the finished product. And there's still sales tax.

If government wants to help the U.S. auto industry, it need do nothing more than eliminate taxes. A politically more likely approach is a massive subsidy of some sort to auto manufacturers, which would be paid for by even higher taxes.

The cumulative effect of taxation is overwhelming. The complaint is often heard that the farmer gets only 5 percent to 10 percent of the retail cost of a loaf of bread; the remainder is assumed to go to middlemen, who are somehow taking advantage of him. In reality, over 35 percent of the bread's cost is taxes, since that's about what government at all levels extracts from the economy (see Figure 5–14). In the case of cigarettes, the figure approaches 95 percent.

Entirely apart from the many hundreds of billions that the government extracts from society every year in direct taxes (almost all of which is spent inefficiently, much of which is wasted completely, and not-a-little of which is used to suppress productive activity), is the cost to individuals and corporations of complying with the federal tax laws. That number is estimated at $120 billion a year. How much is that?

In 1991 "only" $15.6 billion was raised for new stock offerings. So eight times as much was literally wasted on activities and material that serve absolutely no useful purpose. There's no shortage of capital in the country. The government just wastes a large part of the capital we have.

Of course, we receive some benefits for our taxes, but at outrageously inflated prices. Worse yet, most tax revenue goes to pay for subsidies, welfare programs, and endless regulatory bureaucracy that further decrease production.

But taxation and waste have always been with society, which nonetheless has survived and progressed. More to the point are the effects of tax policy on the economy.

TAXES AND THE BUSINESS CYCLE

The healthy side of a depression is the liquidation of distortions that hurt the economy, especially the accumulation of mistakes in the allocation of capital. The details of any tax system—its different rates, credits, preferences, special deductions, deferrals, exemptions, and loopholes—cause people to act and invest in ways they otherwise would not have. In fact, people act in ways they would consider completely irrational were it not for the tax laws; tax considerations motivate people to waste and to misallocate capital on a vast scale.

Suppose, for instance, that a powerful congressman were to introduce and sponsor a bill saying that "All investments in widget factories shall be eligible for a 30 percent tax credit"—meaning that 30 percent of the cost of the investment can be deducted directly from the investor's tax bill. If that sounds a little rich, remember that the governments of numerous countries have enacted even headier benefits to stimulate favored (they like to say "strategic") industries. They may offer 100 percent depreciation over three years, no income tax for ten years, no capital gains taxes and large tax credits on all wages. Of course, since the business environment in countries that need to provide credits is usually terrible, everyone who runs a non-favored business folds his tent and goes to the next country, or restructures his business to qualify for the credits. But that's another story.

Such tax benefits would immediately and directly cause a frenzy of widget plant construction, and induce a lot of people to work at them. There would be considerable "trickle down" as other industries expanded to service the widget factories and their workers. Many people would invest in widgets, with the prospect of saving almost as much in taxes as they risked on the factory, even if it never made a single widget. This is how tax laws create "targeted spending" (a fashionable term in the 1992 elections). And the benefits they offer need not be nearly as radical as those in this example to have a major effect. It sounds like everyone wins.

But there are indirect and delayed consequences, as well. All the capital and labor that has gone into the new factories has, in reality, been diverted from other uses that people would have preferred, absent the tax advantages. And when the market is glutted with widgets, or when the tax benefits run out or are repealed, a wave of widget factory closings takes place, with resulting unemployment and a "reverse trickledown."

Since tax increases are disastrous, you might think that any tax reduction would be a huge plus. That's right, but they are accompanied by the inevitable withdrawal pains of unwinding the distortions caused by the higher taxes. Although lower taxes are hugely beneficial for everyone, they cause widget factories to close, with immediate job losses and write-offs of capital.

REAGAN CUTS, CLINTON BOOSTS

During the Reagan years many tax benefits, including some that had become structural features of the economy, were eliminated. Although the Reaganites boosted many other taxes, they improved the income tax code by simplifying it. If the Internal Revenue Code were to stay unchanged, it would create fewer new distortions in the ways people work and invest, because it's simpler and has fewer special beneficiaries. A lot of the problems the economy experienced in the late '80s and early '90s can be traced to old distortions, cranked in over decades, coming unglued. In the long run the elimination of these distortions can only be very beneficial, but in the short run it is painful for those who own the widget plants, or lent to them, or supplied materials to them, or worked for them, or relied on their operations in any way. And in today's economy, there are a huge number of widget factory equivalents.

Figure 6-1 shows a radical drop in marginal rates in the late 1920s, much as we saw in the '80s.

It is arguable that the radical drop in taxes actually helped precipitate the 1929–1945 depression. That depression was healthy in that it cleansed the economy of many distortions, but it also seemed to stimulate the government into raising taxes again. And higher taxes, among other misguided measures, made the last depression drag on for years, when it could have been sharp but brief.

President Clinton is raising taxes, both from "necessity" and from an inclination to draw more power to the state. His tax increases will have the same effect as Roosevelt's higher taxes in the '30s. Many businesses that could make a go of it under the Reagan regime will have to close.

By making sales taxes and consumer interest non-deductible and by taxing unemployment compensation Reagan's tax bills temporarily slowed the economy and had a deflationary effect. But these effects were relatively minor.

The old law that offered basically unlimited deductibility of interest (against marginal rates that had been as high as 92 percent) naturally encouraged individuals and companies to take on debt. Those same high rates discouraged investors from buying bonds, high yielding stocks and other investments paying current income. Preferential capital gains rates (generally about half the ordinary income rates) encouraged people to try for appreciation, instead. The old tax law favored real estate more than any other investment, because investors could claim accelerated deductions for depreciation even while the property was going up in value. The

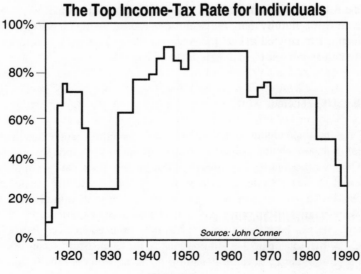

The Top Income-Tax Rate for Individuals

Source: John Conner

Figure 6-1

tremendous tax-motivated buying pressure was a major reason real estate did so well.

Reagan's new law, with a maximum rate of 28 percent and little special treatment for capital gains, provided more of an incentive to seek current return than capital gains on investments. That was a boon for shares with high current yields—mainly big, mature companies—and helped S&P 500–type stocks (and index funds) perform better than the rest of the market. It was good news for utilities, for instance.

People buy bonds mainly for their current yield. The reduction in the top tax rate from 70 percent to 50 percent (in 1982) and then to 28 percent (in 1986) was great news for the bond market. It more than doubled effective yields for people in the top brackets. That drew a lot of money to bonds and helped drive down the very high interest rates prevailing at the time.

The biggest effect fell on real estate, the market that was ripest for a fall. Gigantic amounts of money had flowed into property over decades, especially in the 1970s when inflation magnified real estate's already extraordinary tax benefits. The new tax law took away most of the benefits. The old 19-year depreciation schedule went to 27.5 years for residential property and 31.5 years for nonresidential property. This means less demand for buildings. Without rapid depreciation, followed by conversion of those deductible dollars into favored long-term capital gains, there is no longer any good tax reason for investors to favor real estate over other alternatives.

Further, as with stocks, investment interest expense is now deductible only to the extent of investment income. That really hurts property owners with negative cash flow, which compounds the pressure on almost everyone who bought property in the last ten years.

The residential market, and the standard of living of those with big profits in their homes, was hurt by the IRS limitations on the deductibility of interest on home refinancing. It restricted the refinancing of a house to pay for other goodies. Now the only way to benefit from appreciation will be to sell the house. And after 1990, those who invested in any type of limited partnership, including real estate they did not actively manage, could no longer apply their share of any losses against most other types of income, which created more selling pressure on property.

The Reagan tax reform in general made dividend and interest income more desirable, and the deductions and appreciation potential of tangibles less desirable. The reforms contributed mightily to the strength of stocks and bonds and the weakness of tangibles such as real estate from the late '80s on.

THE CLINTON ADMINISTRATION

So what will be the likely effect of the Clinton administration on our tax policies? Decades of tax-driven distortions were unwound by Reagan's tax reduction and simplification measures at the immediate cost of the real estate collapse, and with the immediate benefit of a tremendous bull market for stocks and bonds. Clinton will almost certainly put that process into reverse, with new tax credits and deductions for certain areas (whatever he and his friends decide are high technology and "sunrise" industries). The revenues lost on incentives for "targeted spending" will be recovered through higher—perhaps much higher—taxes on everything else.

Those additional taxes will drain resources from not-so-favored but productive activity. There's no reason to expect Clinton's tax changes to restore any of the old benefits for real estate. Higher ordinary tax rates will knock the props from under stocks with high yields and from under all bonds. On the other hand, Clinton's tax changes will certainly expand the underground economy, which is a good thing for the country, although the government will denounce its growth as a crime.

A better term for the underground economy might be the "alternative economy," since "underground" has acquired a somewhat pejorative connotation. The alternative economy, which includes everything from barter of services to the millions who don't file tax returns, obey regulations, or purchase licenses to do business, is simply the untaxed, unregulated free market in action. It runs the way business did in the early part of the century, before the income tax, the Federal Reserve, and most regulatory agencies. In the alternative economy, the sellers earn more, the buyers pay less, and the State is shut out. Everyone wins, except those who are fed by the government.

THE LAFFER CURVE

This point of view tends to shock the average person, who has been indoctrinated to believe that the government not only deserves a slice of all economic activity but is also a proxy for society itself. Arthur Laffer, the economist who postulated the "Laffer Curve," apparently labored under that misapprehension, and it seriously flawed his results, which are, nonetheless, worth examining. The reasoning behind the Laffer Curve had a major effect on tax policy in the '80s.

When governments want more revenue, their usual method is to raise taxes. Laffer observed that there is a point at which any further increase in tax rates will yield less revenue, by discouraging economic activity and forcing more of what remains into the untaxed underground economy.

In other words, at a zero tax rate, the incentive to produce would be greatest, because the producers would get to keep all they produced. At a 100 percent tax rate, they would have no incentive to produce at all; if the government tries to take all, it winds up with 100 percent of nothing. So the tax rate at which the government maximizes its revenue is somewhere between zero and 100 percent. For anything less than the maximum revenue the theory holds that there are two tax rates that will yield the same revenue, a low rate (r1) and a high rate (r2). It is the lower tax rate that allows the creation of the most wealth.

You'll notice that Figure 6-2 (the Laffer Curve) shows that some low level of taxation actually has a positive effect on the economy (the area from 0 to rp). This is because Laffer correctly considers some government services—like courts and police—to be essential for the economy to maximize production. But he is incorrect in stating that the government is the only entity that could provide those services, and that taxes are the only way they could be paid for.

The Laffer Curve brings up several interesting points. One, it shows that the interests of government and society not only are not identical, they are to a good degree at odds with each other. As tax rates rise beyond the point needed for Laffer's "essential" services, they reduce society's total output. The analogy is exactly that of a parasite on a host; the more the parasite draws, the weaker the host becomes. And if the parasite eats too much—as the governments of the Soviet bloc and many Third World countries demonstrate—it may actually kill the host, and itself in the process.

The Laffer Curve

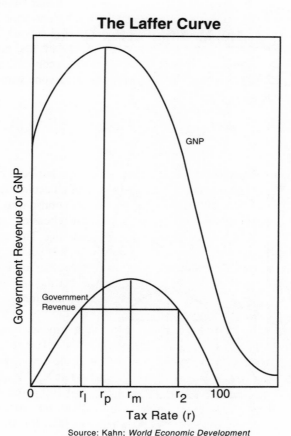

Source: Kahn; *World Economic Development*

Figure 6-2

The real mischief of the Laffer Curve is that it attempts to show the government what it should do to maximize its revenue (point rm), and implies that taxes should be reduced only until government revenue starts falling, rather than until GNP starts falling. I think a curve for greater prosperity would look like Figure 6-3.

It is obvious that it would be best for the economy to have no taxes, but since that leaves nothing for the government, it is unacceptable to them. And since about 50 percent of the U.S. population believe they receive more from the government than they pay into it, it will probably be politically impossible to reduce the size of government much in the short run, despite the urgent need to do so and the purely pragmatic arguments that can be made for it.

Higher taxes seem inevitable during the Clinton administration. Their effect, at a minimum, will be to deepen the economy's malaise. Higher taxes alone may be enough to precipitate the Greater Depression.

The Modified Laffer Curve

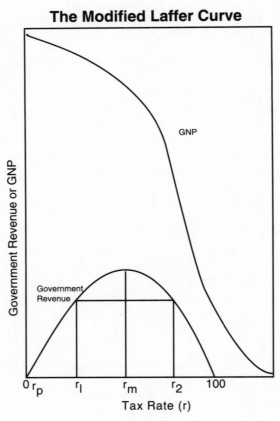

Figure 6-3

Even so, many people find the ethical argument against taxes even more compelling than the pragmatic one.

SLIGHTLY UP FROM SLAVERY

To eliminate misunderstanding as to what taxes are, it is helpful to define the word "theft." One good definition is "the wrongful taking and carrying away of the personal goods of another."* The definition does not go on to say "unless you're the government." There is no difference, in principle, between the State taking property and a street gang doing so, except that the State's theft is "legal" and its agents are immune from prosecution. Many people do not accept that analogy, because the government is widely viewed as being of, for, and by the people, even though it's also acknowledged as acting badly from time to time.

Suppose a mugger demanded your wallet, perhaps because he needed money to buy a new car, and threatened you with violence if you weren't forthcoming. Everyone would call that a criminal act. Suppose, however, the mugger said he wanted the money to buy himself food. Would it still be theft? Suppose now that he said he wanted your wallet to feed another hungry person, not himself. Would it still be theft?

Now let's suppose that this mugger convinces most of his friends that it's okay for him to relieve you of your wallet. Would it still be theft? What if he convinces a majority of citizens? Principles stand on their own. Even if a criminal act is committed for a good purpose, or with the complicity of bystanders, (even if those people call themselves the government), it is still an act of criminal aggression.

It is important to establish an ethical viewpoint on the matter, even if it doesn't change your reaction to the mugger's (or the State's) demands. Just as it's usually unwise to resist a mugger, it's usually unwise to resist the government, which has a lot of force on its side.

That's not to say it's easy to swim against the tide. Every year at tax time promoters of big government haul out an assortment of nostrums to sedate the lambs as they are shorn. One of the worst is "Taxes are the price we pay for civilization," a statement of Supreme Court Justice Oliver Wendell Holmes. It is a splendid example of how, if a lie is big enough and is repeated often enough, it can come to be accepted.

Actually, the truth is almost exactly the opposite. As Mark Skousen, economist and author, has pointed out: "Taxation is the price we pay for *failing* to build a civilized society. The higher the tax level, the greater the failure. A centrally planned totalitarian state is a complete failure of civilization, while a totally voluntary society is its ultimate success."

Taxes are destroyers of civilization and society. They impoverish the average

American College Dictionary (1966).

man. They support welfare programs that anchor the lower classes at the bottom of society. They underwrite a gigantic bureaucracy that serves only to raise costs and quash incentive. They pay for public works programs (once called "pork barrel projects," but now rechristened "infrastructure investment") that are usually ten times more costly than their privately financed counterparts, whether needed or not. They maintain programs that cause huge distortions in the economy (such as deposit insurance for banks and S&Ls). And they foster a climate of fear and dishonesty. The list of evils goes on. But the simple truth is that anything needed or wanted by society would be provided by profit-seeking entrepreneurs, if only the tax collector would retire.

Protesting against taxes because they're a costly or inefficient way of providing services, however, is in good measure futile. It's like saying that the mugger shouldn't rob you because there might be a better way for him to get what he wants.

How serious is the tax problem in the long run? I believe it will become less, not more serious, despite the government's increasingly high tax rates and draconian enforcement measures. The major long-term trend of society is toward decentralization and smaller-scale organizations. The U.S. government will prove no more able to deal with a rapidly evolving economy than was the Soviet government. More and more Americans will see the government as meaningless and irrelevant, as serving no useful purpose.

THE FUTURE OF THE TAX SYSTEM

Of course, that's not the way people in government see things. The IRS has attempted to update and integrate its hundreds of incompatible computer systems, most of which originated in the '60s. When the government's computer systems are modernized, the government will have the capability to track everyone's finances everywhere. That would be a nightmare almost on the scale of Orwell's Big Brother in *1984*. But although the government will try, their success may result in their destruction.

How might that be? Computer programmers, as a group, are among the most original, inventive, and anti-authoritarian people on the planet. Most are independents or work for small companies. Few have warm feelings about the government or the IRS. I would be surprised if, as the IRS's global system is put together, it wasn't seeded with one or more virus programs set to destroy the entire network. In fact, I would be surprised if IRS computers weren't infected with scores of viruses, planted—in numerous possible ways—by different programmers working unbeknownst to each other. Some of these programs are incredibly virulent and practically impossible to defend against.

That may sound like a *deus ex machina* solution to the problem, but I think its likelihood approaches inevitability. The situation is almost analogous to that in H.G. Wells's *War of the Worlds* in which, when vastly superior Martian forces seemed certain to overwhelm Earth, the planet was saved by bacteria that caused the invaders to sicken and die. I wouldn't doubt the IRS has already had several experiences with virus programs. But the spread of such infections would necessarily be limited by the IRS' old systems.

The government and the IRS will increasingly try to use technology to control the average American, but their plans will backfire. In all areas of life, technology has always served as the liberator of the common man, even though it may seem threatening for a time.

Part II

What Can You Do About It?

7

A Low-Risk Portfolio with 1,000 Percent Potential

Man should always divide his wealth into three parts; one-third in land, one-third in commerce and one-third in his own hands.

Babylonian Talmud

To set up an intelligent portfolio, you have to decide not only what, but how much to buy. The answers to both questions center on the concept of diversification.

There are any number of approaches to the problem of how you should diversify, or even if you *should* diversify. Two popular attitudes, which bracket the range of possibilities, are summed up by two contradictory aphorisms. The first, "Don't put all your eggs in one basket," says to diversify broadly and take something of a shotgun approach. The other says, "Put all your eggs in one basket, and then watch the basket very carefully." In other words, use the military principle of concentration of force and, to change metaphors, try to hit long-ball home runs.

At first blush, broad diversification might appear to suit the investor who has already accumulated substantial capital, who is not likely to earn a great deal more, and who prefers to take a more passive approach to the markets. Narrow concentration tends to suit someone still building his capital base, still accumulating capital from his business or profession, who pays closer attention to the markets.

But both approaches are problematic. The first approach incorporates the danger of winding up with a hard-to-monitor hodgepodge that will do no better than the market as a whole. With the second, entirely apart from the problem of choosing the right basket, carefully watching the basket does not guarantee that its bottom won't drop out before your eyes.

There are no easy solutions. But there are two approaches that I use—my own "10 × 10" approach detailed below, and the Permanent Portfolio approach. Both address the dilemma of how to diversify for safety while concentrating assets for returns. You might factor either or both of them into your thinking. Both are variations of what is known as a "hedge portfolio," that is, one structured to hedge against bad times, or at least countercyclical events. It's a useful concept.

HEDGE PORTFOLIOS

To most investors, a well-rounded portfolio means some stocks, some bonds, some real estate, and some cash. That's fine, if you think it will be business-as-usual for the indefinite future. But if you credit the existence of a business cycle, or are just concerned about unexpected events, you do not want all your eggs in a too-conventional basket. If I'm right about what's in store for us over the next few years, stocks, bonds, real estate, and maybe even cash will prove to be suboptimal holdings. And the value and profitability of your business could plunge.

Nevertheless, you don't want to sell most of these assets. You want to live in your house, you like running your business, and you're not about to liquidate your pension. And you surely prefer not to realize a taxable gain on any of them. Further, you have confidence in the future, and your present holdings are probably excellent ways to capitalize on that prospect. Conversely, you don't want to be hurt by a drop over the short run. At a minimum, you want a hedge.

A hedge allows you to keep what you have, secure in the knowledge that if your traditional assets drop substantially in value, you will make it up elsewhere. Allocating a relatively small amount of capital to insure the rest is a corollary to the first rule of investing: "Keep what you have." It is unfortunate that many people learn that rule only after it's too late to apply it.

It is not necessary, or prudent, to invest 100 percent of your capital in search of a 10 percent gain when the same result can be achieved by investing 10 percent for a 100 percent gain. Still, the first policy is exactly what most people, including almost everyone in search of high income, follows. In stable, prosperous times it can be an acceptable strategy, because the risk is proportional to the reward. But, for reasons I've spelled out earlier, that is unlikely to be the case in the '90s. And a conventional portfolio is unlikely to hedge against the unexpected.

A MOST BASIC PORTFOLIO

You must balance four factors against each other in a portfolio: safety, yield, growth, and liquidity.

If you were to buy half gold and half T-Bills, and leave it at that, you would have as risk-free an investment as probably exists today. It would have the advantage of simplicity, and you wouldn't have to devote a lot of time and attention to monitoring your investments. Arguably each of its two components would protect you, albeit in different ways, against both inflation (gold because it's a hard asset, T-Bills because their interest rates compensate for inflation when they're rolled over) and deflation (gold because it can't be defaulted on, T-Bills because their value would rise as other paper assets are destroyed). But neither would do well if the economy lags or if we have genuine prosperity. In any event, half the fun of having money (a distinction: "having," as opposed to either "earning" or "spending") lies in playing with it. Money is like a new car or boat; it's a lot of fun to get it, and it's great to get rid of it, but it ought to be fun in between as well.

THE TEN TIMES TEN (10 × 10) APPROACH

Everyone who devotes any attention to investing inevitably develops his own specialties, approaches, and methods. In other words a style. There are many paths up the mountain, and all intelligent methods have merit. But the degree of merit can vary tremendously with the times. A value investor, who attempts to find dollar bills selling for 50 cents, is going to have a tough time in a mildly inflationary environment when the stock market is booming. A growth investor, who looks for companies with rapidly and consistently compounding earnings, is going to have a tough time during a deflation. A technician, who follows the price action of charts, has a tough time in trendless markets, or periods punctuated by unpredictable events in the world outside.

What we're most likely to see in the '90s are titanic moves in many markets, with hard-to-predict timing and direction. Massive forces of inflation and deflation will vie with one another, and it's impossible to say which will dominate or for how long. In that environment safety, and keeping what you have, will be critical. But safety is unlikely to be found in traditional places, simply because the market will be so radically untraditional.

It makes sense to reorient your assets to deal with the market as it soon will be, not the way it recently was or how we hope it will turn out. This may require you to act contrary to your intuition, since you'll need to sell investments that have established good track records during good times and buy investments with bad performance histories. But that's the very nature of buying low and selling high. You'll never buy low if you demand a good track record.

I've developed what I call the "10 times 10" strategy, which is well suited to the '90s environment. In essence, divide your risk portfolio into ten unrelated areas, each of which has the potential, in your subjective opinion, to increase tenfold in value (move 10–1) over the course of a business cycle. In a way, the strategy seeks to go between the horns of the rifle–shotgun dilemma by diversifying broadly, but only into low-risk, high-potential propositions. Properly applied, this approach should give you the best of all possible worlds. It has certainly served me well. There are several keys to its proper application.

- **10 investments, or investment sectors, 10 percent each**. Do not invest 50 percent of your capital in just one deal that you feel strongly about, since that will put you into the "all your eggs in one basket" pitfall. The biggest mistakes are made on the propositions about which you feel most confident.

  But suppose you can't find ten deals with enough potential in which to invest. Say you can find only three. Should you, then, put a third of your capital into each? No, for several reasons. First, if you can't find many high-potential deals, it may be a sign that the market is overpriced and you're better off waiting. Another reason is that any one deal can go to zero, a complete wipeout. Losing 10 percent of your capital is endurable, but 25 percent, or 50 percent, or even 75 percent is a different matter. I've been tagged for numbers like that in the past, and the experience reemphasizes the first rule of investing: "Keep what you have." And that aphorism brings to mind another: "First make a plan; then, follow the plan." In this case the plan calls for 10 percent per deal, and ad hoc changes will undermine any plan.

- **Unrelated investments**. Buying ten different junior mining stocks doesn't diversify you, except among junior mines. The ten areas should be unrelated so that if, for instance, gold crashes, only a part of your capital will go with it. Ideally, the ten different investment areas should tend to move independently of one another—gold and bonds, or banking stocks and the T-Bill—Eurodollar spread.

  Especially in the current explosive financial atmosphere, almost anything can happen, and the number of stable points around which you can plan your life are decreasing. Today's speculations could be tomorrow's bluechips, and today's bluechips are increasingly speculative. It's enough to turn a skeptical investor into a nihilist.

- **Potential to increase tenfold in value (10–1 potential)**. Since we all make mistakes, your winners must have the potential to more than make up for your losers. With this approach, even if 90 percent of your investments plummet to zero but you have been right about just one, you will have preserved capital. A couple of your choices may go to zero, several others may drop 50 percent or so. But some others will likely double, or quadruple, or better. The emphasis is, obviously, on highly volatile, but also highly depressed, situations.

  And if you stick to investments you think have 10–1 potential, then you'll probably find yourself buying only depressed situations with relatively small downside risk. But high-potential investments, like start-up companies, can and sometimes do go to zero (bankruptcy).

- **Over a business cycle**. What should your time frame be for performance? Business cycles vary in length, but the timing from peak to peak, or trough to trough, usually lasts from five to ten years. The average holding time would therefore be from two and a half to five years, that is from trough to peak, or peak to trough for other kinds of investment.

A long holding period is important for several reasons. It will guard against overtrading and against trying to second-guess yourself. It reduces transaction costs. And, as the government tries to prop up the economy with ever more desperate measures, the short term will become more unpredictable while, paradoxically, the long term becomes more certain.

With the "10 × 10" approach, your net results should be quite satisfying and the risk far less than first seems to be the case. First, diversification always reduces risk, and a disciplined approach to being in ten unrelated areas greatly lessens your risk regardless of the volatility of each component.

Second, you are only likely to get 1,000 percent returns over a business cycle in those investment areas which have already crashed and have hit bottom. The path to low-risk profits is to "buy low and sell high," and this method enables you to put the theory into practice.

Third, by its very nature this approach is contracyclical and acts as a hedge. In good times, it forces you into depressed investments that will offset the drop in value of your real estate, your business, and your pension plan when times turn bad. In bad times, it forces you to take profits, because you'll likely have achieved at least a couple of ten-for-one shots, and forces you to reinvest the proceeds in the victims of the current cycle, such as conventional good-times investments like stocks and real estate.

It should be obvious that this approach does not lend itself to investment vehicles like most mutual funds, or popular, large-capitalization stocks. It relies on volatile, low-capitalization, relatively unknown stocks, supplemented by the use of moderate leverage in assets like commodities, convertibles, options, bonds, or real estate when appropriate.

A CURRENT PORTFOLIO

In early 1993, some of the investments on the list below are excellent values. Others have already exhausted part of their potential and are nearing retirement. In a couple of years almost everything on the list will probably change. Although a hedge portfolio is almost necessarily oriented toward bad times, when those times do arrive you could replace everything with conventional investments. At that point, they will be as cheap and held in as low regard as the investment areas below are at the moment.

Most of the items on the list are subjects of more lengthy discussion elsewhere in this book. Whether they belong here will depend on whether you read this in the summer of 1993 or some time in 1996.

1. *Silver*. This metal is a religious relic from the early days of the hard money movement, but after its canonization in the '70s it was excommunicated during

the '80s. My argument is simple: any commodity that is down over 90 percent in dollar terms and 95 percent in real terms after a ten-year bear market should be bought almost reflexively.

This is a bet on a resurgence of inflation, and/or a monetary crisis where people panic out of the dollar into gold. It also, somewhat paradoxically, constitutes a bet on a conventional boom, with tremendous demand for raw materials.

2. *Agricultural commodities.* Corn, wheat, the soybean complex, coffee, cocoa, and sugar, with prices in real terms near historical lows, belong in your portfolio. Buy equal dollar amounts of each, on very conservative 25–50 percent margin, through any of the exchanges where they trade. This investment bets on high inflation, as well as on various types of political stupidity, like war.

3. *TED spread.* Here you are long a contract of U.S. T-bills for each short contract of Eurodollars. At the moment the spread is also at historical lows.

You are betting on monetary chaos, either very high inflation, or— especially—a radical deflation. Also, in this instance, you believe stocks, bonds, and real estate will drop, and that the banking system will get into real trouble.

T-Bills are the most secure form of dollar debt, since they are the direct short-term obligations of the U.S. Treasury. Eurodollars are the unsecured offshore liabilities of major international banks; they are among the riskiest of dollar assets. Furthermore, T-Bills are exempt from state taxes for U.S. residents, and that adds to their desirability. Accordingly, T-Bills always have lower yields. How much lower is decided by how worried people are that we will have a serious financial crisis, and banks will default on their obligations, like Eurodollars. Figure 7–1 shows the TED spread's price history.

4. *Tokyo short sales.* The Japanese market has already dropped more than 50 percent from its high, so these investments have less upside and more risk than other items on the list. Still, the potential is great.

The way to play it is by shorting a closed-end Japanese fund or buying put warrants traded on the American exchange. This is a bet on deflation, and/or higher interest rates, and/or heightened international tension.

5. *U.S. short sales.* At some point, every other suggestion on this list will be replaced with something else, but I suspect that shorts will remain. Short sales should be restricted to stock promotions, stock frauds, and companies that are on their way to bankruptcy. With this investment you bet on deflation, but stick to companies that would be on their way to the trash can even in the best of times.

6. *Junior gold stocks.* Twice during the last decade, these exploration companies and producers of less than 100,000 oz. of gold p.a. have experienced 10–1 runs; after each run the stocks' prices sank back to previous lows. Junior golds have languished since about 1987. This is a bet on high inflation, and/or a monetary crisis.

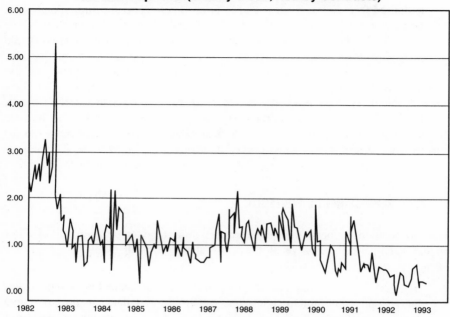

The TED Spread (Weekly Close, Nearby Contracts)

Source: The Interest Rate Strategy by John Pugsley

Figure 7-1

7. *Junior oil stocks.* These exploration companies and producers of less than 5,000 barrels per day haven't fallen as far as the golds since the top of the boom for both gold and oil in 1980, but they have been down longer—with no respite for 13 years. Here you bet on inflation, international tensions, but also, like silver, on a sudden boom.

8. *Politically distressed foreign real estate.* A great opportunity, especially with the rapid and favorable trend away from socialism that's taking place all over the world. It is unfortunate that this area is management-intensive. Also it is difficult to achieve adequate diversification, which is essential, with less than six figures.

   This is a good times-bad times investment at the moment, at least as far as Americans are concerned. Many Third World countries have already had their experiment with socialism, and the lesson is likely to last at least a generation.

9. *Uranium stocks.* A simple method of evaluating metal prices or metal stock prices is to compare the cash cost of production to the market price for the metal. When cost of production exceeds the market price low prices stimulate demand and constrain supply. No new productive capacity is added and existing capacity is idled. Sharp shortages result as substitution is difficult and

the lead time to bring new or idled capacity back on line is long. Uranium has collapsed from $60 to $8 a pound in price. There is no substitute for it. Two producers are Cameco (CCO.T C$20.50) and Uranium Resources (URX.V C$3.50). I believe both of these companies' stock prices will move up 1,000 percent within the next five years.

This list fills only nine of the ten slots in our "10 × 10" portfolio. But that's not a problem, because it always makes sense to have cash in reserve for new opportunities. Now they are fairly easy calls. In a year or two, however, the problem will be whether to sell. Let us look at what might be suitable replacements when each of these investments reaches its potential.

A LIKELY REVERSE-HEDGE PORTFOLIO

Here are some investments that are overpriced now at the top of the cycle but which should be bargains in a few years. Obviously it's crystal ball gazing, but you might keep your eye on the following:

1. Industrial metals. Gold and silver are both plays on instability, inflation, and fear. Copper, aluminum, platinum, palladium, and a whole host of minor metals can also be a play on inflation. But they are sensitive to industrial production as well. Good times tend to mean higher prices for them.
2. Short agricultural commodities. All commodities eventually fall to about their costs of production. Going short when they sell for big premiums to what it costs to produce them is as sure a bet as going long when they sell for big discounts.
3. Reverse TED spread. Here you would be long Eurodollars versus short T-Bills, when the spread is quite high. Another possibility would be to go long financial stocks, like strong banks and strong brokerage firms, which would be hurt in a chaotic environment but will recover.
4. Buy Tokyo stocks. The long-term trend is up. Other excellent prospects will be closed-end funds centering on various developing countries, like Taiwan, Indonesia, and India.
5. Buy U.S. stocks. It is difficult to identify the best groups in which to invest. My inclination would be a closed-end fund selling at a large discount. Another alternative would be venture capital deals.
6. Buy U.S. real estate. Possibilities are commercial space in Manhattan or a few tract houses outside Los Angeles.
7. Buy transports and utilities. These are fuel-sensitive enterprises; their earnings can drop radically as fuel prices go up. Further, the volume of people taking plane rides drops, and the number of people turning off the lights and watching their heating/cooling bills rise, when the economy takes a downturn. The reverse happens when things pick up.

The ''10 × 10'' approach lends itself best to speculative capital and a speculator's mentality. But it should keep you way ahead of the game, over the long run, especially when the markets become volatile. Even if you're dead wrong on nine choices and they all go to zero, if the tenth works out, you will have conserved capital.

Diversification among so many volatile propositions, betting on differing scenarios, has less absolute risk than something that seems conservative but can be torpedoed. Yet most people will still be frightened by it. And, of course, diversification also takes active management, which doesn't suit all investors.

The 10 × 10 portfolio seeks to profit from adversity and, with large profits, to make up for losses you may sustain elsewhere. The Permanent Portfolio, on the other hand, seeks only to maintain the capital you invest in it, which it should accomplish without radical moves or great drama, under almost any circumstances. And it solves some of the perceived problems of the 10 × 10 approach, as well.

THE PERMANENT PORTFOLIO APPROACH

The idea behind the Permanent Portfolio is to set aside the money that you must preserve for the future, money that you can't afford to lose or take risks with, and place a fixed percentage of it in investments that tend to move inversely to each other.

This approach was developed by my friends Harry Browne and Terry Coxon. It amounts to as near a fail-safe, fire-and-forget approach as I've come across. Unlike the ''10 × 10'' approach, which requires that investments be reassessed, bought, and sold over time, while their amounts remain constant, the Permanent Portfolio's components stay the same, and only their amounts are adjusted.

What Browne and Coxon have done is use their best judgment to structure a portfolio that hedges against every eventuality: hyperinflation, deflation, prosperity, depression, malaise, whatever. The approach hinges on two things: (a) a spread of investments that have been chosen to provide protection under any foreseeable economic conditions and (b) maintenance of a fixed percentage of capital in each at all price levels. The idea is to buy and sell as needed to keep the six classes of investment they have chosen in line with the target percentages.

Category	Target Percentage
Gold	20%
Silver	5%
Swiss franc assets	10%
Real estate/resource stocks	15%
U.S. stocks	15%
T-Bills, T-Bonds	35%

Gold should profit from continued inflation, runaway inflation, or other types of monetary crisis. Silver, from rising inflation, prosperity, or possibly from a runaway inflation. Swiss franc assets, from rising inflation or a runaway inflation. Real estate and resource stocks, from rising inflation. U.S. stocks, specially selected for volatility, from prosperity. And Treasury securities, from deflation.

The portfolio solves the problem of when to sell by maintaining a fixed percentage in each asset. For example, if silver ran from its present $4 to $50 over the next few years, you would annually sell enough of this metal to keep it at 5 percent of the portfolio's total dollar value; if you did not, the dollar value of your silver holdings would approach 50 percent. This approach allows you to buy low and sell high automatically and mechanically, without trying to second-guess the markets. At the same time, if any one asset drops in value, you automatically buy more of it at the annual readjustment date.

I suggest you place half of your total investment capital in a permanent portfolio, and liberate the other half for speculative situations. This is a very sound approach. I strongly favor the Permanent Portfolio approach; in fact, I've been a consultant to the Permanent Portfolio Fund since 1982.

The "10 × 10" and the Permanent Portfolio approaches can be combined by allocating "serious" money into the Permanent Portfolio and more-speculative capital into a "10 × 10" portfolio. But the advantages of hedging can also be applied in many other ways, as the next chapter will show.

8

Hedging for More Profit and Less Risk

It's impossible to be sure, at any given moment, whether any market is going up or down. No matter how overpriced a market may be, there are always bulls with good-sounding arguments why it could go twice as high: no matter how "cheap" a market may be, there are always convincing bearish arguments for it to go lower. After all, for every buyer there's a seller (and vice-versa). The same is true for the economy, where a case can be made for both good times and bad times at almost any juncture.

How can you hedge yourself against being on the wrong side of the market? By using "hedge" strategies which are surprisingly little-known, though they're almost always lower risk and higher potential than pure long or short positions.

A "hedge" is a position where you buy X dollars worth of one stock or commodity, and simultaneously short sell (see chapter 12 for details) an equal dollar amount of a different stock or commodity. Since you're both "long" and "short" the market, you don't really care which way it goes. By choosing your positions intelligently, you can be right on both sides of your trade, regardless of overall market conditions.

As fashions change, the first tend to become last and the last to become first. This was recognized in biblical times, and it's equally certain in the investment markets. Regardless of the overall direction of the market, relatively overpriced stocks tend to decline, and underpriced securities tend to rise. Indeed, both movements often happen at once. By being both long one investment and simultaneously short another, you can escape the need to second-guess the direction of the overall market and still profit in either a bull or bear market. The keys to profitable hedging are patience and consistency: patience because it doesn't make sense to be in any market all the time; consistency, because your plan won't work if you don't follow it.

Most of the time, it's a 50/50 bet whether something is going up or down, and you need better than 50/50 odds to make money. The idea is to be in a given investment only when the odds of its going up appear to be 90 percent or better; and to be short when the odds of its going down are equally strong. It is fortunate that odds that strong usually identify investments that are getting ready to move 10-for-one or more as well.

Suppose, for instance, you like the prospects of Stock *X*; you're sure the underlying company will do well. But you're afraid of the market as a whole, which could take Stock *X* down, despite the company prospering. How do you solve the dilemma of whether to buy or to wait?

A hedge might be the answer. Find another company in the same industry, Stock *Z*, which you feel has terrible prospects and perhaps will lose business because of Company *X*'s very success, and whose stock looks to be overpriced. Then buy Stock *X* and short an equal dollar amount of Stock *Z*.

If your assessment is correct, it will not make any difference how the market in general, or the industry in particular, does. You'll make money as long as *X* does better than *Z*—whether they both go up or they both go down. And, if their prices move in opposite directions, you can make money on both and double your profits, even while you've reduced your risk.

Value is relative, not absolute. In other words, you want a position not only because of *what* it is, but because of *what price* it is. For instance, in February 1993, gold is a good buy at $335 and the Nikkei 225* at 16,500 is not; so I suggest owning gold and short-selling Japanese stocks. Several years from now, if gold is at $1,000 and/or the Nikkei is at 5,000, I'll almost certainly be inclined to say the exact opposite: buy the Nikkei index and sell gold.

It's never a question of how many dollars you can get for something you want to sell. The real question is how many shares, or contracts, or acres you can exchange it for. It might, for instance, be hard to say whether corn is cheap or dear at, say, $4 a bushel, unless you know what to compare it with. But we know that wheat usually sells for about twice the price of corn, and soybeans for about triple— because of factors like production costs and protein content. If soybeans sell for $6 while corn is at $4, you can be pretty sure corn is dear, at least relative to beans. By selling corn and buying beans, you're likely to make money.

---

*An index of Japanese stocks, traded on the Chicago Mercantile Exchange

The idea is to pick out very cheap stocks or commodities to buy, and very dear ones to sell simultaneously, with the intention of protecting yourself from general market moves. Buy and sell respectively equal dollar amounts of each and wait for the inevitable, without caring whether the market in general booms or busts.

EXAMPLE ONE

In 1991 I recommended such a hedge in the thrift industry. It provides an ideal illustration of the principle.

Continental Federal, an S&L based close to Washington, D.C., was selling for $5—less than a fourth of its $22 book value, and about a fifth of its previous high of $27. An analysis of its balance sheet showed it could even then have been liquidated for $15. It exceeded all regulatory capital requirements by at least two to one. All but a few of its loans were in the relatively low-risk residential market, and it had already charged off most of its bad loans.

Although management had been competent in making good loans, their overhead expenses were very high at 320 basis points of their $1.1 billion of assets (i.e., about $35 million or 3.2 percent of assets). Typically for a public company, management was treating themselves quite well at shareholders' expense. Why not? They owned only 100,000 of the 2.9 million shares outstanding. Overhead should be no more than 250 basis points (2.5 percent of assets), and a difference of 70 points on $1.1 billion is about $8 million per year. If management were forced to tighten their belts by only that much, the stock could easily sell for at least $12 per share.

A group of shareholders, including myself, joined together to make it happen. Still, because of my misgivings about the economy at large, I did not want to be long Continental Federal without being short an equal dollar amount of something likely to join the choir invisible. GlenFed, the third-largest thrift in the United States, with most of its assets in California, seemed like a good choice in that category.

GlenFed had about $16.5 billion in assets and $950 million in stated capital, which was satisfactory on the surface. But about 80 percent of their capital was debt, on which the interest clock continued to run. At the same time almost any portfolio losses could quickly wipe out shareholders' equity since non-performing assets were already over $700 million, and in California's depressed real estate market, it was clear they could easily suffer large losses. In addition, GlenFed owned numerous hotels, shopping centers, and business parks through a subsidiary, the very worst things to be in at the time. It was all for sale, but there were no bidders, because it seemed likely that the Resolution Trust was going to wind up with GlenFed's properties, and potential buyers could get them more cheaply later.

The hedge worked out well. GlenFed crashed 80 percent, from $5 to $1, while ConFed rose to $22, where it was bought out by Crestar Bank. I wound up making more money using a hedge than I would have simply being right about Continental—and I took much less risk, to boot.

EXAMPLE TWO

All mutual funds are run by management companies, who are responsible for sales, administration, and portfolio decisions. Of several hundred management companies, only about a dozen are themselves public companies, not counting subsidiaries of much larger public firms, like Merrill Lynch. They are all very leveraged as to the amount of money they control. And when stocks and bonds start "heading south" from today's manic levels, half of them could disappear. It is fairly analogous to a gold mining company, in which costs are fixed and profits fluctuate radically with the metal's price.

Fund management companies, like brokerage houses, are an excellent proxy for the kinds of securities in their portfolios. When the value of assets rises, their earnings skyrocket. When the market drops, the whole process goes into reverse.

An effective hedge within this industry might be a fund group specializing in that most-neglected and -abused group, the gold stocks. Of the 34 gold funds, all but one—United Services Group—are either a tiny part of conventional groups, or are run by privately owned managers. United Services (USVSP, Nasdaq, $3.25) is going up for a number of reasons:

1. The company has just been acquired by new management, but the stock remains bombed out from disastrous decisions of the previous managers. USVSP has 4,382,000 shares outstanding, selling at $3.25, for a market cap of about $15 million. Management companies typically sell for between 3 percent and 5 percent of the assets they have under their control. For example, the Templeton Group was just acquired by Franklin Resources for about 4.5 percent of assets. Based on the $650 million USVSP now has under management, its stock is selling for about half of what it should be.

2. United Services manages $650 million at present. Its assets are growing at about $3 million daily, mostly in its government money market and bond funds. A rule of thumb for United Services is that every $10 million gain in assets yields $57,000 (or just under $.013 per share) to the bottom line. When United Services hits $1 billion in assets, that should yield an additional $2 million in operating income, or $.46 a share. At the $5 billion level, that sum should equal about $2 per share in earnings, for a realistic share price of around $20.

3. United Services manages 14 funds at the moment, but over half their assets lie in its two gold funds. When a gold bull market gets underway, not only will the number of accounts multiply but so will the value of the assets, offering double leverage. During a gold bull market, $50–$100 million could flow into these funds per week. And the management fee on gold stocks is a multiple of that for more general funds.

4. United Services' largest and fastest growing funds, after the two gold funds,

consist of government securities. These funds should be big beneficiaries in a financial crisis, since billions will desert garden-variety income funds, which invest mostly in CDs and Eurodollars to maximize yield, and will flow into the safety provided by the very limited number of government-only funds available.

While most fund management groups are way overpriced, United Services should do well because of its concentration in governments and gold.

Which management group might do worst, based on that same reasoning? As the short in the hedge, you should consider Franklin Resources (BEN, $40), the group mentioned above that just bought out Templeton. Several facts about them scare me.

First is a $500 million debt burden, taken on for the acquisition; that will be difficult to bear in a down market, when their asset base starts shrinking.

Second, most of their asset base is in bonds, and most of that base is in California municipals. As chapter 15 spells out, both are candidates for a meltdown.

Third, John Templeton sold his fund group to Franklin Resources. Do you really want to buy something the master is selling? I suspect Templeton got rid of his fund group because he sees the business much the way I describe it in chapter 13.

It's impossible to tell whether this hedge will work out as well as the hedge described in Example One. But I expect profits will accrue on both the long and the short side of the ledger.

I think United Services is a buy in and of itself; Franklin is an excellent short by itself. But you can both reduce your risk, and increase your profits by making both trades at once.

OTHER HEDGES

The market is rife with hedge-strategy candidates, if you keep your eyes open. I discuss another, centering on the prospects of the ecology movement, in chapter 32. Also look at commodities. Think about going long a contract of silver, versus short an equal dollar amount of platinum. Or long palladium versus short copper. The rationale for these hedges is laid out in chapter 21.

Hedges play a big part in my personal investing. The combinations you come up with are limited only by your personal experience and imagination. But the key is to reduce risk, and simultaneously increase profits, whether the markets head up or down.

At a minimum, it would be prudent to take a look at your present holdings and to hedge them. Identify those positions in the most inflated industries and those most likely to be damaged by tough times. Sell off the most overpriced half of these, then take that cash and use it to short issues that are overpromoted, or buried in debt, or run by people of bad character.

The next ten chapters will give you plenty of ideas on what kind of trades are likely to work out on both the long and the short side of the ledger.

9

When to Buy Stocks

If there is anything in speculation which requires courage and power of will, it is selling stocks at high prices.

If there is any axiom which should be borne in mind in speculation, it is this: Don't be afraid to sell after prices have had a big rise and you have a good profit. Let the fellow who buys from you have a chance. And when you do sell, do not rush into the market to buy some other stock equally high with the funds. Take the profits and get out of the market and stay out until there is an opportunity to buy stocks again at prices admittedly cheap. Anyone who thinks he must be in the market all the time can never make any money.

R. W. McNeel
Beating the Stock Market, 1929

I'm not sure whether Mr. McNeel wrote those lines before or after the crash, but my guess is before.

A lot of money has been made in stocks since the lows of 1987, and an immense amount since the beginning, in 1974, of this long bull market. And the market has held up in the face of a persistent recession. A performance that strong leads people to believe that we have embarked upon a new era. Thoughts are turning to buy-and-hold strategies, the kind that would have worked well since 1982. People saw that when the market crashed from 2700 to 1616 (intraday) in 1987, it came back smartly. They then saw that when it went from 3000 to 2360 in 1990, it once again returned to new highs.

The market has stayed high, despite many negatives, for a long time. It has filled a generation of investors with confidence. These investors are track record–oriented, not value-oriented. That is why, if the market drops to depression levels this cycle, most people will ride it down, figuring on another sure recovery. The fact that the market did not recover to 1929 levels until 1954 has been ignored by the general public.

Having said that, it must be noted that time is always on the side of the long-term investor in stocks. It's just that some periods are much less risky and promise higher potential than others. J. P. Morgan knew that when he answered a question about where the market was going with the laconic "It will fluctuate."

J. P. MORGAN MEETS MR. MARKET

Once J. P. Morgan counseled a young protégé who thought they should sell because the market was overpriced. Morgan pointed in the direction of Park Avenue and said: "You see all those houses? They weren't built by bears, they were built by bulls." And of course he was right. The proof is that the Dow Jones Industrial Average (DJIA) has risen about 100-fold in the last century, as Figure 9-1 shows.

If your time horizon is that long, it serves no useful purpose to try second-guessing short-term market swings. The long-term trend since the founding of this country has been up. The ascent of man has been going on for millennia. That ascent will not only continue but accelerate. The earnings and assets of the corporations that create most of the world's wealth will likely rise with it, notwithstanding the problems the markets, the economy, and individual companies will encounter along the way.

Few people, however, plan fifty years ahead, if only because it's more fun to spend a dollar now than five decades from now. The problem for investors in the '90s is not the long-term trend; it's the possibility they could lose 50 percent or more of their capital along the way.

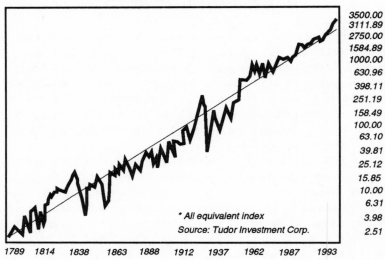

Dow Jones Industrial Average*
Monthly Average: June 1789-1993

* All equivalent index
Source: Tudor Investment Corp.

3500.00
3111.89
2750.00
1584.89
1000.00
630.96
398.11
251.19
158.49
100.00
63.10
39.81
25.12
15.85
10.00
6.31
3.98
2.51

1789   1814   1838   1863   1888   1912   1937   1962   1987   1993

Figure 9-1

In this chapter I want to make the point that with the Dow Jones at roughly 3500, the stock market is, as of spring of 1993, overpriced. I prefer not to be very topical and time-specific in a book. By the time this reaches your hands prices could be half what they now are, and good advice now might be terrible advice in a year because prices had changed, even if the economy remained otherwise identical.

Although prices change constantly, the ways of figuring what's cheap and what's dear in the markets change very little. Let us decide where things stand at this moment, because the principles we'll use were valuable fifty years ago, and they will likely be equally valuable twenty years from now. (I hesitate to say fifty years from now, because of what you will read in chapter 35.)

It's no secret that the market fluctuates; prices change. But it's the same market from year to year with almost exactly the same stocks, the fundamentals of which, as a group, do not vary a great deal. But their prices shift dramatically. Old pros have long recognized this and like to say: "Don't tell me what to buy; just tell me when to buy it."

Nathan Rothschild answered: "Buy when blood is running in the streets." This remains excellent advice, and although almost everyone recognizes its wisdom, few have the nerve to put its theory into practice when the time comes. I'm partial to the approach, but it is not easy for most investors. And even if you have the temperament for applying Rothschild's axiom, you still have to decide how much blood is enough.

Is it possible to apply a mathematical formula to determine when to buy, in effect removing the guesswork? The answer, thanks to Benjamin Graham, is: "Yes, over the long run."

MR. MARKET, THE BRILLIANT NEUROTIC

Even without using the quantitative methods he developed, which are discussed below, Graham* has come as close as anyone can to pinpointing the essence of timing by comparing the market to a man. The man, Mr. Market, is rich, sophisticated, and very smart, but suffers from a manic-depressive nature.

When Mr. Market is feeling on top of the world, he will enthusiastically bid outlandish prices for anything that catches his fancy. Like many rich men, Mr. Market will periodically indulge in all manner of silly extravagances. And because he's an excellent salesman, who usually does very well, many of Mr. Market's friends, neighbors, and relatives join him on these binges.

But like all manic-depressives, Mr. Market's mood inevitably swings. When he's down in the dumps, you can't sell him dollar bills for fifty cents. Every now and then, especially when things have not gone well for a while, Mr. Market gets

---

*Graham, one of the shrewdest speculators of all time, was the author of *Security Analysis* and *The Intelligent Investor* and is generally considered the father of fundamental analysis.

almost suicidal urges and, anticipating the end of the world, decides to give away all his possessions. None of his associates want them, though, because they fear the same thing. That's why they are known as Market Followers.

If you just read about Mr. Market's antics in the paper, you might eventually realize that, although he's rich, smart, and knows everything and everyone, he really is a little crazy. So you don't want to socialize with him, because he's charming enough to make you forget about his radical mood swings. After all, if you become infatuated with Mr. Market, you will inevitably be affected, and drawn in by his moods.

It might be a better idea to take an ad in the paper occasionally and offer to sell Mr. Market things he wants to buy, and buy things from him when he wants to sell, while politely keeping him at arms' length. But even though Mr. Market does idiotic things from time to time, he's no idiot. If he weren't smart, he wouldn't be able to afford his lunatic binges. Most of the time you can't beat him, so don't try. Just watch him from the corner of your eye and wait for the right moment to introduce yourself.

But how can we tell when that might be? Ben Graham, who, as you might guess, watched Mr. Market with a practiced eye, developed one excellent method.

THE GRAHAM APPROACH

Benjamin Graham, the "father of fundamental securities analysis," wasn't the first to use the criteria I'll describe below, but he was certainly the first to formulate and popularize them. Most "value investors" use at least some variation of his approach in figuring out what to buy. But his approach is even more valuable as a method of determining Mr. Market's moods. That's because at times a great many stocks qualify as "good value," and at other times, like now, almost none do. Graham's approach is an excellent market-timing device as well as an excellent way of picking cheap individual stocks.

In brief, Graham's method is to analyze a company's balance sheet and income statement and buy its shares only if they meet certain well-defined criteria for both high value and low risk. He looks at five indicators to decide whether a stock is a good value, that is, whether it's selling for bargain prices. The most important of these is a low share price divided by corporate earnings after tax (P/E ratio). Of course "low" is a relative term, so Graham compares P/Es with interest rates, and isn't interested in a stock unless its earnings yield (the reciprocal of a P/E) is at least twice the current AAA bond yield. In other words, if bonds are throwing off 8 percent, which they were in spring of 1993, a stock would have to be selling at a share price of 6 times its annual earnings (a P/E of 6 or an earnings yield of 16 percent) to qualify. If rates dropped to 6 percent, then earnings yields of 12 percent and 8-to-1 P/Es would be low enough to qualify as a "good value." If long-term interest rates went back to 12 percent, then earnings yields of 24 percent or higher, and P/Es of 4-to-1 or lower would be required to make the cut.

These are low P/Es indeed, at least relative to what people have become used to. Graham realized that such simple, but stringent, criteria would automatically rule out growth stocks, which almost always sell for high P/Es, and companies or industries with unusual accounting procedures. His method would, however, also select companies whose P/Es are low, not because they are bargains, but because of well-known problems. So Graham formulated four other criteria of value that can be used in addition to a low P/E. These are:

1. a P/E less than 40 percent of its previous five-year high,
2. a dividend yield of more than two-thirds the current bond yield,
3. a share price of less than two-thirds book value, and
4. a share price of less than two-thirds net current assets.

But even with those criteria, you might still get hurt, even if the company looks like a bargain, because it's so risky. To Graham, risk equates to debt and a leveraged balance sheet. Hence, Graham insists a company also must have at least one of the following characteristics:

1. The company should have total debt less than book value. But the market is full of anomalies, and as the basic criterion for value is a low P/E, high debt can be offset by other factors.
2. The company's current assets should equal at least twice its current liabilities.
3. The company's earnings should have grown at a compound rate of more than 7 percent for the last ten years and/or
4. The company should have had no more than two drops in earnings of more than 5 percent in the last ten years.

That's value investing in a nutshell—usually companies that have low P/Es, lots of assets and cash, limited debt, and consistent growth in earnings. Solid, meat-and-potatoes, Main Street–type companies; no go-go stocks, no high-flyers, no hyped promotions. And no long-ball home-run attempts either, because Graham suggests selling any stock that goes up 50 percent or more in price. At that point it will almost certainly be unable to meet the buy criteria. The proceeds should be reinvested in one that does.

Obviously this method is not the only way of selecting stocks that can later be sold at a profit. But if you use it consistently, it's very hard to get into any real trouble. And it's an excellent device for market timing. When Mr. Market is on a roll, he has no interest in boring financial stuff, and stock prices reflect it. Later, when he's down and out, he's much more cautious and sticks to value.

When many stocks satisfy Graham's standards, the market as a whole is cheap. In both 1974 and 1982 hundreds of listed stocks would have qualified for purchase. Today I question that there are a dozen.

It's not realistic for the average investor to put together a screen for the whole market using Graham's parameters, but there are three classic barometers of stock-market value that are widely reported, and excellent proxies for such a screen: Price to Earnings ratios, Dividend yields, and Price to Book Value ratios.

PRICE/EARNINGS RATIOS

Being on the wrong side of a bear market is somewhat comparable to the progressive stages of people when they discover they have contracted a terminal disease. First comes denial, then anger and blame, then false hope and grasping at straws, then finally acceptance and resignation. Only then is the market really dead and ready for reincarnation.

Markets have a tendency to go far beyond what's reasonable on both the upside and the downside. We've been seeing the upside part since 1982. I think it's impossible to pick a downside target, because there are so many variables, not least of which is what the government and the Federal Reserve will do.

Both prices and earnings shown in these charts are at the high end of historical experience. When you see an anomaly like that, you risk "Buying high and selling low." The problem isn't so much that the market is "high," a clearly relative thing, as that those levels have been reached at the crest of the longest and shakiest boom in modern history.

DIVIDEND YIELDS

Long-term stock investors who simply bought and held their positions have done very well. Stocks have been the most direct way to capitalize on the tremendous growth of real wealth in this country over the last century. Figure 9-5 shows that dividend payouts have grown at about 3.5 percent compounded during the last 100

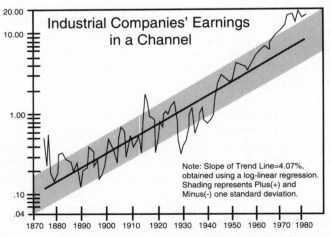

Figure 9-2

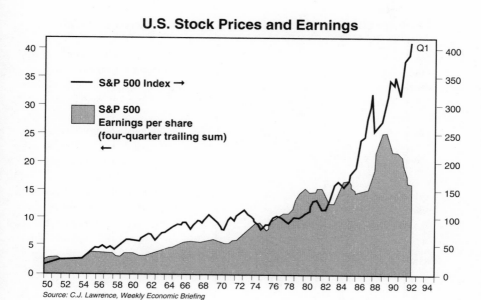

Figure 9-3

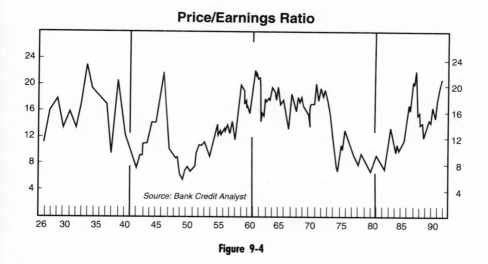

Figure 9-4

years. The total return on the S&P 500 (appreciation and dividends) since 1926 has been more than 10 percent a year in excess of inflation, which has averaged just over 3 percent per year.

Barring an event of cosmic importance, this trend should continue, a reassuring thought for those who own a lot of mutual funds and don't want to sell them.

The S&P 500 and Dividend Yield Ratio as a Measure of Value

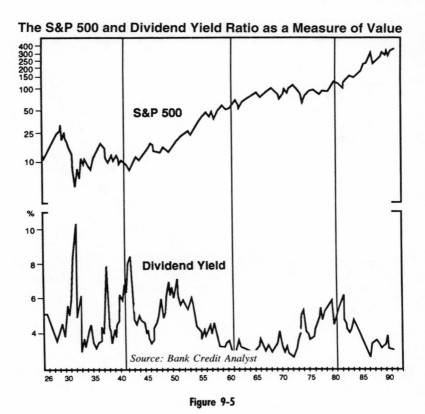

Figure 9-5

But upward progress in companies' dividends—and by implication, earnings, stock prices, and activity in the economy at large—has not been uninterrupted.

Throughout, it has been smart to sell stocks when dividend yields have been low and to buy them when dividend yields have been high.

Historically, stocks have paid more in dividends than bonds have paid in interest. The logical reason is that stocks are inherently riskier than bonds and so have to attract buyers with higher yields.

Figure 9-6 covers the last 120 years. In it you will notice that bonds have only yielded more than stocks consistently since about 1960 using Moody's Aaa bonds and S&P Industrials. Previously stocks and bonds offered about the same current returns, and for a period from about 1915 to the middle of the '50s, bonds paid out as little as 50 percent of stock yields. At present, stocks yield about 40 percent the current return of bonds. Both relatively and absolutely, dividend yields are at an extreme low, which argues that stock prices are still "too high." Figure 9-7 states this in a different way.

It seems reasonable, or it would to Ben Graham, even though Mr. Market might not agree, that the bottom of the cycle will not arrive until the Dow is yielding

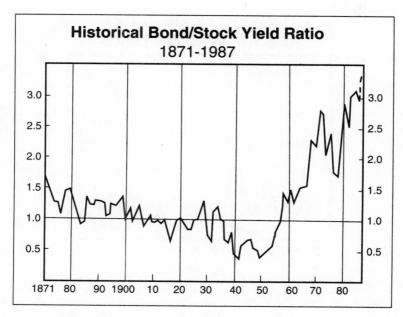

Figure 9-6

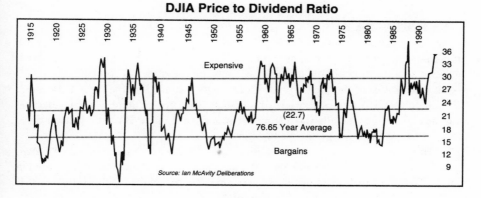

Figure 9-7

the 6 percent it often has at post–World War II market bottoms. Right now it's yielding only 3 percent. That implies a Dow of about 1700, if dividends aren't cut significantly.

Stocks may even come to yield more than bonds, which was the case consistently before World War II, and even through most of the '50s (see Figure 9-8). In

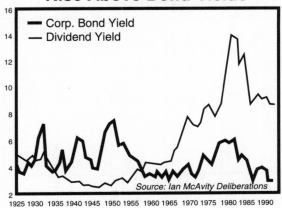

Dividend Yields Could
Rise Above Bond Yields

Figure 9-8

fact, although this annualized chart doesn't show it, the Dow briefly yielded more than 12 percent in 1933, when government bonds were offering only 4 to 5 percent. I'm not expecting a repeat of that performance. But I suspect that there's going to be immense volatility and little joy on Wall Street over the next few years.

PRICE/BOOK VALUE RATIOS

If earnings are an indication of how productively a company is using its assets, book value is an indication of how large those assets are.* Figure 9-9 compares the price/book value ratios of the top 20 percent of the stocks traded on the New York Stock Exchange (NYSE) versus those of the bottom 20 percent; there is a considerable variance. This is especially interesting because the average P/BV ratio is itself close to an all-time high, as Figure 9–10 shows.

This type of variation occurs periodically for reasons more related to crowd psychology than to investment value. We are seeing a variation of what happened in the 1972–1973 bull market, when some companies, called the "Nifty Fifty" (IBM, Xerox, and Texas Instruments, for example) were so favored that they sported P/Es in the 50–100 times range. Were they good companies? Absolutely, with excellent records and sterling prospects. Were they good investments? No, because a good investment is not a function of what something is as much as what its price is. Even as the earnings and assets of those companies continued to compound over the next

*Price/Book Value (P/BV) is share price divided by book value per share.
Book Value Per Share is net worth including intangible assets divided by outstanding shares.

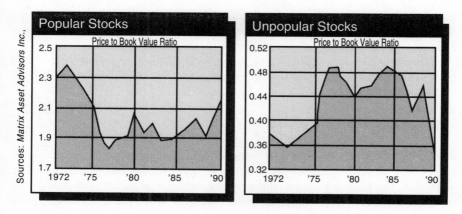

Figure 9-9

Price/Book Value Ratio

Figure 9-10

decade, their stock prices dropped from 50 percent to 90 percent across the board. The prices sank to levels that were as unbelievable on the downside as they had been on the upside just a few years earlier. As of spring 1993, the S&P 400 is selling at 3.5 times book value, an all-time high.

The Dow has often descended to sell at book value; right now it's over twice book. That might imply a bottom of around 1400.

BEAR MARKETS AND BULL MARKETS

Since 1982 the United States has experienced the longest economic expansion in history. We've simultaneously had the longest uninterrupted bull market in stocks on record. The longest previous uninterrupted bull market was the six-year period from 1947 to 1952. At the beginning of that market, it seemed that there was a lot to worry about—such as a resumption of the depression or a major war with a then-expanding U.S.S.R. In retrospect, it's easy to see that the United States had no competition either militarily or economically. Instead, there were tremendous savings and liquidity in a system already wrung out from the depression.

The latest bull market, which is in its twelfth year, is much shakier. The U.S. economy is buried in debt and highly illiquid. It is no longer the only giant among the world's nations. It is riding the crest of a long boom, not recovering from low levels. Unless this is the first time in history that a down market will not follow an up market, something's got to give. Table 9-1 reviews data on all U.S. bear markets since World War I.

The table zeroes in on book value and dividend yield at the tops and bottoms of bear markets. You will note that market peaks had an average P/BV of only 213 percent. The current market, with 253 percent, is second only to the 1929 peak in

Table 9-1 Bear Markets Then and Now

Bear Market Date	Duration (months)	Price to Book (%) Beginning	End	Dividend Yield (%) Beginning	End	% Decline
1919-21	22	248%	138%	4.8	6.1%	48.6%
1929-32	34	418	50	3.3	11.2	89.2
1937-38	13	220	114	4.5	5.0	49.1
1939-42	32	163	87	3.9	6.9	40.4
1961-62	6	190	134	3.1	4.3	27.1
1966	8	209	156	3.2	4.3	25.2
1968-70	18	189	110	3.2	5.0	35.9
1973-74	23	152	77	3.4	6.5	45.1
1976-78	17	127	83	4.1	6.5	26.9
1993	?	270	?	2.9	?	?
Average	**19.2**	**213%**	**105%**	**3.8%**	**6.2%**	**42.8%**

degree of overvaluation. By the time the bear has run his course (over an average of 19.2 months), stocks are typically available at only 105 percent of book, which implies a DJIA of about 1400. Damage as bad as that of the '30s implies a Dow of about 650. That would be, in inflation-adjusted dollars, about where the market bottomed in 1932.

As for dividends, to reach the 6 percent yield levels typical of a market bottom, the DJIA would have to fall to about 1700 (as of early 1993 the DJIA is 3400 and yielding 3 percent). If they rise to the levels of 1932, the DJIA would be in the 900 range. But dividends are usually cut, often radically, during tough times. That is likely to happen this time around, because there is so much debt to be serviced. If they're cut in half, the DJIA may be somewhere between 450 and 900 at the market bottom, depending on how bad it gets.

SO HOW BAD WILL IT GET?

When I'm asked how bad the Greater Depression will be, I usually quip, "Worse than even I anticipate." The longer good times continue, the less likely bad times seem—but the truth is just the opposite.

It's possible that when inflation gets out of control again, we could find hundreds of billions of dollars flowing out of the bond markets into equities, pushing the DJIA much higher. Stocks at least represent real wealth. The corporations will continue to create valuable products.

I would say that the next few years have the potential to treat the market as badly as any since the '30s. But that's not a prediction. You can look at the numbers and draw your own conclusions.

A better strategy is to be out of the stock market until after it has gone down and has been making new lows for many months, when P/E ratios are at a more attractive 10–1, dividends on the Dow are well over 6 percent, and when the average stock is selling for book. Why jump in after a twelve-year boom when all these indicators are at the historic extremes that typically precede a crash?

A COURSE OF ACTION

I trust the point is clear. The market is overpriced, but some stocks have far better prospects than others. Some will likely do better in the next 20 years than did Wal-Mart in the last 20. But how does one choose the right companies? And how does one keep from being washed away in the deluge that may rush between us and the millenium? I think the next chapters have a practical answer to both questions.

The great thing about investing is that you rarely need to be in a hurry. As Warren Buffett, probably the world's foremost investor, says, it's like being in a ball game with no called strikes: you can wait all day, and should swing only at balls you really like. If you wait long enough, the pitcher will get tired and float the makings of a home run up to you.

Questions and Answers

Q: *It's well known that investors like Warren Buffett are buying stocks they see as a sound value in this market. Should we follow their lead?*

A: True enough. Buffett is a value buyer, and there's always some value out there. But he is also noted for buying without much regard for the state of the stock market. When he buys a stock, he pretends he's buying a business, on the premise that he literally doesn't care if the stock markets were to close down for the next five years. This is an excellent formula if you're on the inside of a situation, control it, and have a lot of patience. It also helps if you have several billion dollars to back you up.

It's always possible to point to some well-known investor who's either bullish or bearish. But following the lead of whoever's views have caught the attention of some reporter is a sure formula for failure. The bulls will eventually be right and make money, and the bears will eventually be right and make money, but you will be whipsawed.

The worst policy is simply to follow somebody else's advice or actions because they seem right, or have been right in the past. It is much better to assess the data as best you can and grow from your own mistakes.

10

What Stocks to Buy— and Not to Buy

What's good for the country is good for General Motors, and what's good for General Motors is good for the country.

Charles Wilson (1890–1961)
Industrialist and Secretary of Defense

Free enterprise ended in the United States a good many years ago. Big oil, big steel, big agriculture avoid the open marketplace.

Gore Vidal

THE END OF THE MASS ECONOMY

Chapter 25 presents the case for the next megatrend in the U.S. real estate market, the exodus from cities and suburbs into small towns. This trend has a correlation in the workplace—and the stock market—as well.

The rise of the mass consumer economy in the decades after World War II was accompanied by the growth of large corporations that catered to it. Millions of people who didn't already have a car, a refrigerator, or a house in the suburbs acquired those things. It took large organizations employing huge numbers of people to produce goods on such a grand scale. Happily, those same employees were, in good measure, buyers of what they produced.

But times have changed. Many people now have a couple of cars, a couple of refrigerators, and so much assorted extra consumer junk that they have to use their two-car garages for storage. These consumers will want new "stuff," and will have to replace those things that wear out. But the mass economy that's been the status quo for the last forty years is a thing of the past.

Quality is now more important than quantity. Buick used to advertise its 1955 Roadmaster as having "more road-hugging pounds for the dollar." We don't see ads of that kind anymore. Coincidentally, at about the same time Mercedes literature emphasized that its superb 300SL cost "more per pound than fine filet mignon," a price they justified with its lightness, efficiency, and advanced engineering. At the time, Mercedes was appealing to a niche market and Buick was in the mainstream. Today, a 300SL can't be found for less than $150,000, and the Buick is worth its weight in scrap.

The trend toward quality, and thus items that last, was not prevalent in the '50s. The prices of these two autos were fairly comparable back then. Mercedes prospered partly because it is a technically superior product, and, more recently, because its ownership is considered morally correct.

There's a righteous element in choosing something that will last. It's now considered a sign of moral decrepitude to add to the landfill. Ecological Calvinists believe in austerity and recycling, rather than wealth and consumption. The view that consumption is antisocial is, along with environmental sensitivity, likely to become pervasive. But morality is only an ancillary reason for the trend to higher-quality products.

Technology (the 300SL) is replacing mass (the Roadmaster); that is the major reason industrial commodities have been in a bear market for decades. Technology is rapidly reducing the amount of raw materials needed to achieve a given result. Your camera, your radio, and your automobile are all much lighter, smaller, and more efficient than only a few years ago. Even the clothes you wear have been affected; a few ounces of Gore-Tex do the job of a pound of wool, and do it better. Buildings rely less on steel, concrete, and other materials, and more on precise engineering.

What will happen to the name-brand corporations, such as General Motors, as things change in earnest? Their share of the national pie will continue to shrink. Will they adapt in time to save themselves? The older and larger the organization, the less likely that they'll change.

Corporate culture is enduring. If Alan Alda were to become commandant of the U.S. Marine Corps, his chances of reforming it in his image would be slim. The only certainty would be turmoil while the transformation was being attempted. Efforts to reform old-line members of corporate America would be less traumatic, but in most cases no more successful.

As the mass economy crested, say from 1954 to 1969, the employment rolls of the Fortune 500 went from 8 million to 15 million, and their share of GNP went from 37 percent to 46 percent. During the '70s their share of the GNP rose further to 58 percent, but their total employment rose to only 16.2 million in 1979. Their percentage of the workforce peaked at 21 percent in 1969. Their employment rolls fell consistently through the 1980s, dropping to 11.9 million, only 10.9 percent of the workforce, in 1991. Big Labor has shrunk apace.

The trend away from larger organizations of all types is going to accelerate. That's good for the average person, although it might not seem that good the day he loses his job. The reason is that this trend will lead to a more decentralized, and freer economy.

Big companies have always had an edge when it comes to manipulating and gaining from the government's regulations and tax rules. In fact, they have often been strong proponents of government intervention, because it can help the established companies stave off new competition. Large corporations have an innate advantage in getting government contracts and otherwise feeding at the public trough. It's much easier for Big Government to deal with Big Business and Big Labor on Big Deals. But the tenor of the times has turned against them; only government has continued to grow, because it alone has the legal power to coerce. Like a cancer, it's reaching its largest size at the very time its host, the Mass Economy, is dying.

Meanwhile, although total employment expanded by 20 million new jobs in the 1980s, the growth came from small business. But small business has shown no indication of growing significantly during the '90s, and big business will contract further. Why is small business now stagnant? And where is the growth, if any, going to come from?

Small business is stagnating for several reasons. First, loan capital is tough to come by, even with interest rates very low. Most banks are still in bad shape, despite the government's success in driving short-term rates down to the lowest levels since the early 1960s to help prop them up. Bankers do not want to make relatively risky loans to small businesses when their own balance sheets are in question. And why should they, when they can borrow money from the public at 3 percent and buy government notes yielding 7 percent, with no credit risk or any administrative costs?

Second, regulatory hassles—everything from sexual harassment liability to making the premises accessible to the handicapped to a zero-tolerance environmental policy—have driven the costs, and liability, of doing business beyond the level small outfits can handle. Many businessmen I know would prefer to live off their capital and act as occasional consultants than to go through all the aggravation.

Third, the associated costs of starting a new business—taxes, license fees, legal fees, medical and other insurance—are far higher than in the past. Medical insurance, in particular, has gone from "fringe benefit" to an extremely expensive necessity, amounting to another tax.

All these problems stem from the government. Perversely, they're all likely to get much worse as the malaise of the Greater Depression deepens. That's because today's "New Class" government (see chapter 31) believes it ought to be "activist." And activism is the diametric opposite of a laissez-faire policy, which is the real solution.

What will happen? I anticipate several related trends. In the years to come, there will be many more newly unemployed workers, discharged from both large and small businesses. Those who go back to work will enter into business for themselves, as sole proprietors or with family members, on a very informal basis. They will not, in general, try to grow a business to make a big score, but just run it as a means to get by. They will move to small towns, where costs are lower and they can promote their services informally. They will work out of their homes, which with new technologies is not only easier than ever, but financially more efficient.

There will be a resurgence of the underground economy, which withered, relatively speaking, during the '80s due to the combined effect of lower marginal tax rates and the drug-induced hysteria over the use of cash. In the '90s, the underground economy will make a strong comeback, but this time as much to beat regulations as to save taxes. With the government strapped for revenue and armed with the draconian powers it has acquired in the last decade, however, operating underground is going to be risky.

What effect will this have on the stock market? For one thing, more public offerings will be used by insiders, who intend to cash out rather than grow the business. Those offerings cannot be considered "investor friendly."

One of the world's best-known entrepreneurial aviation engineers recently told me that he really doesn't know what to do about all the regulations he has to contend with, even in the middle of the desert. He felt it would be great if a bunch of like-minded people could get together on a large expanse of land and drop out of the system. He said the government serves no useful purpose he could see. He doesn't want or need any of its services, and certainly has no use for its taxes and regulations. He simply wants out.

This man is an engineer, businessman, and inventor. He's not a libertarian. Although he has never read Ayn Rand's *Atlas Shrugged*, a good litmus test for exposure to free-market ideas, he is looking for Galt's Gulch.* The book describes the collapse of the conventional economy when too many productive people decide that they've "had it." It was written in the 1950s, when the story was science fiction. The trend is now well under way, however, and Rand will prove a prophet.

These trends are gaining momentum, and I don't see any forces likely to change them. And whether they are viewed as "good" or "bad" is in the eye of the beholder. In a Persian fable, a Sufi master meets a sour, bad-tempered traveler coming from a city and asks him what type of people live there. The man responds that they are a horrible, suspicious, and thieving race. The Sufi allows that he is surely right. Later the master comes upon a smiling, pleasant traveler coming from the same city and also asks him what manner of people live there. The man responds that they are gracious, open, and generous. The master allows that he is surely right.

Economic trends are beyond an individual's power to influence. But he can position himself to profit from them, or at least not be adversely affected. Instead of deciding to buy a stock, he can decide to sell it short. Whether the stock is destined to go up or down is of no importance. What counts is whether he is correctly positioned "long" or "short" as it moves.

Getting out of old mass-economy-type common stocks is one way to avoid being hurt by the current megatrend. This includes almost everything in the DJIA and most of the Standard and Poor's 500. General Motors, IBM, and Sears were the wave of the future in the '50s, but that was forty years ago. That's too bad for those

*The mythical valley where Rand's heroes gathered to escape a collapsing U.S. economy.

who have owned their stock since the 1970s. They are now not betting on growth but on the success of extraordinary life-support measures.

But there are other stocks, different in character, that fill the place those companies once had. They are mostly small companies.

BIG STOCKS VERSUS SMALL STOCKS

Two decisions are involved when investing in the market: what to buy, and when to do so. Sometimes one question is much easier to answer than the other. When *Strategic Investing* was published in 1982, I devoted about a third of the book to why stocks were at bargain levels, suggesting readers should invest in large blue-chip companies. Both the *when* and the *what* were fairly obvious. Now small growth stocks are the unquestioned choice for *what*, but the *when* is much less apparent because the market, for reasons we covered in the last chapter, is over-priced.

If you are confident of a company's future, the best time to buy might be whenever you can afford to do so, regardless of whether you think "the market" is high or low. Wal-Mart is a perfect example, a wise purchase anytime in the last twenty years, regardless of where "the market" was. If you look at the long term, with returns of 10-to-1 or 100-to-1, waiting for the "best" time to buy the stock was a way to shoot yourself in the foot.

All the world is looking for Wal-Mart look-alikes, of course. But few discover little Wal-Marts until they're already big enough to join the S&P 500. By the time a

© *M. C. HORSEY & COMPANY, Publisher.*

Figure 10-1

company is that big, holding its stock is no longer a play on growth, it is a guess on the direction of the market as a whole. And that's risky in a market like the current one, which may change precipitously.

Knowing the kind of stocks that probably won't do well in the future narrows the field. Having an idea which stocks will do well helps even more. But with tens of thousands of public companies, it's another matter entirely to pick the handful of issues you should tell your broker to buy. No one would need to know anything about investing other than "Buy the shares of X, period" if picking stocks were easy.

When the time is right, I expect to concentrate my buying in small growth stocks that satisfy the parameters described in the last chapter. The candidates will be the smaller NYSE–type companies, NASDAQ–quoted companies, and the type of outfits that make up the Value Line and Russell 2000 indices. But not start-up ventures, which I discuss in the next chapter.

Over the long run, the returns on secondary stocks are always higher than blue chips (better called "blue gyps" at their current prices). For one reason, it's easier to double from a base of a million than it is to double from a base of a billion. Another reason is that managements of small companies tend to be more entrepreneurial and less bureaucratic. These managements tend to own a lot of the stock, and so are interested in seeing it appreciate.

Also, smaller companies tend to be younger, and youth is quicker to capitalize on evolving trends. The trick is to find them after they've made enough mistakes to know how to survive.

Finally, since the market has increasingly become a creature of institutions, and institutions generally buy large companies only, the small firms are under-owned, solely because they're small. By a happy coincidence, not only do smaller companies have better futures, they are much better values.

As you can see in Figure 10-2, the blue chips represented by the S&P 500, have outperformed the small-capitalization growth stocks, represented by the Value Line, by 100 percent over the last decade.

For blue chips to outperform growth stocks is historically anomalous, since small stocks are usually relatively much cheaper at the bottom (as in 1982), and then substantially outperform the big stocks during bull markets, until they are relatively overpriced at the top. Exactly the opposite has happened over the last ten years.

Here is a great opportunity. The trend will reverse over the next decade. As a result, quality secondary stocks now have much higher potential and, at least over the long run, lower risk than today's blue chips.

A bear market is probably imminent, and it serves no purpose to buy stocks that will go down, even if they don't go down as far as some others. They're better value than the blue chips now, but small stocks could be hurt very badly in the next few years.

The big danger with small companies during bad economic times is that they may not survive. It would take a tour de force of incompetence, probably even beyond the ineptitude of their recent managements, to put GM or IBM under; but

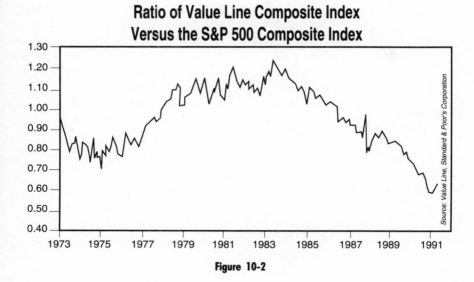

Figure 10-2

management of a small company must scramble constantly to keep from getting in back of the eight ball. If it does get into big trouble, a small company cannot expect help from the government, unlike companies considered "too big to be allowed to fail." It's hard enough for a small company to raise capital in good times but nearly impossible in bad. Usually it is undercapitalized, management is often inexperienced and, even if it can turn out a good product, it frequently does not know how to merchandise it. Little institutional support exists for the stock in the best of times, and when the public loses interest, there may be no buyers for the shares of a small company once you need to sell. These are just a sampling of the problems.

It also explains why successful companies can offer such spectacular returns. The next chapter deals with the most volatile sector of the small-stock market.

11

Venture Capital and Low-Priced Stocks

Security is mostly a superstition. It does not exist in nature. Life is either a daring adventure or nothing.

Helen Keller
"The Open Door"

The fortunes made by ground-floor investors in Steve Jobs's Apple, Ray Kroc's McDonald's, Ross Perot's Electronic Data Systems (EDS), and in hundreds of other household corporate names are legend. And it is obvious that every member of the Fortune 500 was a start-up once. Should you, therefore, attempt to become an amateur venture capitalist? The answer is almost certainly no, at least not in the way most people try to do it.

In 1992 there were 670,000 new business incorporations, not counting new proprietorships and partnerships. Most of them will fail within the next five years. Most of the rest will never become more than marginal enterprises. About the only thing they have in common, other than an entrepreneur excited about an idea, is a desperate need for money. Relatively few of them will ever get it, or at least get enough of it.

It is true that start-up money eventually accounts for most of the world's wealth. Morgan Stanley estimates that venture capital showed the highest compound rate of return of any investment (18 percent) from 1945 to 1991. But the vast majority of the money invested disappears without a trace, a total loss to those who risk it. The trick, of course, is to make sure your money is not part of those losses. That's easier said than done. Let's look at where venture capital comes from and then address how to make the most of the situation.

Start-up businesses have three sources of money, other than the entrepreneurs' own pockets, which should, of course, make a major contribution.

CATEGORY ONE: **Friends, neighbors, and relatives**.

This is where most venture capital money does, and should, originate. After all, an entrepreneur's previous associates are in the best possible position to assess his or her abilities and help guide the entrepreneur as the venture progresses. And if an entrepreneur cannot garner serious seed money from the usual suspects, that should be the end of the story.

This is not only the most obvious but the best source of financing for any new business. The entrepreneur will get the best terms possible and incur the minimum of costs, fees, and commissions, if he manages to survive the libraryful of government rules about what can be said and done, where, and with whom. These regulations were supposedly put in place to protect the investor, although their effect is to discourage and limit investment.

CATEGORY TWO: **Professional venture capitalists**.

Hundreds of groups make it their full-time job to look at deals and determine which of them merit funding. But there are thousands of times more people who want money than who are willing to invest it. Capitalists know this, and their lending terms often reflect the fact. Unless it's an unusually strong deal, with proven people and meaningful money already invested, an entrepreneur can expect venture capitalists to keep him on a short leash, if he's lucky enough to get any money at all.

Entrepreneurs, all of whom believe they are starting up the next McDonald's, are always shocked when people with money don't fall all over themselves to pay up for only a small portion of the equity. A typical venture capital deal, however, is made only after months of investigation. And when the money arrives, it's most often a loan, not equity, with personal guarantees from the entrepreneur, whose stock is placed in a voting trust controlled by the investors. The capitalists will probably require control of the board, possibly require fees for their time in supervising the company, and certainly seek a considerable amount of equity as a bonus.

These rigorous terms often become a blessing in disguise. Entirely apart from the fact that it is better for an entrepreneur to own 30 percent of something real than 100 percent of an idea, it can be a big advantage to have sophisticated professional investors (as opposed to friends, neighbors, and relatives) on the team. They once made their own mistakes and can guide the entrepreneur away from pitfalls. The investors have connections that may prove to be invaluable; and they have a real interest in defending their investment, which means they'll be there to ensure it goes right. And when really big money is needed, venture capitalists are usually in a position to arrange a public offering.

CATEGORY THREE: **Public offerings**.

Few investors want to give an entrepreneur money just to finance his dream. An entrepreneur may want to devote the rest of his life to his company, but most investors want to know what their investment is worth from day to day, and they need liquidity to take advantage of it. So a public offering gives early investors a way out, and it gives late investors with less sophistication, or a different risk profile, a way in.

I've played the venture capital game as a first, second, and third category investor as well as an entrepreneur. I treat investments in Category One (friends and relatives) as lottery tickets and do not expect to hit the jackpot more than once in a blue moon. Investments in Category Two are the province of professional capitalists and not within the scope of this book. But everyone and anyone can get into Category Three (public offerings). This is the area of venture capital where you obtain an education quite cheaply and stand to make meaningful money with the least risk. Not, however, in the way most people might think.

LOW-PRICED STOCKS

When large national brokerage firms do an IPO (Initial Public Offering), it is usually for a company that has been in business for some years, not for a start-up, which entails too much risk. Pioneers are romantic heroes, but they are also the guys who wind up with arrows in their backs.

New issues offered by established brokers have typically been nurtured by professional venture capitalists for some years, have gone through childhood and early adolescence, and still have plenty of growth ahead of them. But as with all adolescents and young adults, there's a lot of unpredictability, and the chances of accidental or violent death are fairly high.

These new issues may or may not be a good deal, depending on how they're priced, but at least they have some kind of track record and can be analyzed like stocks in general.

Here, however, I want to address low-priced stocks. They used to be called "penny stocks." In general, these companies have almost always skipped Category Two financing, and sometimes even Category One financing; they're raw start-ups, fresh out of the idea stage: a different game entirely.

In the past, most were priced under $1, which served to warn even the most unsophisticated investors that the stocks were speculative. The SEC, in its efforts to protect investors from themselves, has enacted new rules (SEC Rule 15c2-6) to redefine penny stocks. Stocks selling for less than $5 a share, with less than $2 million in net tangible assets, and without a NASDAQ or exchange listing, are defined as penny stocks.

To avoid onerous rules against penny stocks, promoters simply repackage the deals so that the stocks are priced at more than $5 (for example, 500,000 shares at $5, instead of 5,000,000 at $.50), more money is raised to meet the asset test, and enough professional fees are paid to get on NASDAQ. Nothing has changed except the size of the meltdown. As usual, the new rules offer opportunities to promoters rather than protection to investors.

Now price alone no longer serves as a warning flag, and investors are reduced to wading through a prospectus. Of course that's important, and everyone should do it. But, again to comply with SEC regulations, a prospectus is often the size of a Russian novel and so filled with legalese, disclaimers, and boilerplate clauses that very few investors actually ever read them or know what to look for even if they do.

Low-priced venture-capital stocks, especially those in Vancouver, received a lot of adverse media attention in the '80s. This was nothing new. In the 1950s it was Salt Lake, in the late '60s Spokane, in the early '70s Montreal, and in the late '70s Denver—each became an epicenter of speculative activity sparked by uranium, silver, gold, and oil, respectively, because those commodities were produced locally. Each boom stimulated the floating of hundreds of new companies as promoters moved in to take advantage of the situation.

Like the tulip mania, the South Sea Bubble, or New York in 1968, the quality of the deals declined as the madness built, and the occasions of fraud increased. When the underlying commodities collapsed, the stock markets that had been built around them were devastated. That, of course, caused recriminations and brought in the regulators to make sure it could never happen again.

But the primary purpose of a stock market is not fraud. It is to raise money for new business. Most articles on the subject represent that scams are the norm, not the exception. Vancouver, in particular, received a lot of attention once it became the leading venue for new companies. And it deserves some attention here.

VANCOUVER: A SHOPPING MALL FOR DEALS

During the 1980s, when the pace was a deal per minute, Vancouver became the world's epicenter for start-up deals. It was a veritable one-stop shopping center for venture capital, and the concept made sense. No one can effectively check out deals offered by hundreds of different brokers all over the continent. It was a little like the mall phenomenon in the retailing business.

Where's the best place to open up a restaurant or a clothing store or a gas station? Most people would advise: open a store where others do not exist, because there will be less competition, or because an area without a store arguably "needs" one. Wrong. Usually the best place to start a restaurant, or whatever, is right next to a bunch of similar enterprises. Provided it is well run, the new store won't suffer from the competition, it will gain from it, since people will be drawn to an area known for that kind of product and for offering a wide selection. An isolated store has to fight to draw customers. In contrast, a complex of stores draws them naturally. It's the same with venture capital. This is what the concept of a market is all about.

That was Vancouver's attraction at the top of the last new-issue boom, and it will serve that function again in the future. But now it can equally well serve as a mall for depressed "vulture capital" deals.

Vancouver presents some advantages unavailable in the United States; foreign investors have every reason to prefer Canada over America. Foreigners have experienced U.S. government conduct best described as "flakey." Stunts like freezing Iranian assets in 1979, the comic opera with Libya, the Iran-Contra sideshow, the posturing with Japan, the destruction of common-law principles in an effort to entrap alleged drug dealers, the Marc Rich affair, and a host of others do not serve to create an atmosphere of confidence. Sophisticated speculators are cautious about putting a large stake into a country going the way of a banana republic. They have no way of knowing when they, or their countrymen, might incur the wrath of Washington and be smitten with some irrational, reactive, punitive legislation.

Now, the Canadian government is really no better than ours, but Canada is not in a position to act like a great imperial power. Canada makes investors feel safe, since they know their assets are less likely to be held hostage due to some ill-advised adventure in a nothing-nowhere corner of the Third World. A great many Vancouver-listed companies are actually U.S. operations that are traded in Canada, since regulations have made it too costly to raise capital in America.

Venture-capital markets like Vancouver inevitably develop bad reputations because of the high risk. Most of the companies they trade eventually go bankrupt, albeit with radical share price swings along the way. Successful companies almost always de-list and move on to a major exchange, so only raw start-ups and the walking wounded stay in Vancouver. Most amateur venture capitalists, therefore, wind up losing their money, since even legitimate companies have an extremely high rate of failure. The risks of investing in Vancouver are not a function of inadequate regulation, but rather due to the nature of the companies involved. It is unfortunate that the concept of a public venture-capital market has been largely discredited in the process.

But if you are familiar with the way a penny-stock market works, you can use it to your advantage. The first thing to keep in mind is that most small stocks trade just a few thousand shares a day, which amounts to peanuts in dollar value. Some days there may be no trading at all. That can make for explosive moves.

When something extraordinary hits, like a favorable article in the press, a massive number of buy orders will appear. But the number of sellers is still at the old level. As a result, no stock is available and the price skyrockets until word of the new price and volume activity spreads to old shareholders. When they do get the word, the old shareholders, overwhelmed by their good fortune, all move to put their shares on the market. But by that time most of the new buyers have already bought, and the price crashes. The only people who make real money are either very lucky or very hip to the way the market is structured. And, of course, the brokers and the transfer agents, who collect fees for shuffling certificates in the short-lived paper blizzard.

Short sellers, of which more in the next chapter, also play an important role. When professional market players, brokers, and floor traders see an influx of unexplained buying, they try to determine the source. If there's nothing new with the fundamentals of the company except for its discovery by a new group of investors, they become confident that the scenario I've just described is unfolding, and they start shorting the stock as it appears to be topping. That's good in that they keep it from "spiking" quite as high as it otherwise would. Later, when the shorts step in to cover and take their profits, they also keep the stock from falling as low as it otherwise would.

And there are other factors. How many of the issued shares are free-trading, and how many are restricted? It is important to know when the restricted shares will become free-trading, since a lot of them will be unloaded by people tired of holding them. Will a price run-up make it profitable to exercise any warrants or options? If so, more extra paper may be offered on the market. Does the company have a strong promoter constantly making the rounds to tell the corporation's story, to discourage selling and stimulate new buying? The market's memory is short, and unless people are constantly reminded of why they bought a stock, they forget and sell to buy the next hot deal, or maybe just a new refrigerator.

The factors mentioned above are "for informational purposes only," because there's almost never a good reason to buy a stock under those conditions. Keep these dynamics of trading in small-market-capitalization stocks in mind, however, as you read the next chapter.

Here are the real dangers of small stocks, as well as the ways you can profit from them.

Almost none of the marginal public companies ever have a chance. They typically fall into one or both of these classes: (a) those that don't have a chance by structure, or are the products of fools, and (b) those that don't have a chance by intention, or are the products of knaves.

I cover the second group in the next chapter. First, consider legitimate penny stocks. It's worth looking at why even stocks issued by well-intentioned promoters have the odds stacked against them, and why they're almost always never worth buying. And also why, occasionally, they can be incredible buys.

BORN LOSERS

Most small public start-up companies, that is, new businesses that should be getting their money from Category One investors, raise some money, try to make a go of it, and go bust. Only one in a thousand of the little deals floated to the public each year has a prayer of turning into the next Xerox. They usually have big hopes and dreams, lots of smoke and talk. But that's the nature of speculation; you pay your money and you take your chances.

The small public offerings always have great projections, but their plans usually have a fatal flaw, like a person with a complex and exquisite recipe for wild rabbit stew who has overlooked the technical detail that first one must catch a rabbit. Most businessmen bite the dust several times before arriving at a winning formula, if they ever do. Starting a successful business is incredibly tough, whether it's a private or a public company.

Even if everything else is perfect, issues of low-priced stocks are almost always, by their very nature, undercapitalized. And undercapitalization is by far the prime reason a new business of any type goes under. Once again, the SEC rules play a major role in the failures that cost investors so dearly by demanding expensive up-front documentation.

Most entrepreneurs do not have a grip on the true magnitude of the expenses involved in going public. And that's not even counting the problems presented by an inexperienced management or a flawed business plan or a thousand other things that are to be expected with any start-up venture.

The average small Initial Public Offering falls between $300,000 and $1,000,000. It takes a minimum of $100,000 for the legal and accounting work necessary to go public. A minimum of 10 percent of a small offering goes to the broker. The office expenses (rent, equipment, employee salaries, taxes, insurance, and continuing legal and accounting fees) probably amount to $20,000 per month for even the smallest operation, so six months of the business eats up $120,000 on General and Administrative (G&A) expenses. Many small companies are already out of money, before allowing for the costs of the business itself, such as inventory, advertising, and shipping.

In addition, a public company requires a stock promotion budget, which could be the largest expense of all. There is almost always a promotion budget, because the founding shareholders, the underwriter, and the clients who bought the public offering all want liquidity. The reason the broker and his clients bought the stock was not to fund the dream of the entrepreneur but to sell their shares to someone else for a higher price. Few penny-stock brokers will fund a company unless the entrepreneur can show them where new buyers are going to come from.

After all that expense, where is the money to make the business grow and become successful? There simply isn't a lot left over. That's why most penny stocks, even those taken public with the best intentions, meet a sad fate. A lack of capital alone kills most of them. They don't have a chance from the very start because they are improperly structured financially. And once they're behind the eight ball, the stock is probably on its way to zero. Some might think the SEC's new $2,000,000 rule mentioned above would solve this problem. But it just squeezes out legitimate deals that need less money while fattening the promotion budgets and payrolls of others.

Most small public companies, and there are thousands of them in the "pink sheets" and on all the Canadian exchanges except the Toronto Exchange, should never have been sold to the public. It is just common sense. Really good deals are done with private money; anyone with enough experience to start a new business probably has his own money or has associates who do, and that's where the good deals stay. Why go through the initial and continuing expense and aggravation of going public unless there's no alternative?

As a result, like medieval monks, the public must be content with the poorest and worst of everything. Not only that, they wind up buying a weak deal after substantial dilution, because all the insiders own shares purchased early for nominal prices. Despite all these drawbacks, when the rare opportunity arises in these stocks, it can be extraordinary. And those opportunities are worth monitoring the penny stock industry for. In fact, penny stocks can occasionally resemble real stocks.

THE BUY SIDE

As an intellectual exercise, it is interesting to note how the market value of stocks can fluctuate without any relationship to the underlying value of the company. Here are three of many examples.

In *Strategic Investing* (pp. 310–15) in 1982, I used IBM as a case history. IBM is as relevant to the junior industrial market today as it was to the blue chips in 1982. IBM stock had fallen 35 percent in dollar terms and 67 percent in real (after inflation) terms from its high in 1968 to its low in November 1981. And those decreases occurred in spite of the fact IBM's earnings quadrupled in the same period and its dividends increased over seven times. The numbers were even more skewed by the time the bear market hit bottom in August 1982.

I also featured electric utilities when they were typically selling for half of book value, five times earnings, and 15 percent in current dividends. You couldn't give them away at the time. Within five years they showed a total return of about four to one, at which point people were stumbling all over themselves to invest.

Real price anomalies do not happen every day, but they can be extraordinary when they do. The Limited, now one of America's top retailers, sold for one-sixth of book value at the market bottom in 1974 and now sells at four times book and twenty-two times earnings, after having run up 200 times in price.

The list of examples can go on as long as you like. When markets are at cyclical bottoms, no one cares what the fundamentals are, and if they are told, they discount and disregard them, like Mr. Market in chapter 9. The same is true to a vastly exaggerated extent of those few penny stocks that survive. Just as their prices are usually much higher than the reality merits early in their histories, the reverse is true at market bottoms.

Some low-priced deals actually work in spite of themselves because of the tenacity or acumen of the principals. Entrepreneurs may be too inexperienced or too committed to know or care that the odds are stacked against them. But that's no excuse to buy their stock during the Initial Public Offering, even if you are confident the venture will succeed. The stock will almost certainly be available later for as little as 10 cents on the dollar.

When a large company falls on tough times, there will be fewer market makers for its stock, but there will always be some, and analysts will still track it. But there is often no interest or support whatsoever for penny stocks once the promotion ends, even if the company is doing well.

There's always a time, usually several occasions, in a company's history when its stock price is far below the value of the company as a business. Finding those companies, at those times, is how Warren Buffett has made billions. Although the value on big companies can be excellent, it is even more extraordinary with small ones because no one watches them. Even during the best of times, there are few sophisticated players who pay attention to them. Few investors can play in Buffett's league, with scores of millions. But many people *can* think about becoming takeover artists when a business is worth several million but might have a market value of only several hundred thousand.

Figure 11-1 describes a Vancouver-listed company I've watched for years. This company had been a going business for ten years before coming to market to raise money for expansion, which is unusual. What's not unusual is the price history.

The entrepreneur linked up with a promoter who, in exchange for a large share position, used his connections to raise C$2.4 million through the Vancouver Stock Exchange. The promoter then hyped the stock, sold, and went on to the next deal. The entrepreneur continued running the business as before. At its peak in 1986 at C$30 (after adjustment for a subsequent reverse split of the stock) AIM Safety had a market value of C$39 million. By 1990 the price per share was only C$0.22, and the market value had fallen to C$600,000. Since 1990 its revenues have exploded from C$600,000 to C$8.4 million in 1993. The company is now negotiating with a Fortune 500 company, which is marketing their products, to be taken over at US $5.25 per share or 15 times earnings, whichever is greater. 1993 earnings are projected at upward of C$0.75 per share. At C$0.22 the stock was as good a deal—from a strictly business perspective—as you would ever hope to see anywhere. Why weren't there many takers? So many small companies had collapsed by 1989, on their way to zero, that even sophisticated players figured this one was no different. But eventually, reality asserts itself, on the upside as well as on the downside.

Why do managements of small companies not buy these shares personally, and even take their companies private? At market bottoms, they are among the most discouraged observers and often have little personal cash, having depleted their reserves just to get the company through the same tough times that devastated its stock.

There will be outstanding opportunity for investors with modest means to take over small companies in the years to come and become small-scale Icahns, Buffetts, or Kluges in the process. One reason the pickings will be so rich is because of the SEC, which has taken all manner of actions to destroy the market for penny stocks. They have made it almost impossible for U.S. investors to become aware of stocks on Canadian exchanges. American brokers can only solicit for penny stocks with great difficulty. And the SEC has closed down scores of brokers who specialize in them.

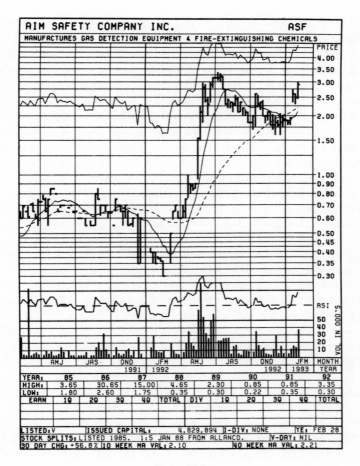

Figure 11-1

Of course, the SEC's intentions were to protect the public from the many abuses. But in the process they collapsed the prices of many struggling but legitimate companies. And the new regulations and rules made it next to impossible for these fledgling companies to raise new money. But the silver lining is that, like all government intervention in markets, it created huge distortions from which speculators can profit.

Searching for value among collapsed penny stocks isn't nearly as exciting as climbing aboard while they're being promoted, but it's much, much safer and much more profitable. After all, the object of investing is profit, not excitement.

Excitement, as well as profit, is always available by short-selling bad companies, the subject of the next chapter.

There is a closed-end mutual fund that allows you to participate in venture capital funding simply by owning its shares. Allied Capital (ALLC, $16½) comes close to being a "set-and-forget" proposition. It's a venture-capital fund that makes loans to smaller but established companies out of the start-up category, frequently with guarantees from the borrower's principals.

In addition to 10 percent to 14 percent interest rates, the fund typically receives warrants on the common as a bonus. I've been around the venture-capital game long enough to realize that this, not the direct purchase of the risky common of junior industrial companies, is how to play. The management has been investing for thirty years now. They look at about 8,000 deals each year, of which they actually loan money to only 10 or 15. Their default rate is less than 1 percent of assets annually, an outstanding performance due to their exacting criteria. If you had put $10,000 with them in 1960, it would have been worth $2 million by 1991, for a 27 percent rate of return, compounded annually.

Can they keep it up? The main constraint on a fund of this nature is size. In other words, it's much easier to double a million dollars than to double a billion. But Allied has a policy of paying substantial dividends from ordinary income, as well as capital gains. That policy has kept total assets down to a manageable level.

12

Reverse Venture Capitalism

That which is about to fall, deserves to be pushed.

Friedrich Nietzsche

Risk varies inversely with knowledge.

Irving Fisher (1867–1947)
The Theory of Interest, 1930,

A "short sale" is the sale of a security not owned by the seller in anticipation of a decline in its price. It's the reverse of a normal trade. In practice, when you order your broker to "sell short" a given stock, the broker will lend you the shares from his own inventory or borrow them from another customer or from another broker. The shares are then delivered to the investor going short, and the proceeds are used as margin for the loan. Purchasing shares to close the position is known as "covering."

Most short sellers attempt to pick stocks that are fundamentally overpriced. They short stocks with high price/earnings ratios, high price/book value ratios, and low dividend yields—the opposite of those Ben Graham would buy. These include stocks that are currently fashionable that they feel will soon go out of fashion and stocks that should get hurt under an anticipated economic scenario. In fact, most stocks in 1993 are good short-sale candidates.

A good strategy, but shorting based on market timing or traditional parameters of value offers no certainty of profit. After all, even in a market as ripe for a fall as Japan's in 1987, stock prices doubled again before the crash started in 1989. If you sell short only because you believe that the market is overpriced, J. P. Morgan would like a word with you at the beginning of chapter 9. There is a better way.

PROFIT FROM STOCK FRAUDS—THE RIGHT WAY

There are more overpriced junk stocks trading than underpriced potential growth stocks. But occasionally I find something with so little substance combined with such a high price that it's appropriate to use an indelicate term such as "stock fraud." No doubt there will be criminals as long as there are people; a certain number of them will, without fail, find their way into the securities business.

Fraud, not just the very high risks of the market, is what really gives the penny stocks a bad name: deals put together by people with bad intentions. These "contrepreneurs" are con men disguised as entrepreneurs who have no intention of growing a business. Their sole purpose is to artificially inflate the price of an intrinsically worthless stock in order to unload it on the public. In fact, after they've sold all their own stock, the promoters often short stock to any late-arriving buyers, secure in the knowledge it will drop to zero.

At that point, someone who bought a big block might call his broker with orders to sell and, after an embarrassing pause on the salesman's part, would hear those dreaded words: "To whom?" There's no bid because there are no buyers. And there are no buyers because the insiders have gotten rid of their paper, the promotional budget is spent, there's no real business in the shell, and brokers are directing clients' attention elsewhere.

This is something few newcomers realize until a promotion ends or a bear market begins. During the October 1987 unpleasantness, even many NYSE stocks were "no bid" for hours at a time. It can happen much more easily in Vancouver.

If the bad guys put as much effort into growing a business as they put into weaving a story to incite greed in the hearts of the credulous, their companies would probably be legitimately successful. But some people would rather steal money than earn it, even if earning it is easier.

Contrepreneurs have devised numerous variations of stock fraud. Phony accounting is a favorite. Sales can be fabricated with purchase orders from shell companies offshore. Inventory can be created by borrowing it when the auditors visit, or moving it from one location to another just ahead of the auditors. Assets can be manufactured by valuing some widget at a ridiculous figure. Press releases are widely distributed to create confidence and the appearance of activity.

The mining business lends itself particularly well to all this. Few people have any understanding of mining technology or how to interpret drill and assay results or how to compute the economics of a project. Ore deposits can and do peter out and reappear unpredictably, making it easy to blame the company's failure on "bad luck." It's possible to salt properties and tamper with results and deceive even experts. There's always the prospect of hitting a bonanza, which makes mining the perfect place to sell blue sky.

Of course frauds are not unique to penny stocks. You may recall the 1970 Home-Stake drilling scandal, which took millions of dollars from prominent show-business personalities. The fraud was so well executed that even professionals visiting the company believed it was a real oil operation. In the 1960s Billie Sol Estes convinced government inspectors and thousands of investors that he had millions of gallons of nonexistent soybean oil by phonying the measuring devices. The ZZZZ Best fraud in the '80s ended with its twenty-three-year-old CEO being sentenced to decades of hard time for running a fantasy cleaning business. Those are some frauds that quickly come to mind, and none was a penny-stock deal.

In the most cleverly executed promotions, the assets are real but vastly overvalued. That way it's easier to inflate the price of the stock and it precludes most legal repercussions. Who's to say, after all, what something is really worth? Even the finest companies regularly go from being grossly overpriced to grotesquely underpriced. But knowing the true value of something is the key to making a killing in the market and to not getting killed.

Valuing assets accurately is not easy to do; otherwise the tens of thousands of security analysts worldwide would be unemployed. Or they would at least consistently choose stocks that go up, which they don't.

But there's more than one way to skin a cat. Armed with a knowledge of how the game is played, there's no reason not to play. You can join the insiders and sell these shares. Or short-sell them, to be precise.

What can the average investor do when he suspects a fraud is being perpetrated? What should you do when you become aware of a bad stock being promoted by bad people? Fortunately, an immediate, direct, and profitable remedy is available. It doesn't require the services of either a policeman or a lawyer. When you find a bad stock, you short it.

HOW TO PICK BAD DEALS

I hope I've made clear that it's almost always foolish to buy a new issue of a start-up company, and almost always better to short start-up stocks at the right moment. How can you find the really suitable shorts?

Why not put yourself in the position of a reverse venture capitalist who doesn't look for deals to buy but deals to short? There are thousands and thousands of deals you can choose from, traded over-the-counter and on Canadian exchanges. Let's look at the qualities necessary for shorting public deals that, applied cool-headedly, will result in far surer profits than buying.

A venture capitalist looks at four major factors when he invests money; you should consider the same factors to determine a good short. Find people who you'd expect to be wearing ski masks when they visit the local convenience store, if it weren't for the fact they had been introduced to the markets. Look for a start-up with little or no revenue and high expenses. Look for lots of debt and minimal cash. Look for a market cap out of all proportion to the possible value of the underlying business.

1. **People**—A company is no better than the people who run it; it *is* the people who run it. Good people make for good business, and bad people make for bad business.

Look at it this way. You can have a company with great people, a great business plan, and adequate capital, and it still can come to a bad end. Those things tilt the odds of success in your favor, but Murphy's Law can still make a hash out of it. On the other hand, if you can find a company that has bad people behind it and whose business plan is a lie, then it's a cosmic certainty the company will end in disaster.

The first step, whether buying or shorting a stock, therefore, is to look at the ethics of the people involved. Look at their past deals and see how many of them have worked out. Ask around to find out their general reputation. If it's a big investment, hire an investigator to run a check on them; it could be the cheapest money you'll ever spend. Ross Perot was crucified in the press for investigating prospective employees. But to anyone who is concerned with business ethics and who has been around the block a few times, it's plain common sense. Yet few investors do it.

People of good will naturally assume that others have similar intentions. Every investor who does a large number of deals eventually gets bagged. Even John Templeton, one of the world's shrewdest and most-experienced investors, readily admits being taken to school. It happens to the best of us.

I've sat across the table hearing lies so transparent that I felt insulted to be thought that stupid, only to realize my intelligence was not in question. Some people are pathological liars so twisted that lies are their preferred way of dealing with reality. Some literally can't tell the difference between the truth and a lie. Even if they know the factual difference, they can't see any moral difference. Although they have no personal ethics, skilled contrepreneurs are often clever, credible, and so apparently sincere that they are very hard to spot. They're so slick that sometimes the only way you can tell they are lying is that their lips are moving.

This is why I almost always visit a company before making a substantial investment. The times I've gotten hurt have been the times I should have dug deeper. The loss of a day and airfare is trivial compared to the amount of money to be won or lost.

2. **Income statements**—Most low-priced stocks do not have much of an operating history. But they do have income statements (even if there's no income), balance sheets (even if there's no cash), and, most important, notes in small print at the end of the financial statement. There's a big difference between what a company has shown it can do over at least three years and what management says it hopes it can do. Their projections are always based on the best-case scenarios.

I'm all for optimism in business; a pessimist is doomed before he starts. But if all they have is blue sky, let them get their money from friends and relatives; put yours on the opposite bet. Nobody has enough money to back every dream that comes along, and companies without proven growth are just a step or two away from dreams. The most successful investors are those who stick with companies that have proven, consistent records of growth.

Analyzing the income statement of a start-up company is particularly easy because the key is held by the "burn rate"—how much money they are spending each month. Divide the burn rate into the cash they have to determine how many months it will take for the money to disappear, and the price of the stock along with it.

3. **Balance sheet**—When a stock is being promoted, little is said about the quality of its balance sheet or how much cash and debt the company has. More likely, attention is directed away from those topics. Blue sky is much more exciting than numbers, and the prospect of earning millions gets more attention than a little cash in the bank. It's amazing how many people will buy a stock without checking to see if the cash to do all those marvelous things is on hand, or whether there's a lot of debt, with interest eating away at the company like a cancer.

Sophisticated investors simply walk away from companies with debt problems. But a smart reverse venture capitalist will seek them out as prime targets for shorting.

4. **Value**—"Value" includes the first three points above plus whatever you want to assign to a company's prospects or blue sky. Value is what you would pay for the entire business if you were a businessman using your own money.

When you look at a company, pay no attention to the share price. Instead look at the market capitalization, that is, the number of shares times the price per share. Then ask yourself: "Would I pay X million dollars for this company if I were buying the whole business, were going to run it myself, and I couldn't sell the stock for five years?" If the answer isn't a resounding "Yes!" don't buy. And short only if the answer is a resounding "No." There are 50,000 public companies in North America alone; you can afford to be very particular.

A careless investor will buy a company selling for 50 cents per share with 100 million shares out, but pass on an identical deal at $5 per share, but with only 1 million shares issued, because the share price made the deal seem "too expensive"—the exact opposite of the facts.

SIGNS OF A GOOD SHORT

Evaluating companies in this manner is most relevant for small companies you can visit and appraise personally. It is less critical with NYSE-listed companies, as their size and momentum enable them to survive incompetent management for long periods.

How can you identify which of 50,000 public companies are worthy of detailed analysis? The companies almost come looking for you, because their promoters try so hard to drum up buyers. A number of fairly reliable indicators will draw your attention to short-sale candidates.

1. The company's promo package, for example, will include reprints of the front page of some national publication where the company ran an ad, implying that the paid advertisement placed there was actually an article about the company.
2. Obvious anomalies, like a mining company with an office in Florida or New Jersey. Both are traditional locations for stock fraud.
3. A company listed on a foreign exchange prominently advertising that it has been granted a 12G3B(2) number by the SEC. That's intended to imply approval by the SEC, when, in fact, any non-U.S. company that has been public more than three months can get such a number by asking for it.
4. You may find frequent ads announcing what a good deal the company's stock is.
5. The company has a large market capitalization. More than, say, $10 million, even though it has been in its present line of business only a few months.

If you ever receive an unsolicited phone call from an unfamiliar broker touting some nothing/nowhere company that's going to earn a million dollars if it can just make payroll this week, you'll know what to do. Don't hang up; get all the information and then short all you can. But do so with a different broker.

All these things serve to draw in the ignorant and gullible, while they scare off anyone who's been around the block once or twice. But few people who buy low-priced stocks have detailed knowledge of them, relying instead on the SEC to safeguard their interests. The pros in the game know this and make the most of it.

Promotion plays a big role in the low-priced stock market.

PROMOTION

There are only two ways to increase a stock price: by creating real value in the company, which draws buyers naturally, or by engaging in a promotion campaign designed to lure buyers in.

Stock promotion has gained a bad name over the years; in polite circles it's now called "corporate public relations." But despite its frequent unethical use, promotion can be critically important to building a successful business.

A high stock price makes it possible to raise capital with less dilution of existing shareholders, which builds shareholders' loyalty. Legitimate promotion can enable a company to trade fewer of its shares in exchange for another company in a takeover or merger. The more successfully a company promotes its stock, the more it's able to do. But building a company's assets is not the priority of contrepreneurs when they promote a stock to unreasonable levels.

Remember that there are only two reasons for boosting the price of a stock: to raise money or make an acquisition, and to "off paper," in the vernacular of fraud artists. That's why it's important to know the real intentions of the people behind a deal.

In fact, it's instructive fun to toy with a contrepreneur by first getting him to say his company does not need money (they never need money), then asking why, if he doesn't need money, he wants to boost the stock price. One always encounters a panicked moment of silence as the contrepreneur tries to backpedal to a tenable position.

WHY ISN'T EVERYONE A SHORT PERSON?

Why isn't shorting more popular?

First, few people seem to understand the concept of selling something that doesn't belong to them.

Second, most people see it, incorrectly, if understandably, as wishing to harm a company and its shareholders.

Third, people are naturally optimistic. And it's easy to be optimistic when promoters are telling you all the good things that could happen, while it takes a lot of hard work to pinpoint the flaws.

Fourth, investors are aware of the stock market's historic tendency to rise, and they feel they're on the wrong side of a bet.

Fifth, brokerage houses do not promote the concept. To intimate that some stocks might be overpriced can only confuse and scare a lot of investors. Further, brokers are in business to sell stocks and get their clients "long." Getting them "short" is counterintuitive. Shorting a stock won't make a broker any friends among other brokers, or among other companies who fear their stock might be next, or among the legion of people who already own it. Who needs more enemies?

Sixth, and perhaps most important, shorting stock presents a lot of regulatory problems. Short selling is considered "speculative" by the authorities, who believe it's their duty to help the market go higher, whether it deserves to or not. You can't, for instance, short on most exchanges except on an uptick because of SEC rules. This plays right into the hands of contrepreneurs, who can ensure that a market never sees an uptick, just because they keep selling their paper.

Regulations also make it nearly impossible for the average investor to short stocks that aren't on an exchange or on NASDAQ. As a result, some of the juiciest promotions totally escape market discipline.

In addition, the kind of research that leads to good short opportunities can have bizarre consequences today.

Equity Funding, an NYSE-listed stock in the '70s, is a classic example. The company defrauded major brokerage firms and thousands of their clients by creating insurance policies from thin air. They were exposed by analyst Ray Dirks, whom I mention at greater length in chapter 17. The SEC harassed Dirks for years because he made the fruits of his research available to his clients before alerting the SEC. This early insider-trading case is a reminder of the chilling effect the SEC has on the disclosure of data.

Seventh, and finally, saying unkind things, or even just telling the truth, about stock frauds can have legal repercussions. Contrepreneurs can usually be relied on to sue anyone exposing their malfeasance. The promoter starts legal action because, when confronted with the cruel facts by his now-uneasy investors, he can say, "It's all a bunch of lies. How could you believe that about me? I've sued the SOB to make him retract it!" The threat of a costly and aggravating lawsuit is enough to give most people second thoughts.

The contrepreneur also brings suit to serve as a warning to others who might try to unmask his game. Many have a jailhouse mentality that makes much of being macho, of being a bad person to mess with. Death threats are sometimes made to those threatening to expose fraudulent schemes.

These are the main reasons shorting isn't widely popular. But none of them need deter you from profiting as a private investor. In fact, because they ensure less competition, they aid your efforts as a speculator.

WHY BE A SHORT SELLER?

The main reason for shorting stocks is the reason you are in the stock market in the first place: personal profit. There are, of course, risks peculiar to shorting, and I'll cover them below. But on the whole, this is perhaps the single, most-profitable thing you can do in the market year in and year out, in good times and bad.

If you short a stock at $10 and it goes to zero, you've made $10. Most people would rather buy a stock at $10 in hopes of its going to $100, of course, and that's actually another reason why shorting is unpopular. It appears to have limited profit potential with a theoretically unlimited loss potential. Sophisticated players, however, prefer a low-risk $10 gain to a nonexistent $90 profit. The problem of the theoretically unlimited loss can be solved by instructing your broker to buy the stock back if the market goes against you by more than a predetermined amount.

When you short a fraud, you have reality firmly on your side. You can be certain that an overpriced promotion eventually must crash. In fact, for that reason shortselling can be far more conservative than any buy-and-hold strategy. You can, unfortunately, never be certain that the price of an undervalued company will go up.

There are other reasons for shorting that provide psychic profit to supplement the financial gain. Most of us like to do well by doing good.

1. **Public service**—Anything worth doing should be done at a profit; altruism leads only to hypocrisy. If you can't profit, monetarily or psychically, from curing a perceived problem, that's a strong indication it's really a nonproblem and probably not worth bothering with.

Stocks go higher only because there is more buying than selling; every share sold, and shorted, makes it that much harder to take a stock higher. By depressing a stock's price, short sellers keep the poor suckers who are lured into buying the stock from paying as much, and therefore eventually losing as much, as they otherwise would.

2. **Market liquidity**—Ideally, a fraud sold short never has to be covered because the stock goes to zero. The short seller, therefore, may be able to make a profit and defer the tax liability, which can be a substantial fringe benefit. But most of the time the opportunity cost, and the risk, of holding for a complete wipeout makes covering, or buying back, the shares a more probable outcome.

That means short sellers may be willing buyers when no one else would dream of making such a purchase. Sometimes short covering provides the only market for a defrauded long investor to sell stock into after the contrepreneur has walked away from the deal.

3. **Doing justice**—Enough short selling can, by itself, cause a fraud to come unglued, not only saving unwary investors but bringing financial grief to the villains. As is usually the case, a genuine public service lines the benefactor's pockets. This is an important point, because if vigilant short sellers can consistently take the profit out of frauds, they can effectively remove frauds from the market and perhaps even bankrupt the perpetrators.

It's strange that short sellers have traditionally been viewed with suspicion. They're often portrayed as destroyers of companies. But only a very stupid short seller will attack a viable enterprise, because the odds are stacked against him. Why bother when so many pieces of rotten fruit are ready to fall of their own weight?

As I hope I've illustrated, the facts are totally at variance with conventional wisdom. Shorts are the natural policemen of the marketplace, holding the high moral ground. With typical perversity, however, regulatory agencies make shorting hard. They have imposed stiff margin requirements to discourage shorting. They make it difficult to short except on an uptick, which generally plays right into the contrepreneur's hands. They foster an atmosphere that is intended to make shorting seem unpatriotic.

RISKS

Are there any risks to shorting? Not in the long run, but very definitely in the short run. The standard risks include a call from the broker demanding a return of the stock you borrowed, because all the owners want theirs back. This is unusual, but a "short squeeze" can be a disaster when it happens, because the stock's price can go through the roof as panicking shorts are forced to cover at any price. That is why it's wise to stay away from shorting stocks that already have a large short interest. (Short interest is published monthly in the *Wall Street Journal*.)

Shorting a fraud backed by a well-oiled promotional machine can be like standing in front of a freight train. These guys love to trap shorts who position themselves too early. And if contrepreneurs can force massive short covering by driving a stock to truly absurd levels, the stock can be driven higher yet. The titanic battles that emerge between longs and shorts are fun to watch; and that's what I prefer to do, rather than participate. The most prudent policy is to wait until it looks as though the promotion is over, and then make them choke on their own paper.

Contrepreneurs deserve no mercy. They've given regulatory agencies an excuse to arrogate more power. They have nearly destroyed the prospects of legitimate start-ups to raise money publicly in North America, especially in Vancouver. Investors are a little bit like Mark Twain's cat, which once sat on a hot stove and got burned. From that experience it learned a lesson, and it never sat on a stove again, hot or cold. That is why, although stock fraud will always exist, it's a cyclical phenomenon, sometimes waiting for a new generation of investors in need of a learning experience

As with other specialized investments, you will do well to build a relationship with a broker who knows how the game is played. It's understandable, of course, that you would want to give your business to your next-door neighbor or brother-in-law if he is in the business, but doing so is usually not smart.

Last, watch the commissions you pay. Some U.S. brokers will tag you with 10 percent on low-priced stocks, and that borders on the criminal. If you do any trading in Canadian stocks, you should have an account with a Canadian broker. The commissions in Vancouver are nominally 3.3 percent, but 50 percent discounts are widely available. Beware of brokers who represent investment bankers (many Canadian brokers do) since their real money is made from issuing stocks and their loyalty lies with those issues.

13

Mutual Funds: An Accident Waiting to Happen

Mutual funds have long been tipped as the unsophisticated investor's solution to the stock market and the sophisticated investor's answer to achieving effortless diversification. Since we have had a massive supercyclical bull market from the market's bottom at DJIA 40 in 1933, with jet-propelled rises after the more-recent bottoms in 1974 and 1982, the fund industry has done everyone a favor by making it easy to participate.

The New York Stock Exchange has been with us for 200 years, but the American mutual fund business got under way only in 1924. Ever since, the fund industry has been a barometer of the stock market in general, rising and falling with it. Just five years after the creation of the first fund, the 1929 crash wiped out most of the industry; it's tough to make money managing assets when 90 percent of them disappear in just four years.

But the industry survived. In 1940 there were 68 funds managing assets of $450 million, spread over 296,000 shareholder accounts. Not counting Money Markets, which are another story, the business grew slowly to about 540 funds by 1982, then exploded to more than 3,100 today. The amount of money under fund management invested in stocks and bonds has gone from $70 billion in 1982 to over $1,100 billion in 1993. Even during the last fund boom, which also preceeded a market meltdown, the "go-go" era of the late '60s when Bernie Cornfeld had legions of aggressive salesmen opening accounts for everyone who had two nickels to rub together, there were only a few hundred funds. Today there are ten times as many, and there are hundreds more funds than there are stocks on the NYSE. Mutual funds have been growing at the rate of about one per business day for a decade. The funds have become a phenomenon.

It's arguable that people who were buying funds in the early '80s were value buyers who could see the market was depressed and were making a reasonable bet on recovery; at the time, funds had terrible ten-year track records. Buying them took courage and a contrary nature. That's no longer the case; almost every fund has a great record, and people are piling in because they see recent performance as a predictor of even better results to come.

Billions and billions have been pouring into mutual funds monthly since the late '80s. Up to about 1982, money flowed into mutual funds in small amounts. Purchases ranged up to about $1 billion per month from the start of the bull market in 1982 to 1991. The $280 billion flowing into them in 1991 alone was more than the industry's total asset value in 1983.

Since the beginning of 1991, money has been flooding into stock and bond funds at the combined rate of about $4 billion a month, and by the end of 1992 at more than $15 billion a month. Mutual funds have become a mania.

American Mutual-Funds Assets

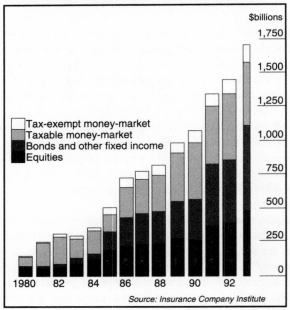

Figure 13-1

Number of Mutual Funds

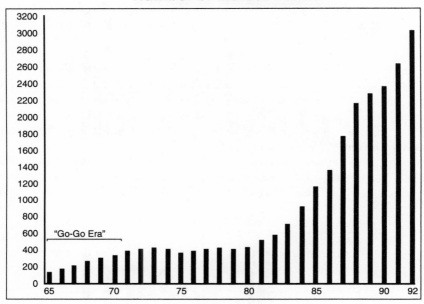

Figure 13-2

The huge growth in the size and number of funds has been a bonanza for the management companies that run them. Their revenue has risen tenfold in about as many years. My guess is, those revenues could well drop more than 50 percent in the next few years.

A quarter of all American families now have mutual fund accounts. With about 70 million accounts open, further growth is going to have to come from homeless people. Why is this growth important? Any industry that expands quickly warrants your attention because major distortions are created along the way. And major distortions are a great opportunity for the speculator.

INSTITUTIONAL MONEY

The stock market has increasingly been dominated by institutions (pension funds, mutual funds, and large money managers) since the '60s, and particularly by mutual funds since the middle of the '80s. Institutional money tends to be performance-driven "hot money," subject to the groupthink of a few thousand managers. That's changed the character of the market, making it much more short-term–oriented, with trading volume ten times higher than it was before the '80s mutual fund boom.

Share ownership by individual investors, on the other hand, tends to stabilize the market since it's both diverse and there is relatively little turnover. Individuals

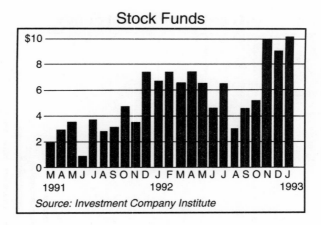

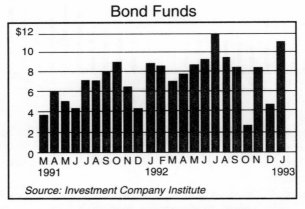

Figure 13-3   Stock and Bond Funds Net Growth

tend to buy and hold, partly because the transaction costs are high for an individual, and partly because, unlike institutions, they have to be concerned with capital gains taxes. Also, one tends to be less cavalier with one's own money.

Individual investors account for very little of today's trading volume, except indirectly through the purchase of mutual funds. Retail brokers earn most of their commissions not by trading stocks, but by trading derivative products like options, doing partnerships and underwritings, and selling managed accounts and mutual funds. The real volume in the stock market is from pension funds, mutual funds, and the like. There's nothing wrong with that, but opportunities arise because the funds tend to concentrate on similar kinds of stocks.

Institutional players do not buy equal amounts of each of the perhaps 50,000 public companies traded in North America; 90 percent of those companies never draw their attention. Gigantic institutions have little alternative but to buy the shares

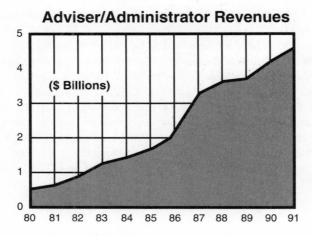

Adviser/Administrator Revenues

Source: Lipper Analytical Services

Figure 13-4

of gigantic companies in gigantic block trades. The companies suitable for that kind of activity are almost exclusively those corporations that compose the DJIA 30, or at least the S&P 500. In fact, many of the stocks in these leading indices are purchased solely because they're part of the indices; so the big market capitalization stocks draw mutual fund purchases and grow even bigger. That's what the index funds are all about.

So, because of the institutions, what has developed since the middle of the 1980s is a somewhat broader form of the "two-tier" market that existed in the early 1970s when the "one-decision" stocks, a.k.a. the "Nifty Fifty," were all the rage. It's no accident that those stocks were among the most-devastated issues during the 1973–74 bear market. And their present equivalents, the big-capitalization stocks the funds are concentrated in, will likely be badly hurt in the next major decline.

The "two-tier" market phenomenon itself is an indication that the market is past its peak. When times start getting tough, portfolio managers discard the weakest companies first. They retain the highest quality and/or biggest issues because they are the most liquid. The "quality" issues become priced out of all proportion to their real value as a result of this seemingly rational pruning. But size is no longer a guarantee against failure; it's as likely a harbinger of failure for reasons explained in chapter 10.

If "everyone" owns a stock, then all the potential buyers have already bought; and there's only one thing they can do: sell. Perversely, they'll all sell at once. Fund managers all read the same literature, went to the same schools where they took similar courses, and now belong to the same clubs. They generally hold similar values and socialize with each other. They are bound by the same regulations and are subject to all manner of peer pressure, perhaps the reason many favor yellow suspenders. They tend to see things similarly. When they do something, they tend to act similarly.

Fund managers have all been buying for the last decade, and stocks have gone up. Now that they dominate the market, who will absorb the large blocks they'll sell when that becomes fashionable or unavoidable? To whom can the institutions sell? Certainly not to the public. The public will be redeeming their own fund shares, causing funds to sell their holdings to generate cash to meet the redemptions.

When an institution sells, the only likely buyer is another fund; but they'll all be selling together, for the same reasons. That kind of thing can put a market into freefall. Vacuums could develop under stocks with heavy institutional ownership. Their chart patterns would resemble the glide path of an ICBM on re-entry. Index funds will likely lead the way.

INDEX FUNDS

In a stock market as overvalued as this one, it's hard to pick the worst place to have your money; there are so many choices. But where is the really dumb money likely to flow, money that's thrown at the market without a thought to the fundamentals? Index funds.

Index funds basically buy the shares of the stocks in the S&P 500 index, or a similar index, in order to duplicate and track the index' performance. They originated late in the 1970s as a response to the paradox that mutual funds are unable to consistently equal the performance of the market as a whole, especially after their fees, costs, and commissions are factored in.

The index funds have kept investors from being buried in popular but correspondingly overpriced stocks. Simultaneously, they bought blocks of unloved companies that happened to be in the S&P, and these stocks often turned out to be bargains. Costs were low, since the funds didn't have to hire analysts. And you knew that, unlike specialty and sector funds, if "the market" went up, you were making money, a good feeling during a prolonged bull market.

So index funds grew to the point where they started to influence the market. When a new stock is added to the S&P, a portion of index fund dollars must buy it, which drives it higher, regardless of its merits. When a stock is bumped off the list, it automatically triggers index fund sales.

There's no reason to place much confidence in the managers of most of today's thousands of funds. Most of them were in school during the last bear market, and few of them have ever seen anything but a bull market. But at least most of them try to buy issues that appear cheap by some criteria. Nothing is as brainless as an index fund, which tends to hold overpriced issues by the very fact that it must buy the stocks that every other index fund is buying. Just as bad, the companies in the indexes are mostly big "mass economy" organizations, the very kind likely to get hurt the worst in the years to come.

When a bear market arrives in earnest, index funds are going to see some of the biggest redemption demands. The shareholders of specialty and sector funds, having bought them because they like biotech or foreign stocks or whatever tend to have some knowledge of what their funds hold. The shareholders of guru funds, like Templeton or Magellan, might stay with them because they have confidence in the management. But index fund shareholders tend to be the least knowledgeable and the most fickle; they own index funds only because they want to be "in the market." The S&P 500 could go from being one of the best performing areas of the market to one of the worst. A good part of its rise and fall will have been due to index funds.

TRACK RECORDS

People invest in mutual funds because they believe the funds relieve them of the need to be cautious. They hope the funds will beat the market, which a lot of mutual fund advertising seems to promise. The industry as a whole, however, underperforms the market; that was, you will recall, one of the reasons for the creation of index funds.

Funds as a whole almost necessarily must underperform the market for at least two reasons:

First, all mutual funds charge a management fee (which can run to 1 percent or more), and many also charge a 12b-1 fee, which can run up to another 1.25 percent, and is used for advertising to bring in more shareholders. Whether the market is up or down, these charges eat away at your capital each day.

Second, most funds always keep a portion of their portfolios in cash, which tends to dampen performance during bull markets. Of course, that same cash reserve can cushion losses during bear markets, but funds tend to be most in cash at the bottom, and less at the top. This upside down teeterboard will whipsaw a fund's portfolio.

Nonetheless, you'll always find funds bragging about their performance, as if the past is a good indication of the management team or management philosophy's likely performance in the future. Exceptional managers and management philosophies exist, but the average fund buyer mistakes a bull market for genius. Few of the more than 3,100 funds are managed by geniuses. What we have experienced instead is one of the most spectacular bull markets in history. The law of averages, and the direction of the market, are far more important than any other factor in determining the fate of your money with most funds. You should, therefore, largely disregard fund performance histories for several reasons:

1. Funds are the market. The money management industry has grown so large that it is, in effect, the market. And if you are the market, it's impossible by definition to beat the market, especially after a host of fees. True, in any given year, some funds will greatly outperform or underperform the pack, but, with prominent

exceptions, that's not so much because their managers are smart but because fashions in the market happened to favor what was already in their portfolios.

2. Sectors rise and fall. Markets go in cycles, and so do the sectors that make up the broader market. An obvious example is gold funds. Gold funds have been the top performers during many quarters of the last couple of decades. Naturally, this fact is exploited in a mutual fund's advertising at the appropriate moment and brings in a lot of shareholders. But gold shares have been the worst performers equally often. This is true of all types of funds.

3. Managers lose their magic. While it's true that some managers have significantly outperformed the market over long periods, their very success can undermine their performance. Funds that are really successful get so big that they can't buy the small volatile companies that often accounted for their original success; they get in their own way. Success also spawns lots of imitators that invest in the same stock sectors, driving up prices and making them poorer values.

Common sense tells us that it is impossible for several thousand experienced managers to appear within a decade. The world just isn't populated with clones of Buffett, Allmon, Templeton, and Lynch. Most funds are run by managers who didn't have to deal with the 1973–1974 bear market, possibly not even the 80–82 unpleasantness. And, of course, there's nobody left who sees the 1930s as other than ancient history.

Nevertheless, some funds are still a good value today. The closed-end funds listed in the Country Fund Table are worth considering in any market because they're closed-ends, of which more later.

USING FUNDS PROPERLY

Please don't misunderstand my point on mutual funds; they're a great invention with real value. But, especially now, they are being used unwisely, as "set-and-forget" devices that will outwit the market and insulate shareholders from losses.

It is almost always a bad idea to substitute someone else's judgment for your own in the hope it will prove to be wiser. A better idea is to improve your own judgment. That usually means making your own mistakes.

The best use of mutual funds is to make investing more convenient once you know what you want. But you must have your own investment philosophy. Until you develop one, your results will be no better choosing funds than individual stocks. It makes sense to pay managers a fee for saving you the trouble of reading lots of reports, talking to scores of company executives, and making hundreds of buy-and-sell decisions. Those are details that can be left to the fund managers— once you determine what market sector you like and what selection methods your fund is going to use.

Generally I recommend specialized funds, that do something that would be very difficult for an individual to replicate. For instance, some mutual funds invest only in companies with certain characteristics, such as growth or yield stocks. Some are run according to clearly defined principles of stock selection. The idea may be to buy only those stocks with the "best" chart patterns, or only those companies that conform to the parameters laid down by Benjamin Graham.* Or only stocks selling for low P/Es. Or dozens of other supposed methods of picking winners. As long as you can count on management to adhere to the stated purpose, you know exactly what you're getting.

I covered my own methods of selecting stocks in the preceeding chapters, and in *Strategic Investing*. I tend to restrict my buying to closed-end "sector" funds, which limit themselves to certain industries or countries.

From time to time, certain sectors, such as oil in the early '70s, gold in the late '70s, technology from 1982 to 1983, or biotech in 1991 to 1992 became fashionable. Trying to guess what's going to be hot is never easy. But it's often easier to determine the prospects of an industry as a whole than any one company in it. That's the advantage of a sector fund; you get diversification within an industry, and you're hiring a staff to do all the things necessary to sort the companies out. You're not trying to substitute their market judgment for yours; rather you're using their superior technical expertise. You're counting on them to crunch the company's financials to determine if it will survive long enough to realize its potential.

There are hundreds of open-end funds that specialize in one sector or another, and others that specialize in some "patented" approach to the market. But closed-end funds offer the same features and are more advantageous to own. It is surprising that few people know much about them.

OPEN-END VERSUS CLOSED-END FUNDS

Here's a rule of thumb: Restrict yourself to closed-end funds.

The vast majority of funds are of the open-ended variety. An open-end fund can issue an unlimited number of shares and redeems them itself at their net asset value. On the other hand, a closed-end fund has a fixed number of shares that are bought and sold like a common stock. If an investor wants to liquidate, he must sell them on the open market for whatever they bring.

Just like an ordinary stock, the price of closed-end shares is set by the psychology of the market, and there's no necessary relationship between the price of a closed-end and the value of its assets. Just like any stock, closed-end funds sometimes sell at big premiums or big discounts to their underlying assets, depending on the market's enthusiasm for what they hold. But unlike typical stocks, the assets of a closed-end fund are publicly traded securities, priced daily; it's easy, therefore, to tell precisely what a closed-end fund's assets are worth. You can often buy a dollar's worth of assets for a huge discount, sometimes as much as 20 to 40

*See discussion of Benjamin Graham, chapter 9.

percent, when the market loses interest in the sector the fund owns. When psychologies change the discount can turn into a premium, sometimes ranging to well over 50 percent on some funds.

Big discounts usually show up only when the market itself is depressed, and premiums when it's overpriced. The fluctuations in the premium-discount of closed-end funds offer a powerful form of leverage without borrowing and, as a bonus, an excellent signal when to buy and sell.

Markets regularly go from being maniacally overpriced to depressively underpriced. Closed-end funds generally amplify bull markets by going to premiums, and bear markets by going to discounts. Stocks that are already at bargain levels can be bought even more cheaply through a closed-end selling at a discount, and an overvalued market can be sold at even higher levels because of the premiums likely to be attached to closed-end funds.

If you like to "buy low and sell high," closed-ends offer a way to "buy lower and sell higher." They offer some of the leverage of options, but without the risk and costs.

There are about 400 closed-end mutual funds available at the moment; most of them, conveniently, specialize in a specific sector. Almost all the funds investing in specific countries, especially if their markets are small or illiquid, are closed-ends. This points out another advantage: a closed-end fund's manager knows exactly how much money he has to invest; he doesn't have to keep chasing more and more marginal securities to invest new funds that roll in, as do open-end managers. In small markets, it may be very hard to buy stocks at reasonable prices if millions of dollars start flowing into an open-end fund, and when they flow out, it would simply be impossible to sell shares to redeem the fund's outflows.

In particular, the closed-end funds specializing in certain countries will present spectacular opportunities as the world restructures along the lines discussed in chapter 27.

For your reference, I'm including a list of closed-ends that invest strictly in foreign equity markets. There are also about one hundred that invest in foreign bond markets. The historical discount and premium figures serve to give a rough idea of how volatile a particular fund may be.

Questions and Answers

Q: *What do you think of the "Telephone Switch" programs and other methods of trading funds?*

A: There are now a number of services that use various methods—mostly interpreting charts—to determine whether you should buy or sell different funds. There's no reason to believe these tout sheets will be any more successful than those catering to common stocks, or horses at the race track. The popularity of these fund trading services with the public is, however, an excellent indicator of how overpriced and manic the market is.

Table 13-1 Country Fund Table

Name	Price	% Discount/ Premium (%D/P)	Past % D/P	Specialty
Argentina	11	+15%	−1% / +20%	Argentina
Asia Pacific	13.5	+2%	−30% / +30%	Asia
Austria	7	−6%	−20% / +40%	Austria
Brazil	13.5	−6%	−50% / +20%	Brazil
Brazil Equity	10	+3%	N.A. / +25%	Brazil
Chile	33	−2%	−25% / +25%	Chile
China	14	−13.4%	−15% / +5%	China
Emerging Germany	7.5	−5%	−15% / N.A.	Germany (small cos)
Emerging Mexico	17.5	0	−20% / +5%	Mexico
Europe	10	−5%	−20% / +5%	Europe
First Australia	8	−3%	−30% / +15%	Australia
First Iberian	6.5	−15%	−15% / +40%	Spain/Portugal
First Israel	13	−15%	N.A.	N.A.
First Philippine	10.5	−25%	−40% / +20%	Philippines
France Growth	10	−10%	−20% / +5%	France
Future Germany	12	−9%	−20% / +15%	Germany
GT Greater Europe	9	−15%	−20% / +15%	Europe
Germany	11	+11%	−10% / +50%	Germany
Greater China	13	−7%	−5% / N.A.	China
Growth of Spain	8.5	−13%	−30% / +1%	Spain
India Growth	15	0	−20% / +20%	India
Indonesia	9	+16%	−20% / +20%	Indonesia
Irish Investment	7	−16%	−25% / N.A.	Ireland
Italy	9	+10%	−40% / +30%	Italy
Jakarta Growth	7	+9.5%	−25% / +20%	Indonesia
Japan Equity	8.5	−10%	−10% / N.A.	Japan
Japan OTC	8	−1%	−30% / +20%	Japan (small cos)
Jardine Fleming China	15	−6%	−15% / +5%	China
Korea	15	+32%	−5% / +100%	Korea
Korea Invest.	11.5	+15%	−10% / +15%	Korea
Latin Amer. Equities	14	−6%	−12% / N.A.	Latin Amer.
Latin Amer. Investment	25	−3%	−30% / +15%	Latin Amer.
Latin Amer. Discount	14	−8%	−10% / N.A.	Latin Amer.
Malaysia	16.5	+10%	−25% / +50%	Malaysia
Mexico	24	−8%	−50% / +100%	Mexico

Table 13-1   Country Fund Table (*Continued*)

Name	Price	% Discount/ Premium (%D/P)	Past % D/P	Specialty
Mexico Equit. & Income	16	− 5%	− 20% / + 1%	Mexico
Morgan Stanley Emerg. Mkts.	17	+ 10%	N.A. / + 20%	Third World
New Germany	10.5	− 5%	− 15% / + 40%	Germany (small cos)
Portugal	8	− 10%	− 20% / + 20%	Portugal
ROC Taiwan	9	+ 5%	− 30% / + 20%	Taiwan
Scudder New Asia	15	0	− 30% / + 5%	Asia and Japan
Scudder New Europe	8	− 15%	− 20% / N.A.	Europe (small cos)
Singapore	11	− 2%	− 20% / N.A.	Singapore
Spain	9		− 10% / + 100%	Spain
Swiss Helvetia	14	− 6%	− 25% / + 10%	Switzerland
Taiwan	20	+ 7%	− 10% / + 100%	Taiwan
Templeton Emerg. Mkts.	16	+ 24%	− 20% / + 30%	Third World
Thai	20	− 10%	N.A. / + 100%	Thailand
Turkish Inv.	5	+ 18%	− 25% / + 20%	Turkey
United Kingdom	9.5	− 10%	− 25% / N.A.	U.K.

Q: *Is there any reason to buy a "load" fund?*

A: No. The commission you pay, often as much as 8.5 percent of the sales price, which equals 9.3 percent of the amount actually going into the fund, serves no purpose besides lining your broker's pocket. It's true that sometimes the only way you can get into a given fund is by paying the commission, but with more than 3,000 funds available, you can often find an equally desirable no-load, or closed-end, equivalent.

Q: *Are there any advantages to open-end funds?*

A: Mainly convenience. It's an advantage to send in odd amounts of cash when you feel like it. And it's a plus to switch between funds in the same family with only a phone call. Whether those factors outweigh the advantages of closed-ends depends on your approach and situation. Open-ends have a place, but it's limited, using the methods I suggest.

All things being equal, a closed-end fund, purchased at a discount from asset value, is as good a deal as you're likely to get in the stock market.

The Allmon Trust (GSO, $10) buys proven growth stocks, and manager Charles Allmon is perhaps the best in the business at picking them. Although he doesn't claim to be a market timer, he has an excellent sense of when the market is cheap or dear. He is currently mostly in cash because he feels that at 3500, the market is absurdly overpriced. When it drops to reasonable levels, his fund will be one of the few with cash to buy it.

14

Money Market Funds as Hot Potatoes

Ready money *is* Aladdin's lamp.

Lord Byron (1788–1824)
Don Juan, 12

Money Market Funds (MMFs) are mutual funds that invest solely in short-term debt instruments. Currently there are more than 900 available with $600 billion in assets and almost all of them provide checking, daily interest, and other facilities offered by bank accounts. It's hard to open a newspaper or magazine without finding an article on their advantages. My visceral reaction when the popular financial press is interested in something is to look elsewhere. After all, few things that "everybody" knows are worth knowing. Nevertheless, there are so many different MMFs that some are still worth considering.

In *Strategic Investing* I urged readers to use only MMFs that invest strictly in high-grade securities. It's possible to pick up slightly more yield by investing in low-grade paper, but only at the risk of a significant portion of your capital. I have no problem with risking capital when there's a reasonable prospect of increasing it by a multiple. But risking it to gain a few basis points is a sucker's bet.

As the problems with the debt in the economy, discussed in chapter 5, start to seriously hurt the markets, people will start wondering why they ever allowed themselves to be deluded into buying funds based on the yield alone. To an unsophisticated investor, a fund with a higher yield is a "better" fund; he never wonders about the quality or the length to maturity of the assets he is investing in.

Especially since short-term interest rates descended to the 3 percent area in 1992, the public has moved billions of dollars into MMFs, investing in risky but higher yielding paper (such as Eurodollar CDs), as well as into bond funds, using them as an alternative to MMFs. The current steep yield curve means long-term bonds promise to pay well over twice the return on short-term paper of the same credit quality.

Does all this make any difference? It certainly will if interest rates go up. MMFs and bond funds are essentially the same, except for the maturity dates of the paper they own. Bond funds own paper maturing anywhere from a year to thirty years out. Money market funds own paper maturing in less than a year.

MMFs are safer than bond funds for two reasons. First, because the maturity of their investments is shorter, there is less innate risk. Obviously, the shorter the time money is invested, the less chance something might go wrong. Second, also because of the short maturity, a radical change in interest rates will have only a minor effect on value; a doubling of rates will basically halve the value of long bonds, however.

Unsophisticated investors, who read the ads in *Money* magazine, tend to think one MMF is as good as another, except for differences in yield. And they believe that bond funds are basically the same as, but better than, MMFs because decreasing interest rates during the early '90s have made them look that way; falling rates have added substantial capital gains to investors' already high yields. Such investors, who now think they have a neat, high-yielding alternative to a bank account, will find they bought into a risky, volatile speculation once credit and interest rate conditions begin to change.

Here's the point. MMFs and bond funds compete to gain investors by offering the highest yields possible. That means they have a powerful incentive to buy "junk" paper to improve the yields, because the managers get paid based on the number of dollars they have under management, not on the safety of their fund's assets. And the public puts its money where it gets the highest yield, since it apparently believes safety isn't an issue. After all, it's well known that no one has—yet—lost a penny in an MMF.

To keep yields at competitive levels, fund managers have had to both lengthen maturities and go to riskier paper. The next time a money fund experiences a default in its portfolio, the manager may not be in a position to make good on it, as happened in March 1990 with the T. Rowe Price MMF, among others. And that may lead to a full-blown panic.

The possibility of a major financial accident in MMFs has existed for about a decade, since they have grown so big, but so far nobody has been hurt. And the longer things go without mishap, the more confident the public becomes. How confident should they be? Let's look at the type of paper MMFs buy. There are basically seven types.

1. **Short-term U.S. Treasuries**—It's hard to conceive of them defaulting unless there's a domestic revolution or the government loses a major war. That they are redeemable only in paper dollars, which have no intrinsic worth, is beside the

point. In today's moving paper fantasy, you must pretend U.S. Treasuries are "good as gold," since they are, by far, the safest way to own dollars.

2. **U.S. Government Agency Obligations**—Government agencies, such as the Small Business Administration (SBA), and Government National Mortgage Association (GNMA) sell their own securities in the market, much as would a private corporation. Their debt is not Treasury debt, but in some cases it is guaranteed or collateralized by the U.S. government, (one reason why the national debt and annual deficits are always understated). While almost as good as Treasury debt, those securities offer a higher yield. But, keep in mind, if they were absolutely as good as the Treasury's, they wouldn't have to yield more.

3. **Repurchase Agreements** (Repos)—Banks and brokers keep debt instruments in inventory much as a clothier stocks sweaters; this inventory is financed almost entirely by borrowing. A repo is a loan made to a financial institution with a debt instrument for collateral. If the underlying instrument defaults, or drops significantly in value, then your mutual fund's security could melt away. Of course the institution it lent the money to must stand good for it, but an upset in the market is exactly the type of thing that could cause the borrower to collapse as well. A major risk here, even if the collateral is U.S. Treasury Bills, is that your fund may not have the collateral in its possession at the time a borrower goes under for some reason, in which case the fund must wait in line with other creditors.

4. **Bankers' Acceptances**—A means by which banks finance inventory for businesses, they are basically self-liquidating loans, and are a major area of banking activity. The loan is secured first by a pledge of merchandise being purchased by the borrower, the value of the product, second by the credit of the borrower, often by the supplier or customer for the merchandise, and last by the credit of the bank offering the loan for sale. When times are good, it is a sound piece of paper. When times are bad, however, the inventory in question could fall drastically in value, and the buyer and/or seller could go into default—along with the bank. If that happens, your fund is left holding the bag.

5. **Certificates of Deposit** (CDs)—These liabilities of domestic banks or S&Ls are covered by FDIC insurance only up to $100,000, but MMFs typically buy them in $10,000,000 minimums i.e., no more than 1 percent insured. CDs bought by MMFs have to be considered very risky.

6. **Commercial paper**—The unsecured promissory notes of major corporations. As business cyclically slows down, a lot of corporations that have borrowed heavily are going to be almost as sorry as the lenders.

7. **Eurodollars**—These are the unsecured foreign obligations of international banks, the same banks that have lent the money in question to countries in South America, Africa, and the old Eastern Bloc. Eurodollars are the riskiest and least secure short-term paper. They are the same instruments you would short against an equal amount of T-Bills to put on a TED spread (see chapter 7).

It wouldn't take an actual default to hurt CDs, commercial paper, or Eurodollars. Just the fear of default would depress values and hurt investors in most MMFs.

The bottom line: choose your money fund as wisely as you select any other mutual fund, because significant risks of loss are involved. An MMF should be used only as a secure parking place for dollars; the appropriate amount of risk is zero.

AVAILABLE FUNDS

In *Strategic Investing*, in 1982, I suggested that it was probably OK to put money in a fund as long as it had no exposure to CDs, commercial paper, and Eurodollars. I restricted my list of purchase candidates to funds holding U.S. Treasuries, U.S. Government obligations, and repos. Since the last ten years have been excellent for the financial markets, a more aggressive approach would have worked and would have offered a slightly higher yield. But the future promises to be increasingly stormy, and there is no point in taking chances for small advantages at the end of the longest, but shakiest, boom in modern history. It is more important than ever to monitor the portfolio of your fund, especially with investor confidence running so high that, during most of late 1992 and early 1993, there was only a 30-basis-point difference between T-Bills and Eurodollars. Do not count on a subscription to some money-market newsletter to keep you out of trouble, either. By and large, they tend to be running dogs of the industry.

At the present time there are only three funds that stick exclusively to investing in Treasury Bills: Treasury-Bill Portfolio, Capital Preservation Fund, and Neuberger & Berman Government. The proliferation of MMFs in recent years, like bond funds, has been mostly in the junk area, which itself is interesting.

Table 14-1 shows the returns of the three T-bill funds during 1992 versus the rest of the field.

The gross return is what the fund credits to your account after all expenses; the net return is what you keep after subtracting 28 percent for the government. This figure is more important for investors in a higher bracket, less important for those in a lower bracket. You'll notice that Treasury-Bill Portfolio Fund provided the highest net return. Its net was the same as its gross. It performed considerably better than any other kind of MMF, including the highest pure tax-exempt fund. This is a

Table 14-1   1992 Money Market Fund Yields

Fund	Gross Return	Net Return
Treasury-Bill Portfolio Fund	8.1%	8.1%
Capital Preservation	8.1%	5.8%
Neuberger & Berman	7.6%	5.5%
Highest-yielding fund	9.2%	6.6%
Highest tax-exempt fund	6.1%	6.1%

considerable accomplishment in a field where yield typically equates directly to risk. Clearly, based on the greatest degree of safety and the highest net yield, the Treasury-Bill Portfolio Fund would appear to be the only logical choice for an MMF. This will be even more true as taxes skyrocket under Clinton.

TREASURY-BILL PORTFOLIO FUND

How were they able to do this? There are, surprisingly, provisions in the tax code that allow a mutual fund to accrue income to the benefit of shareholders, without making a taxable distribution. Very few funds, and no other money-market fund that I'm aware of, take advantage of these provisions, since they operate on the assumption that they are in the investment-management business, not the tax-planning business. Investment advisor Harry Browne speculates there are three reasons why that is the case.

First, when the MMF industry started, it wanted its product to look as cashlike and riskless as possible, so they priced shares at $1.00 and paid out earnings daily as taxable dividends, precluding the use of any tax strategies. Treasury-Bill Portfolio, on the other hand, adds its daily income to the redemption value of shares, to achieve tax deferral for its shareholders. Its price ($64.57 in March 1993) fluctuates as dividends are added to the asset value.

Second, fund managers do not like to confuse potential clients; and going into the arcane tax law might scare away as many people as doing so would attract.

Third, tax planning is an extra administrative nuisance for fund managers. If, however, they see that Treasury-Bill Portfolio Fund grows rapidly—it was started in September 1987 and currently has $200 million—there will undoubtedly be imitators.

A final tax benefit of the fund is that when you do make a withdrawal, you take your interest earnings as a capital gain. If you have capital losses on other investments, you can offset your gains.

You can obtain a prospectus by writing to Permanent Portfolio's address, Box 5847, Austin, TX 78763, or by calling 800-531-5142, or 512-453-7558.

WHEN INTEREST RATES GO UP?

At some point, interest rates are likely to return to, and then surpass, the levels of the early '80s. People who were complaining in the early '90s about the 3 percent MMF yields will celebrate; they'll again receive 10 percent to 20 percent returns. But they will be drinking from a mirage. A 3 percent interest return, say 2 percent after taxes, is a real loss of only 1 percent when inflation is 3 percent. But 20 percent interest, say 14 percent after taxes, is a real loss of 7 percent when inflation is 20 percent. The higher yield looks better. And it feels better for a while, because you're inadvertently living out of capital. But if the situation continues, the principal in the account, even if all the after-tax interest were reinvested, will not, eventually, buy a stick of gum.

And the risk in a world of 20 percent yields comes from defaults as well as from inflation. A debtor who can crack an interest nut of 3 percent might have real trouble at 20 percent.

At that point you can expect some serious defaults in the portfolios of many MMFs. Management companies will try to contain them, in order to avert panic, but the numbers could be overwhelming. What will happen to interest rates if a scared public starts moving out of MMFs in a big way? They'll go through the roof, which will compound the problem.

The top-quality government funds will benefit from such a panic situation. Money would flow into them, seeking safety. But they are not safe either, because the dollar is already in trouble. There are two other alternatives: foreign currency MMFs and Swiss annuities.

FOREIGN CURRENCY MMFS

I explain how to hold assets abroad in chapters 18 and 27. But a very practical alternative method exists to, in effect, hold foreign currency here through any of the seven MMFs that specialize in that market. These MMFs can be a critical part of your portfolio, because it diversifies you out of the dollar. And since the late '80s, the yields on most foreign currencies have been up to two or three times higher than yields on U.S. dollar instruments. Unfortunately, however, those funds invest in the same type of assets as ordinary MMFs, just in different currencies. My cautions concerning them are, therefore, similar.

Different currencies will do better or worse than the dollar, but most will do better. Owning foreign currencies is an intelligent diversification.

You should look at the following funds:
1. Fidelity D–Mark Performance
2. Fidelity Yen Performance
3. Fidelity Sterling Performance
4. Keystone Aussie: Short-Term Income
5. Huntington Income Portfolio: Hard Currency
6. Huntington Income Portfolio: Global Currency
7. Huntington Income Portfolio: High Income

SWISS ANNUITIES

If you were to choose one currency to diversify into, it should be the Swiss franc. There's every reason to believe it will rise to parity with and above the dollar in the years to come. There's no reason for its long-term uptrend, from $0.23 in 1971 to $0.65 in 1993, to reverse.

It's impossible to predict what will happen in the near term, but you should use every opportunity to trade your dollars for stronger, better-managed currencies. Although no currency is convertible into gold, the Swiss authorities have enough gold, so that if they choose to back the franc, they could do so about twice over at current prices.

The question is not whether to diversify out of the dollar, but how best to do it. The best way to own Swiss francs is through an "annuity" issued by a Swiss insurance company. I put the word *annuity* in quotes because the product has little relationship with the traditional products familiar to most Americans. The Swiss annuity presents several distinct advantages.

1. There is no Swiss withholding tax on the interest earned, unlike Swiss bank accounts and Swiss government bonds, and there is no U.S. tax payable on interest until you withdraw it.
2. No requirement exists for you to report your account to the IRS, as is the case with foreign bank and brokerage accounts. A Swiss annuity is as close as you will come to holding a private offshore investment. All Swiss banking secrecy laws apply.
3. Under most circumstances the annuity, properly structured, is safe from lawsuits and creditors. And that's increasingly important in the Age of Envy.
4. Principal and interest are guaranteed by substantial Swiss insurance companies. These firms have long been noted for their conservative balance sheets and invest heavily in Swiss government bonds. Interest rates are competitive (6 to 7 percent as of early 1993). That's a big premium over bank accounts either here or in Switzerland, especially after taking taxes into account.
5. You have the option of switching the account to U.S. dollars, German Marks, or ECUs.
6. The account is 100 percent liquid. There's no up-front fee and no redemption fee after the first year. Your money starts earning immediately, and you can withdraw it at any time. You pay a SF500 fee only if you withdraw your investment during the first year.

These are important pluses. It's absolutely critical that you diversify politically and geographically, and this may be the most practical way to do it, while securing an extraordinary combination of safety, privacy, tax shelter, high current return, and capital gain potential.

For more information contact JM Lattmann, A.G., Box 170-C, Germaniastr. 55, 8033 Zurich, Switzerland. Tel 011-411-363-2510, Fax 011-411-361-4074.

15

Income—Bonds as a Triple Threat to Capital

> Long term Government bonds are like an Exacta bet on 10 Presidential elections, 6½ Senate turnovers, and 20 House elections. I would rather go to the race track than make that bet.
>
> Ian MacAvity

The quest for yield preoccupies most Americans with money to invest. Few are aware that their quest for income may end in a meltdown of their capital. Investments bought for yield, as substitutes for bank CDs or savings accounts, are not thought of as risky.

The problem, of course, is not the desire for income itself. Interest should be something you earn, not something you pay. But those few who are paying attention to risk are watching only gradual and subtle risks, like the risk that inflation will outpace their return. The real hazards, however, are likely to be sudden, and catastrophic.

This chapter will underline the big risks but will also show you how you can have the best of all worlds—higher current returns and more security. Let's look at the bond market first.

CERTIFICATES OF GUARANTEED CONFISCATION

The $64,000 question of the '90s may not be which way stocks, gold, commodities, or real estate are headed. Each of these markets is worth, literally, trillions, and none is going to zero—or even approaching it—even under the worst possible scenario. All except stocks are real, tangible assets; and although stocks are paper certificates, they represent the ownership of tangible assets.

The bond market, however, with the exception of convertibles, represents a claim only on dollars, not tangible assets or shares. When the dollar and the economy were stable, this was not very important. The potential for a rapid meltdown in the value of the dollar has long been perceived as merely theoretical, with consequences far off in the future, if ever. As Keynes is famous for having said, "In the long run, we are all dead."* But Keynes's tempestuous storm is now just around the corner, and you and I will live to see it.

The bond market alone—not counting mortgages, bank debt, commercial paper, and other forms of credit whose claim is on dollars—totals about $5.5 trillion. It is significantly larger than the stock market's $4 trillion. What would happen if the dollars represented by bonds ceased to have value? What would happen if the floating abstraction called the dollar were to vanish? In other words, since the dollar rests on confidence, what would happen if that confidence were to evaporate?

The real key to what will happen to the economy is probably held by the bond market, not only because of its gigantic size, but also because bonds are payable in dollars, and the future of those dollars is problematical.

So, which way bonds?

BONDS FOR INCOME

The bottom line on bonds is that they're a triple bet—on the solvency of the issuer, on the value of the currency, and on the level of interest rates. Any one of these bets can prove risky, but bonds combine them in a triple threat to capital.

The level of debt, which brings into question the solvency of bond issuers from the U.S. government on down, and the near inevitability of inflation are dealt with throughout this book. If interest rates were "high enough," always a subjective matter, then bonds could still be an interesting speculation. But, as of March 1993, rates are at their lowest levels (and bonds at their highest levels) since the early 1960s.

Based on the level of rates alone, bonds are about as overpriced as the U.S. stock market in 1968 or the Japanese market in 1989.

Is it possible that the United States could have a runaway inflation, wiping out the $5.5 trillion in bonds now outstanding? Yes, because the American authorities could create an unlimited number of dollars, much as the governments in scores of other countries have done with their own currencies. But there is a big difference. I don't know of any country that has ever had a runaway inflation that also had a large bond market. That is due in part to the fact that no one will buy bonds in a currency with a history of frequent disappearances. Countries with badly managed currencies never develop bond markets to start with. But the lack of bond markets in these

*"This *long run* is a misleading guide to current affairs. *In the long run* we are all dead. Economists set themselves too easy, too useless a task if in tempestuous seasons they can only tell us that when the storm is long past the ocean is flat again." —John Maynard Keynes, *A Tract on Monetary Reform*, 1924.

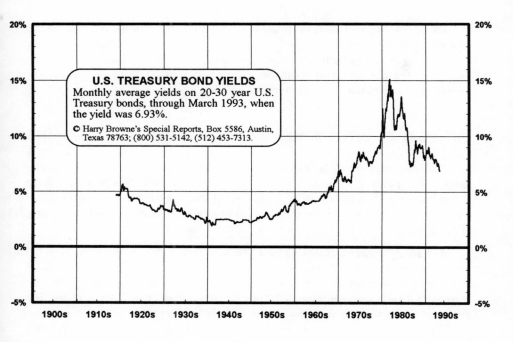

U.S. TREASURY BOND YIELDS
Monthly average yields on 20-30 year U.S.
Treasury bonds, through March 1993, when
the yield was 6.93%.
© Harry Browne's Special Reports, Box 5586, Austin,
Texas 78763; (800) 531-5142, (512) 453-7313.

Figure 15-1

countries is also due to the fact that inflation itself can be deflationary, which seems like a paradox.

Interest rates roughly keep pace with inflation. Suppose conditions return to the levels of the early '80s, with 15 percent inflation and 15 percent bond rates. What happens to the $5.5 trillions of bonds now outstanding, with average coupons of about 8 percent? They'll fall roughly 50 percent in price, wiping out $2.25 trillion. That means that $2.25 trillion in purchasing power that someone was relying on has also disappeared. The "someone" is banks, pension funds, and insurance companies, as well as the public at large.

As people make fewer purchases the level of business activity drops. Lower levels of business activity make it harder for many to service their mortgages or bank debt, and defaults rise, compounding the problem. Banks lend less, and the money supply contracts. Where do the dollars go? A wag might say they die and go to money heaven, and there's actually a lot of truth to that. If the dollars represented something real, they would still be in existence, albeit in someone else's hands. The paradox is that some of the value lost by bondholders is gained by the remaining dollars. Inflation has a deflationary affect.

The bond market in 1993 is more than three times as large as it was in the early '80s, the last time we had a crisis. Because the markets are so much larger now, the crisis to come will be much more serious.

How will it end? That remains an open question, because we can't be certain how the government will try to pull the economy through this business cycle. Nor can we know whether their measures will succeed one more time.

But there are things you can do to insulate yourself from the meltdown, whether it's inflationary or deflationary.

WHY ARE PEOPLE BUYING BONDS?

The risks in bonds are clear. But it's almost always a mistake to act on a single-minded, fixed idea. Let's look at bonds the way most buyers do, with a view more to their rewards than their risks. People buying them at the 8 percent level aren't doing so, after all, from a perverse desire to lose money. Today's bond buyers are, or have been, in the market for one or more of the following reasons.

1. **"Real" Interest Rates Appear High**—"Real" interest rates (the nominal rate minus the rate of inflation) are higher in 1993, at 5 percent (8 percent minus inflation of 3 percent) than they were in 1980, when T-Bonds were yielding 12 percent (but inflation was running 12 percent, leaving a "real" return of 0). The argument is often made that you should lock in this high real return.

Apparent "real" yields, however, are largely irrelevant to making or losing money if you buy bonds now. The best time to have bought bonds in the last 50 years was from 1980 to 1982, when the apparent real rate of return was negative. The inflation rate can skyrocket quickly back to double-digit levels, much as it did in the '70s. Those who lock in 8 percent coupon bonds now because they show a "real" 5 percent return might, I suspect, realize a real 10 percent negative return in a few years. Worse, as rates go up to match inflation, they could produce a 50 percent loss on capital as bonds retreat to their previous lows.

Remember if you bought 2 percent government bonds in the deflationary 1930s for a real yield of perhaps 10 percent (prices were dropping; "inflation" was running about −9 percent), you would have had your head handed to you when nominal rates moved up to just 3 percent.

2. **Deflation Insurance**—Prices of many things—notably commodities, real estate, some wages, and many technological processes like computer power—fell through most of the '80s, while the rate of increase in the CPI itself has gradually decreased from a peak of more than 13 percent in 1980 to about 3 percent today. There's a prospect of actual deflation, not just disinflation. If a real deflation, like that of the 1930s, got under way, yields could conceivably drop substantially from the current 8 percent. If hundreds of billions of dollars in bonds were to default in a deflation, the remaining good obligations would arguably be worth more. Bonds are perceived as an insurance policy against deflation.

There is actual danger of a full-scale deflation, and with all the debt outstanding today, anything could happen. The government could declare a total repayment moratorium, including even its own obligations. Or maybe it would attempt some type of wholesale bailout. In a number of realistic scenarios the bond market would crash amid a credit shortage, despite an outright deflation.

Bond prices are like any other prices; they go up because there are more buyers than sellers, not necessarily because there is an inflation, a deflation, prosperity, a depression, or what-have-you.

3. **A Bet on Stability and Prosperity**—Bonds were in a super bear market, a slow-motion crash, from the 1930s until the early '80s. In addition, the dollar itself has lost about 90 percent of its value in the last fifty years, and over 75 percent since 1967 alone (i.e., the CPI has risen from 100 to 426). But the last ten years have been good for bond prices, if not for dollars. Since all trends eventually reverse, the reasoning is that a new bull market began in the early 1980s.

This is all true, of course. However, the long bear market was caused by chronic political meddling, and that got worse in the '80s, even while bond prices rose. The bear market in bonds has been controlled by a force comparable to that which draws a man toward the ground if he falls from a fifty-story building. He may hit an awning on the way down, and bounce back a way, but the law of gravity hasn't been repealed.

This bear market will end, but not necessarily before the dollar reaches zero. I can't see how the current resurgence of confidence in the future has any relevance to the fate of the dollar in the next five years. Confidence is mostly a matter of psychology, and crowd psychology can turn on a dime.

4. **A Play on Lower Tax Rates**—This item is now really history. Few people believe taxes are going to be cut at this point, but that was the trend throughout the '80s.

Interest on bonds has long been subject to ordinary income tax, and for many years taxes confiscated from 50 percent to 92 percent of a bond buyer's income; that was a major disincentive to investing in bonds. In the '80s, however, marginal tax rates dropped dramatically, to the 30 percent area. Many people who had never considered bonds before were induced to buy them, and this new buying helped drive down interest rates. In addition, lower corporate taxes gave companies extra earnings, thereby increasing the desirability of their bonds and decreasing their need to borrow.

When President Clinton increases marginal rates, this process will go into reverse. That will make bonds a poor holding for income, but they will remain excellent vehicles for speculation.

BONDS AS A SPECULATION

It makes little sense to put a substantial part of your assets into long-term bonds at less than 8 percent. The interest is inadequate to compensate for the risks, and bonds can be very volatile; you stand to lose as much capital in a day of market movement as you could gain in a year of interest payments.

Bonds should be viewed as vehicles for speculation on the direction of long-term rates, not something for those investors who want safety and capital conservation. They are political footballs that will be passed dozens of times in the years to come by the intellectuals making a game out of "fine tuning" the economy. You can bet that the ball is going to be dropped at some point.

If you want to speculate on interest rates, which is what owners of long-term bonds are doing, whether they know it or not, you're probably better off doing so in the futures pits in Chicago; at least there you are forced to confront the degree of risk you are taking.

In a hallway in my house I display worthless bonds issued by the governments of Hungary, China, Russia, and the Confederate States, among others. Not one was redeemed, because the issuing governments disappeared; but it wouldn't have made any difference if the governments had survived, because their currencies didn't. I also have hundreds of worthless banknotes, some in very large denominations, from scores of countries where these notes are no longer circulated or honored. It's entirely possible that they'll be joined someday by U.S. Treasury bonds and Federal Reserve Notes.

There is one type of bond, however, that can have a prominent place in your portfolio; convertible bonds.

CONVERTIBLES

Corporate bonds that are convertible into common stock, at a given price, are hybrid securities, offering the yield and security of a debt instrument combined with the potential upside of equity. Roughly 1,200 different convertibles are traded in the United States, and probably an equal number are available in various Eurocurrencies.

Convertibles are available in two flavors: bonds and preferreds. Preferreds are advantageous mainly to corporate investors, since they can claim tax deductions for 70 percent of the dividend they receive. Unless you do business through a corporation, bonds are almost always more desirable, everything else being equal, because they offer higher after-tax yields and better conversion terms. And they are more senior securities.

Experienced investors never buy a common stock without first checking to see whether a company also offers a convertible, for several reasons.

1. Commissions are lower on bonds than stocks and are generally fixed at $5 per unit when sold on an agency basis.
2. The interest coupon is guaranteed, and interest accumulates if a company is unable to pay it currently. Preferreds do not pay interest; they pay dividends. Dividends, even on preferreds, are often passed and lost forever, unless it's a cumulative preferred.
3. A convertible often offers as much, or nearly as much, upside as the common, depending on its conversion terms.

4. While they share most of the upside of the common, convertibles have much less risk. This is true not just because of their senior status but because of their yield. At worst they trade at their investment value as pure bonds.
5. A convertible almost always offers a substantial yield advantage over the common. Why buy the common when it is possible, in addition to the other advantages, to pick up 5 percent to 10 percent in current yield?
6. Convertible bonds have a specific date and price at which they must be redeemed by the issuer. A convertible can often be bought at a substantial discount from par, which means there should be a guaranteed capital gain when it is eventually redeemed by the issuer, even if it hasn't already been converted into common.

With all these plus factors, you are probably wondering why anybody buys anything but convertibles. There are several reasons. One reason is ignorance. Most people are only vaguely aware of convertibles. Few convertibles are quoted in the general newspapers. Convertibles take some explaining, and brokers like to keep things simple rather than risk confusing a customer; they're in sales, not the education business.

Although institutions understand the game, the market for convertibles is usually too small and too illiquid to allow them to play. In addition, most convertibles are issued by second-tier companies needing to offer a sweetener to raise capital; most institutions like to stay with S&P 500 outfits. But as was pointed out in chapter 10, smaller companies are more likely to have what you want.

These disadvantages serve to keep the prices of convertibles lower than they would be in a completely efficient market. And that makes them excellent candidates not only for the speculator but for the income investor.

One other factor should be considered, which could be of immense importance in the 1990s. Even the highest-grade "straight" bond is worth nothing but a certain number of dollars; you may get the dollars, but they are likely to be worth much, much less in the future. Considering the trillions of dollars of bonds outstanding, if a real dollar panic ever hits, their owners may not be able to get out of them at all. Owners of convertibles, however, have the option of trading their bonds for shares in the underlying corporation.

As unlikely as it may seem at the moment, convertibles could evolve from low-grade securities whose downside is limited by the fact they can trade as bonds, to the only type of bonds with some degree of safety, because they can be converted into stock.

SOME SPECIFICS

If you are interested in any company or any industry at any time in the future, always check to see whether a convertible exists before buying. Few investors do, and they later regret their oversight. The ideal time to buy a convertible occurs when stocks are low and interest rates high. Conveniently, these things usually happen together. The year 1982 was the last major bottom.

It's not my intention to give how-to advice in this book. That information can be gained from brokers' pamphlets and magazines, among other places. But convertibles have several noteworthy characteristics.

Yield to maturity—Total return if it's held to redemption, including capital gains and interest. This is important because the underlying stock may never rise to its conversion price. Hence yield to maturity shows your worst case should the convertible trade strictly as a bond, provided the underlying company doesn't fail.

Conversion price—The price at which the underlying common is at parity with the bond.

Conversion premium—The percentage by which the common needs to increase before it hits its conversion price. The higher the premium, the more the convertible trades like a bond; the lower the premium, the more it will follow the stock price.

A few convertibles deserve special comment at the moment. I note some convertibles on smaller oil stocks in chapter 23. Smaller defense companies, of the type discussed in chapter 30, also have a lot of convertibles. My most favored group, however, is convertibles issued by gold mining companies. The shares of these gold companies are depressed right now and possess massive upside potential. If, in the worst case, you convert to stock, you should do very well indeed. In the meantime, your money earns a satisfying income.

At present, these are the gold mining converts available:

ISSUE	PRICE	% Yield	PREMIUM	% Yield of Common Stock
Battle Mt. 6% of 2005	$70	10%	140%	1.7%
Coeur d'Alene 6% of 2002	$78	7.8%	88%	1.4%
Coeur d'Alene 7% of 2002	$96	7.3%	40%	1.4%
Echo Bay $1.75 Preferred	$22½	7.8%	75%	1.6%
FMC 6.75% of 2005	$84	8.0%	210%	1.2%
Freeport Copper & Gold Conv. 0% of 2011	$33	0%	0%	2.8%
Freeport Copper & Gold Preferred	$29	6.1%	36%	2.8%
Hecla 0% of 2004	$37	0.0%	134%	0%

If convertibles are the best, or perhaps the only, type of bond to consider, then municipals are among the worst.

MUNICIPAL BONDS

Municipal debt literally went hyperbolic in the '80s. (See Figure 15-2.) Lots of it will be defaulted on, and the remainder will be paid off only through gigantic tax boosts.

Taxes rose sharply in the last decade, as illustrated in Figure 15-3, but they could look like small potatoes in the years to come.

The fiscal problems of state and local governments are well known; most state and local governments are deep in debt and running large deficits—even after raising taxes faster than the federal government over the last thirty years. (See Figure 15-4.)

Despite a compound growth in taxes, of, on average, 7 percent during each of the last seven years, state and local government spending has outstripped its revenue increases. The deficits governments are running today are far greater than the surpluses they achieved in the boom years, as Figure 15-5 shows.

I see no reason for the trend to change soon. In fact, it's likely to accelerate for at least three reasons: (1) a declining economy will reduce tax revenues; (2) a declining economy will be met with demands for higher welfare payments and other

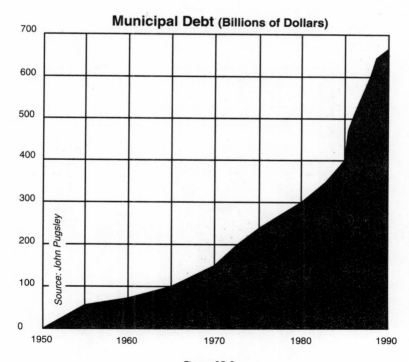

Figure 15-2

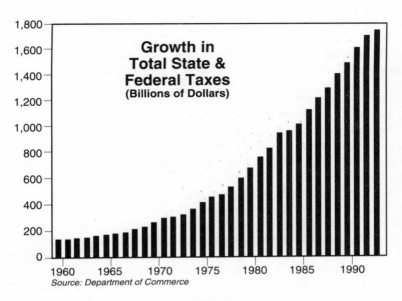

Source: Department of Commerce

Figure 15-3

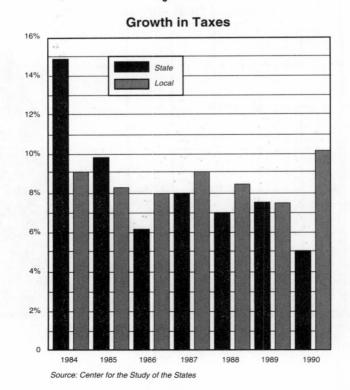

Source: Center for the Study of the States

Figure 15-4

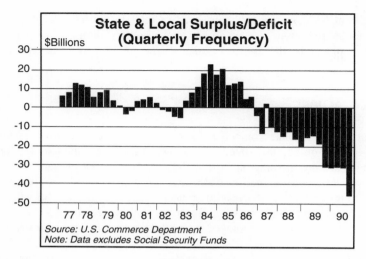

Figure 15-5

state funds; (3) federal government subsidies to the states have dropped from a high of 26 percent in 1980 to 17 percent last year, even though federal grants rose from $85 billion to over $131 billion. Federal grants could start dropping in dollar terms as federal deficits worsen, which will put more pressure on the states to increase revenue from citizens, putting more of a drag on the economy.

Of course, state and local governments cannot keep borrowing and taxing indefinitely. Even the Soviets found that bankruptcy is a fact of the real world. And since state governments cannot print money like the federal government, they are likely to reach a crisis point much earlier.

As a result, it is more important than ever to insulate yourself from profligate state governments. You should seriously consider moving yourself and your capital to a state with no, or at least a low, tax burden.

The growing numbers of people working for the state are a sure indicator of bad things to come, even though politicians tout it as "creating jobs." You may be shocked to know that the 80,000 local governments in this country now employ 18.5 million people, or more people than work in manufacturing, and only slightly fewer than work in the retail trade. Sure, many of them repair the roads, put out fires, teach children, and do other things required by the market. But many self-righteously enforce destructive regulations, collect taxes, and shuffle paper to the bedevilment of those who are taxed to pay their salaries. Nationally, the number of state employees increased 19 percent in the '80s, compared to a 9 percent population increase.

You want to stay away from places like California, Massachusetts, New Jersey, New York, Ohio, Maine, Oregon, Hawaii, Minnesota, and Indiana, in particular. They all have high taxes, and the trend is higher.

Also avoid Connecticut and Texas. The average state government per capita expenditure increased 48.8 percent from 1982 to 1988. Connecticut at 73.2 percent and Texas at 58.7 percent ran way ahead of that. In the past, local governments tended to be run more conservatively because they didn't have the unlimited borrowing power or the ability of the federal government to print money. No longer.

PRACTICAL ACTIONS

The best way to insulate yourself is to ignore municipal bond investments and to live in a low, or no, tax state. The sooner the better, since some states, like California, are now attempting to tax the pensions of out-of-state retirees if the money was originally earned in California. Of course, most people are not in a position to relocate themselves based on tax considerations; they live where they do for professional and family reasons. But many do have that freedom. For example, if you're retiring, are self-employed, can relocate your business, or invest professionally.

People vote intelligently with their feet. In the last ten years, the population growth of states with the highest taxes was 2.4 percent less than the average national population growth; those states with the lowest taxes had population increases of 9.0 percent higher than the national average. My suspicion is that productive individuals and businesses, that is, those with high incomes, have been moving one way, and those seeking fat benefits and subsidies have been moving the other way.

States with no income tax include Florida, Wyoming, Nevada, Washington, New Hampshire, and Texas, although Texas may be getting an income tax soon.

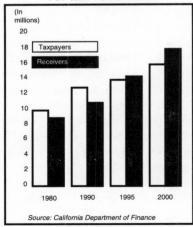

California taxpayers vs. tax receivers

Source: California Department of Finance

Figure 15-6

Smart places to live might be Nevada or Washington, close to the Oregon border, or in Wyoming, close to the Montana line. You would pay no income tax where you live, but could make all your purchases where no sales tax is levied.

When you crunch all the numbers, you might find that it's worth making a move from a financial point of view alone, not counting intangibles like lifestyle and the gratification of denying revenue to grasping state bureaucrats.

Right now the typical "quality" muni bond (that is, those that make up the futures index, yields about 6 percent. With tax advantages, that equates to a pre-tax yield of around 9.25 percent. But I wouldn't want to own the debt of entities as shaky as these. You'll recall that California recently had to pay its debt with script instead of dollars. As the economy slows, many states may find themselves in the same position.

WHAT ABOUT HIGH-YIELD, OR "JUNK," BONDS?

Junk bonds are those with a major agency risk rating of less than BBB* or its equivalent. Before these bonds proliferated in the '80s, junk bonds were a very good deal because their only slightly higher default rate was offset by their higher yields and the possibility that the debt would be upgraded. But because junk was not rated BBB or better, most institutions couldn't buy it, so it was cheap.

Michael Milken, who became famous for selling many billions worth of low-rated bonds, realized that the only thing that can happen to a AAA bond is to be downgraded and lose value overnight. A sound but lower-rated bond could be upgraded. Junk bonds were an excellent deal for both borrower and lender.

As with most good things in the market, the situation eventually grew manic. As the '80s wore on, the risk/reward equation for junk turned negative, due to the huge amounts of new debt being issued.

Junk bonds are priced much more in relation to the issuers' viability than to interest rates. If rates rise a lot, these bonds will plummet in order to stay competitive. But a bond that has a poor risk/reward ratio at 100 may offer excellent value at 50 or 75. Higher rates, however, will slow down business and hurt the issuers' fundamental prospects. So junk bonds must be chosen carefully.

If you like a certain stock or industry, it pays to check to see if any junk bonds are available just as you would look for convertibles. Because the market questions the ability of issuing companies to redeem their junk bonds, their prices fluctuate with the underlying stocks almost like convertibles. Like convertibles, junk bonds offer high current yield and far more security than the common.

Junk bonds were a central issue in the Wall Street "scandals" of the '80s. It's worth taking a closer look at them, with an eye to the wider implications for the economy and the market.

*Debt rated less than BBB is regarded as speculative with respect to capacity to pay interest and repay principal in accordance with the terms of the obligation. BB is lower risk while C carries the highest risk.

16

Wall Street Ethics

The liberty of man consists solely in this: that he obeys natural laws because he has *himself* recognized them as such, and not because they have been externally imposed upon him by any extrinsic will whatever, divine or human, collective or individual.

Michael Bakunin, *God and the State*, 1871

Even though the SEC still prosecutes a couple of dozen new cases a year, the media furor about insider trading has died down from the hysteric levels it reached in 1990, when Michael Milken went to jail. The media have always found a ready audience, especially among the envious, the unsuccessful, and the hostile, for tales of scandal among the rich and famous. The desire to see the mighty laid low is certainly one of the more perverse characteristics of human psychology. People on the bottom of the heap, whether viewed economically or psychologically, are especially prone to envy. They seem to think it makes more room for them at the top, even as it redeems their failure by showing that it must be necessary to lie, cheat, and steal to gain wealth.

Envy is no more prevalent than it was in the past; envy is human. But some social structures bring out the worst in people. In the old Soviet Union or Nazi Germany or Salem during the witch-hunting days or Spain during the Inquisition, it was possible to report someone to the authorities and see him "cut down to size." In other times and places, like America and England during the nineteenth century, other peoples' opinions had little or no effect on the lives of the intended victim.

It is unfortunate that the United States appears to be entering a period (see chapter 32) more similar to the sordid past of other countries than to its own better days. If the so-called robber barons of the nineteenth century were alive today, they would have spent more time arguing in court and serving time in jail and less time building steel mills and railroads. If that had been the case, the whole country would be far poorer today.

"Ethics," in the current vernacular, relates to investing in two main ways. One has to do in general with investing in trendy areas like pollution control, or "soft" technologies, or in companies that give money to politically correct causes, such as saving the whales and rain forests and not investing in currently unfashionable areas, such as chemicals and defense.

The other investment-related area of ethics that concerns the public and the media involves such things as insider trading, program trading, parking, greenmail, golden parachutes, proxy fights, regulation, and management featherbedding.

Ethics is the study of what is morally right and wrong. There's a lot of confusion on the subject. To get my philosophical bearings, I naturally turned to our national repository of wisdom and moral rectitude: the popular media. Its definitive statement on this subject and an accurate reflection of the public's attitude as well is given in the 1986 movie *Wall Street*. It is instructive to examine the film as more than entertainment. Let's go to the movies.

WALL STREET, THE MOVIE

Wall Street chronicles the rise of a young stockbroker, Bud Fox, to a position as protégé of corporate raider/speculator Gordon Gekko, Bud's supposed corruption in the process, and his subsequent return to grace. On a psychological level it is the story of how a "good guy," represented by Fox's father, and a "bad guy," represented by Gordon Gekko, vie for possession of Bud's soul. It's a sad story, because the "good guy" wins.

Fox's father, an unintelligent, pigheaded, envy-driven loser who is a populist union steward, mentions to Bud that the FAA is going to exonerate his employer, Blue Star Airlines, for an accident that had been hanging over them. He gratuitously allows how he had always believed it was "those greedy, cost-cutting" airplane manufacturers that were really to blame. His views provide a good insight into the filmmaker's values. Another is offered when the elder Fox says: "The only difference between the Empire State Building and the pyramids is that the Egyptians didn't have unions." Sure. And the only difference between McDonald's and a Gulag bread line is the sesame seed bun.

Knowledge of the unannounced FAA decision is valuable data. Bud wangles an appointment with Gekko, using a box of Cuban cigars his straight-arrow Dad must have liberated with a bribe to a customs inspector, as a door-opener. To ingratiate himself further, he discloses the Blue Star decision to Gekko, who naturally buys the stock in anticipation and makes a bundle. This is presented as an illegal and unethical use of inside information. Was it illegal? Who knows?

The very concept of inside information is undefined and undefinable. The rationale against insider trading is the creation of a "level trading field" for all players, so no one knows anything before anyone else and there are no "unfair" advantages.

Would acting on the elder Fox's information have been illegal if he had told not just one person, but everyone he knew? What if he took out ads and tried to inform the world at large? What about those people who did not read the paper; would they have grounds for a lawsuit because they were not given the opportunity to buy? That decision rests on the whim of some regulator. Shouldn't it also be "inside information" if the few people who are the first to hear an official announcement immediately act on it? What if Gekko had simply had a hunch about the decision and bought Blue Star based on that hunch alone; how could he prove he *didn't* have illegal data?

Is the use of insider information ethical? Absolutely, whenever the data is honestly gained and no confidence is betrayed by disclosing or using it. Because the whole concept of inside information is a floating abstraction, it's a witch hunter's dream and a natural for government lawyers. It takes millions of dollars of legal fees to reach an arbitrary decision on legalities alone. And, as with most regulatory law, concepts of ethics, justice, and property rights never even enter the equation.

In the movie's next supposed moral dilemma, Gekko convinces Fox to follow an Australian speculator around town to learn what stocks he's buying and buy them first. The confused Fox comments: "Inside information, isn't it?" before embarking on field research that resulted in more successful trades. Is it inside information to follow someone around town and conjecture what he's likely to buy based on whom he visits? I can't see how, but who cares, because it's information honestly acquired.

In the next instance Fox, posing as a cleaning man, gains access to a law office and copies some files detailing a takeover. Inside information? It's academic, because that act is simple theft. The movie is unable to distinguish between detective work and burglary. The fact that a theft has been committed—the only real, common-law crime in the whole movie—is never acknowledged.

A HERO IN THE SLIME

The viewer's attention does not focus on the vapid, dishonest yuppie Bud Fox, played by actor Charlie Sheen, but on the dynamic Gordon Gekko. Gekko is not a particularly nice guy. He is materialistic, cheats on his wife, and doesn't give suckers an even break. And he probably doesn't care where or how Fox gets his information. But do you care where Standard and Poor's obtain their data? No. You care only that it is accurate, and you make the reasonable assumption it is not the product of theft. Gekko encourages Fox to get information that isn't common knowledge. That's what makes for success in many legitimate endeavors. But he never sends him out to steal.

In fact, Gekko does nothing unethical in the movie except lie to the union people when he's about to take over Blue Star. But for that exception we can make a case that Gekko, his personality aside, was actually a moral hero. Look beyond the nasty patina the film paints him with. Gekko rewarded Fox for doing what appeared to be good work. He paid for value received.

A criminal takes what he has not earned, offering nothing in exchange. Whether someone is a criminal or not has little to do with whether he violates some law.

Gekko's infamous "greed is good" speech at the annual general meeting of Teldar Paper should be given at every annual corporate meeting. Gekko explains how money is concentrated life, representing all the good things one ever hopes to have and provide. And since love, life, and money are good, so is the desire—greed—to have as much of them as possible. Gekko's speech is also an accurate and excellent presentation of why takeovers are usually a good thing. Gekko points to Teldar's numerous vice presidents who are paid six figures to shuffle memos and build little satrapies* with money that should be given to the shareholders as dividends. Gekko makes it clear that if he wins they will be fired. Gekko is absolutely right, and his actions throughout the movie can only serve to better the lot of thousands, maybe millions, of people. In that regard, at least, the country could use a thousand Gordon Gekkos.

Fox is understandably unhappy with Gekko because of his lie about Blue Star. He decides to turn state's evidence against Gekko when the SEC gets both him and Gekko in its sights. He wires himself, presumably to get a reduced sentence, and induces Gekko to say compromising things. Here the only morally unambiguous and satisfying point in the whole movie is made: Gekko, quite correctly, beats the daylights out of the sleazy young Fox.

The distasteful movie ends with Fox completely caving in to the ethical morass endorsed today as "correct," and personified by his father. He says: "Maybe I can learn how to create, instead of living off the buying and selling of others." Maybe he's planning to retire to a hippie commune to create candles and baskets. Maybe he would prefer Cuba, where buying and selling are illegal.

It is strange how the public rarely analyzes moral issues; something is considered "wrong" because a preacher or an official says it is. No one considers whether the "authorities" might have based their judgment on a false premise or a hidden personal agenda. Sometimes things are believed to be wrong because "everyone" assumes as much, as everyone once assumed the sun revolved around the earth. And, after a while, that unchallenged assumption becomes part of the social contract.

Now Gordon Gekko, and everything he's supposed to stand for, has become a cultural totem for everything that's wrong with the U.S. financial system. Try defending Gekko sometime and watch the reaction you get; better you should try to defend Stalin. People have a hard time getting past their emotional reaction and weighing the rights and wrongs of a situation.

---

*The province of a subordinate, despotic ruler.

Especially with the increasing influence of the popular media, that unreasoned emotional response can only hurt the markets, the economy, and the unlucky individuals who are singled out.

MICHAEL MILKEN AS ROLE MODEL

Milken was the object of an intense government investigation costing hundreds of thousands of man hours and many millions of dollars. It became a political issue with a life of its own, and Milken had to be punished for something. After all, someone who made $500 million in one year can't live happily ever after, even if he earned it honestly.

The fact that Milken could be prosecuted in the first place should give nightmares to anyone who believes in justice. But the most disappointing element in this whole melodrama was Milken's response to the government's Star Chamber methods: he agreed to a $200 million fine, agreed to a $400 million "contribution" to a fund for the "victims" of his actions, pleaded guilty to six trivial and technical violations, and issued an apology for having been naughty. It is interesting that all six counts rested on the testimony of two witnesses who agreed to turn state's evidence against their former associates. Whether these moral cripples told the truth, or lied to please the government and save their hides, will never be determined because a trial never took place.

Drexel Burnham, the firm Milken put on the map, didn't get much of a trial either when it was forced to pay a $650 million fine. Drexel is now out of business because of a resulting lack of capital. It's scary how easily government types can arrange to keep some firms in business, and destroy others.

I regret that Milken didn't take the opportunity to play Howard Roark or John Galt, exposing his antagonists as the real criminals and revealing the sanctimonious hypocrisy of the establishment. The idea might have been on his mind for a while when, after trouble first started, he distributed thousands of copies of *The Incredible Bread Machine*, a highly principled libertarian defense of the free market.

But then Milken backed off. Maybe he did so at the advice of his conventional lawyers. Lawyers sometimes informally act as agents of the State (that is, like normal securities attorneys) on the defendant's payroll. Maybe Milken really became convinced what he did was wrong. Maybe he thought it was wrong all along and was just in it for the money. Maybe he's never been anything but a sharp bond salesman devoid of moral principles. Or, maybe, he just figured that battling the government for the rest of his life, using a public defender after they had seized all his assets under RICO, wouldn't be worth the trouble. It's hard to say what one "should" do in a situation like his. But he certainly conducted himself far more honorably than other defendants, many of whom were just common-law criminals, who turned state's evidence. Or, for that matter, the prosecutors, the judge, and practically everyone else involved in the whole mess.

Milken's troubles should be instructive to any of us who become too successful, too high profile, and the object of hysteria in the Age of Envy. As it turned out, Milken was sentenced to ten years, in addition to the $600 million he had already paid in fines. It was, therefore, with considerable chagrin that presiding Judge Kimba Wood announced that the loss Milken supposedly caused his investors was, at most, just over $300,000. And even that figure could be arrived at only by using the government's Kafkaesque securities laws.* In the meantime stoolpigeons who turned state's evidence got off with relative wrist slaps, presumably as reward for becoming what amounts to paid informers.

Milken was railroaded for political crimes, a victim of the institutionalization of envy in this country. Milken and Drexel Burnham, by financing numerous hostile takeovers to the great profit of many, probably did more in a few years to clean up corporate misdealing than scores of thousands of regulators have done since Day One at huge cost to all concerned. That's why the regulators and corporate America wanted to crucify him.

In the next chapter, I address a number of related concerns. Form your own opinion of the ethical implications of each and see if you've been guilty of flying on automatic pilot to the land of groupthink.

*Franz Kafka wrote of entrapment by surreal bureaucracies.

17

Envy and Wall Street Ethics

Government is the great fiction, through which everybody endeavours to live at
the expense of everybody else.

Frédéric Bastiat (1801-1850)
Essays on Political Economy

No one should be entrusted with power, inasmuch as anyone invested with
authority must, through the force of an immutable social law, become an
oppressor and exploiter of society.

Michael Bakunin, *Statism and Anarchy*, 1873

Every great robbery that was ever perpetrated upon a people has been by virtue
of and in the name of law.

Albert Parsons, on being sentenced to hang, 1886

INSIDE INFORMATION

The term *insider trading* is as nebulous and as open to arbitrary interpretation as the
Internal Revenue Code. A brief definition is "to trade on material, non-public
information." That sounds simple enough, but in its broadest sense, it means you
are a potential criminal for attempting to profit from researching a company beyond
its public statements.

You may remember the case of Ray Dirks (see chapter 12) who nearly had his
career ruined when his research uncovered a massive fraud at Equity Funding, a
popular stock of the day. His "mistake" was that he told his clients to sell before he
informed the SEC and the market at large. He had no obligation to either the SEC or
the market at large, and he acted in the *only* ethical fashion, by alerting the people
who paid him to do market research, to whom he had a clear obligation, before
everyone else heard the news and drove Equity's stock to zero. The same principle
holds if you have inside information that could send a stock up.

Far from making the market a safer place for your money, the rules on insider
information and trading have a chilling effect on the amount and the quality of

available information. Their existence discourages all concerned from delving for, disclosing, or acting on information. And the entire market is based on information.

The case of Robert Freeman is perhaps even more disgraceful than that of Michael Milken. Freeman was sentenced to four months and a $1 million fine for being on the other end of a telephone when someone commented "Your bunny has a good nose" in response to his conjecture as to whether a KKR buyout would succeed. The hysteria has made it dangerous to overhear, much less repeat, rumors; it is potentially dangerous even to form opinions that cannot be grounded in a company's annual report. You can never know whether some witch-hunting prosecutor might decide to make a hobby out of you.

The Milken insider trading scandal was shameful, but not for the reasons the prosecution put forward. There's no indication that Milken caused injury, except to the lax managers he evicted through the takeovers he financed. In fact, many of Milken's supposed victims were signatories to the numerous full-page ads that appeared in support of him after his indictment.

The problem, ethically, should not be how information is used, but how it is acquired. Whether information is "inside" has no moral significance as long as it is honestly acquired. The market is a register of information, and impeding the free flow of knowledge in any way makes that register less efficient. That, and a morass of regulation, open the door to real corruption.

Insider trading has never cost a shareholder a penny. Other actions taken by insiders have, however, cost shareholders many billions. Regardless of the rhetoric, the name of the game in hostile takeovers and proxy battles is always management versus the shareholders.

MANAGEMENT VERSUS SHAREHOLDERS

It's strange how little scrutiny investors devote to a company's management and directors. We naturally, and logically, assume they are working in the best interests of their employer, if only because that is what they are paid to do. Apart from this moral obligation, they have a legal duty as fiduciaries to act in the interests of shareholders and to maximize the company's value. Good management is ten times more important to a company's success than any other consideration. When a company does well it is rarely dumb luck.

As important as it is to scrutinize corporate management, there are limits to what you can do. Hiring a private investigator, for instance, is practical or appropriate only when you are taking a very large position. Fortunately, studying the track record of the board of a company often allows you to determine whether you are dealing with honest, competent people or with sleazy bozos who could easily be wearing ski masks on their next visit to the local convenience store. Yet most people do not give the issue a lot of thought, since if they are unhappy with the way a company is run, they can sell their shares and forget about it.

When the people running a company look at the millions or billions of dollars they control, some of them convince themselves they "deserve" a little more than a mere salary. Or perhaps a lot more. So there are lots of expense account dinners, the offices are redecorated, and the company leases a BMW for everyone. And salaries are increased. If management is bold and the company big enough, they will buy a jet, an executive retreat, and a bunch of country club memberships. Management starts to forget whom they are working for, and if the directors aren't completely independent, no one reminds them.

Management may then decide they are underappreciated by the shareholders, who assume the status of a nuisance, and the game is on in earnest. It is similar to the housekeeper who decides that, because she runs your house, she should sleep in the master bedroom.

There are lots of ways management can, and does, take the shareholders to school. They may, for instance, buy assets from the company at below market value, or sell assets they own to it at inflated values. If they intend to disclose these transactions, they will have some corrupt third party phony-up a "fairness opinion." Or they may decide *not* to disclose that they are a party to these dealings and rely on friends, relatives and offshore corporations to hide their tracks.

Management and directors can act overtly by voting themselves big bonuses, but there are many more subtle ways—I'd like to find a more delicate way of saying this—to loot the company's treasury. Perhaps they will issue themselves cheap stock options, so that if the stock somehow still manages to go up, they make millions. If it goes down, they just reset a lower option price and wait for a better market.

I'm touching on only a few of the most obvious techniques a self-dealing management can use to exhaust a company. Since management hires the accountants, retains the legal counsel, and writes the news releases and quarterly reports, it takes some real digging for a shareholder to find out what's going on, much less prove it and put a stop to it. The unfortunate fact is that all the methods used by those with a criminal mindset to plunder a company can contribute to a company's genuine best interests when applied by honest and well-intentioned managers. Corporate law is rather like a gun; the purpose to which it is put depends completely on the character of the person holding it. And sometimes that person's character doesn't emerge until after the fact or until there is enough money on the table.

Mark this well: The interests of management are often not only different from those of shareholders but antithetical to them. Let's look more closely at management buyouts, which were popular during the '80s.

MANAGEMENT BUYOUTS

I presume you're as sick as I am of hearing pundits decry the greed that supposedly characterized the '80s. It's not greed if a politically correct Jane Fonda or Bruce Springsteen makes $50 million a year, but it is for a stockbroker or a manager to make 2 percent of that. I'm a freedom fighter, you're a rebel, he's a terrorist.

There's no reason why corporate executives shouldn't make huge sums if they're responsible for the shareholders doing the same. That's not what always happens. Large sums of money can tempt managers running a corporation to violate their fiduciary duty to their employers, the shareholders. Especially in large bureaucratic companies, the top people tend to be power-seekers adept at politicking and infighting. They do not create value; they schmooze, cajole, flatter, maneuver and scheme. They are immortalized in song and story everywhere from *How to Succeed in Business Without Really Trying* to *What Makes Sammy Run*.

For every Warren Buffett or Boone Pickens, there are scores of Roger Smiths, the recent ex-chairman of GM, and Wesley Mooches of *Atlas Shrugged*, anti-heroes in the Randian mold. When characters such as these see vast sums in a corporate till, they stop seeing the shareholders as employers and start viewing them as adversaries. This attitude tilts the odds against shareholders in the battle for investment survival. Louis XIV said, "L'etat, c'est moi!" Corporate managements tend to equate their own interests and those of the corporation in the same way.

Management buyouts are one of the most egregious examples of this conflict. Only management can be expected to know a company's real prospects, and its assets' real value. That presents an overwhelming conflict of interest in a leveraged buyout, since management is at once the buyer and the supposed representative of the seller. Management is supposed to realize top dollar for the shareholders but is also trying to buy as cheaply as possible. A common ploy is to buy the company by borrowing the money from the company; to add insult to injury, management stays on the shareholders' payroll while doing so.

But even if a company is really worth what management is willing to pay for it, why not sell off its pieces to the highest bidders and pass the proceeds on to the shareholders? There could be several reasons. Managers don't want to see the employer that's feathering their nests go away, which would happen if they liquidated assets. Even more likely, managers realize they can buy the assets on the cheap with money borrowed from the shareholders. Also, by taking the company private, they can effectively bury any of their past misdeeds. This can be the most powerful reason of all.

Any management group attempting to take a company private should immediately be dismissed and investigated, at a minimum for breach of trust. Perversely, this ultimate form of "insider trading" is one of the few that's actually unethical, and, paradoxically, almost the only insider trading that's legal. When the very concept of justice has been inverted, what can keep management honest?

Most investors would say: "That's why we have regulators. The SEC. The government."

THE REGULATORS

Few, if any, government agencies serve a useful purpose that couldn't, and wouldn't, be satisfied by entrepreneurs in a free market. This is emphatically true of the Securities and Exchange Commission, which attracts small-minded, self-aggrandizing obstructionists more powerfully than the Mafia attracts thugs.

Whenever investors read about, or get hurt by, a stock fraud, their first reaction is to go to the SEC for more regulation. That is, at best, naïve and reactive. As the late Col. E. C. Harwood of the American Institute for Economic Research said, the SEC could as easily be an acronym for "Swindlers Encouragement Conspiracy" as for "Securities and Exchange Commission." In point of fact, the SEC is not the market's guardian, but its worst enemy, costing investors far more than the worst con artists. This is true for two reasons.

First, the existence of the agency gives investors a false sense of security. Small investors, especially, feel that Big Brother is watching out for them because the SEC monitors offerings and stock and bond trading. When responsibility is taken away from people, they tend to act less responsibly. The average investor will receive a gigantic prospectus full of legalistic gobbledegook, find it largely incomprehensible, and believe that anything so intimidating that complies with SEC regulations must be solid. In other words, the very existence of the SEC tends to lower an investor's guard and leave him more vulnerable.

Second, the SEC has a multibillion dollar annual budget. That money is directly and indirectly extracted from the marketplace, so it cannot be used to fund productive investment. And that sum cannot compare to the real costs of regulation, which amount, I suspect, to scores of billions annually. The money is lost to legal fees, usually running from $200 to, in some cases, more than $1,000 an hour, for services with no productive value; to thousands of tons of printing that no one reads; to uncountable man-years spent on bureaucratic trivia; and to years of costly delay endured by businesses trying to raise money. The SEC isn't the solution. It is most of the problem.

Investment frauds should be prosecuted exactly like any other form of fraud. The concept of "crime" has been defined through centuries of common law. A myriad of arbitrary and counterproductive rules are redundant.

The billions regulators cost both investors and taxpayers every year buy very little of positive worth. Getting regulators to investigate a potential fraud is next to impossible; they have their own agendas. Perhaps if management lined the shareholders up against a wall and machinegunned them, it might be cause for an inquiry, but only if there was also a lot of press coverage.

Like all bureaucrats, regulators respond mainly to political pressure. Aggrieved shareholders do not elect them and are usually too disparate to force them into action. If one or more shareholders wants to press an issue against management, he has to invest 100 percent of the time and money required yet receives no more benefit than the shareholders who remain on the sidelines. Management, however, controls the treasury and can bring pressure to bear on both lawmakers and regulators to act in their favor.

MANAGEMENT AND THE LAW

Political jurisdictions compete to provide a favorable environment for corporations. Sound good? It's not, unless you naïvely think that what's good for management is good for the shareholders. Management prefers jurisdictions where the law keeps the owners from becoming a nuisance.

That is why most corporations are headquartered in Delaware; laws in that state make it easy for management to get its way, as opposed to guarding the rights of shareholders. Delaware receives about 20 percent of its budget from the corporation business, and its officials know what side their bread is buttered on. In 1989, for instance, Delaware's courts allowed the management of Time to merge with Warner in order to reject a $200 per share cash takeover offer from Paramount; the stock subsequently dropped 60 percent, and even now trades at the equivalent of $120, after a four for one split. Why did the directors of Time refuse Paramount's offer? To keep their jobs, which would have disappeared in a hostile takeover. Warner's "white knight" aided management by assisting in the rape of the shareholders.

Other states have proven even more oppressive to shareholders by passing anti-takeover rules such as precluding the deductibility of interest on takeover debt, or imposing confiscatory taxes on profits, or requiring any dissident to buy the company at an arbitrarily determined price. Such anti-takeover measures universally and without exception entrench managers and ensure their jobs and retirement plans. And corrupt managements grant themselves outrageous golden parachutes with the complicity of their friends in public office.

Such maneuvers are all at the expense, and to the detriment of, shareholders as they reduce the value of a company to a prospective outside buyer. When Pennsylvania, the fourth most-popular situs for the incorporation of Fortune 500 companies, was passing such a law, with especially important provisions protecting "stakeholders," the man in charge of investing Pennsylvania's state employees retirement money said: "I could not invest another penny in companies incorporated in Pennsylvania because of my legal duties to present and future retirees."

"STAKEHOLDERS"

We have recently witnessed the conjuring of something called "the stakeholder." The concept may be bogus and silly, but it's nonetheless quite important. State stakeholder laws require that the supposed interests of employees, suppliers, customers, communities, and the environment be taken into consideration before an outsider can take over a company. Like "poison pills," "golden parachutes," and the paying of "greenmail," they serve absolutely no useful purpose except to keep management entrenched. Many managements support these measures under the guise of being good "corporate citizens."

The more firmly management becomes entrenched, the less urgency they feel to innovate, to keep the payroll lean and the shareholders, or even the customers, happy. And they become more tempted to milk the corporation, secure in the knowledge that the most shareholders can do is sell their stock in the open market, at the depressed prices likely to prevail as a result of management policies.

Other People's Money, a movie with Danny Devito, strikes a different tone than *Wall Street*. Like *Wall Street*, the climactic scene is a shareholders' meeting, where Devito (the "bad guy") is pitted against Gregory Peck (the "good guy"). In the words of my colleague Harry Browne: "Mr. Peck is his usual insufferable, moralistic, holier-than-thou, deadly serious, I'm-such-a-good-person-because-I-care-about-people self. The only person who can play that part better is Albert Gore."

Entrenched manager Peck tries to convince shareholders that the company's wire and cable division should remain in business, despite the fact that it's costing the company huge amounts and is responsible for the meltdown of its stock. As one of his main arguments, Peck offers the fact that "stakeholders" are a big family out of a Norman Rockwell painting, and should not be inconvenienced by technological change or the fact that nobody needs their products any longer.

Devito points out that the division is just an albatross around everyone's neck. But his real point strikes at the malaise afflicting society: "What about the future of the community and the employees (i.e., "stakeholders")? I can answer that question in two words: *Who cares?* Do you think *they* care about *you*? Did the town lower your taxes when you were going through tough times? The employees are making twice what they were ten years ago, while your stock is worth only one sixth what it was then. Are they shedding tears over your losses? They've never worried about you; why should you worry about them?"

That speech should be appended to Gordon Gekko's and be read at all annual general meetings.

Will the trend toward stakeholder rights continue? I believe it will. If so, shares will be valued only on their discounted dividend stream, not on their value to an outsider. Shares could then be priced to again yield considerably more than bonds, as was the case until about 1960. After all, they are junior securities that are last in any line of creditors. And cash for dividends is available only after management has paid for all the greenmail, provided all the golden parachutes, and settled all the stakeholder suits.

So if the regulators and lawmakers are a detriment to the shareholder—entirely apart from the regulations and taxes they impose—where will help come from? Hope of rescue lies with the "takeover artist," the "predator," and "corporate raider." They are the true heroes in the story. They are the people Mike Milken financed.

THE RAIDER

There are only three ways in which a corporation has value to a shareholder: because it may be liquidated, because it may be bought out, or because it may pay dividends. Raiders keep managements honest by making buyouts and/or conducting liquidations when the stock price falls enough to make the exercise profitable.

Management's sanctimonious blather about defending "your" corporation from someone who wants to buy it for above-market prices is always self-serving.

Most companies subject to takeovers are vulnerable only because their stock price is low relative to their assets. And that happens when the assets are being misallocated and the market has no confidence in management's abilities to correct the error. In fact, a company can usually be acquired only if management owns no more than a token amount of stock. And if the managers are not also owners, why should they care what the business is worth, as long as they keep their jobs? Most managers of big corporations own very little stock in them; arguably, that is because they can see it's a poor long-term investment.

Ludwig von Mises, the main proponent of the Austrian School of economics, commented almost half a century ago: "A successful corporation is ultimately never controlled by hired managers. . . . the emergence of an omnipotent managerial class is not a phenomenon of the unhampered market economy. It [is], on the contrary, an outgrowth of the interventionist policies consciously aiming at the elimination of the influence of the shareholders and their virtual expropriation." This is, he said, "the preliminary step on the way toward the substitution of government control of business for free enterprise."

He draws the distinction between laissez-faire capitalism and corporate, or state, capitalism—sometimes known as fascism, which is the direction this country is heading. Certainly, laissez-faire has few defenders. Conservatives such as William F. Buckley and George Will posture as defenders of the free market, but they act as some of its most insidious betrayers. They are state capitalists who believe in taxation and regulation as philosophical principles. But taxation and regulation make it hard for a worker to accumulate capital and then jump through all the legal and regulatory hoops necessary to go into competition with established companies.

The raider's major weapon against inefficient and corrupt management is the proxy contest, in which a dissident slate of directors endeavors to show the average shareholder why he should "throw the bums out." Most proxy documents are written in lawyerese; they're not easy reading but are usually very educational. Shareholders, however, are frequently ignorant or apathetic, and few have a grip on the philosophical issues involved, which is a pity. Your vote counts far more on these ballots and the issues are much more clear cut and relevant than they're likely to be in a political contest. If you get a proxy, read it carefully and act.

The much-maligned raiders and hostile-takeover artists are almost always the good guys. They aren't acting out of altruism, but for personal profit. That's precisely how the market polices itself. It's a pity shareholders almost always seem to vote in favor of management. They should almost always vote against them.

Another major tool of the raider is high-yield, a.k.a. "junk," debt.

"JUNK" DEBT

What about the more than $200 billion in debt that was created through the efforts of Milken and others who followed his lead? Isn't debt one of the big problems facing the economy, and aren't junk bonds yet another reason to disapprove of Mr. Milken and the predators he financed? I think not.

These risky bonds can be excellent speculations, depending on your evaluation of the business cycle, interest rate trends, and the prospects of the underlying company. But that is not at issue. Junk bonds were originally created because they were a perfect tool, in most cases the only practical tool, for rescuing companies protected by laws entrenching management. The debt did weaken a company's balance sheet, but that was the concern of its new owners, not the regulators, or society. Taking on a lot of debt to buy something is risky. But it forces the new management to cut fat, close inefficient plants, fire redundant workers, and sell off marginal divisions to someone who can do something productive with them. Junk was used primarily to merge or acquire companies; sometimes it was used to break up a big company into several smaller ones. The result almost always rationalized operations and made them more efficient.

There will be plenty of bankruptcies as a result of all this debt, but so what? Just because a corporate structure collapses doesn't mean that the buildings, people, technologies, and materials it controls vanish. Only the equity of the investors who embraced high-risk leverage by holding the stock of a junk bond issuer disappears. Only they are disciplined by the market. The corporation's assets become available to new investors, who can then buy them cheaply and thereby have a leg up in running them profitably.

In the end, even many fired workers benefit, because they're forced to put their energies to better use at a new job. And such a change is easier during good times, when buyouts typically are done and jobs and money are more available, than during bad times.

"PARKING" STOCK

This term usually refers to the practice of buying stock in another's name to avoid alerting management that a stock is under accumulation for a takeover. A reasonable person might ask how parking stock is any different from holding your hand close to your chest in a card game. Certainly it doesn't harm any existing shareholders, since they are under no obligation to sell their stock, which is probably going up because of the added buying pressure caused by the dreaded parking.

Then why is parking "wrong?" Because of the Williams Act of 1967, which states that once any group acting in concert accumulates more than 5 percent of a company's stock, the group must halt buying and alert management of its intentions. This gives the officers and directors time to arrange for a "poison pill" to preclude shareholders from getting the higher-than-market price the outsiders would be willing to pay after buying as much stock as possible in a quiet fashion. A poison-pill will likely cause the outside group to sell their stock, depressing the market. The Williams whose name the act bears is, incidentally, the same corrupt senator who later did time for bribery in the Abscam affair.

"Parking" is another artificial noncrime forbidden by the establishment in order to safeguard itself.

THE BOTTOM LINE

Making a distinction between the real abuses, such as self-dealing on the part of management and widespread betrayal of fiduciary trust, and the perceived abuses, such as hostile takeovers, insider trading, and parking stock, that have drawn the public's attention over the last decade is important.

Investors may come to view public companies simply as vehicles for the enrichment of the managers who run them. That will make it harder for small companies to raise money for legitimate ventures. It will also tend to allow the small group of pension and mutual fund managers, with no direct interest in seeing that management keeps its hands out of the cookie jar, to increasingly control the markets. If they don't like what they see, they'll just blow their shares into the market. Or, worse, since they often went to the same schools, belong to the same clubs and move in the same circles as management, they might have some complicity in the whole matter if only by turning a blind eye. I'm not a conspiracy buff, but these possibilities are real. It conjures up the kind of corporate-controlled dystopia put forward in movies like *Rollerball* and *Robocop*.

This raises something even more important. In 1989 the Carter-Ward scandal was uncovered. Two corrupt stock promoters had bribed the manager of a mutual fund to buy massive amounts of companies they controlled. The fund manager succumbed to some of the same moral problems confronting all corporate managers: "Gee, I'm only making $30,000 a year, but I'm responsible for many millions. Now, suppose I . . . .''. That attitude partially accounted for the hundreds of billions of S&L losses. Could the same cancer be eating at the managers of investment funds? There's an excellent chance it may be. The pillage and rapine in the savings and loan scandal may become endemic to corporate America.

Laws and regulations create distortions and the opportunity for corruption. And laws making hostile takeovers impractical will go a long way toward destroying America's capital markets—an ominous thought at the end of one of the longest booms in history.

Three strategies will protect you from the damage the stock market will suffer. First, short selling. Second, correctly anticipating the way money leaving stocks will flow, and positioning yourself in these alternative investments early on. Third, investing only in sound companies with ethical management owning a substantial share of the company. Managers inclined to view other shareholders as partners rather than inconveniences.

I've discussed short selling and management ethics; the next few chapters will cover investment alternatives to the stock market.

18

Back to the Future With Gold

> The more the state "plans" the more difficult planning becomes for the individual.
>
> F. A. Hayek
> *The Road to Serfdom*, 1944, Ch. VI

Throughout history—with only rare exceptions, like the years since 1971 when the U.S. dollar dropped all links to gold—few people perceived gold as an investment or a speculation. It was simply money, cash in its most basic form. It was a medium of exchange and a store of value. People did not accumulate gold because it could make them wealthy, but because it was a convenient, liquid way to keep the wealth they had.

Gold has not been viewed in this way in recent years, because the government suppressed its price. Meanwhile, the government's inflated currency ballooned the price of everything but gold for decades, until 1971. Then, when U.S. Government gold sales could no longer keep the price fixed at $35 per ounce, the metal's price shot up to regain a natural relationship to the prices of other goods. In those days gold was an ideal speculation, with minimal risk but a huge upside. Moreover, most people wouldn't discover gold until the early birds needed someone to sell to.

Gold has been in a free market for more than two decades now; the frenzy of the '70s, which took the metal from $35 to more than $800, has disappeared. And enough time has now passed for gold to not only find a new equilibrium but again to become underpriced.

Before looking at where the metal's price is likely to go over the next few years, it would pay to consider some fundamentals.

The Questions: Any discussion of gold always comes back to certain basic questions: Why is gold money? Why is gold valuable? Why can't money be whatever we say it is? (The last question is usually asked by government officials because they don't know the answer to the first two.) Why does gold give rise to all kinds of controversy not associated with, say, platinum or lead? Why is the stuff an emotional, political statement for those who love it and for those who hate it?

The Answers: Over thousands of years, in billions of transactions by millions of men, many commodities have been used as money: stones, salt, cattle, and seashells among them. But wherever gold was available, it tended to displace other media of exchange. Like any successful money, gold never needed to be decreed "legal tender" by a government; it was recognized as the most desirable money by common consent because of its unique properties.

Certain materials have proven especially well suited for certain uses. Aluminum is good for airplanes, bricks for construction, paper for books, and gold for money. If bricks were used for airplanes and aluminum for books, the results would be as suboptimal as when paper is used for money.

In fact, the properties required of money were first described by Aristotle in the fifth century B.C.

1. It is durable. It won't evaporate, mildew, rust, crumble, break, or rot. Gold, more than any other solid element, is chemically inert. This is why foodstuffs, oil, or artwork can't be used as money.
2. It is divisible. One ounce of gold—whether bullion, coin, or dust—is worth exactly 1/100th of one hundred ounces. When a diamond is split, its value may be destroyed. You can't make change for a piece of land.
3. It is convenient. Gold allows its owner physically to carry the wealth of a lifetime with him. Real estate stays where it is. An equivalent value of copper, lead, zinc, silver, and most other metals would be too heavy.
4. It is consistent. Only one grade exists for 24 carat gold, so there is no danger of owning 24 carat gold varying in quality. Twenty-four carat gold (pure gold) is the same in every time and place since gold is a natural element, unlike gems, artwork, land, grain, or other commodities.
5. It has intrinsic value. Gold finds new industrial uses each year. Of all the metals, it is the most malleable (able to be hammered into sheets less than 5-millionth's of an inch thick), most ductile (a single ounce can be drawn into a wire 35 miles long), and the least reactive (it can stand indefinite immersion in seawater, does not tarnish in air, and can withstand almost any acid). Next to silver, it's the most conductive of heat and electricity and the most reflective of light.

    These superlatives make gold very useful, entirely apart from its value as jewelry through the last 5,000 years—as well as a medium of exchange and a store of value. Arguments that gold's value is "mystical" are silly; it is one of the 92 natural elements and has some unique properties.

    One important last point was not listed by Aristotle, probably only because he lived before the creation of paper and banking.

6. Gold cannot be created by government. Gold can, of course, be debased with impurities or falsified in weight, and governments strapped for revenue have tried those tricks. But a trader can protect himself with a pair of scales or a vial of acid, although a familiar and trustworthy hallmark on a coin saves him that trouble. Unlike currency, gold cannot lose value because of government mismanagement. On the contrary, it tends to gain value because of government mismanagement.

But isn't that all academic, since gold isn't presently used as money anywhere in the world? I think not. Even though the concept still receives little discussion, and none in "official" circles, gold is likely in the foreseeable future to reassume its traditional role as money worldwide. When that happens, its purchasing power is likely to be much higher than it is at the moment.

THE RETURN OF GOLD AS MONEY

The U.S. economy will continue to lose ground relative to others in the future not because we'll necessarily do badly in absolute terms, but because others will grow more quickly. That is a natural evolution and is not important to individual Americans, except from an historical or psychological point of view.

The dollar, however, is certain to lose its place as the international reserve currency, and that *will* affect individual Americans. This is so because dollars are merely the unsecured liabilities of a bankrupt government. The world has more than 200 governments, and the United States government is no longer special or different, nor is it necessarily more trusted. It is just bigger.

Foreign governments that keep their reserves in dollars recognize that the United States can create dollars at will, and the larger the gap between the U.S. government's spending and its tax revenues, the more likely it will create vast amounts of paper dollars. The potential instability leaves the dollar less desirable as a reserve currency, for the same reason the Brazilian cruzado is no one's first choice.

But some form of reserve currency is needed. Most national currencies are like the chips used by Las Vegas casinos: good only within the house that issues them. Chips have real value mostly because they are redeemable in dollars, a common denominator everyone recognizes. Dollars are the reserve currencies in casinos. Similarly, nonreserve currencies are either worth almost nothing outside their homeland, like the Russian ruble, or sell for varying discounts, like minor European currencies. Currencies like the mark and the yen have been better managed than the dollar. Consequently, these currencies are beginning to replace the U.S. unit for trade in many areas.

As the dollar fluctuates unpredictably against the stronger currencies, while constantly losing value in absolute terms, it becomes less suitable as a medium of exchange or as a store of value. Middle Eastern oil producers have often stated a desire to stop pricing their product in dollars.

But what would they price it in? Is there any other suitable common denominator? Other currencies are controlled by other governments, just like the dollar. Does it make any sense to have assets in a unit that could be radically devalued overnight, for any political reason? Retaining reserves in other currencies means holding somebody else's promise, and the mark and the yen are no more immune to inflation than the dollar. Entirely apart from economic common sense, no government wants to use another's currency, for nationalistic reasons.

Before the collapse of the U.S.S.R., rumors circulated that the Soviets were toying with the idea of creating a gold-backed ruble, to free them from relying on other currencies to settle payments. It was a straw in the wind, and proof that when governments are desperate enough, even they will resort to common sense.

Using the dollar as the international reserve currency before 1971, when it could be exchanged for a fixed amount of a recognized asset, gold, made some sense while the United States was the world's preeminent economic power. Now the U.S. is coequal with the Germans and Japanese. In fact Taiwan, a country of 20 million, now has the world's largest foreign exchange holdings. There are no longer any good reasons for central banks to hold their assets in a currency like the dollar. There's really no practical alternative to gold.

That's not what officials at the World Bank and the International Monetary Fund believe, of course. But they also believed that their "paper gold," as they termed a creation called Special Drawing Rights (SDRs), could act as an international reserve currency. We hear little about that accounting fiction these days. If a dollar can be called an "IOU nothing," the SDR can be called a "Somebody owes you nothing."

Like people who are sick of fighting after a war, no one wants to hear about concepts like risk and debt after a depression. It is my guess that following the Greater Depression, unbacked currency, of whatever description, will no longer be in vogue. "Dollar," "pound," "mark" and "yen" will again be just convenient names (receipts) for a fixed amount of gold on deposit in a specific location. Since the last depression they have had no intrinsic value, and their issuers will give you nothing for them. Only redeemability imposes the discipline to limit the amount of currency that can be created. Eventually, the market value of paper dollars will reach their intrinsic value.

Before the last depression, the British pound was the world's premier currency, and it was logical to think of the gold price in terms of pounds as well as dollars. Today, the relationship of gold to the pound is largely unwatched, academic and irrelevant, except to Englishmen.

That is one reason it makes sense to look at gold in foreign currency terms. The dollar has become just another piece of paper you buy and sell when convenient. For an American to keep track of prices in dollar terms alone will prove as delusional as a Brazilian measuring value in just cruzados.

In terms of yen, marks, and other strong currencies, gold is far cheaper now than it was when it bottomed in 1985, or in 1982. To a German, a Japanese, or a Swiss, gold is even more of a bargain than it is to an American, since their currencies have tripled against the dollar since 1971, even while they've lost over half their domestic purchasing power. For them, US$350 gold is selling at about $50 an ounce in 1971 terms.

Since the financial center of gravity is shifting to countries with strong currencies, it will be cheap, as well as logical, to use gold as an international reserve currency. If you were running the central bank of Germany, Japan or Britain, would you choose to hold dollars, which are backed only by the credit of the U.S. government and are created as fast as they are needed, or gold?

GOLD AND OTHER GOVERNMENTS

Each of the world's major economic-political blocs should move to gold over the next decade. And in the twenty-first century, gold will be a noninvestment again, as it was in the nineteenth, because gold will once more be used, in a daily context, as money.

Gold and the Ex-U.S.S.R.

The local currencies now circulating in what used to be the Soviet Union, and the ruble in particular, are nearly worthless due to a lack of confidence in their value. The easiest, and perhaps the only, way to salvage the situation is to back the ruble with gold. Figure it out. How do you expect the average Soviet citizen to react as his life's savings in rubles become completely worthless? And why would another fabricated currency that replaced the ruble be better managed?

The Russians may still have some gold reserves to provide some value to the ruble. But that seems unlikely, since they appear to have been selling off 100 percent of their production as fast as it's come out of the ground, just to keep going over the years.

A major reason South America has been a perennial hotbed of revolution is that chronic runaway inflation makes it impossible for poor people to save and gain a stake in the system. Of course they are always targets of revolutionary rhetoric, which will soon be a major problem in the ex-U.S.S.R. If the ruble was gold-convertible, internally as well as externally, it could be traded in the West for items citizens, and the government, want. That would make it much easier for the average man to focus his attention on production and savings, rather than theft and politicking, to improve his station in life.

Gold and the Japanese

The Japanese stock and real estate markets are still worth not billions, but trillions, more than they should reasonably be worth. The Japanese government also has the lowest gold reserves of any major government (754 metric tons—23.45 million

London Gold Price in Four Currencies

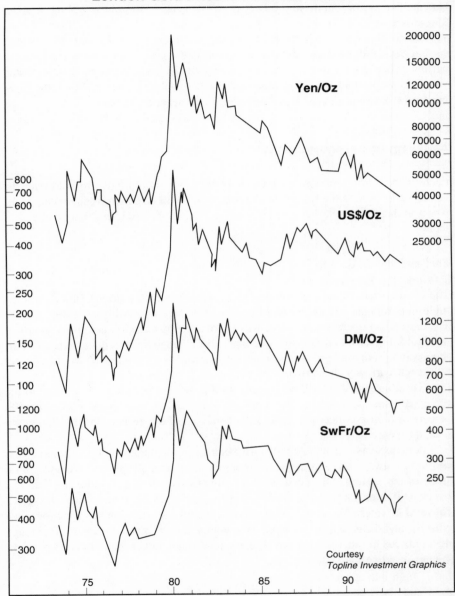

Courtesy
Topline Investment Graphics

Figure 18-1

ounces—worth $8.2 billion at US$350, equalling only 13 percent of reserves). The rest of their reserves are primarily in the U.S. dollar. The average for industrial countries is 48.5 percent in gold. Having seen the value of their dollars collapse more than 50 percent since 1985, and while observing American spending habits, the Japanese authorities have good reason to start moving out of dollars. But there are few currencies suitable for a government, or its central bank, to buy except gold.

Japanese investors are realizing how overvalued their markets have become, and some experienced fund managers are likely to start thinking about getting into an asset that, in yen, is now nearly as cheap as it was in 1971, that has value in and of itself, that tends to be contracyclical, and that they don't own much of. The fact that the Japanese have very little gold now is actually a positive factor, because, not having it, they're not in a position to sell it. And with an increasing desire to diversify assets for safety, it's very likely they will increase their buying.

Japanese savings accounts alone—not counting stocks and real estate—are estimated at about $2 trillion. If only 5 percent of this sum invested in gold, just as a hedge or for diversification, it would take five years worth of the current total annual production of gold worldwide to meet the demand.

Gold and the Europeans

High-level bureaucrats of the EEC have been trying unsuccessfully to structure a common monetary policy since the late '80s. But trying to coordinate currencies is an impossible task, since countries have wide variations in money growth and interest rates. Perhaps someone will get a bright idea, and suggest: "Before the First World War, when the lira, the mark, the franc and the pound were all just names for a certain amount of gold, all of this was a nonproblem. Maybe we ought to go back to a gold coin standard and dispense with all this silly palavering."

At first this might seem a too-rational and workable solution for men who depend on confusion for their paychecks and press appearances. They would have to stop playing big shots who make policy for everyone else, and do something productive for a living, but far stranger things have just happened in Eastern Europe, and more quickly than anyone could have guessed.

Reality has a way of asserting itself, even in politics. Much as politicians dislike and distrust the market, they distrust each other more, and the EEC is likely to be the first area where gold will be reinstituted as money. In the case of a real crisis, the market would certainly trust gold over the assurances of political leaders. Europeans will likely use gold as a solution to their monetary problems at a price that is high enough to make their current reserves worth something.

There will be steady accumulation of gold by strong hands in the years to come. Central banks will show less interest in supporting weak currencies, and will put their own self-interest first, building positions in the metal. They will finance its purchase mainly by dumping the dollar.

WHERE IS THE PRICE OF GOLD GOING?

Since gold broke free of the U.S. government's price controls in 1971, it has had two major "legs" up and two down. From 1971 to 1974, the first leg up, the metal went from $35 to $200, an increase of about 450 percent. During the subsequent down leg, from January 1975 to the middle of 1976, the metal dropped to $100 for a loss of 50 percent. The second leg took it above $800 in 1980, a rise of 700 percent. In the thirteen years since then, it has fluctuated between $300 and $500. The natural question arises: What next?

In the kind of crazy *fin de siècle* environment we can expect, nobody will quite believe the volatility of all kinds of prices. Quite likely the price of gold and the DJIA will cross again, as they did in 1980 and nearly did in 1933, neither of which was a particularly mellow year.

Gold fluctuated between $300 and $500 throughout the '80s. It was fairly valued relative to other commodities for much of that time. But $400 in, say, 1983 would buy substantially more than $600 does in 1993, and gold has fallen back to the lower end of its range. On the basis of purchasing power it is now undervalued at around $350.

Figure 18-2

It's helpful to look at historical precedents to determine what gold might be worth. An ounce of gold would, for instance, buy a top quality suit in the 19th century; today it would take two to three ounces. A gold sovereign (weighing .235 of an ounce) would buy three high-quality dinners in the London of 1914; today the $85 it represents might get you one.

But the markets are constantly undervaluing, then overvaluing absolutely everything. The '80s were boom years with plummeting interest rates and a soaring stock market. It was the worst of times for gold. It would be simpleminded to say that, just because the '70s were good to gold and the '80s bad, that the '90s will be good again. Yet I'm confident that will be the case. The great gold superbull market that started in 1971 will eventually come to an end with the reacceptance of the metal as money.

With the world financial system as unstable as it is, gold's next move will likely take it far above what it "should" be worth.

GOLD'S WORTH IN DOLLARS

Where will the U.S. government borrow the hundreds of billions they will need to stay afloat for the rest of the decade? Higher taxes will not be popular in the midst of a dramatically declining standard of living and would only weaken the economy. Monetizing government paper on a hundred-billion-dollar-scale would be very inflationary and would turn the world's financial and debt markets inside out. The government will tax, borrow, and inflate anyway, of course. But it will prove impossible to borrow at anything like present interest rates. Who will lend to a bankrupt, and in totally unsecured dollars?

The United States is not without resources, however. It still has the largest gold reserves, 261 million ounces. One gambit might be to make new bond issues redeemable in gold; the government could then borrow money at around 3 percent. That could keep the game going for at least a while.

Will it happen? Not before a true crisis forces the issue. Before 1933, all U.S. government debt was redeemable for gold, because the dollar was just another name for 1/20th of an ounce of the metal. But if the government returned to a gold standard, it would have to fix a redemption price. Right now that price would come to $350. But what might the price be in the future, especially if the dollar itself, not just a series of bonds, were to be as good as gold?

Let's consider a few points that bear on the price of gold. They don't constitute a rigorous proof that the price of gold is worth any particular number, but anecdotal evidence can put things in perspective. It becomes clear that neither the world in general, nor the U.S. government in particular, is awash in gold.

The ratio of gold to dollars—another way of saying the gold price—has varied between 20-to-one and 800-to-one in the years since 1932. Take a look at a few current ratios.

1. **Ratio of U.S. government gold assets to money supply** (M1)—U.S. M1 (the basic money supply, including currency and checking account deposits) is approximately $1,000 billion, and U.S. gold reserves are 261 million ounces. Dividing one into the other gives a gold price of about $4,000 per ounce, if each dollar were redeemable with a fixed quantity of the metal, as was the case before the creation of the Federal Reserve. That is unlikely to happen until we have a total collapse of the present monetary system.

It bears repeating that the only practical way to eliminate inflation is to let the dollar represent a fixed amount of gold on deposit. It would obviate the role of government in the economy. Actually, there's no more logic to the government making money than there is to it making cars, or bread or anything else.

2. **Ratio of U.S. government gold assets to annual interest on U.S. government debt**. Liquidating its gold (at $350) would cover annual interest payments alone ($200 billion in 1992 and rising) on government debt for only 5.5 months. The annual interest bill alone is enough to buy the next ten years worth of total world gold production.

3. **Ratio of U.S. government gold to the annual government deficit**. The government's stockpile of 261 million ounces of gold is worth $91.35 billion at $350 gold. That may seem like a lot, but it amounts to only about 25 percent of just one year's annual deficit.

4. **Ratio of U.S. government gold assets to its liabilities**. The U.S. government's debt is $4.2 trillion. If that debt were to be redeemed in gold, the government's 261 million ounces would have to each be worth $16,000 an ounce.

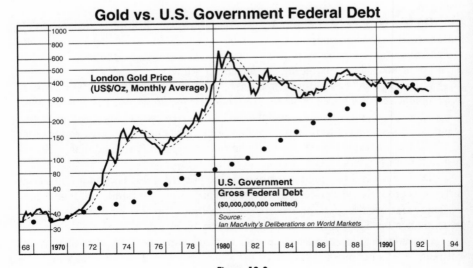

Gold vs. U.S. Government Federal Debt

Figure 18-3

At $350, the government's total gold holdings wouldn't last long. It's reasonable that the government again will raise the gold price radically (as Roosevelt did from $20.50 to $35 in 1933, and Nixon did from $35 to $42.22 in 1971). Gold is the government's major liquid asset.

It's also interesting to compare gold prices to the amount of debt.

You will note that gold has proven to be overpriced when its price level has risen faster than the federal debt has grown. The ratio of the U.S. federal debt relative to gold's price is the highest it has been since the early '70s, when the metal's great bull market began. (See Figure 18-3.)

There is no one-for-one predictive value to these relationships, but it is clear that high levels of debt, high monetary growth, and a shaky financial system set an excellent stage for high gold prices. Relative to those things, the price of gold is "low" at the moment.

5. **Ratio of U.S. gold to the foreign trade deficit**. If the U.S. government were to make the dollar redeemable in gold to foreigners alone, as was the case before Nixon closed the gold window in 1971, the government's 261 million ounces would evaporate in thirteen months with gold priced at $350, and the deficit running at $80 billion a year, about what it averaged in the '90s so far.

The trade deficit, in itself, is no cause for alarm except to mercantilists and rabble-rousing politicians; at times it's more economic to buy a lot of cars and TVs from foreigners, and at other times it's economic for them to buy grain and jumbo jets from Americans. No country buys exactly as much merchandise as it sells in a given year. In the past, however, an international gold standard kept things in balance. Once you had spent all your gold, you had to stop shopping. Prices dropped within your country, presenting bargains for foreigners, and gold would flow back in.

In the current environment of paper currencies, however, the trade deficit does present a problem. It leaves a lot of dollars (i.e., liabilities of the U.S. government) in the hands of foreigners who, unlike Americans, will sell them readily if they fear a drop in the dollar's value. The value of the unbacked dollar depends entirely on the confidence of its holders. The U.S. government, just like a stock promoter, dreads to see shareholders sell. In both cases, the price of the paper drops toward its intrinsic value. Gold obviates the trade deficit problem since it's fungible: American gold is the same as Japanese gold is the same as Brazilian gold. Unlike different currencies gold is always valued at its intrinsic worth.

During the late '80s, both the Taiwanese and Japanese governments bought large amounts of gold in the United States to reduce their trade surplus. The American government protested that this disguised the real size of their trade surplus. But the protest gave rise to a sense of cognitive dissonance. Why is the export of gold to redress a trade imbalance any less valid than the export of airplanes, wheat, or coal? Especially if the point is made by a government whose official attitude is that gold is nonmoney, or quasimoney at best, and still carries it on their books at the fictional price of $42.22?

A MODEST PROPOSAL

All these ratios hint at astronomical gold prices. The numbers stretch credibility. But, at the same time, a much higher gold price does buy the U.S. government some additional time (albeit not much, unless it learns to spend less). Despite some politically delicate consequences, such as multimillionaire jewelers and billionaire miners, a high gold price is an attractive alternative for the U.S. government. The amount of gold produced would go through the roof, probably doubling and redoubling again in short order, but the amounts mined would still be trivial compared to the number of unbacked dollars and other currencies outstanding. Even if the U.S. government were to distribute its gold reserves to its citizens—the true owners, anyway—it would amount only to an ounce per person.

More gold production would be inevitable in a sound monetary system. It is true, of course, that a gigantic new supply of gold in a society can cause an inflation as effectively as a new supply of paper money. That happened in Europe when the Spaniards brought home the gold they looted from the Inca and Aztec empires. But that form of inflation is a nonrecurring event. A great increase in the supply of gold would reduce its value, which would eventually reduce production. An equilibrium would again be found. But inflation could never be chronic if gold were used as money.

GOLD DURING INFLATION, DEFLATION, AND CHAOS

New production and industrial consumption are relatively unimportant determinants of gold's price, even though many pundits make much of them. Unlike any other metal, most of the gold that has ever been mined is sitting in the vaults of central banks and the safe deposit boxes of investors. It's not being "used" for anything; it's *raison d'être* is simply to be an asset. What determines the price of gold, therefore, is the desire of its owners to own it or to liquidate it and own something else.

And that, in turn, depends on the inflation rate (how fast paper money is losing value), the chances of a credit collapse (the likelihood of deflation wiping out paper assets), and the general level of confidence in the future.

Inflation has decreased since its cyclical highs of 13.3 percent in 1979, 12.5 percent in 1980 and 8.9 percent in 1981. It averaged 4 percent from 1982 to 1992. The mildly inflationary equilibrium we've experienced over the last few years cannot last in the face of the titanic forces set in motion by the business cycle discussed in chapter 3. A "soft landing" is improbable.

The most likely alternatives are much higher inflation or uncontrolled deflation. Some time soon, creation of more currency and credit will be the only way the government can fund its deficits, transfer programs, bank bailouts and other mega-disasters waiting in the wings. And if we have a financial accident, that in itself will be an excuse for the authorities to expand the money supply. Even if they fear doing so, it will be more palatable than the alternative. High rates of inflation would send gold rocketing, much as they did in the '70s.

Could the disinflation of the '80s snowball into a wholesale deflation in the '90s? Yes. Some analysts reason that if disinflation was bad for gold, then deflation like that of the '30s would be disastrous. But a serious deflation would likely also cause the price of gold to explode. It is the only financial asset that's not simultaneously someone else's liability. And if we have a deflation this time. it will not be possible to buy government paper and wait in safety, as was possible during the '30s, for at least two reasons.

First, a deflation would set off all kinds of spending programs and bailouts. The U.S. government would go from being a questionable risk to a bad risk as it was forced to borrow on a huge scale to finance emergency spending, much of which is already mandated by law, while tax revenues were falling. Second, a deflation would almost certainly result in calls to reinflate as rapidly as possible—a course of action unlikely to inspire confidence in the dollar. Gold would soar in a serious deflation.

Gold is a big winner in either scenario; it is a matchless crisis hedge. It's the only financial asset that's completely invisible and private. There are no social security numbers stamped on gold coins, and they leave no paper trail when they change hands. Unlike real estate, for instance, a government cannot easily find gold to tax or confiscate. Unlike stocks, gold doesn't represent a value that can be dissipated or mismanaged. Unlike bonds, gold cannot default. And unlike currency, gold cannot be inflated away.

There are not many low-risk places for wealth to hide today. But plenty of wealth exists and, as the world's greatest coward, capital will look for a place to hide when things get scary. Gold is the perfect financial asset in times of uncertainty.

This is not the 1970s, when gold was a great speculation. You should view gold as a vehicle for savings and for conservation of capital. When you save, you're not expecting to hit a long-ball home run; you are simply trying to put away assets for future consumption. You want safety. You do not want to have to trust a government, a bank, or the management of some corporation. You want the asset itself, something you can hold in your own hands.

Gold is not a trading vehicle; it's a core holding. Buy it as privately as possible, put it away, and forget about it.

HOW TO BUY GOLD

You can accumulate gold using the commodity exchanges, in 100-ounce contracts, but that makes no sense unless you are dealing in large quantities. For practical purposes, you want to have the metal in your own possession, except for what you might store abroad. And you want coins, not bullion, for the same reason coin has always been used in transactions: it's more convenient, and you know exactly what you are getting without using a scale or calipers.

Which coins should you buy? I suggest strictly bullion-type coins that trade for close to their intrinsic value. That would include Austrian 100 Coronas (containing .98 oz. of gold) and Krugerrands, which are both available for 2 to 3 percent over the bullion price and represent the best value. Maple Leafs and Eagles (each one ounce) trade in the 5 percent premium range. Sovereigns, which are the world's most-recognized gold coin, and seminumismatic to boot, are an excellent value at a 4 to 5 percent premium; an additional convenience is their small size (.2354 oz. of gold). You should emphasize sovereigns in your purchases.

Few Americans today own meaningful amounts of gold coins. Take a straw poll among 10 or 15 neighbors; it's unlikely any of them have even seen a gold coin, much less buy them monthly. For 99 percent of the population the importance of owning gold is in the "you'll find out" department.

WHEN TO SELL

Determining when to sell an investment is at least as hard as figuring when to buy. With gold, more than almost anything else, you will be tempted to hold it, or buy more, when you should sell. That's because the next major run in gold—the last one, I believe, before we return to a gold standard—will take place in a chaotic environment. The metal will grace the covers of *Time* and *Business Week*, and everyone will try to buy it in a panic. I hope to look around then and find some other value that's very cheap, something worth trading my gold for. Maybe it will be corporate convertible bonds with 20 percent yields. Maybe it will be Japanese stocks for a fraction of book value. Maybe it will be real estate, when it once again shows large cash-on-cash returns.

No one can know what it will be, but something will be very cheap when gold is very dear. Say gold is triple its present level and the investment of the future is one-third its current price; that is, arguably, a nine-for-one return on capital. It may not be possible to get out of gold and into something else at the best possible moment. But if you keep looking with an open mind, it will be worth the effort.

This decade should see the final bull market in gold, with a total restructuring of the world's financial system. It is hard to envision just another cyclical extension of what's been going on for the last 20 years, although it also seemed unlikely back in the early '80s when the economy not only muddled through but gave birth to Yuppies.

The grand finale of the upcoming last leg of the gold bull market should be reminiscent of the better scenes from the movie *Rollover*, if not *Road Warrior*. I expect to see gold well over $1,000 during the next few years; and I suspect I'm being conservative in that forecast, which is typical at the close of a long bear market.

Questions and Answers

Q: *But isn't the world going to employ electronic money anyway, and won't that obviate the whole question of what's used for currency?*

A: "Banknotes" originated as receipts, issued by private banks, for gold deposited with them; the paper receipts were more convenient than gold for some applications. But they weren't a substitute for gold any more than a receipt from a storage company for your furniture is a substitute for the couch you want to sit on. Similarly, bookkeeping entries indicate the transfer of wealth, like gold sitting in a vault, or real estate, without actually moving the wealth itself. But they aren't substitutes *for* the wealth.

Using computers to help keep accounts is an excellent idea; but employing a more-advanced technology to accomplish something doesn't change the original purpose. The blips have to represent something tangible or they will have the same fate as other artificial currencies, except on an even larger scale as they are so much easier to create and manipulate.

Q: *But how can gold be a good money since it doesn't pay interest?*

A: Paper and electronic blips do not pay interest either; money earns interest. Interest is simply the time value of money, the premium a borrower is willing to pay to have the use of the money now, while the lender defers using it to the future. Anything that is used as money, therefore, can and would earn an interest rate. So would gold.

Historically, gold (or those currencies which were backed by gold) has earned interest at about 3 percent, for the most secure form of deposit. It is hard to say why that is the usual percentage; perhaps because the rate at which real wealth has tended to grow over long periods is 3 percent and, coincidentally, that's also the rate at which the supply of gold has tended to expand.

Q: *Should I buy and store precious metals outside the United States?*

A: You should buy investments wherever, and from whomever, the best combination of service and low cost is available, whether the vendor is in the States or elsewhere. It is, however, very prudent to store a substantial share of your long-term assets outside the U.S. Precious metals lend themselves to that better than most other investments. They should be considered a core holding for the foreseeable future.

The main arguments for keeping investments abroad are political and geographic diversification. The best countries to look at include Canada, the United Kingdom, Switzerland, the Netherlands, and Hong Kong. The best way to proceed is to get on a plane and take a nice vacation while you learn the ropes first hand. The days of opening a foreign bank account by mail are gone. With today's climate, you won't find many quality institutions willing to take your business, nor advisors willing to help you with the details. The only advice I can offer is to stick with long-established, recognized institutions. As a general rule, stay far away from those that solicit your business. And be aware of the tax and reporting rules the United States imposes. One plus in favor of gold coins is that, stored in a safe deposit box, they are not a reportable asset under current Treasury regulations, as are foreign bank and brokerage accounts.

Although there are hassles involved with having assets abroad, it is smart to diversify internationally.

Q: *Why hasn't gold moved during recent crises, like the October 1987 stock market crash or the 1990 Kuwait action?*

A: As always, the answer comes down to the balance of buyers and sellers. A good guess is that the Iraqi, Saudi, and Soviet governments have been recent sellers to pay bills and buy essentials like food and guns.

The U.S. government hasn't yet had to sell gold to generate cash, but it will try to keep the price down for other reasons during crises. With the collapse of the dollar to close to all-time lows against most important foreign currencies, the government probably feels that holding the line on gold is psychologically more important than ever.

During the October 1987 crash, for instance, there was relatively little the United States could do to support the stock market; the government and the Federal Reserve do not trade stocks. But they could ensure that gold did not take off. The last thing they wanted was a gold rush at the same time the stock market collapsed. But even though they succeeded in keeping the price down in 1987, they will not succeed in future downturns. The government was unable to control the price of gold at $35 in the early '70s. It has less power now, and the situation is much shakier.

You should be interested in value, not price trends. Gold actually went below $35 in 1971, just before the beginning of a decade-long bull market. The metal will probably hit some insanely high number on its final run in the next few years, as the world's whole financial structure is washed out and reformed.

Q: *Is it true the old Soviet republics have huge reserves that will be mined in the near future and depress the market?*

A: Skilled observers of mining figure that relatively few Russian mines can be operated profitably. Before Russian production expands, because of Western technology and capital, it is likely to collapse further, because mining concerns are unable to obtain essential spare parts or even fuel.

The Russians have lived for generations in an atmosphere of "they pretend to pay us, we pretend to work." Many individual Russians will eventually become competent entrepreneurs, but large-scale mining needs steady workers. In fact, in Russia most responsible positions are held by women, since the men are usually drunk. Smelting operations in the old U.S.S.R.'s major mining region have killed every tree and river within 200 km downwind. Gold recoveries are minimal, and wastage is phenomenal. Russian mining is a catalogue of horrors, and you won't see

Western companies put meaningful money into the old U.S.S.R. for another decade, at least until their coming civil war is over.

Q: *What about production from the rest of the world?*

A: It's odd that during the '70s, the argument was made that there was not enough gold in the world to use as money. There was some truth to that claim then, but at $1,000 to $1,500 prices it is reasonable to anticipate that adequate supply will not be a problem.

In a free-market society, the government would not regulate money any more than clothing or food. And the "price" of money, that is gold, would be set the same way as the price of every other commodity, by supply and demand. If there were a "need" for more money, miners would find it profitable to produce more; if not, mines would close down. Miners would earn a businessman's return, unless they discovered a bonanza. Money and mining would be self-regulating, and central banks would be redundant.

Most mines today have "all in" (including administration, depreciation, and interest) production costs of around US$350 per ounce. Few new mines are going into production, and their production is trivial compared to the continuing decline in South Africa, which accounts for half the world's gold production. With the tenor of the political situation in that part of the world, no new investment is being made that would turn the trend around.

Q: *So gold is likely to cure the world's monetary ills forever?*

A: Forever is a long time, but it will make the difference for the foreseeable future. As with all commodities, technology will constantly reduce gold's production costs and develop new supplies. Few people give adequate credit to the continuing

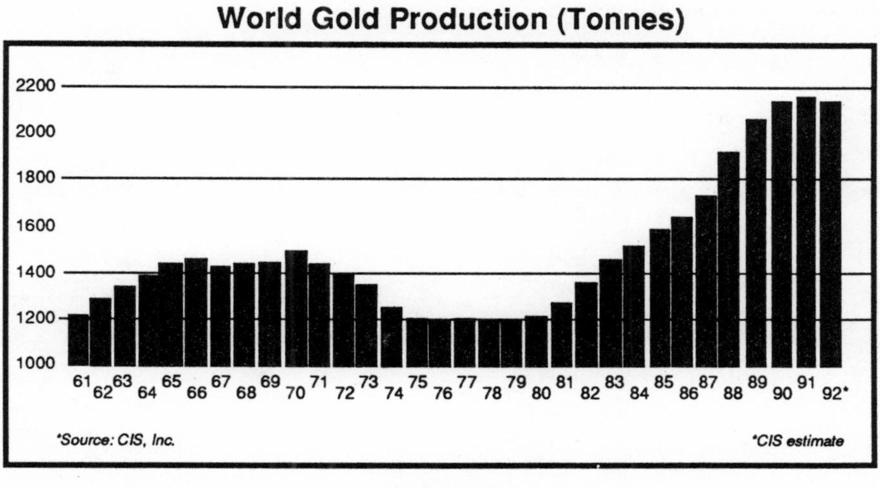

World Gold Production (Tonnes)

Source: CIS, Inc. *CIS estimate

Figure 18-4

development of technology. In the case of gold, they still believe an old prospector with a mule wanders around the desert looking for a narrow-vein, underground deposit. Almost all new mines today are large volume, open-pit, heap-leach operations. Still, that may change again over the decades to come.

At least three breakthroughs could eventually greatly expand the supply of gold.

1. *Biotechnology*—This science is already influencing mining by the development of bacteria that can transform a troublesome sulfide ore deposit into one recoverable with oxide techniques. In the future, genetic engineering will induce seaweed or other ocean flora to concentrate gold, much as spinach concentrates iron or kelp iodine.

2. *Space exploration*—Many asteroids contain large concentrations of heavy metals. With the limitless power of the sun, zero gravity, huge volumes, and no externalities like pollution control, taxes, or land use charges, mining costs in space should be very low.

3. *Fusion*—It's already feasible to transmute elements. But the energy involved makes it uneconomic. Fusion should realize the alchemists' dream.

Eventually technology will totally overturn the entire basis of life as we know it (see chapter 35), possibly even including the nature of money. But don't rush to change any of your near-term plans. Although the laws of science and technology may decree that in the distant future the price of gold could be the equivalent of about $1 a pound—a gold price of somewhere beyond a thousand 1993 dollars an ounce is a likely target before the decade is over and the world's monetary system is restructured. Not really a lot, only a triple, especially by comparison to the 2,500 percent move the metal made during the '70s.

More on gold production in the next chapter, because that is where returns of ten- or fifty-to-one can be had.

19

1,000 Percent Returns on Gold Stocks

No price is too low for a bear or too high for a bull.

Proverb

The art of investing emphasizes inaction as much as it does action. Success is a long-term proposition, and most of your time should be spent patiently hunting for the fattest prizes, not frenetically chasing after every mangy stray. Given transaction costs and the vagaries of your own mind set, an even-odds bet is inevitably a fool's bet. You want anomalies where risk and reward are heavily weighted in your favor, where the arguments that you'll be right are so compelling that you are almost forced to act. You should, in other words, look for propositions that resemble gold at $35 in 1971. In 1993, junior gold stocks (those which mainly interest themselves in exploration and have limited current production) fit the bill.

You should purchase gold for one set of reasons; you should buy gold stocks for another. Gold stocks and gold relate as a chicken does to an egg: much the same, but utterly different.

On the one hand, gold securities are no different from shoe, computer, retail, airline, utility, or any other stock group. They go in and out of fashion. They are alternately underpriced and overpriced. They represent ownership in a business, which is sometimes profitable and sometimes not.

On the other hand, the differences between gold stocks and any other groups of stocks are significant. Golds are the only group, other than possibly defense and environmental issues, that can amount to an ideological statement as much as an investment. Few people are likely to become impassioned over the prospects of furniture manufacturers or toy makers, but gold stock investors can be fervent. Because it is a small industry, only a little buying or selling can cause wild swings in prices. And because gold stocks are a direct, though somewhat unpredictable, inflation/chaos hedge, they can get large amounts of money moving in and out as quickly as mass emotions can change.

You can look at the gold stocks as a hedge, a speculation, or even as a long-term growth opportunity, in the case of the right companies. The industry certainly lends itself to my hedge strategy, described in chapter 8.

SELECTING THE "WHAT"

Gold stocks are probably the world's most volatile class of securities. Timing is more critical with them than with anything else you might buy. Figures 19-1 and 19-2 illustrate the point:

The law of gravity eventually overcomes all but the soundest stocks, however, and most high-flying resource stocks eventually have charts like Figures 19-3 and 19-4.

Junior resource stocks can be a good substitute for the lottery. Even in a horrible market, there's always something like Consolidated Stikine Silver, which went from $.28 to $15 in three months based on its spectacular 1988 drill results in the remote Eskay Creek area of northern British Columbia. Such drill results usually surprise everybody, including the company's own geologists. Besides, even if you owned Stikine at $.28, which itself would have been a fluke, since there was no rationale for owning it when it was trading at $.28, you probably would have sold it as soon as you saw it go to $.56, thinking you were a genius for having doubled your money.

If the game of investing in resource stocks were easy to play, everybody now doing so would have retired a multimillionaire years ago. Unfortunately, though, most of the would-be Stikines blow the treasury on Lear Jet rides or misplaced drillholes. Unable to file annual reports with the stock exchange, such companies are delisted and turn into wallpaper.

Consider the following stories.

1.   The good news: ABM Gold controls Sonora, Golden Bell, and Inca in the Mother Lode region of California. Each has reserves of over 1 million ounces.

The bad news came out later. The Sonora Mine, which cost $85 million to build, will never be able to pay off the $46 million debt it incurred to build the mine, unless the metal goes to $375 and stays there. The stock went from a peak of $15¼ in 1987 to its current 0.07 cents, despite the reserves on its undeveloped properties (which may be academic for environmental reasons) and the ability of its Sonora Mine to produce 125,000 ounces a year.

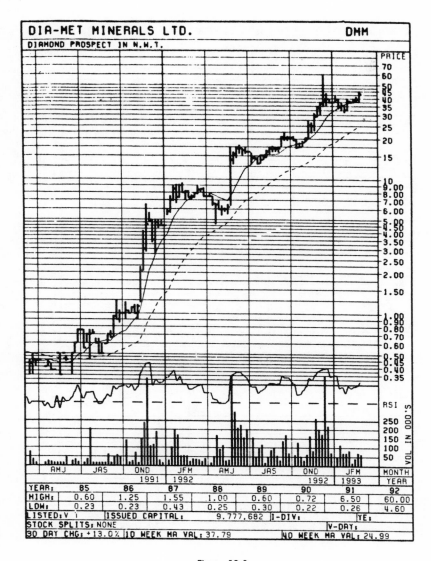

Figure 19-1

2. The good news: Aurizon, after a merger, had two mines in Quebec that both went into production in 1987. Their prospects took them from adjusted prices of 25 cents in 1985 to $14 in 1987.

    The bad news is that management took on $30 million worth of Swiss franc–denominated debt, which rose against the dollar, while both mines encountered runaway costs and every technical problem possible. By 1990 the stock traded at 0.31 cents.

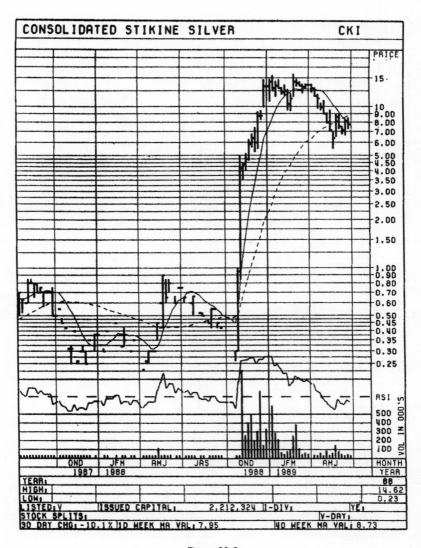

Figure 19-2

3. The good news: Galactic Resources peaked in 1987, when the stock reached $18, as they put the Summitville Mine in Colorado into production. They were acquiring many more properties and seemed on their way to becoming a major.

    The bad news is that they took on a large amount of debt, which they were unable to service. Meanwhile, the environmental costs of closing down their Summitville Mine, which was totally uneconomic, were more than the company was worth. The stock was trading at 5 cents by 1993.

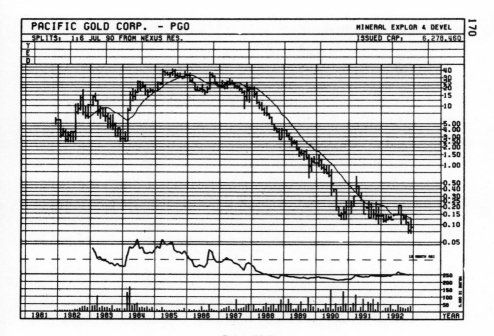

Figure 19-3

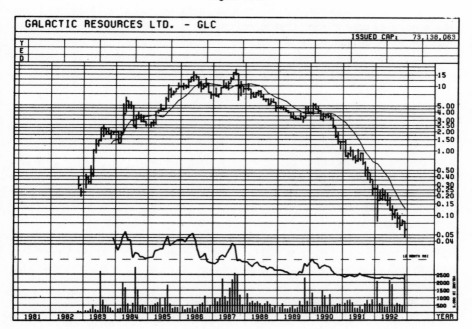

Figure 19-4

4. The good news: Geddes Resources proved up a gigantic (120 million tons) and high grade (1.7% copper, 1.2% zinc, .8% cobalt and 0.06 oz. gold) polymetallic deposit. Depending on the metal prices, that ore is worth perhaps $150 a ton. This property, plus the market's confidence in its excellent management, took the stock from 5 cents in 1986, to $5.25 in 1987.

    The bad news is that because its property is located in remote northwest British Columbia, the capital costs will be around $450 million to develop. And since the mine is on a "scenic river," development will trigger no end of legal hassles. The stock now trades at 50 cents on the reality.

5. The good news: In the 1970s City Resources found a very large deposit (approaching 2 million ounces) on Graham Island in British Columbia, on which they spent $20 million proving it up.

    The bad news is that they'll almost certainly never be allowed to mine it because of a combination of metallurgical, environmental, and political problems. The land is considered sacred by the Indians. The stock has fallen from $10 to 3 cents.

6. The good news: Quartz Mountain proved up its very large low-grade property in Oregon, which took the stock from 18 cents in 1984 to $6.50 in 1987.

    The bad news, which came out later, is that the mine will not be economic until gold goes well over $400 because of the environmental obstacles to new mines in Oregon. That took the stock down to $0.03 by 1993.

All of these companies have spent many millions proving up their ore bodies and/or building their mines. That money appeared to be intelligently spent at one time, but was ultimately wasted. There are hundreds of similar stories. Some speculators who bought "right" on these companies made thousands of percent on their money. Those who didn't suffered near-wipeouts.

TIMING THE "WHEN"

It's possible to profit either by choosing a company with proven properties and management, or just by getting lucky. I've learned to prefer the former. As Damon Runyan said, "The race may not go to the swift, nor the battle to the strong, nor the bread to the wise. But that's the way to bet." But knowing *what* to buy is still only half the game; even more important is knowing *when* to buy.

Analyzing small mining issues is not a skill that can be learned overnight. In addition to all the problems of picking general stocks that we've discussed, you have to know enough about the gold mining business to at least decide what questions to ask. Interpreting the answers is something else again.

None of this will make any difference during a real gold bull market; when a strong wind blows, even the turkeys fly. There's nothing wrong with any of these companies that a much higher gold price couldn't cure.

Say a company, back in 1980, sold 10 million shares at $5 and also took on $10 million in debt to finance production of its 1 million ounces in Ontario. It might have seemed like an excellent idea at the time, since cash production costs might have looked like $250 per ounce, which (at 50,000 ounces per year) would yield cash flow (after direct costs but before taxes and depreciation) of $12.5 million—or $1.25 per share—at $500 gold. After all, investors might reason, what were the chances gold could drop below the $250 break-even level?

Ten years later, costs have escalated to at least $400, if only because of inflation. And with gold at $350, cash flow is now a negative $2.5 million per year. The company can't even service the debt it has, much less pay it off. The mine has no current value at all, and its shares probably sell for 2 percent or 3 percent of their previous high. All of the original investors' capital has been lost, and the debt might even be settled for a few cents on the dollar.

Although the company was a terrible investment in the early '80s, when it looked like a great deal, in the early '90s it can be a wonderful investment, although it looks terrible. Whether anything is a good investment is more a function of *what price* it is than of *what* it is. At $5 it was a terrible investment; at 5 cents, or even 50 cents, it's a great speculation.

If you now assume $500 gold, with $400 costs, that same mine will earn $5 million per year, or 50 cents per share. If you can buy the shares at 10 cents, you have 50 or 100 to one upside if gold just returns to $500.

At least as of early 1993, sentiment on gold is bearish; sentiment on major gold stocks is *very* bearish; sentiment on the juniors is so negative that I can describe it only as a historical anomaly. In relative terms, the junior gold stocks are as cheap as the U.S. stock market was in late 1974, or New York real estate in 1975. Just because those markets later exploded in price does not mean that the small gold stock market will. But the odds favor a comeback. Junior gold stocks are down an average of 97 percent, as of early 1993, from the peak they reached in the summer of 1987. When gold returns, this market will switch from panic back to mania. And when it happens, the percentage gains are likely to be huge and will accrue quickly.

The best way to play the game is to own shares of a company with costs that are a fraction that of mines in North America, and with a property that's ten times as big.

THE FUTURE OF MINING

The future of the mining industry will not be in North America; it lies in Third World countries. It's not possible to predict what things will be like in 10 or 20 years, but right now Third World countries are very accommodating to industries that the developed world shuns. Costs of all types are vastly lower. Natural resource companies are much more likely to be left unmolested, since they constitute a major source of income and foreign exchange for both the government and the people. In developed countries, natural resource companies are marginal and can be thrown to the political wolves with seeming impunity.

You may have a certain understandable reluctance about, in effect, sending your money to exotic locales with questionable reputations. But that's precisely why these are the places to go. Although momentum has been building toward Latin America in particular since the middle of the '80s, prices are still low and few investors and prospectors have picked over the available properties. The desperate economic state of these countries means that there will be none of the obstructionism that makes mining a nightmare in North America.

In fact, the days of the mining industry are probably numbered in the developed world. The "Green" movement has become so virulent that the lawyers who arrange for permitting and environmental statements are now more important than the geologists who find deposits or the engineers who place them into production. Creating a successful mine in North America is less a technical than a legal and public relations achievement. The process of permitting, as opposed to finding or engineering, a mine is among the most time-consuming, expensive, and risky aspects of the whole business. That's true even in isolated areas, far from the paths of most backpackers. "Environmentalists" love the idea of preserving windblown landscapes in the middle of nowhere, even though few of them venture beyond the suburbs.

Most Third World countries, on the other hand, have already learned about the practical effects of nationalization, high taxes, huge bureaucracies, and socialist policies—generally from firsthand experience. Chastened by poverty, Third World countries offer workable environmental policies and freedom from constant legal harassment. Furthermore, most mines are in unpopulated areas. A company need not worry about locals holding hearings and filing suits because they do not want a gold mine next door. There are also many positive advantages. Only in Third World countries can miners find important tax holidays and very cheap labor.

Political risk was a real factor in the '50s, '60s and '70s, but not now. It is worth reemphasizing that less risk exists in most of these countries than in the United States, which now has punitive regulatory requirements for new mines. The days of undeveloped countries nationalizing property are over. The real danger to mining is indirect expropriation in developed countries, through legal battles and costly regulation.

As the world economy turns increasingly global, countries will be classed according to the intelligence of their economic policies rather than to their distance from New York. That being the case, it's wise to exchange U.S. producers for companies whose properties are in countries on their way up. This is why Freeport, for instance, sold all its U.S. gold properties. It felt the proceeds could be used better in Indonesia.

Of course there are disadvantages to mining in the Third World. Telephones generally are few and unreliable. Planes fly sporadically. Medical facilities are unsophisticated. If you need a tool more complicated than a screwdriver, you have to import it. But these countries are privatizing rapidly, and conditions are improving.

All things considered, it typically costs twice as much to produce gold in North America as it does in the Third World. Nevertheless, investors will pay more for North American production because they perceive it to be more stable and less risky. A mistake. They have inverted the concept of political risk. I have little doubt that in the future, the situation will be reversed and investors will quite properly pay a premium for production in places like Chile, where profit margins are far higher. For now, the better part of an investor's resources portfolio should be concentrated in Third World natural resource issues.

HOW TO SELECT MINING STOCKS

Companies with proven ore bodies usually lack the excitement that turns investors into adrenaline junkies. However, stable companies cause fewer embarrassments. After all, once a company has found an economic deposit, most of the high drama is over and the rest is largely engineering and mechanics.

The worst case, barring extremely bad luck or bad management, should be that the deposit is farmed out to a major and the company merely collects its percentage, using the proceeds to finance more new properties. The best case is that management can put the property into successful production themselves and then proceed to find other properties, eventually growing the company into a major. In the former case, the shareholders should not get hurt; and in the second case they do extremely well, with rewards of ten- or twenty-for-one on their money, albeit over a long term. American Barrick, which started out as a Vancouver penny stock, is the best recent example of this ideal scenario.

Juniors sell to, or co-venture, projects with majors because they lack capital or expertise. Majors sell to, or co-venture, with juniors for a larger variety of reasons. Maybe a project is too small for them, or maybe they want to devote their manpower and capital to something of higher priority. Maybe the project is geographically distant from their other operations, or maybe someone in top management wants to terminate the career of the project's manager for political reasons.

Little companies can become big companies only by putting their mines into production. In order to do that, they need to raise tens of millions of dollars, which is extremely hard for a small company to do. It can become a chicken-or-egg problem. What often happens is that little companies are acquired by, or merge with, a major.

Ranking junior golds is extremely tough, since lightning strikes unpredictably in the mining business. A company on the edge of bankruptcy, whose shares are trading for pennies, can pull a magic drill hole on borrowed money and be trading for $10 within a week. And the prices of small company stocks often reflect perceptions (read *promotion*) over the short run more than they do reality. Furthermore, of the thousands of little companies supposed to be in the mining business, few have the money or management necessary even to stay out of bankruptcy court, much less find a valuable ore body and place it in production. Most of your money, therefore, should be in juniors that either are producing or have a proven ore body and soon will be. You want juniors that have the potential to turn into majors.

In general, I prefer buying stocks with small caps just because they're more volatile; it takes less buying to drive a stock worth $1 million to $10 million than it does to take one from $10 million to $100 million. This is especially true since retail buyers will typically place an equal amount of their funds into each stock they are interested in, whether it's a giant like Newmont or some little penny stock with nothing but a good story. The percentage gains in the small cap stocks are, therefore, usually much greater. That is the good news about little companies.

The bad news is that institutions do not buy little companies precisely because they are so small; they cannot buy a significant position without driving the stock up, and then they have no one to sell to because the market is so illiquid.

About 2,000 gold stocks are traded in Canada, about 500 in the United States, about 500 in Australia, and about 100 in South Africa. Those companies, in turn, have properties all around the world. How can an investor possibly monitor them? He can't unless he is a full-time professional. But the full-time analysts stick to the majors almost exclusively. The managers of the thirty-five mutual funds that invest primarily in gold issues are still smarting from the bear market that began in 1987. When they buy something now, it tends to be big, stable, and well known.

Largely because of the buying of these mutual funds, the majors tend to be overpriced relative to the juniors. "Relative" is the key word. When the market turns and billions of dollars try to get into those funds overnight, even the majors will go through the roof. But the second- and third-tier companies, which are currently suffering from a lack of support, is where the real leverage is.

I find it useful to classify mining companies into four groups.

FOUR CLASSES OF GOLD STOCK

1. MAJORS are large established companies with at least 200,000 ounces of annual production and current earnings. These are usually listed on the NYSE and are covered by security analysts at the major wire houses. When someone decides he wants a gold stock, these are the issues he'll turn to (see Table 19-1). The list is not inclusive; I have left off large mining companies like ASARCO and Amax because they're not "pure" gold plays, even though they mine a considerable amount of gold.

2. SECOND TIER/ DEVELOPMENTALS. This category includes companies that are due to be in production in the near term, or have only recently gone into production, or do not produce enough to make the major category. Some institutions own them. They are on NASDAQ and Toronto rather than the NYSE. Major

Table 19-1   Senior Producers

Name	Price	Number of Shares (millions)	Market Capitalization (millions) of US$
Agnico Eagle	C$ 6.50	131mm	US$ 163
Amax Gold	US$ 8.50	75	642
American Barrick	US$18.25	285	5,200
Battle Mountain	US$ 7.25	80	570
Cambior	C$14.25	36	405
Coeur d'Alene	US$15.75	15.5	244
Echo Bay	US$ 6.25	105	671
First Miss Gold	US$ 6.25	18	113
FMC Gold	US$ 5.00	74	360
Freeport Copper	US$21.00	192	4,025
Glamis	C$ 6.75	18	95
Hecla	US$10.25	32	330
Hemlo	C$ 9.25	97	720
Homestake	US$14.50	137	1,990
LAC	C$ 7.25	147	1,085
Newmont Gold	US$40.00	105	4,200
Newmont Mining	US$44.00	68	3,010
Pegasus	US$17.00	32	540
Placer Dome	C$18.75	237	3,535
Royal Oak	C$ 4.70	70	262
TVX Mining	C$ 3.20	134	341

brokers do not really follow them, but solid specialty brokers do. Few have earnings—yet. But that's why they are interesting; their prices now are very low relative to what those earnings will be once they are in production, with numbers running from 5 to 15 times estimated earnings.

3. THIRD TIER/ EXPLORATION. These outfits clearly have a worthwhile property, which has had substantial geological work done on it. But they haven't drilled it out to find exactly how large it is, nor have they done the metallurgical and engineering studies to ascertain whether a profitable mine can be built, nor do they have the capital to develop it. For those reasons, any estimate of when they expect to pour the first gold bar is pure conjecture.

These are not candidates for institutional buying until they have a "bankable feasibility study" with production and profit projections, which will move them up to the second tier.

4. WILDCAT EXPLORATION. These companies have a long way to go before some mutual fund will put dollar one into them. Most companies in this category, 90 percent of all public "mining" companies, have inexperienced man-

Table 19-2　Second Tier/Developmentals

Name	Symbol	Price	Previous High
Aurizon	ARZ.T	C$　.30	C$13.50
Avino	AVO.V	C$　.25	C$ 3.75
Bema	BGO.T	C$ 1.00	C$ 5.25
Cornucopia	CNP.T	C$ 1.00	C$ 9.50
Crown	CRO.T	C$ 5.00	C$13.00
Equinox	EQX.T	C$ 2.15	C$ 5.50
Euro Nevada	EN.T	C$17.00	—
Franco Nevada	FN.T	C$37.00	—
Golden Star	GSC.T	C$ 9.75	—
Granges	GXL.T	C$ 1.90	C$19.25
Hycroft	HYR.T	C$　.80	C$15.00
Imperial Met	IPM.T	C$　.25	C$ 1.80
Minven	MVG.T	C$　.25	C$15.25
Miramar	MAE.V	C$ 1.25	C$ 6.25
Queenstake	QTR.T	C$ 2.75	C$10.00
Rayrock	RAY.T	C$10.50	C$14.50
Redstone	RR.T	C$ 4.00	C$ 5.50
United Keno	UKH.T	C$　.60	C$20.00
Viceroy	VOY.T	C$ 6.75	C$25.00

Table 19-3　Third Tier/Exploration

Name	Symbol	Price	Previous High
All North	ANH.V	C$　.15	C$ 6.85
Arizona Star	AZS.V	C$　.65	C$ 2.15
Athena	AGC.V	C$　.40	C$ 4.40
Atlanta	AAG.T	C$　.50	C$ 6.60
Biron Bay	BBQ.A	C$　.60	C$ 3.00
Carson Gold	CQG.V	C$ 3.20	C$ 5.20
Cathedral	CAT.T	C$　.70	C$ 3.50
Columbia	COB.V	C$　.25	C$10.80
Colony Pacific	CYX.T	C$　.15	C$ 2.45
Coral	CLH.T	C$　.55	C$10.50
Chase	CQS.V	C$ 3.50	C$ 8.00
Geddes	GDD.T	C$　.65	C$ 5.25
Minera Rayrock	MRN.T	C$ 2.00	C$13.40
Newhawk	NHG.T	C$ 1.00	C$ 8.25
St. Genevieve	SGV.T	C$　.80	C$11.00
St. George	SGE.V	C$　.40	C$ 4.15
Venezuelan Gold	VZG.V	C$11.00	C$11.00

agement, little money, and completely unproven properties. When the markets get hot, none of that will make the slightest difference. Smart players will make millions on complete garbage.

Wildcat plays can go completely wild if a drill hole hits. But, on the other hand, in a bad market the wildcats can disappear without a trace. This is where the biggest gains are to be made. But you really have to know what you're doing.

TILTING THE ODDS

Most investors who own mining stocks tend to do so only at the height of a mania, which is a mistake. They buy some stocks based on promotion, then hold on in the dumb hope they will go higher. That may work for growth stocks over the long term, but doing so becomes a formula for disaster with the volatile golds. You should do several things as you increase your involvement with these issues.

1. Consider subscribing to one or more of the publications (listed in the appendix) that follow the gold market. Knowledge is your first line of defense against losses, and the editors make understanding that market a priority along with recommending gold stocks.
2. Make sure you are on the mailing list of every company you own, read their press releases, and visit the industry shows. Call the companies, and consider flying to Vancouver, Reno, Toronto, or Denver, where 99 percent of these companies are located. Spend a few days talking to management. Impose upon them if necessary , and let them explain exactly why their stock should go up.
3. Call your local college or university and inquire about relevant courses. In particular, write the University of Nevada—Reno, Division of Continuing

Table 19-4 Wildcat Exploration

Name	Symbol	Price	Previous High
Abo	ABU.V	C$.10	C$ 1.50
Adrian	ADL.V	C$.80	C$ 9.75
Arbor	AOR.V	C$.20	C$ 5.00
Canalaska	CKE.V	C$.25	C$ 1.05
Carlin Gold	CIO.V	C$.50	C$ 2.65
Golden Queen	GQM.T	C$.20	C$ 3.10
Greater Lenora	GEN.T	C$.50	C$10.50
MVP	MVP.T	C$.03	C$ 4.00
Noramco	NNN.T	C$.50	C$14.75
Northgate	NGX.T	C$.75	C$13.00
Solomon	SRB.V	C$.50	C$ 3.00
Victoria	VIT.V	C$.35	C$ 2.00
Westview	WVW.V	C$.25	C$ 3.45

Education, Reno, NV 89557, and the University of Colorado, Continuing Education, P.O. Box 178, Boulder, CO 80309. This is an active, time-consuming approach, but it will pay off. If you're not as yet in a position to interpret the data you receive, at least use a broker who can. If he can't, you are using the wrong broker.

4.   Get a good broker who stays on top of these companies. (Most people use someone like their brother-in-law at Dean Witter.) With gold stocks that is a big mistake because gold is a specialist's market. There are probably only about a hundred brokers in North America who qualify, most of them in Canada. Those brokers I know and do business with are listed in the appendix. Take an hour, call them all, and compare their commissions, services, knowledgeability, and bedside manner. Choose the one who will serve you best and move your account there, unless you are absolutely convinced your present broker is better. Some brokers pretend to be experts but do not dirty their hands with field trips or even talk to management.

5.   Consider opening a managed account with someone who has an interest in the juniors. It is tough running your own portfolio when there are about 3,000 stocks to choose from worldwide. Managed accounts are much more flexible than mutual funds and, at the moment, only BGR Precious Metals (discussed at the end of this chapter) holds a meaningful number of juniors.

MINING TECHNICALITIES

If you have an interest in science and technology, you can learn a lot by visiting mines, reading industry publications, and talking to management. Eventually you pick up numerous details about techniques of fire assaying, the problems of mine ventilation, and other rather arcane subjects.

Geostatistics, for instance, is the science of determining how much ore you have, its grade, and how much drilling and sampling you have to do in order to prove it. If you look into this subject, you might know enough to question a company that speculates it has, for instance, 10 million tons of 0.1 oz./ton ore. How closely spaced are the drill holes? Is the ore body disseminated evenly, or is it characterized by lots of deceptive little high-grade pockets? Of the several statistical methods available, which was used to infer tonnage and grade from the drill holes? How can we be certain that the samples taken from the drill core (which is about two inches in diameter and can be many hundreds of feet in length) were representative? How finely were samples ground before assaying to overcome the "nugget effect"?

An investor would usually never think of asking many of these and similar questions, all critical, to determining the value of a property and from there, the value of a stock. These questions become relevant only after you have acquainted yourself with geochemistry, which gives an indication of whether there might be an ore body based on the composition of soil samples and the presence of certain trace minerals in rock, and geophysics, or how to interpret gravity anomalies. And both precede metallurgy, which tells you whether it is possible to refine an ore economically and which of numerous technologies to use. Mine construction is another, totally different field. And even then it might all be for nought if environmental and permitting problems can't be solved.

The irony involved in gaining knowledge on a subject is that the more you learn, the less you think you know. While your competence improves, your confidence in any particular project will likely lessen, because more knowledge draws your attention to what can go wrong. That is why the best salesmen and promoters often do not clutter their minds with facts. The facts could temper their enthusiasm and their certainty and compromise their abilities to convince others. But too little knowledge is usually fatal for the buyer.

You must follow the same drill whether you are looking at biotech, computer, oil, manufacturing or any other stock. You may recall Robert Pirsig's book *Zen and the Art of Motorcycle Maintenance*. In the book he makes the point that anyone who endeavors to become a good motorcycle mechanic must, almost of necessity, become a true renaissance man. If you're going to tighten bolts properly and avoid stripping the threads or overcompressing a gasket, you will do well to learn something about metallurgy. And if you learn about metallurgy, you will be learning more about chemistry. Chemistry might lead to physics, which might lead to astronomy, which in turn might lead to philosophy, which might take you to literature. And so an ignorant, greasy motorcycle mechanic might realistically transform himself through his interest in truly mastering his trade, and in pursuing all new questions to an answer. All knowledge is interrelated.

You will be happier with your results if you dig into the fundamentals of the businesses of the companies you own. You will understand the reasons for what's happening in the market, and no longer feel that things happen unpredictably and inexplicably. The knowledge will also make it easier for you to determine a company's true value, regardless of what the market is doing.

If fundamentals have anything at all to do with it, and they do in the long run, and if investor psychology continues to go from hot to cold to hot every few years, and it will, you stand to make a great deal of money buying shares of small mining companies now.

A SELECTION OF GOLDS

The selection of stocks I've compiled in the tables above have varying degrees of merit. Some of these outfits are selling at or below their current cash values per share. Others have big properties that are already well into the developmental stage and only need higher gold prices or a deal with a major. Some are producing mines that are strapped by low gold prices. Which should you own? Some of the stocks listed in the previous four tables may become worthless for any of the reasons that turn mining stock certificates into wallpaper, but all of these companies have real prospects.

Despite the fact that most of the outfits in these tables are selling for 10 percent or less of their previous highs, they all have more developed properties, more experienced management, and sometimes even more cash than they did when the market was hot. One reason some of these companies are selling for less than cash is that they raised money at much higher prices in years gone by and have not spent it.

If you believe a resurgence in gold prices will occur, and mining stocks will explode in their usual leveraged way, then you'll want to own the stocks in these tables. They should average a 1,000 percent gain in the next several years. If you looked at a chart book in 1987 and asked yourself why you didn't back up the truck at the 1985 bottom, then the prices on this list should have some personal relevance. One of the nice things about a radically fluctuating market is that it constantly offers opportunities to apply your "learning experiences."

Conditions in 1993 are as different from the peak in the summer of 1987 as possible. I do not know that this is the exact bottom, but only liars ever buy at the exact bottom. When prices do turn, however, these stocks will likely pop 25 percent to 50 percent overnight just because the markets are so thin and the market capitalizations are now so small. Check the current market capitalizations with your broker.

In general, the lower the market cap, the more volatile the stock. If you bought $10,000 worth of some of these stocks, as small as they now are and as lightly as they trade, your buying alone could double their trading price. The same amount of money going into a major would barely be a round lot trade.

Questions and Answers

Q: *When is the best time to buy into these stocks?*

A: When any market as volatile as golds is down 98 percent from a previous peak, you can forget about trying to squeeze the last few nickels out of the market with cyclical timing. But the North American golds do have an annual cycle. They're typically weaker in late December for two basic reasons: (a) Unless it's been a good year for gold, most companies will have spent money but earned little. Their stocks will be down, and they will become candidates for year end tax-loss selling. At that point the whole group winds up being sold for whatever they will bring, solely for tax reasons. (b) In the dead of winter properties in northern climes aren't being drilled. Therefore there's no news, no excitement, and no psychologically compelling reason to buy or stay in.

There is a class of professional players, few of whom care about the mining business in itself, who make an excellent living capitalizing on this fact alone from year to year. I recommend a longer time horizon, however, unless you plan to make trading a profession.

Q: *Have gold stocks lost some of their traditional ability to act as a hedge, since they crashed along with everything else in October 1987?*

A: Instead of replaying their performance of the '30s or of 1973 to 1974, when the golds showed great strength in the face of a bear market in industrials, golds crashed in 1987.

The first question: How did the golds get high enough to crash in 1987? Actually, it was similar to the penny silver stocks during the '60s. When industrials of every description were going through the roof, the speculative fever, and lots of supermoney created by the boom, flowed into Spokane and sent the average piece of moose pasture on that exchange upward more than 100 times. Spokane silver stocks exploded not because silver itself doubled, but because stocks as a whole were in an historic bull market. The mountain of funny money created by the '60s market boom flowed over into these little silver stocks as objects of speculative interest. They crashed with the rest of the market in 1970. That's also what happened with the gold stocks in October 1987.

This underscores, I suppose, the futility of trying to predict what will happen in the future based on what has happened in the past. Which time in the past? Why couldn't this time present a variation on the theme? Could what occurred in the past have done so for different reasons than we suspect? I've never credited the simple-minded theory of contracyclicality about gold shares (that is, when the general stock market goes down, golds go up, and vice-versa) if only because there have been so many times in the past when both have risen together, such as 1933 to 1937, 1971 to 1973, and 1982 to 1983.

Q: *What about Australian gold stocks?*

A: The Australians as a group are often excellent bargains, having shown current dividends in the 10 percent area a number of times. In part their value derives from the fact that so little attention is paid to them in North America; outside buying usually comes from London. But it is tough enough to stay on top of the situation in North America without also monitoring the conditions on the other side of the planet, where it's hard to meet management or visit the property.

Q: *Should I leverage my gains by using margin?*

A: Margin debt is, in general, a trap for a long-term investor. Not only is the interest clock always ticking, but you might be squeezed out in the short run before you have time to be right in the long run.

Margin buying and selling is particularly dangerous with the junior gold stocks, since most of them tend to be low priced. Once a stock falls below a certain price (C$2 in Canada, and usually U.S. $5 in the U.S.), it is no longer marginable. If someone has 10,000 shares of a C$2 stock with a $5,000 debit against it, everything is fine until it goes to C$1.90. At that point the stock must have 100 percent margin, and the broker must sell until the debit is paid off. Of course this happens in lots of accounts at the same time, and the bid falls away even further. The stock might hit $1.25 before everyone gets enough paper off to cover the debit.

GOLD STOCK FUNDS: AN ANOMALY

As emphasized in chapter 13, institutions dominate today's market and are likely to do so at least until the present financial system self-destructs. The question is how best to take advantage of the situation. Gold stocks present a very convenient answer.

If there's danger in owning stocks that already have a heavy institutional ownership, opportunity can be found in buying those shares the institutions decided not to purchase. When a stock is heavily owned by institutions, the only thing they can do is sell; when they don't own something, all they can do is buy. When that happens, the chart patterns of the favored stocks resemble a launched space rocket. I'm not saying that a stock that is 50 percent in professional hands is necessarily a bad deal; it could skyrocket if that ownership goes to 75 percent. At the same time, it does not guarantee a stock will become an institutional favorite because it is not preferred now. However, gold stocks will again have their day in the institutional sun, for a number of reasons.

First, some gold stocks will come into their own as growth stocks, with expanding earnings. Many companies have the potential to be consistent low-cost producers, veritable money machines even with present gold prices. As these companies mature they will expand their assets and earnings along with their reserves and production. That will happen even if we never see a real bull market in gold, and it will attract attention.

Second, if the world financial and monetary systems become as chaotic as I expect, the institutions—including pension funds, insurance companies, large money managers, and garden variety mutual funds—will seek a small position in these stocks as a disaster hedge. The theory is that putting 5 percent of assets into something that is contracyclical and highly volatile acts as an insurance policy on the other 95 percent.

Third, the present generation of managers is now familiar enough with mining shares to consider buying them. That wasn't true even as recently as ten years ago. They could pile into these stocks the way they do into any other group, if that's where the action is.

The key question is how much in the way of gold stocks do institutions now own, and what amount of buying could likely come into them?

At present only about 10 percent of all gold shares are institutionally owned, compared to an average of 39 percent for all other groups. Since that figure includes big companies like Homestake (about 20 percent), it becomes obvious how very little support the little stocks have from "big money." This 10 percent stake is grossly out of proportion to the percentage in any other industry; the next lowest is distillers, at 15.4 percent. Nor is it simply a prejudice against either extractive or highly cyclical industries, since they own 52 percent of aluminum, 45 percent of forest products, 61 percent of fertilizers, and 48 percent of coal. They have 31 percent of the related copper industry.

The pressure will arrive from two directions at once: from conventional institutions buying gold shares as either a hedge or a profit play, and from the public buying funds that already specialize in gold shares.

As late as the early '70s there was only one gold fund, International Investors; in 1982 there were still only five; but now there are thirty-five. The assets of these funds have risen tenfold, from about $200 million to $2 billion, since 1980, a time when gold has been in a bear market. As the gold market itself turns around, the growth of these funds could be truly spectacular.

When the public starts moving out of conventional funds, where will the money flow? Most of it into money market funds, but a lot of it into gold funds, which will, in turn, be forced to buy gold shares as assets pour in. The public has become quite enamored of "switch fund" trading whereby the customer, with just a phone call, can have his assets transferred to a fund that's "hot" from one that's not. Literally hundreds of millions of dollars could find their way into the gold funds simply because, in the near future, they will likely be the only funds going up.

This is in distinct contrast to previous gold bull markets, where the buyers were typically idealogues or cognescenti. Those buyers will still be there in greater numbers than ever, thanks to the education the public has gotten since the dollar was first devalued in 1971. But the new legion of trend-following mutual fund traders greatly outnumbers them, and they will flood the gold funds with new capital, simply because they follow trends.

If the institutions own about 10 percent of the approximately $30 billion worth of gold stocks outstanding, a small percentage, then what percentage of their net worth is in them? At present, the market value of all the stocks traded in the United States is about $5 trillion (or $5,000 billion); the institutions own $2 trillion, or 39 percent of this amount, including about $3 billion in golds. In other words, about .15 percent of their assets. The funds have more than 7 percent of their assets in computers and 5 percent in drugs.

Regarding the number of institutional owners, the way Standard & Poor's, whose numbers I'm using, sees it, about 1,650 institutions own IBM, and the typical "name" U.S. company is owned by between 100 and 800 of them. The golds are the most "underowned" group of stocks on the board; only about 0.15 percent of institutional capital is currently in them divided among perhaps 100 institutions. When this market really gets underway, many institutions that currently have no participation are going to want gold shares. But there are very few shares to go around. Looking at it another way, the institutions own only 10 percent of the shares of the mining companies, compared to 38 percent of the market as a whole; they could do a whole lot more buying.

Either as a percentage of the industry, or as a percentage of the funds' assets, gold shares are underowned relative to the market. As a public-spirited citizen, you'll want to be in a position to accommodate our nation's fund managers when they're scrambling to buy these shares at much higher prices.

Questions and Answers

Q: *Which are the best gold stock mutual funds?*

A: The 35 open-end funds specializing in gold stocks are all basically proxies for the major producers. None of them has a meaningful position in the juniors, nor will they until trading volume in the small stocks increases substantially. That's because either a sudden influx or withdrawal of shareholder funds could leave them with liquidity problems.

The best answer, if you don't want to do it yourself, is a managed account or a closed-end fund. There are two closed-end funds in the gold area right now, both traded in Toronto. One, the Central Fund of Canada (CEF.A, C$4.85) holds only gold and silver bullion. It is a convenient way to buy the metals in the form of a stock certificate. It generally sells for a small discount from the value of its holdings, so it is arguably the cheapest way to buy gold.

However, I really want to call your attention to BGR Precious Metals (BPT.A, C$7.75). BGR is a closed-end fund, listed on the Toronto Stock Exchange, which invests almost exclusively in secondary and tertiary gold mining companies. It typically sells at a 10 percent to 15 percent discount from net asset value, but when the gold shares again get popular, it will go to a large premium. This is really the only vehicle currently available which can give you a "spread" of the juniors.

20

South Africa and Its Gold Stocks

Together, hand in hand, with our matches and our necklaces,* we shall liberate this country.

Winnie Mandela

Far more than most places, South Africa illustrates the effect of politics on investment. To most people, investing in South Africa means investing in their gold stocks (although the Johannesburg Stock Exchange lists more than 900 other stocks). Gold stocks anywhere are volatile enough, but international sanctions, internal turmoil, and currency controls have made South African golds as volatile as penny stocks, despite huge production and substantial dividends.

In the 1990s, politics will have a bigger effect than ever on investments here, and it will not be beneficial. Let's first take a look at the country, then at its mines.

WHITHER SOUTH AFRICA?

Apartheid, the system of legalized racial separation, has been a dead letter in practice for years. The only remnant of it in 1993 is that blacks still do not have the vote. But that is also going to change; soon the country's 32 million blacks, or rather, their leaders, will be calling the shots. What does that mean?

*"Necklaces" are tires soaked in gasoline, placed around the neck of a politically incorrect person—all of whom have been black so far—and ignited.

217

There are probably a hundred credible scenarios of South Africa's future, but one I've never bought is the simplistic white-vs.-black race war. First, there are eight major black tribes and two white tribes, the English and the Afrikaners, each with its own splinter groups. Further, especially among the blacks, lines are increasingly drawn between urban and rural. Apart from that, of the 42 million population, there are 3 million Cape Coloured, who generally align with the 5 million whites, and 1 million East Indians, located mostly around Durban, who generally align with the opportunity of the moment.

All these groups break down along still more lines. Most whites can see the writing on the wall. But a hard-core minority centers on the Afrikaner Resistance Movement (AWB), composed mostly of rural Afrikaners, ex-Rhodesians, and white immigrants from Mozambique, who will not countenance black rule under almost any circumstance. This group basically wants independence for the Orange Free State and has lots of support within the armed forces and police.

The African National Congress (ANC), now led by Nelson Mandela, is the black group that captures most of the Western press's attention. Its orientation is that of most socialists thirty years ago. The Pan African Congress (PAC) is a somewhat smaller group populated mostly by unreformed Leninists. The black group most closely aligned with free-market principles is Inkatha, based among the Zulus and led by Chief Gatsha Buthelezi. Regardless of what the other blacks or whites decide, the Zulus will do what suits them and will take no guff from anyone. Since the Zulus constitute the largest tribe of blacks, and are the most united group besides, we should hear more about them than we do. But Buthelezi's pro-capitalist views do not suit the western media nearly as well as those of the ANC. There's an excellent chance that Zululand will attempt to break off from the rest of the country.

There are plenty of other complications, such as the existence of four nominally independent tribal homelands within South Africa: Ciskei, Transkei, Bophuthatswana, and Venda. They're not recognized internationally, and each is basically a dictatorship in the best African tradition, with its own army, police and domestic policies. They may, or may not, acquiesce to being reincorporated into Azania, as the ANC prefers to call South Africa.

Last, but far from least, about half the black population is under eighteen. There's no more dangerous creature on the face of the earth than a young, unmarried male, especially if he has grown up poor, uneducated, and unemployed in an urban environment controlled by rich folks of a different race whom he believes are responsible for his poverty.

The bottom line is that Azania will probably experience the same cycle as has almost every other newly independent black African state: strongman rule, state control of the economy, wealth redistribution schemes, gigantic bureaucracy supporting a cadre of kleptocrats, capital flight and gradual economic implosion. Still, I think it is unlikely to be as bad as what happened in Tanzania or Mozambique, if only because the *zeitgeist* just isn't what it was in the '60s and '70s. Even the most insular and ideological socialists know what happened to the Soviet Union. And most of the whites will stay on, if only because the Afrikaners have roots in South Africa that go back further than those of most of the blacks.

Although the turmoil here can only help the price of gold, it can only hurt the shares of local gold mines.

SOUTH AFRICAN GOLD MINES

As of now, South African gold mines are probably the most leveraged in the world. They're old (many go back more than fifty years) and deep (some more than two miles underground). Many are close to mined out, and the average cash cost of production is closing in on $350 an ounce. The revenue that many generate from uranium is worth next to nothing, since that metal is off 75 percent from its peak.

Two things are really going to clobber the mines in the future: labor costs and taxes. Labor costs in the mines have exploded over the last two decades. Black miners now earn close to what whites receive for comparable work. When the new government takes over, that trend is going to accelerate, not only in the mines but throughout the economy. A great deal of the mine labor is now imported from other countries in the region, especially Mozambique. This situation will end and the mines will be forced to use domestic labor, which will be higher paid, less skilled, and more demanding.

South Africa is already a highly taxed and highly regulated economy. Indeed, from an economic point of view, apartheid was just a welfare scheme intended to benefit poor whites at the expense of blacks. Chances are that taxes will go up even further, which isn't going to help the mines.

Many things will improve in South Africa now that sanctions and travel restrictions have been discarded by the international community. But South Africa's huge import duties, export regulations, commodity marketing boards, and foreign exchange controls cause a more effective embargo than could its enemies abroad. And now a left-leaning government can just take over the ready-made superstructure. That's pretty much what happened in Rhodesia.

I was a big fan of South African gold mines in the 1970s, when *Crisis Investing* was written. At that time many were yielding current dividends of (this is not a misprint) 30 percent to 60 percent, and those dividends doubled and redoubled several times as gold rose to its 1980 highs. Although I expect another spectacular run in the gold market, most of the profits this time are not going to go into shareholders' pockets. As Table 20-1 shows, although South African golds are priced at bargain levels by historical standards, they are no longer the value they once were. Because we are entering a bullish environment for gold, South African gold stocks are not going down. When the gold boom gets under way in earnest, they should double or triple. But they will not likely repeat their performance of the 1970s.

Table 20-1

Name	Price in US$ March 31, 1993	1980 High	1976 Low
Blyvoor	1.45	25.50	3.73
Bracken	0.45	5.64	0.88
Durban Deep	5.00	44.35	2.16
East Rand Proprietary (ERPM)	3.50	40.32	2.35
Grootvlei	1.90	13.50	0.43
Harmony	4.00	28.87	2.27
Loraine	1.00	9.67	0.54
St. Helena	7.50	56.85	10.19
Stilfontein	1.00	30.64	1.31
Western Areas	1.80	11.04	0.94

There are about 100 South African gold stocks. Table 20-1 does not include a complete listing of South African gold mines or of all the relevant information about any one mine, but it should give you a frame of reference. I suggest you look at these numbers closely. Compare current prices with previous highs and lows, and you'll find many are at or below their 1976 lows—reached when gold hit the bear market bottom of $103, which was simultaneous with the riots in Soweto—and many stocks are off 85 percent to 90 percent from their highs.

Since the mines in South Africa now are older, deeper and producing lower-grade ore than in the '70s, and gold has less percentage upside potential than it did in the '70s, these stocks ought to be priced to yield higher current dividends than they did back then. But the share prices have retreated only to the levels of fifteen years ago, and earnings and dividends are much lower.

To illustrate my point regarding the relative volatility of short-life and/or high-cost mines, the price chart and dividend histories of St. Helena and Loraine can be compared to Vaal Reefs and Kloof, long-life, low-cost "supermines." Notice that St. Helena and Loraine are down 95 percent from their peaks and sell at their lowest prices ever. Vaal Reefs and Kloof have held up much better, supported in good measure by their dividends.

Despite South Africa's problems, I expect all these mines to return to at least their previous highs in both price and dividends. The mines in Table 20-1 are in a class with Loraine and St. Helena, which is where the leverage is.

One practice of South African mines, as well as most mines that can control the grade of ore they mine, is to mine lower-grade ore when the price of gold is up. This procyclical practice is probably the opposite of what you would expect to happen. In the case of diamonds, for instance, the De Beers syndicate withdraws supply at the bottom of the market and increases it when prices are high. But with gold, the immediate consequence of high prices is less production. The higher the gold price goes, the less gold the South Africans will mine, since they utilize rich ore at low

St. Helena—US$ ADR

Source: Yorkton Securities

Figure 20-1

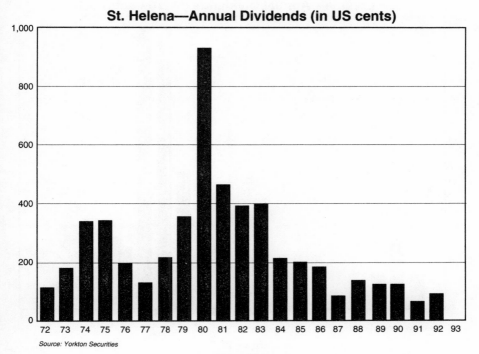

St. Helena—Annual Dividends (in US cents)

Source: Yorkton Securities

Figure 20-2

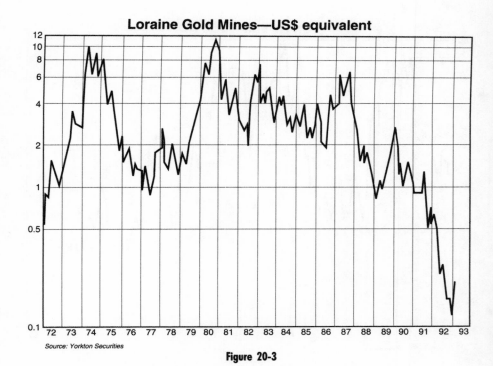

Loraine Gold Mines—US$ equivalent

Source: Yorkton Securities

Figure 20-3

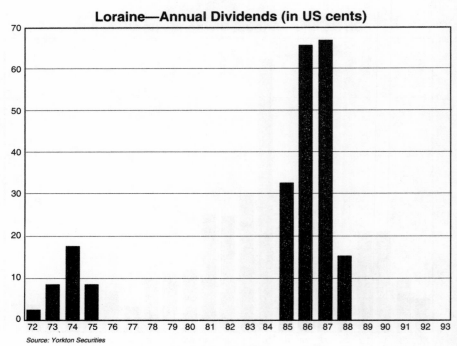

Loraine—Annual Dividends (in US cents)

Source: Yorkton Securities

Figure 20-4

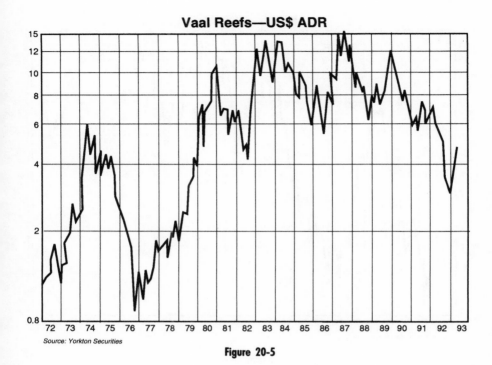

Vaal Reefs—US$ ADR

Source: Yorkton Securities

Figure 20-5

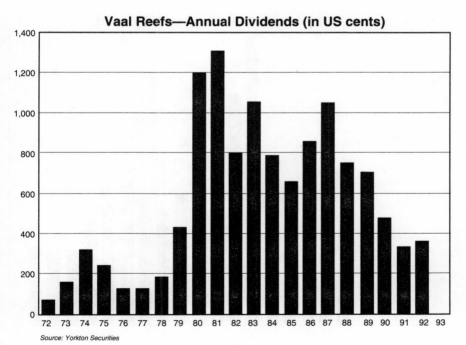

Vaal Reefs—Annual Dividends (in US cents)

Source: Yorkton Securities

Figure 20-6

223

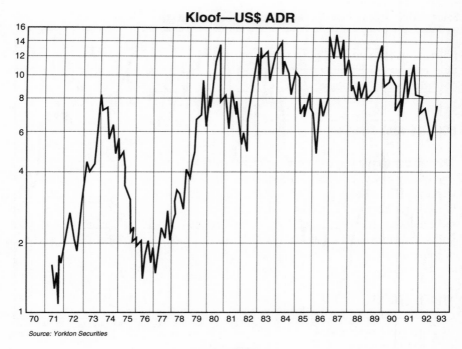

Figure 20-7

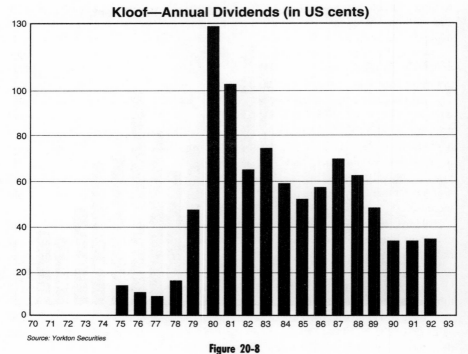

Figure 20-8

prices to operate profitably, and poor ore at high gold prices to maximize the life of their reserves. Right now most of the South African mines, including all the high-cost producers, are "high grading."

POLITICS AND TIMING

The critical element in profiting from these stocks has always been timing. That's true of any stock, of course, but of these more than others because of the political element. Historically the time to buy South African gold stocks has been when blood is running in the streets. Although that overused catch phrase is figurative in most markets, it should be applied literally with these stocks. It is no accident that political disturbances and economic difficulties tend to go together here more than in most places.

WHICH STOCKS?

The few conventional investment advisors who monitor South African golds invariably wind up favoring the long-life, low-cost, heavily capitalized "supermines," like Vaal Reefs (30+ year-life, $150 cost/oz. with 190 million shares and $800 million of market capitalization) or Driefontein (50+ year life, $120 cost/oz, with 102 million shares out, an $800 million market capitalization). That approach makes sense with most mining stocks, but not with those in South Africa.

First, if you're not going to hold the stock for 30 years, and if you're afraid the country's political/economic system may not last even five, why pay a huge premium for 30+ years of reserves?

Second, since you are presumably buying these stocks to get leverage on gold, why pay a large premium for less leverage in a low-cost mine? If gold is $350 and costs are $150, profit is $200 per ounce; if gold rises to $550, profits double. But in a mine where costs are $300, profits would multiply by a factor of six. The increase in dividends would track profits in both cases. But where a blue chip may be yielding only 10 percent now, with the prospect of only doubling that dividend, a high-cost mine may be yielding 20 percent now, with the prospect of a sixfold increase.

Third, since to most buyers a mine is a mine is a mine, a small-capitalization company like Loraine (16.4 mil. shares at $0.30, or $5 mil.) or Stilfontein (13.1 mil. shares at $0.65, or $10 million total capitalization) is likely to attract almost as much buying as a Vaal Reefs or a Driefontein, especially when the market gets hot. Obviously, a million dollars flowing into the shares of a little company is going to move the stock a lot more than it would a big one.

I suggest you watch these stocks closely. The returns won't be as spectacular as those of the North American–listed stocks, timing is even more important, and they have some unique risks. But many have 10-to-1 potential nonetheless.

21

Silver and Company

Whoever could make two ears of corn grow upon a spot of ground where only one grew before, would deserve better of mankind than the whole race of politicians put together.

Jonathan Swift

When the price of any commodity is neither more nor less than what is sufficient to pay the rent of the land, the wages of labour, and the profits of the stock employed in raising, preparing, and bringing it to market, according to their natural rates, the commodity is then sold for what may be called its natural price.

Adam Smith

SILVER

Silver was the metal of the '70s. It ran from its officially fixed price of $1.29 in 1971 to close to $50 in 1980, at its manic top. Forty-to-one shots, even over a ten-year period, are a rare treat indeed, and that run made silver a lot of friends for life—folks for whom the metal, along with gold, was as much of an ideological statement or religious artifact as it was an investment.

It is unfortunate that the apotheosis was fleeting, and the last thirteen years have treated silver's admirers almost as badly as the preceding ten treated them well. In fact, with silver under $4.00 at the moment, it's down over 90 percent from its peak in dollar terms, and well over 95 percent in real terms, since the dollar has lost about 50 percent of its purchasing power since 1980. The real (after inflation) figure is what counts.

Figure 21-1 shows silver's rise from controlled levels in the '60s, through its fall from grace over the last decade. Several times, after a sharp fall or a long period of quiescence, the metal experienced a significant rally, each time from lower levels. The world financial system was on thin ice throughout the '80s, and silver has long had a quasi-monetary role as a so-called "poor man's gold." There was good reason to suspect, therefore, whenever silver rallied, that it was more than just a rally. It might be a resumption of the great bull market, on its way to a final climax.

Take a look at Figure 21-1 for a minute. Investors who are shell-shocked by the last thirteen years' price history will say, not unreasonably, that there's no good reason why the downtrend should end just now. Maybe, they conjecture, we will see $3, or less, before the absolute bottom. Maybe. But what difference does it make? The general price level has more than tripled since 1971, and has about quadrupled since 1967; silver fluctuated mostly between its "official" price of $1.29 and just over $2 for the six-year period from 1967 to 1973. In real terms silver is cheaper now at $4 in 1993 than it was 25 years ago (see Figure 21-2). In fact, it's selling for the equivalent of less than one 1967 dollar per ounce.

PAST AS PROLOGUE

Most of the world's raw materials are, like silver, extremely cheap in real terms. The long-term trend of commodity prices is being driven inevitably downward by technological efficiencies in both production and consumption. But the fear and greed that accompany the kind of monetary crisis we're likely to see can easily swamp the long-term trend for brief periods.

The government arbitrarily pegged silver at $1.29 per ounce for decades. But decreasing supply, increasing demand, and a depreciating dollar put upward pressure on the price of silver. By the middle of the 1960s, the distortions became apparent, as U.S. coinage, which was 90 percent silver at the time, started to disappear from circulation. The government attributed this disappearance of silver coins to the rise of vending machines, even though they certainly knew it was caused by hoarding. Even with two billion ounces of silver in their stockpile, plus all the circulating coinage that was available for melting, the government couldn't keep the price down.

By 1974 silver's price had risen to $6, in the general commodity boom that peaked early that year. It drifted off to between $4 and $5 over the next five years, until it started a lunatic assault on the $50 level in the late '70s. When gold collapsed 50 percent from $200 in early 1975 to just over $100 in late 1976, and platinum did even worse, silver was almost stable; it was the strongest of the metals during the '70s.

Today anyone who is looking at precious metals, and that's almost nobody, is thinking about gold, platinum, and, to a lesser degree, palladium. Silver is discredited, a dead duck. Even copper receives more respect. Silver is, relatively and absolutely, the weakest not only of all the metals but of all the commodities. The gold/silver ratio is at an all-time high of around 90 to 1 (see Figure 21-3). Silver is selling far below its cost of production, and nobody could care less. It is, in other words, a classic bottom.

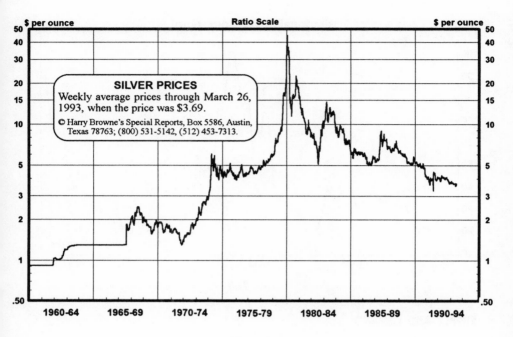

SILVER PRICES
Weekly average prices through March 26,
1993, when the price was $3.69.

© Harry Browne's Special Reports, Box 5586, Austin,
Texas 78763; (800) 531-5142, (512) 453-7313.

Figure 21-1

Real Silver Prices
(In Constant 1850 Dollars)

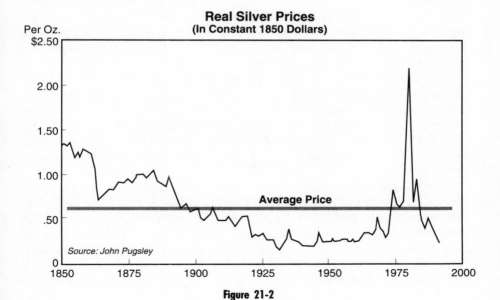

Figure 21-2

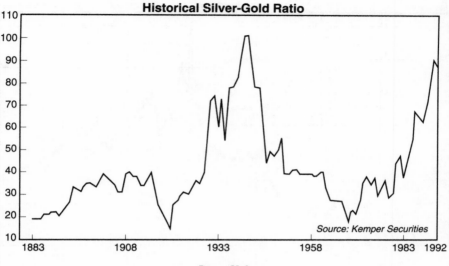

Figure 21-3

SUPPLY AND DEMAND

The arguments for and against silver have always revolved around supply and demand. Just as a substantial supply/demand deficit supported the bulls when the metal was priced at several times current levels, a supply/demand surplus makes people feel the metal is going nowhere now. The '70s bull market was driven largely by a lack of supply, and the '80s bear market, by a surfeit of supply with dropping demand. My conjecture is that the '90s will show a steady supply and surging demand, mostly from investors.

Throughout the '70s worldwide production averaged between 300 and 350 million ounces per year; estimates are that annual production is now around 375 million ounces. The world went from a production deficit of 100 to 200 million ounces per year for many years to a surplus of 50 to 100 million during most of the '80s. Since 1990, the supply/demand picture has again reverted to a deficit approaching 50 million oz/year, Table 21-1 shows. There are 31,000 ounces to a metric tonne.

Consumption dropped radically in the industrial world in response to the high prices of the late '70s and early '80s. Free world consumption ran in the 400 to 500 million ounce range throughout the '60s and '70s, and then collapsed to the 350 million range following the 1980 price spike. In the United States, consumption ran about 200 million ounces a year in 1970, and it has been dropping consistently since then to the 115 million ounce range at present.

What will happen next? My guess is that over the last decade all the fat was cut

Table 21-1   Supply/Demand: Silver (000 Tonnes)

	1987	1988	1989	1990	1991	1992E	1993P
Mine Production	10.90	11.10	11.40	11.70	11.50	11.70	12.00
Other:							
a) Scrap	3.50	3.80	3.60	3.40	3.60	3.60	3.60
b) Coin Melt	0.30	0.30	0.20	0.15	0.10	0.10	0.10
	3.80	4.10	3.80	3.55	3.70	3.70	3.70
Indian Dishording	0.50	0.40	0.10	—	—	—	—
Government Disposals	0.60	0.30	0.30	0.30	0.30	0.35	0.30
Net Imports from E. Bloc	0.20	0.20	0.20	0.30	0.40	0.35	0.35
Total Supply	16.00	16.10	15.80	15.85	15.90	16.10	16.35
Industrial Demand	13.40	14.30	14.50	15.80	15.90	16.30	16.80
Coinage	0.90	0.80	0.80	1.00	0.90	0.85	1.00
Total Demand	14.30	15.10	15.30	16.80	16.80	17.15	17.80
Implied Stock Increase,							
Commercial and Private	1.70	0.90	0.60	−1.00	−0.80	−1.10	−1.60
Average Price ($ 1oz)	7.04	6.54	5.50	4.83	4.04	3.96A	N/A
WBMS, USBM, KSI estimates							

Source: Kemper Securities.

out of silver consumption. Hereafter, development of new uses, many in response to the low price, should reverse the trend again. A nasty recession, not to mention the Greater Depression, will hurt industrial demand. On the other hand, almost all silver production is a byproduct of base metals mining, which should drop substantially when times get tough.

Meanwhile, the monetary chaos likely to accompany such an event should drive a lot of buying into silver. At current prices it will be a natural refuge from inflation and bank collapses, for the average man and sophisticated speculator alike.

There are big "X Factors," of course, but most of them are likely to be favorable. As the Third World in general, and China in particular, industrialize and become more prosperous, they will use more silver and more of every other raw material. By now everyone has heard the argument about what will happen to consumption when a billion Chinese start taking family pictures. The bottom line is that consumption is likely to keep heading up from these levels.

What is really going to make silver move is the desire of investors/hoarders/speculators to hold it or sell it. And the point is that when the world economy is on the ragged edge, at a time when the metal's real price is down 95 percent from its high, at a twenty-year low in dollar terms, an all-time low in real terms, and this after a ten-year bear market, then the next move will be on the upside. And the potential for a meteoric move is great. It has been twenty years since silver looked this good.

WHAT TO DO

There are three basic approaches to capitalizing on the situation: coins, stocks, and bonds. Any of them is a suitable vehicle, depending on how much risk you want to take. You can also trade silver futures (see chapter 22), and silver options are also available.

Coins

Pre-1966 (after 1966 they're all a copper-nickel combination designed to resemble silver) U.S. silver dimes, quarters and half-dollars have sold for about 1 percent to 5 percent above melt value through most of the last decade. That in itself is an indicator of how depressed the market is, because in the past they carried a premium of up to 35 percent. About 715 ounces of silver are in a $1,000 face amount bag, and with $4.00 silver, a bag will cost about $2,900. If someone asked me now what is the most prudent and intelligent thing to do with a few thousand dollars, I would say to buy these coins, put them away and forget about them.

Stocks

Most gold and base-metal mines produce significant amounts of silver, although revenues from silver are trivial at $4.00 per ounce. If silver rises, most mining stocks will get a boost. The real leverage is with the outfits that specialize in the metal. Table 21-2 shows the U.S. companies to watch.

ASARCO is by far the biggest silver producer of the group, at roughly 9.3 million ounces per year, but since that amounts to only about 3 percent of its gross revenue, it isn't a very direct silver play. Most of its revenue comes from the smelting, refining, and mining of copper, lead, and zinc.

Hecla is perceived as a silver company, producing 4.5 million ounces annually, but its revenues from its 100,000 ounces of gold production are close to double those from silver.

Sunshine is the most-leveraged company, fairly loaded with debt. It is interesting that its 2.4 million ounces of silver production account for only 20 percent of its annual revenues. They also mine some gold and copper, but the bulk of their earnings now comes from oil and gas. What should attract your attention about Sunshine are its debt and its preferred stock.

SUNSHINE CONVERTIBLES

You can buy Sunshine common, but there are several better ways of profiting from a turnaround in the fortunes of the company and its products. Sunshine has about $200 million of long-term debt. Their 8 percent of 2006 bonds trade at $27.

Table 21-2

	Symbol	Price	1980–1993 Range	
			Hi	*Lo*
Asarco	AR	25⅜	48.50	10
Coeur D'Alene	CDE	12⅞	36.00	1.5
Hecla	HL	8⅛	26.60	6
Sunshine	SSC	¾	26.25	½

Assuming Sunshine survives (I think it will) these bonds, with 30 percent current yields provide an extraordinary return. How risky are these bonds? Risk is relative, of course. They're less risky than the stock, but they're still junk bonds.

Sunshine also has an issue of 8.1 million shares of a cumulative preferred. This security, trading on the NYSE at about $3½, is slated to pay $1.19 in dividends, either cash or the equivalent in common stock; currently the dividend is being passed, but accumulated. As a bonus to the yield, this preferred is redeemable at $11.94 per share when the company elects to redeem. Obviously, as the company's fortunes improve, the preferred will appreciate.

CONCLUSION

The last time silver sold at these prices was a generation ago. The supply/demand balance isn't what it was then, but it's turning after ten years of surplus. What's really going to move the metal is the desire of people to hold it, and the right conditions could easily take it to $10 or $20. It's guessing to pick either a price or a date, but you're now looking at a major bottom in the market. Use one of the methods above to take advantage of it.

COPPER

In *Strategic Investing* I recommended buying heavily margined, distant-delivery copper futures when the metal was in the 60-cent range. In 1982, copper's price was substantially below the cost of production in most places, about $.90, and it was just a matter of waiting for the inevitable to happen. In early 1987 it did, albeit after a somewhat longer wait than I had anticipated, with the red metal exploding to over $1.50 by late 1988. At this point, with copper trading at $1, there's little speculative appeal, for several reasons.

First, huge production increases are coming on stream all over the world. Gigantic mines in Indonesia, Chile, and elsewhere will be cranking out hundreds of thousands of tons of copper per annum.

Second, all the new deposits are very low-cost, $0.40–$0.70 per pound. That means the mines will stay in production and new ones will keep coming on stream, unless the price drops well below those levels. A lot of inefficient copper mines will join the ranks of the departed, but the big new projects are not going away.

If anything, the cost of producing copper will drop further because of new leaching technology (Solvent Extraction-Electro Winning, or SX-EW) similar to that used in gold mines, except that it employs sulfuric acid, which is almost free, instead of a cyanide solution. Like the heap-leach gold mines, leach-process copper mines can use extremely low-grade ore. A further advantage of the SX-EW process is its environmental friendliness. It eliminates the need for costly (about 30 cents per pound) and incredibly dirty smelting.

Third, copper consumption follows a downturn in the world economy. There's an old saying that every bull market has a copper roof, since consumption of this industrial metal peaks at the top of an economic boom.

Fourth, copper isn't a particularly high-tech metal. It's a refugee from the industrial revolution, with relatively few new uses being developed. Worse, old uses are disappearing. The largest copper mine in the world now is AT&T and the rest of the world's telephone companies, all of whom will eventually tear out all their copper wire laid during the last century and replace it with optical fiber.

Currently I do not view copper as a good speculation.

PALLADIUM, PLATINUM—AND NONSENSE

There are six PGMs, or "platinum group metals"—platinum, palladium, rhodium, ruthenium, indium, and osmium. They share similar atomic structures and, as a result, related electrochemical properties and uses. The production of the PGMs is trivial next to that of gold (at about 60 million oz. per year). Platinum production is around 4 million ounces, palladium about 3 million, and all the others together less than 500,000 ounces.

Platinum received a lot of attention in the 1980s, moving from about $150 through most of the 1970s to as high as $650 in 1988, at which time the public was inundated with ads from coin dealers hyping platinum coins and bars. At the time that hype alone served as a tipoff that you did not want to get involved. It is a mistake to participate in markets where there is an immense amount of newfound attention, where the commodity is subjected to intense analysis, where there are wild price moves, and where the public is buying, unless you approach with an eye to going short.

What is platinum worth? There's no fundamental reason for platinum to sell at a premium to gold, and there's good reason to think it could fall substantially. In fact, platinum was once used to counterfeit gold coins because it cost so much less.

The bulls' argument for higher platinum prices hinges mainly around two factors: continuing problems in South Africa, which produces 85 percent of the

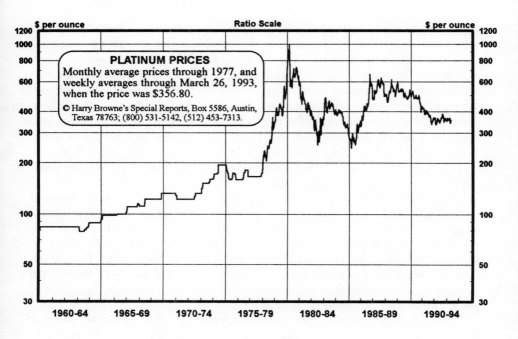

Figure 21-4

world's supply, and increasing demand by investors. Although platinum typically moves with gold whenever people start panicking out of currency and into hard assets, it is purely an industrial metal. Even silver and copper have more traditional use as money. Platinum is certainly more comparable to silver than to gold; central banks do not hold it in their reserves, and it is not money. That means that all the platinum being hoarded will eventually be unloaded when the price is right, just as was silver. It makes as much sense to hoard indium, gallium, or cobalt as it does platinum. Any industrial metal can be profitable if you buy it at the right price. But platinum, selling at a substantial premium, or even parity, to gold, with rising production, a potential collapse in consumption and prices reflecting an artificial mania created by producers and retailers, doesn't qualify. (See Figure 21–4.)

Demand

Demand for platinum grew from 2.6 million ounces, in 1976, to only 2.7 million in 1985 and 3.9 million in 1991. But included, since 1982, in that growth is a new category of demand: hoarding. Hoarding, the same thing as investment, amounted to 45,000 ounces in 1982, 90,000 ounces in 1983, 170,000 ounces in 1984, 430,000 ounces in 1985, 325,000 in 1986, 622,000 in 1987, and 677,000 in 1988.

Investment demand has dropped off in '89, '90 and '91; 75 percent of investment comes from Japan, and the weakness of their financial markets has hurt platinum demand. The minting of platinum coins and medallions by Engelhard and a number of countries, including Mexico, China, Australia, Canada, Switzerland, and the Isle of Man, has made hoarding easy. Investors may have accumulated several million ounces of inventory, which will be ready to come onto the market when fashions change. The price chart of platinum could wind up looking like silver's over the last few years. Like any other industrial metal, when the price gets high enough or when fashions change, when the economy takes a serious downturn or as more progress is made toward better and cheaper automotive catalytic converters, that hoarded platinum is going back on the market.

The main industrial use for platinum is as a catalyst in the petrochemical industry and especially in the pollution-control systems of cars. Development is proceeding on methanol fuels, ceramic engines, greatly improved ignition and injection systems, and a number of other technologies that will either eliminate or significantly reduce the need for current catalytic technology. Apart from those facts, the world has a surfeit of cars, and it's a declining industry. And most of the platinum used in converters will be recovered. You are unlikely to hear of that possibility from popularizers of platinum coins.

In other words, the main reason the metal's boosters say it's going up, and that there's a shortage—investment demand—is just a large surplus disguised as investment inventory. But the investment demand that creates a self-fulfilling prophecy of higher prices also serves to reduce industrial demand and increase production. High platinum prices cause substitution of the metal wherever technically feasible, which is exactly what happened to silver when its price went out of control in the late '70s and early '80s. And it will certainly cause a large increase in supply, which also happened to silver. The platinum Koalas and Maple Leafs now being bought as curiosities or as speculations will be melted down. At some point, the price could collapse by a large percentage, again just like silver.

I find it amusing to see platinum demand projected out years into the future. Typical estimates simply extrapolate industrial demand on a straight line curve. There's absolutely no way of even guessing what it will be with the current shaky world economy. Autocatalyst usage could drop in half—as could all its other usages, which are purely industrial, except for jewelry, about 1.3 million ounces in 1991. But more than 80 percent of jewelry usage is in Japan, and it's hard to envision Japanese demand will continue as their stock and real estate markets collapse.

Supply

Supply, on the other hand, is likely to be much more predictable because of the large capital costs of building a mine. Unlike gold, whose production has been remarkably stable over the last 100 years, annual production of platinum has exploded since WW II, rising from 310,000 ounces in 1946 to present levels of about 4 million ounces. The metal's price strength has stimulated a great deal of exploration activity all over the world and it can mostly be produced at around $200 per ounce.

Most of the new production is coming from outside South Africa, which increasingly obviates the argument about the metal's political risk. With a potential surplus of perhaps 2 million ounces per year, as automotive and Japanese jewelry consumption drops, even while new mine production rises and unloading by investors increases, the price of platinum could collapse in the next few years. This is not to say it won't go higher over the short run.

The best argument for the price of platinum rising faster than gold is that there is much less of it around than gold. Just as with stocks, a million dollars flowing into something with a small capitalization will send the price flying, whereas with something the size of Exxon there might not even be an uptick. That's why platinum has usually gone to premiums over gold in bull markets, and discounts in bear markets. Rhodium is an even better example. That obscure PGM became important to the manufacture of catalytic converters, and its price ran from $250 an ounce in the early '80s to $7,000 an ounce in 1991, before retreating to around $2,000 an ounce. But volatility has nothing to do with these metals' merits as long-term investments.

Why bother trying to second-guess these things? In a good speculation you can build an overwhelming case that something is a one-way street, preferably something that has reached an extreme in price.

PALLADIUM

The problems of the platinum market lead to some conclusions about palladium. Palladium has similar, perhaps even better, potential for a supply cut-off than platinum, since 60 percent comes from the former U.S.S.R., and most of the rest from South Africa. Palladium is substituted for gold in dentistry and for both platinum and rhodium in auto catalysts because of its relatively low cost. With about the same production, most of the same uses, one-fourth the cost per ounce, and without the overhanging speculative inventories, it seems to me the better deal. Who knows, someone may start minting palladium coins and create an artificial shortage.

The bottom line is that I think you are better off buying a futures contract of palladium than of platinum, and you are unlikely to get hurt if you do so at present palladium price levels ($100 per ounce).

22

The Raw Materials of Civilization

> The actual price at which any commodity is commonly sold is called its market price. It may either be above or below, or exactly the same with its natural price.
>
> Adam Smith

The commodities traded on North America's twelve futures exchanges are the raw materials of civilization. They belong in your portfolio as much as do stocks, bonds, cash, real estate, gold, and other assets. Broad diversification is important, yet most people are completely undiversified into commodities, which they consider "speculative."

There is no question that futures can be speculative; the leverage available makes it possible to turn $10,000 into $1 million with a good move. For instance, from mid-1972 to late 1974, each 112,000-pound sugar contract went from being worth $5,600 at $0.05, to $72,000 at $0.60. With maximum leverage $10,000 would have positioned you in fifteen contracts, leading to a million dollar profit—if you had had the nerve, and the patience, to stay in the market for thirty months. Almost every commodity shows similar movement cyclically.

Taking a very long-term view, raw material prices have continuously dropped since the industrial revolution, as technology made them cheaper to produce. But what's basically been a 200-year bear market has always been punctuated with explosive reversals of the trend due to manmade and natural disasters. Owning commodities usually amounts to a bet on the Four Horsemen. There's a time and a place for everything.

We can't predict when things will skyrocket, but we can analyze when the odds are high that something will happen, and what the cost of waiting for it to happen will be. The most important question about any investment is: What is the downside? At the prices prevailing in early 1993, with the Commodity Research Bureau (CRB) Index of 23 commodities selling at 200, I see little downside in commodities. But before considering putting any money in these markets, it makes sense to look at why they move the way they do, often going from panic lows to manic highs.

GOVERNMENT: FRIEND OF THE SPECULATOR

Two factors move the commodity markets: natural forces, and politics. In a free market, we would deal only with the former, primarily crop yields, which is largely a question of predicting the weather. That is not easy to do, but basically amounts to knowing that in good years you get high crop yields, and a drop in prices; in bad years you get low yields and higher prices. Natural forces aren't necessarily predictable, but at least they do not insult intuitive common sense when they move markets.

Government quotas, subsidies, supports, taxes, and marketing regulations are the greatest cause of commodities' volatility; they alternatively cause disruptive shortages and wasteful surpluses. Government intervention gives the appearance of stability over the short-run, but at great cost to both the producer and consumer in the long-run. This offers great opportunities to speculators.

Sometimes government will artificially depress prices for years, as they did with gold and silver throughout the 1960s; the eventual result is an upward explosion in price as the commodities play catch-up. The losers in that example were the taxpayers, whose funds are used to suppress prices, the mining industry, while prices were held down, and precious metal users, after prices rose. Astute speculators saw the distortion and captured their profits as, during the 1970s, silver ran from $1.29 to nearly $50 and gold ran from $35 to over $800.

Sometimes government will artificially support prices for years, as they are now doing with sugar. Because of taxes and quotas, sugar imports cost American consumers about $.22 a pound, even though the world market price averaged about 8 cents through the '80s. The losers are U.S. consumers, who typically pay about $3 billion extra per year, low-cost foreign producers, and the environment of the Florida Everglades, which suffers tremendous pollution and water level disruption from the artificial and uneconomic sugar industry. The winners are domestic growers, who lobby ferociously and, eventually, the speculators who are positioned when the U.S. government is once again forced to capitulate and sugar prices drop.

Sometimes government will subsidize farmers in ways that are harder to quantify in dollars. In California, for instance, most crops are grown on desert land that is productive only because of irrigation. The farmers are granted the water at trivial cost, while in some years city dwellers have to limit the length of showers they take. When market forces reassert themselves, you can expect produce price rises to reflect higher costs. Although it will be disruptive at the time, society will gain as the water is used in more productive areas. Of course, there will be huge profits for properly positioned speculators.

The resurgence of free market ideas, combined with the massive losses the government runs on agricultural programs, should lead to a decrease in government economic intervention. If this happens, inefficient subsidized farmers will find a new line of work, production surpluses will disappear, government agricultural expenditures will plummet, and the whole current commodities mess would stabilize. That will probably happen sometime in the '90s, from lack of government funds rather than from any intellectual convictions.

Even trivial, but politically connected, industries are tremendously costly. For instance, U.S. beekeepers cost taxpayers up to $100 million per year. The $60 billion spent by the Department of Agriculture (USDA) each year is almost entirely wasted and misallocated. From 1980 to 1992, direct federal agricultural subsidies alone were over $162 billion, plus interest, of course, since all the money is borrowed at this point.

The net result of government farm subsidies and regulations is not only that the United States has been damaged economically but (to the chagrin of jingoists who used to say, "They may have the oil, but we have the food") that America has been substantially compromised as an agricultural power. Planted acreage for corn has dropped from 82 million acres in 1982 to 75 million in 1992; for oats, from 14 million to 11 million; for wheat, from 86 million to 70 million.

One major reason acreage has dropped is the USDA's "set aside" program, intended to restrict supply in order to raise prices. But raising prices in the United States shrinks demand as foreigners buy their food elsewhere. So the USDA naturally has a program of export subsidies, as well. Despite the billions of dollars misallocated to subsidize exports, the export of grains collapsed during the '80s. Soybean exports went from 929 million bushels in 1981 to 560 million in 1991; corn, from 1,997 million bushels to 1,725; wheat, from 1,771 million bushels, to 1,068.

Meanwhile, Argentina, Brazil, Canada, and Australia have stepped up their exports of these commodities. Paradoxically, the U.S. is on its way to officially becoming a net importer of raw foodstuffs. I say "official" because the United States has undoubtedly run a multibillion dollar agricultural balance-of-trade deficit for years due to imports of marijuana, cocaine, and opium products. But that's another story.

Governments worldwide meddle in agriculture. There are plenty of inefficient but politically well-connected farmers everywhere, producing surpluses at taxpayers' expense.

The Organization for Economic Cooperation and Development reported that in 1990 its 24 member countries paid $176 billion in subsidies to farmers, equaling 44 percent of the total value of all crops and livestock they produced. The United States accounted for $36 billion, and the European Community paid subsidies of $82 billion, equaling 48 percent of output. The Japanese paid subsidies of $31 billion, equaling 68 percent of total production. These subsidies amounting, on average, to half the value of the goods produced are economically unsustainable, and eventually governments will be forced to eliminate them. As subsidies are eliminated, commodity prices will tend to rise—at least initially—as inefficient farmers and marginal land are squeezed out. That would not hurt consumers if their taxes no longer had to support the immense costs of subsidies. But perhaps that would be too simple. Rather than just deregulate, it would be more in character for the powers that be to create the conditions for a famine in order to get prices up to subsidize inefficient farmers. You may think I'm stretching the point. But the U.S. government caused the slaughter and burial of whole herds of livestock, and poured tons of milk in the gutter during the '30s in a futile attempt to raise prices, even while many people couldn't afford to eat.

One thing is certain: the USDA doesn't grow any food. Yet this bureaucracy has grown like a cancer. In 1900, when over 39 percent of the American population lived on farms, the USDA had a budget of $4 million; today, when less than 2 percent of Americans live on farms, it has a budget of more than $60 billion. Total farm income in 1991 was only $45 billion. In 1950 there were 10 million farmers and the USDA employed 84,000 people. Today the USDA has a staff of 129,000 but there are only 2.9 million farmers.

Why is agriculture such a heavily subsidized industry? Governments everywhere want to limit imports and add to exports, so they encourage the uneconomic production of food; it's about as intelligent as Honduras subsidizing an automotive industry. In addition, the rulers of each silly political subdivision want domestic food security in case they start a war or do something to cause an embargo by their neighbors. And producers always want to sell their product for as much as possible, while consumers want it to sell for as little as possible. So there's a natural tendency for government to try to make everyone happy. For an apple with a market price of X, they may try to give the producer 2X, while selling to the consumer for 1/2X, making up for the difference with taxes, debt, and inflated currency.

Sometimes subsidies are intended to "create employment," which may be the most stupid purpose of all, since "advanced" countries were able to advance because people down on the farm were liberated to do something else. The United States has progressed from a nation of many small, poor farmers to a few, mostly large and wealthy farmers. It would be better if their numbers dropped to 1 percent, or less. And the same is true of every industry; the key to immense wealth is to have fewer people producing more, but selling it for lower prices, even while earning higher incomes through efficiency.

Some government officials are aware of the consequences of all these subsidies. But they also realize that eliminating subsidies would unwind all the distortions and misallocations of capital that have been cranked into the system over decades. That would be a good thing, but no politician wants to see it happen while he's in office. So the ticking bomb is handed off to the next administration.

THE SECULAR TREND

When you compare the prices of manufactured goods to the prices of the raw commodities used to make them, it is immediately apparent that the real price of raw materials has gone down considerably, relative to the products they're made into. Of course, just because something is cheap doesn't mean it's a bargain. Commodities have been getting cheaper for the last two centuries, and there are at least two good reasons—improving technology and increasing capital—why the trend should continue for a long time to come.

First, as technology advances, yields will be greater for ever-lower inputs of capital and labor. Slash-and-burn techniques were replaced by plowing; the oxcart was replaced by the tractor. Specially formulated and systematically applied fertilizers have supplanted sporadic ox droppings; genetically selected seeds have largely replaced the homegrown varieties. Pesticides and herbicides are eliminating damage by pests, and new breakthroughs are being made practically every day to increase yields and reduce costs. Grain yields per acre, for instance, have tripled over the past few decades and may double over the next twenty years. Technology is now, and has always been, the driving force that increases wealth and standards of living.

That relates to the second long-term trend driving down prices: the accumulation of capital. The more wealth in a society, the less each additional increment is worth; abundance leads to low prices. A surfeit of capital enables producers to invest in the land, labor, and technology required to produce more. That's why a hamburger in New York costs maybe 25 percent of what one does in Zaire's Kinshasa, despite the fact the average New Yorker earns 100 times as much money as the average Zaïrois.

The secular trend for commodities is down, but that has nothing to do with what happens over the next couple of years. Just as the Greater Depression is countercyclical to the ascent of man, higher commodity prices are countercyclical to the long-term trends I have described. Yet this short-term trend could make you a fortune over the next few years.

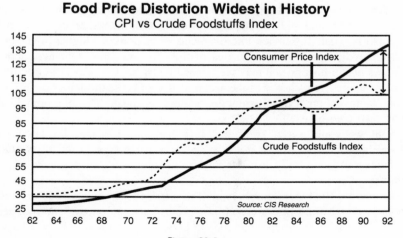

Food Price Distortion Widest in History
CPI vs Crude Foodstuffs Index

Source: CIS Research

Figure 22-1

A BREAK IN THE TREND

There are people, including almost everyone in the Green movement (even though the Club of Rome had to recant much of its gloomy *Limits to Growth Report* of 1972), who believe massive shortages are inevitable. These people generally trot out only those arguments that fit their ideology, whether the arguments are rigorously researched, or not. They have a vested political interest in representing us all grubbing for roots and berries to stave off starvation while slowly freezing in the dark, because our fear of such a future allows the imposition of all kinds of government controls. The fact that government actions are almost the only way to cause such a nightmare in the first place is beside the point. These types consider control an end in itself.

But it is true that current farming methods do have their own set of problems. The suburbs continue to eat into the most productive farmland each year. Vast amounts of agriculture, and most of that in California and Arizona, depend on irrigation. That water is heavily subsidized and will become unavailable as economic and population pressures build. Chemical fertilizers have an adverse long-term effect on the soil, which is itself a living system. Pesticides and herbicides destroy the bacteria, insects, worms, and other life forms that make the soil a system. They also slowly poison groundwater, even while their intended prey grow resistant to them. Hybridized strains of plants, although they tend to have very high yields, usually are not as hardy as their naturally evolved progenitors and could be devastated by some new pest. And since mass crops today are grown from just a few varieties in vast monocultures, rather than from many localized varieties as in the past, any problems that arise are disseminated widely.

But none of this argues for the end of the world, just for higher prices. These and other problems can, and almost certainly will, be solved by technology, capital, and time. Or perhaps they'll just become nonproblems, as technology leapfrogs over them. That is what happened when coal appeared, just in time to obviate the need for wood from rapidly disappearing forests. Oil, in turn, relieved the problems presented by coal. Efficiency improvements in response to higher prices quashed the supposedly apocalyptic oil crises of the '70s and '80s. Our next short-term crisis, no matter how grim it may seem when it arrives, will appear as primitive and trivial a hundred years hence as the accumulation of horse droppings on city streets, before the invention of the automobile, seems to us today. The long run will almost surely take care of itself.

But we could suffer from bad luck and bad management, as I pointed out in chapter 1, because that's what government brings to the party. Government intervention usually leads to disastrous shortages or to equally disastrous surpluses.

Remember that few famines really ever resulted from natural causes; low food supplies or high food prices are almost exclusively caused by state intervention. Somalia has an acute famine, and the old U.S.S.R., which used to be a large food exporter before 1917, has had a chronic one for the last seventy-five years. The causes are identical.

Meanwhile, the governments of the West create massive agricultural surpluses through subsidies and import/export shell games. Its consequence, I do not doubt, will be a solution like Roosevelt's was, pouring milk in the gutter and burying piglets—a costly, stupid, debacle.

The question of "whither agricultural prices" over the next few years is analogous to the inflation-deflation argument. Although real prices will drop long-term, a major contracyclical development will no doubt occur to send them skyhigh over the next few years. The continuing collapse of the dollar since 1985 has driven commodities denominated in either real terms ("constant" dollars) or strong foreign currencies to almost their lowest levels in history.

You can profit by taking positions in the commodities, which are at extremely low levels, much as you would an undervalued stock, and holding them until they become cyclically "overvalued." How do you know when to take a position? Two factors are crucial: historical price and production costs.

HISTORICAL PRICES AND TRADING VOLUME

People have become complacent with the bargain-basement commodity prices of the eighties, especially since 1990. Just as everyone thought the high prices for oil, real estate, and practically every kind of hard asset would last forever in the late 1970s, they now expect that depressed commodity prices are here to stay. And it doesn't matter if they know better intellectually, because the markets move on emotions, mainly fear and greed.

Historical prices are important to watch if you believe that the way to profit in the markets is to "buy low and sell high." Everyone will pay lip service to that truism, but before taking a position, few actually examine the price history of a stock to determine how cheap or dear it is relative to where it's been in the past. Historical prices cannot tell you when to buy, but they are a great help in showing you when not to buy.

Prices have been flirting with historical lows for years, and when the market moves, the next move is likely to occur with a vengeance and make up for lost time. Figure 22-2 tells the story:

Volume is another related indicator; prices and volume tend to track each other in most markets. High volume usually indicates a high level of interest from investors. Low volume correlates with lack of investor interest and low prices.

The volume of financial futures contracts has expanded greatly in both absolute and relative terms over the last few years, while the absolute and relative volume of agricultural commodity contracts has tumbled. That is a tipoff that financials are "high" and tangibles are "low," exactly the opposite of patterns at the beginning of the '80s.

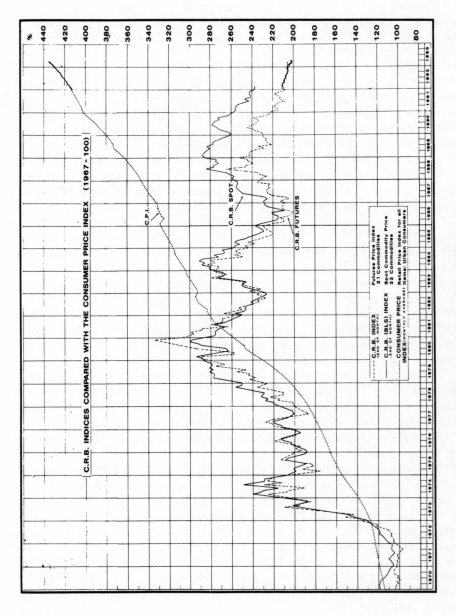

Figure 22-2 Long-term Chart of Futures vs. CPI

COSTS OF PRODUCTION

The second factor to watch in order to determine when to buy and sell is costs of production. All commodity prices tend to fluctuate with their costs of production. If the market price is too "low," farmers will grow something else or leave the business. If the market price is too "high," farmers will plant fence row to fence row to take advantage of it. At the same time, consumers adjust their demand based on prices.

Two types of costs are involved in farming: fixed and variable. Fixed costs are mainly represented by land; variable costs are such things as seed, fertilizer, and labor. In some areas total costs per acre are high because land is rich and therefore expensive, but because yields are also high, cost per unit of produce can be low. In other areas the yields per acre may be low, but since land (fixed) costs are also low, the costs per bushel can be comparable. Areas under intensive irrigation such as the Southwest, have very high costs but can yield between two and three times what poor lands do.

The farmer cannot control the prices he receives, and has only marginal control over costs; the main variable he can influence is yields per acre. That is the underlying reason yields have more than doubled in most commodities over the last two decades.

There's obviously a lot of leeway in what constitutes "costs," depending on whether a farmer owns or rents his land, what taxes or subsidies he can qualify for, what accounting systems are used, what happens to currency values, and the level of interest rates, among many other factors. The following are some ranges of costs at the moment: corn—$2.50–$3.25 per bushel; soybeans—$5.25–$6.50 per bushel; wheat—$3.50–$4.50 per bushel; and cotton—$0.65–$0.75 per pound.

As of early 1993, almost every basic agricultural commodity is selling for less than its costs of production. That means the next big move is likely to be up. In addition, farmers will receive a huge boost from inflation. Agricultural commodities are a sound long-term holding. But your psychology and the methods you use to take advantage of price moves are of far more importance than the direction of the markets. That is why most people walk away from the futures markets with empty pockets.

LOSERS

Only a few people are involved in the futures markets. On the one hand that is a pity, since the possibilities of profiting through periodic buying and selling of the raw materials of civilization are vast. But because most people seem to have a hard time using adequate margin, trading discipline, and conservative strategies, it's perhaps just as well.

Many people seem to feel the futures markets are too risky and/or unpredictable. They are undoubtedly right; the worst investment you can make is one you do not understand. If you are not willing to do some homework, then it's wisest to stay away from futures. But the best solution, if you care about your financial well-being, is to dig in and familiarize yourself.

Every study I'm aware of shows that between 80 percent and 95 percent of the amateurs who trade futures lose money. That is why I do not believe in "trading" commodities. Between the market's short-term randomness, commissions, and your own psychology whipsawing your trades, it is unlikely the results will be very good.

Trying to second-guess and trade the markets are one thing. Accumulating the raw materials of civilization for the long-term when they are selling for historic lows and at below production costs, as a bet on the incompetence of government, is something else entirely.

It's all a matter of timing, or rather, the absence of it. If you buy right and have patience, you do not need timing. Buying straw hats in the winter isn't so much a question of timing, as it is a matter of patience.

In *Strategic Investing* I recommended buying commodities; the Commodities Research Bureau (CRB) Index was at about 220 in 1982. It was a good call; the index was close to a historic low. It subsequently ran to 280 in 1984, retreated to 200 in 1986, and rose to 270 again by 1989. Now, in 1993, the market is presenting another, even better, cyclical opportunity with the CRB index at around 200.

TIME FRAMES

Humans tend to believe that a trend in motion will continue indefinitely, and the longer it continues, the more confident they become. Most people buy investments only after they've established "good track records," that is, after they've already risen greatly in price. That is also a major reason why it's not easy to win the battle for investment survival; investors are always fighting their emotions. It takes courage to buy things that are cheap and in disfavor, and sell those everybody thinks are sure winners.

It is interesting that the vast majority of commodity speculators are losers, but the vast majority of real estate buyers have been winners. Why do these markets seem to offer different odds? In part the long-term trend of commodities has always been down, but has been rising for real estate. Those long-term trends are likely to continue, regardless of what will happen in the '90s. But other factors also affect the odds of success in these two areas.

Commodity traders have the odds loaded against them. Transaction costs are, cumulatively, very high; commodity traders often wind up spending 50 percent to 100 percent of their starting capital in commissions annually. Tax treatments are typically punitive. Real estate buyers have long been treated to massive tax breaks, whereas commodities buyers are penalized. They must, for instance, pay taxes on profitable open positions each year, even if they do not sell them. Commodities, unlike property, never provide rental income. And while leverage is great with both, real estate speculators do not have to post more margin money if their property values decline.

The biggest single factor, however, is probably psychological, namely the length of the investors' time horizon. Players in real estate tend to be in for the long haul; those in commodities watch the screens by the moment, and often scalp for the smallest profit.

If you are on the right side of a market, you want to let your profits run and give the trend time to be your friend. That is a major reason why real estate has treated the average investor so well since the last depression. Property has always been a production to sell, so most people are loath to do so unless they have to and they tend hold onto real estate during temporary downturns; its very illiquidity helps investors during a bull market. As soon as a major bull market gets under way, most commodity investors are on the phone to their brokers to cut their profits.

I suggest, therefore, that you treat selected commodities the way most people treat a good piece of property. Buy a contract of wheat, or a selection of commodities, at the right price for cash, and hold on until the market turns manic and everyone wants to buy it from you. The holding time for commodities isn't anywhere near what it would be for property, but real estate techniques are the model for success. The maximum holding time for a commodity is one year—enough time to give farmers a chance to plant and take advantage of high prices.

A PROPER METHOD

Because the long-term trend in commodities is down, it makes no sense to participate unless prices are clearly at some extreme. When they are, you want to be a patient, well-capitalized long-term trader. You want to use these markets to go for long-ball homers, not to scalp for a few cents here and there while being eaten up by commissions.

The key to success in all investing is to correctly determine the relative value of one thing to everything else. To do that, you have to look at the fundamentals. Commodity traders know that fundamentals have little to do with short-term price movements but they do affect long-term price trends. Although most speculators use a lot of leverage (margin), you should use little leverage (margin). And while most traders use only charts and technical indicators, you should use the fundamentals.

A PROPER COMMODITY PORTFOLIO

To establish a position in commodities you can buy (or sell) on conservative margin or you can buy (or sell) options on the commodities. Table 22-1 shows how a portfolio might look as this book goes to press, buying an equal dollar amount, by contract value, of each of the most undervalued commodities. As some prices rise, you would automatically lighten up on them, while adding contracts to positions of those that drop, in order to keep the total dollar amount invested in each commodity

Table 22-1

Future		Contract Size	Price	Value	Margin	Number of Contracts	Total Value
Cocoa	MR 94	10 tn	$1050/tn	$10,500	$2,000	3	$31,500
Coffee	MR 94	37,500 lb	$0.75/lb	$28,125	$3,000	1	$28,125
Corn	DC 94	5,000 bu	$2.50/bu	$12,500	$1,000	3	$37,500
Cotton	MR 94	50,000 lb	$.62/lb	$31,000	$2,000	1	$31,000
Oats	DC 93	5,000 bu	$1.50/bu	$ 7,500	$1,000	5	$37,500
OJ	MY 94	15,000 lb	$0.90/lb	$13,500	$3,000	3	$40,500
Palladium	DC 93	100 oz	$120.00/oz	$12,000	$1,500	3	$36,000
Silver	MY 94	5,000 oz	$4.00/oz	$20,000	$2,000	2	$40,000
Soybeans	MR 94	5,000 bu	$6.00/bu	$30,000	$2,500	1	$30,000
Sugar	MR 94	112,000 lb	$0.11/lb	$12,320	$1,200	3	$36,900
Wheat	DC 93	5,000 bu	$3.15/bu	$15,750	$1,500	2	$31,500

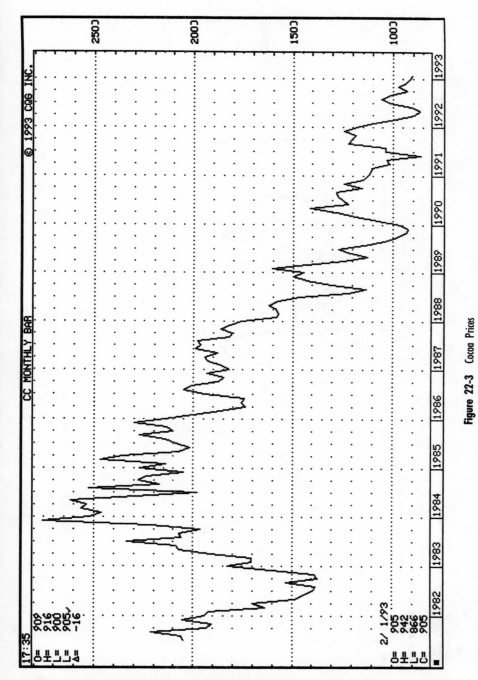

Figure 22-3 Cocoa Prices

Commodity Information Systems, Inc.; tel. (405) 235-5687

(C) Copyright 1993 CQG INC.

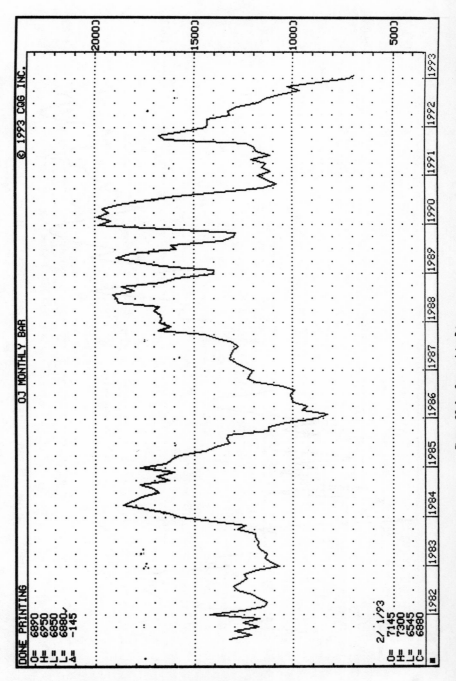

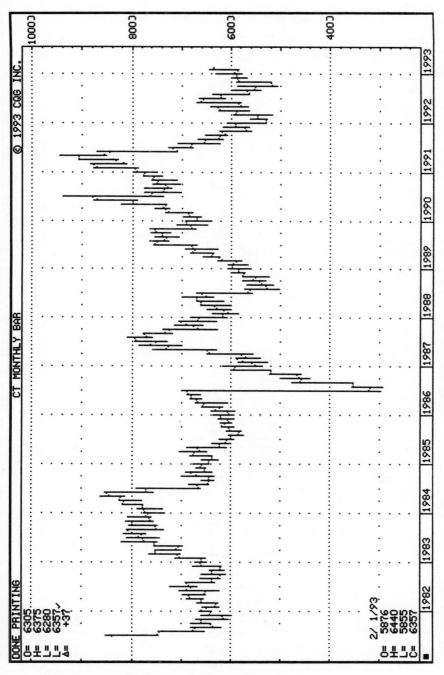

Figure 22-5   Cotton Prices

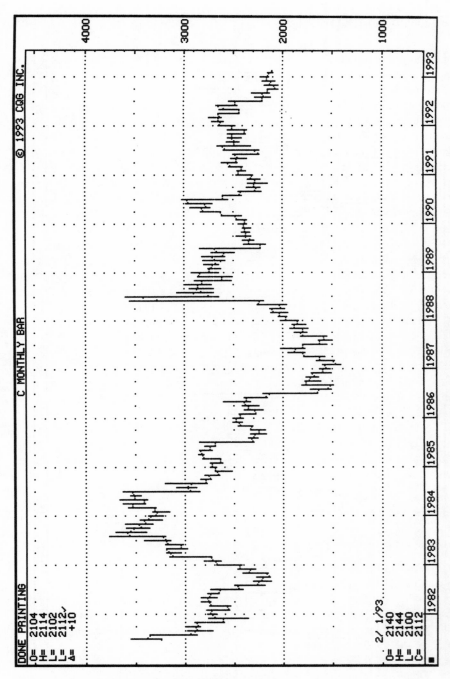

Figure 22-6   Corn Prices

Commodity Information Systems, Inc.; tel. (405) 235-5687

equal. You might adjust your positions monthly. This is a mechanical method that leads you to automatically buy the most depressed commodities while taking profits on the priciest.

Some of the dollar amounts may be intimidating. You might, therefore, prefer to position yourself in copper, corn, silver, soybeans, and wheat on the Mid-America Exchange, where contracts are from one-fifth to one-half regular size. Commission costs, however, are almost the full amount, and prices aren't usually as good. In any event, to purchase roughly equal dollar amounts of each commodity on the major exchanges,—one cotton contract for five oat, three sugar, three cocoa, two silver, two wheat, etc., would cost over $375,000 (roughly $35,000 per commodity) if you posted 100 percent margin. The minimum margin would be about $45,000.

It's a bad idea to use minimum margins; you should be in a position to at least treble the minimum margins. This is a game for only the relatively well-financed investor who understands the risks and is willing to wait patiently. A glance at Figures 22-3 through 22-6 illustrates how low most commodities are, especially if you adjust the prices for the Consumer Price Index (CPI).

Should this basket of underpriced commodities return to their previous dollar highs, the value of the portfolio would about triple, yielding an over $700,000 profit. Should they return to highs in inflation-adjusted terms, that number would look more like $1.5 million. Bear in mind, however, that although we are very close to the bottom, barring a wholesale deflation, there's no way you will get out near a top, barring dumb luck. Still, the odds are very much in favor of a patient bull at this point.

One last note. The collapse of the dollar since 1985 against most major currencies hasn't resulted in any increase in raw materials prices. The dollar's long-term weakness, I suspect, will drive the last nail in the long commodity bear market's coffin.

Questions and Answers

Q: *What about buying farmland as a hedge against higher agricultural prices?*

A: The price of U.S. farmland, in real terms, is at 1930s levels after a long decline since 1980. The explosion of commodity prices in the '70s resulted in farmland doubling and tripling; farming was very profitable for a while. The decline in the dollar's value is likely to accelerate in coming years. It would be unusual to have even more of the generally excellent weather that helped depress prices through much of the 1980s. This argues for higher commodity prices and higher prices for farmland.

You do not want, however, to invest in farmland in California or the Southwest that is under intensive irrigation. These lands are economic only with subsidized water. When economic and political pressures, from city residents who suffer shortages as a result, raise the prices or reduce the supplies and subsidies of that water, a great deal of land will revert to desert.

23

Energy and Its Producers

The natural price . . . is as it were, the central price, to which the prices of all
commodities are continually gravitating.

Adam Smith

I'm not a specialist in oil. An investment interests me only when it's either too
cheap or too dear to ignore. The last time I recommended oil stocks as a group
occurred in *Crisis Investing*, written in 1978. The timing was good since the juniors
I pinpointed subsequently tripled in price by the time the boom crested in 1980.
Since then they have cyclically collapsed, in the best tradition of all resource-based
industries. But now, in 1993, the smaller oil companies again present as good value
as they did back in 1978. It's been a long wait but, if I'm right, the oils have a lot of
catching up to do. And that should be true in spite of a weak overall market.

Speaking as a generalist, a speculator unattached to any investment, except for
its price relative to its value, small oil stocks should have your attention. Let's look
at oil and then at the companies that produce it.

OIL

One part of analyzing commodities is getting a grip on their fundamental values:
supply and demand, cost of production, and historic price range. It's perhaps a little
harder to evaluate oil than other raw materials. For one thing, its price has recently
been very volatile. Crude oil fluctuated around $2 or $3 a barrel for many years
before the 1971 dollar devaluation set off the first "shortage" in the early '70s. It

Real Oil Price
(1981 Dollars per Barrel)

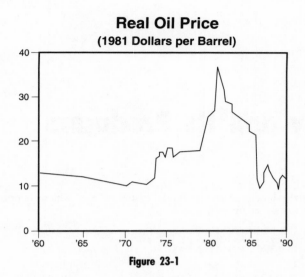

Figure 23-1

then shot up to the $35 level in the early 80s, which is about $60 in 1993 terms, and crashed to $9 in 1986. It has floated around $15 for the last few years, and seems to have settled in the $20 area since 1991. What's the stuff really worth? Figure 23-1, in constant dollars, puts prices in perspective.

Real Price of Gasoline
(1982 dollars per gallon)

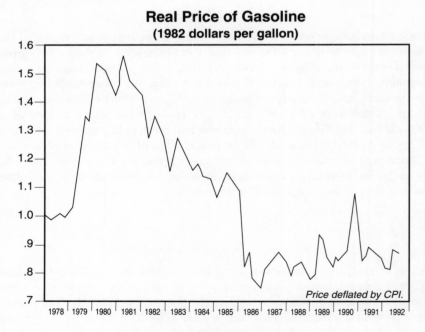

Price deflated by CPI.

Figure 23-2

Oil at $20 isn't at a panic bottom, but it doesn't present a lot of risk, either. In real, constant terms, the black goo is about as cheap as it's ever been. Its typical pre-1971 prices in today's dollars translates to around $7 to $10. You can buy gas now, in constant dollars, as cheaply as you could back in the "gas war" days of the sixties; I just miss the free steak knives. And it's real prices that count, as any Brazilian who's tried to keep track of prices in cruzados can tell you.

The basic elements of the fundamental value of crude are inflation, economic growth, the financial status of major producers, the prospects of war and peace, technological innovation, production costs, and the amount of low-cost reserves available for pumping.

U.S. CONSUMPTION AND PRODUCTION

The Dallas Fed, which specializes in analysis of the oil market, calculates that if the mineral's price stayed around the $15 figure it averaged during most of 1988, U.S. oil consumption would move from its current 17 million barrels per day (m/b/d) to 23 m/b/d over the long run, even without economic growth. They also calculate that it will take $27 oil to keep U.S. consumption at the 17 m/b/d level, even if there's no growth. Figure 23-3 illustrates that conclusion.

They are probably right, and oil is still cheap in the $20 area, even though I do not generally have much confidence in "sophisticated" projections. Perhaps you recall that a decade ago Texaco made some projections at $30 oil that showed it going to at least $60; economists at the World Bank were talking $90. Most projections are extrapolations of current trends; that can be done just as well with a straight rule as a computer. They cannot take the unpredictable events that happen in the real world into account.

Assume, for example, that the Salt Lake "cold fusion" experiment had been

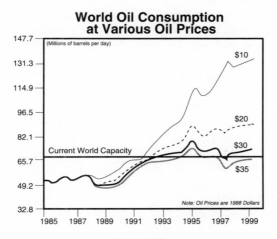

Figure 23-3

successful in some significant respect. It would not only have sent palladium through the roof (it tacked on $40 in early 1989 just on hope) but it would, in time, have reduced the price of oil to its value as a chemical feedstock. Probably a dozen political, economic, or technological events are on the horizon that could radically change reality itself, not to mention the price of oil. No one can predict what will, or will not happen, or when.

That is not to say that events and prices are totally random, since cause does have effect, even if in many cases indirect and delayed. Degree of predictability is what makes speculation different from gambling. But guessing the future of oil prices is no easier than for any other commodity; 90 percent of the time it's an even odds bet and not worth making.

In the long run, it depends on supply and demand, as with anything else. But barring a genuine *force majeure*, long-term oil consumption trends take about ten years to reverse, by most estimates. That's because of the stupendous investment that has been made over many years in both capital goods and consumable items that depend on oil production, distribution, and use. The demand for oil is basically inelastic (consumption changes little, regardless of the price) over the short run, and elastic (consumption changes a lot, depending on price) only over the long run, pretty much as shown in Figure 23-3. Oil is similar to most industrial commodities, and unlike agricultural goods, in that respect.

That still brings us back to the question of where the price of oil is headed. I tend to be a bottom-fisher as opposed to a trend-follower, so I was very bullish in July 1986 after oil prices bounced off a low at under $10. Now, at $20, I'm still a long-term bull on the mineral. But the value is clearly greater in the oil stocks.

THE DECLINE OF BIG OIL IN THE UNITED STATES

Neither the world in general nor the United States in particular is ever going to run out of oil. Shortages will appear only in the event of major government intervention: wars, price controls, embargo, or production quotas. That is because, in a free market, availability is rationed by price. At $5 there would be a huge shortage of oil because everyone would want more, and production would cease; at $100 there would be a glut because everyone would cut consumption to the bone, and production would skyrocket. But left to regulate itself that type of price imbalance never happens in a free market because supply and demand prevent it.

Notwithstanding those points, it is inevitable that the geological supply of oil, the amount of reserves remaining in the ground, as opposed to economic reserves, which depend on the price of oil, will decrease every year. Easy to drill, conveniently located fields were exploited long ago. And all fields eventually deplete and run dry.

Texas, for instance, has been the leading oil state for decades. But in 1988 it produced the lowest amount (698 million barrels) that it had brought forth in forty-

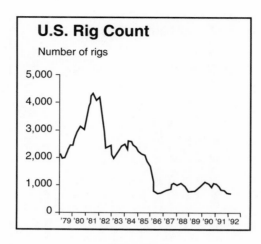

U.S. Rig Count

Number of rigs

Figure 23-4

five years. That production was 25 million barrels less than it was in 1987, and way down from its peak of 1.29 billion in 1972. This trend cannot reverse, even with much higher oil prices, because Texas—like most of the lower forty-eight—has already been extensively explored over the last century; the U.S. is the most heavily drilled piece of geography on earth. Figure 23-4 tells the story.

The rig count tracks the number of new wells being drilled. It is currently 596, the lowest in 52 years; it last stood at that level during World War II, and then only for lack of steel. Even in 1986, when oil went under $10, the rig count never went below 735. Oil imports (7.355 million barrels per day) are at their highest level since 1978; domestic production has fallen to levels last seen in 1961 (7.21 million b/d). The number of crews looking for new deposits fell about 30 percent in 1991 and 1992. Figures 23-5 through 23-7 tell the longer-term story.

The decline in new wells is partly due to advances in the acquisition and interpretation of seismic and geological data; geologists can see below the surface far better than before, and drill fewer holes that turn out dry. So less capital and labor are needed for a given amount of production. The United States is, however, almost drilled out. In the 1950s the average new field ran about 4 million barrels; today the average new field is less than 500,000 barrels. From 1960 to 1980, thirty-six fields of over 100 million barrels were discovered in the United States, despite oil averaging only $3 per barrel most of that time. Since 1980 only three fields of that size have been discovered, even after more intense exploration and a peak oil price of $35 in 1980.

Four times as many wells have been drilled in the United States as the rest of the world combined. They are small wells, averaging only 12.5 b/d, as opposed to the foreign average of 172 b/d. Other countries will eventually move on to their smaller fields; in the United States those fields are being drilled now.

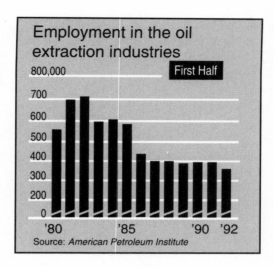

Figure 23-5

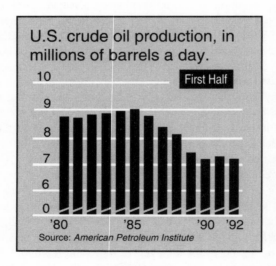

Figure 23-6

Please do not misunderstand me. I'm not in any way endorsing the Ralph Nader/ Barry Commoner/ Jeremy Rifkin/ Club of Rome line that we will all freeze in the dark once we exhaust our resources. Predictions of that nature have been around for more than a century, and they are generally made by those in quest of political power. Their motives are questionable, since they seem willfully ignorant of how the price mechanism both rations demand and creates new supply. We will not run out of oil, but its real price is likely to trend higher because of geological reality.

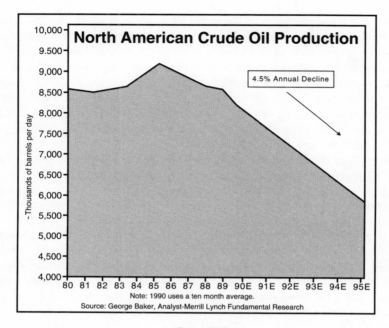

Figure 23-7

It's really nothing to worry about. There's little doubt that—at the right oil price—hundreds of billions more barrels will be recovered from abandoned fields in the United States alone. Technology will advance and new discoveries, like those in Alaska, which is now the biggest producing state, will be made. But the political and environmental problems are increasingly significant, and discovery costs will rise further once the easy oil is found. Production in the United States, which used to be the world's biggest producer, will continue to drop unless prices go much higher.

WORLDWIDE SUPPLY AND DEMAND

On the demand side, the United States used 15.7 million b/d in 1985, 17.4 m/b/d in 1989, and an estimated 17.7 in 1992. About 50 percent of U.S.-consumed oil is imported. But the real growth in consumption will come from outside the United States because that is where 95 percent of the world's population lives, particularly in the Third World. World consumption, now at about 60 million b/d, will likely continue rising at perhaps 2 percent to 3 percent per year, barring some major technological breakthrough.

Even in a very severe economic decline, which is probable, consumption will take only a temporary dip because consumption in places like China, India, Korea, Indonesia, and Brazil will make up for any decreased demand from currently industrialized countries. Most of the world's oil consumption is accounted for by the 800 million people in developed countries, 15 percent of the world's population; demand can only increase as 3 to 4 billion more people join the industrialized world.

It is a paradox that oil is worth more to the poor people of the world than to the rich. A farmer in the Third World who uses a barrel of diesel each month to pump water to irrigate his fields may be willing to pay two, five, or ten times current prices. Not to do so means starvation; his demand is highly inelastic. A suburban U.S. commuter will think about car pooling, take fewer discretionary trips to the shopping mall and turn down his thermostat.

Figure 23-3 shows that the Dallas Fed estimates it will take oil prices of over $30 (1988 dollars) to prevent demand from exceeding current world production capacity by the mid-'90s. The oil price required to keep world-wide consumption at present levels is much higher than that required for the United States alone. The international part of the oil equation makes the situation politically volatile.

The production of oil is highly distorted since in most of the world governments directly control its production, for example, the Organization of Petroleum Exporting Countries (OPEC). Nations produce these commodities at any cost because costs are incurred in a soft, controlled local currency, but revenue is generated in dollars. And it's the dollars that count, since dollars buy the guns, Mercedes, and New York townhouses the ruling classes fancy.

The production cost of a barrel of oil is a function of a variety of factors. Is the oil located under downtown Los Angeles or the Arctic Ocean? How deep is it? Which government wants what level of royalties and/or taxes? Is the well good for 10 or 10,000, barrels per day? How hungry are the oil companies for new fields? How many dry holes does it take to get a producer? Costs are all over the lot, but in most places today looking for new oil is a marginal activity.

OIL POLITICS

Many political pundits make a big deal about the part oil plays in the U.S. trade deficit and the "strategic dependence" of the U.S. on oil.

In a free market world it would be academic whether oil came from Saudi Arabia or Texas, because payment would be made in gold by whoever needed the commodity, and it would concern only the buyer, the seller, and the economics of transportation. The concept of a national balance of trade would be meaningless. But in today's highly politicized world the trade balance has meaning. Payment is made in dollars. And dollars are the unsecured liability of a bankrupt U.S. government. OPEC's share of world oil reserves has grown from 68 percent in 1979 to 77 percent today, which adds an even greater political element. Growing U.S. imports can only put more pressure on the dollar and more upward pressure on oil prices. It is possible that exporters will, at some point, price oil in another currency. It is also possible that another embargo could occur should one of the U.S. government's foreign policy adventures go wrong.

Oil is perhaps the most political commodity. Where it is produced can affect its value more than any other factor, as demonstrated by the 1991 problems with Iraq, when oil spiked briefly to $40. The world may still be on a honeymoon following the collapse of communism, but it's hardly the end of history. The fundamental cause of war and revolution still exists, namely, politics. And, to a lesser extent, just plain geography.

Political chaos and its effect on oil prices favor investment in North American–based oil companies.

OIL RELATIVE TO OIL COMPANIES

The case for oil is bullish. Why not simply buy the crude, on the New York Mercantile Exchange where it's traded in 1,000-barrel contracts, as a long-term speculation? There are several reasons why oil stocks are a more attractive holding than the commodity itself at the moment.

1. Buying any asset that doesn't show earnings is a pure bet on higher prices. It is a speculation that should be reserved for commodities and stocks that are extraordinarily depressed and are a sure bet to rise in price (in other words, companies and commodities with little downside, not just investments for which you can build only a long-term case). Regardless of its other merits, oil doesn't qualify at $20, the way it did at $10 in the panic sell-off of 1986.

2. Buying a commodity incurs the cost of lost interest on your capital, whereas buying a stock often offers a current return. And specialized securities like Master Limited Partnerships (MLPs), oil royalty trusts, and the convertibles of junior oil companies are paying current yields of, typically, 10 percent. Good junior oil companies, like those listed later in this chapter, are selling for just a few times cash flow, with a substantial prospect of capital gains.

At present stock prices, it makes a lot more sense to buy reserves in the ground than to buy the commodity on an exchange. Ten years ago, when oil stocks were the hottest game in town, the opposite was true. In fact, oil stocks back then were a superb short sale.

3. It usually makes no sense to buy a commodity when you can buy its producer for a discount. The best example of this, and the facts may be partially apocryphal, is Daimler-Benz in November 1923, at the peak of the classic German hyperinflation. The market cap of the company was supposedly only slightly more than the retail price of a single car rolling off its assembly lines. Usually, if you want a Mercedes, it would make sense simply to buy one, but in this case it would have been better to buy the whole company and get all the cars for free. The prices of small oil companies aren't quite that depressed, but they are down 75 percent to 90 percent from their peaks. And they provide a leveraged way of participating in an uptrend in the oil price without the risks of the futures market.

4. That leverage is greatly compounded by the fact that pension funds and mutual funds do not buy commodities, but they do buy the stocks of their producers.

In 1993, at what should prove to be the tail end of a long bear market in oil and oil stocks, these securities are very underowned. When the psychology changes, the small oil companies have the potential to move almost as radically as do small gold mining companies. When Wall Street tries to invest in them, it will be like trying to squeeze the Hoover Dam reservoir through a garden hose.

5. Even if the price of energy stays flat or goes down, an individual oil company could increase its earnings consistently by increasing its production through successful drilling or acquisition. An exceptional company can increase earnings despite the price of its product. Obviously this is a double-edged sword, though, so it pays to choose your companies wisely. Random selection only works in a runaway bull market.

JUNIORS OR MAJORS?

The protracted oil industry bear market has been directly or indirectly responsible for the bankruptcy of several governments, scores of banks, thousands of companies, and a large number of individuals. The bottom in oil prices may have occurred in 1986 at $10, but the companies that produce it have stayed weak. But if a given company can withstand a bear market for the better part of a decade, the chances are it's pretty lean and mean, and that management has absorbed some valuable lessons.

And it is about time the petroleum industry again had its day in the sun. Despite the problems other industries face now that the debt-fueled '80s boom is over, it is hard to see how things can get much worse for the oil companies; they've already had a depression. Look at Figure 23-8 to see the industry's relative strength; it is about 75 percent weaker than the stock market as a whole. The figure represents the larger oil companies; smaller companies have been even less successful.

If the time has come to buy, which are the stocks you want? Probably not the majors; they will do fine in a resource bull market, but they are so large that their stock prices change direction as slowly as a supertanker. And they are, in general, poorly managed, at least from the shareholders' point of view. As is often the case, management treats shareholders as an inconvenience. The middle- and small-sized independents tend to have more entrepreneurial management, in the mold of T. Boone Pickens. Because of their small size, when they add assets to their relatively small base, it has a major impact.

The ability of the surviving juniors to add assets is a strong factor at present. Large U.S. oil companies are divesting themselves of U.S. properties. A major just cannot operate hundreds or thousands of small stripper wells scattered across the countryside, for the same reason a fund manager doesn't buy small cap stocks; they are unable to monitor and control them effectively.

The majors need their expertise and capital to compete for the megafields that are opening up in the Third World, where the return on time and capital is higher by an order of magnitude than in the United States. Big oil is, therefore, happy to sell small properties for a discount so it can capture a big multiple by redeploying the

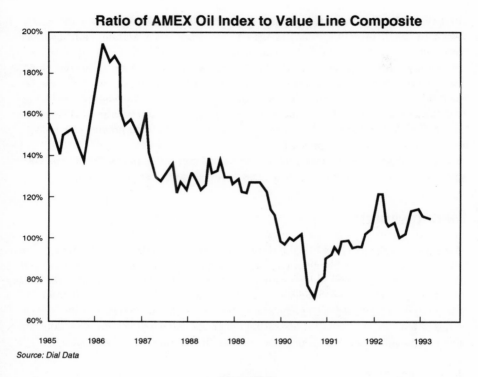

Ratio of AMEX Oil Index to Value Line Composite

Source: Dial Data

Figure 23-8

funds elsewhere. Foreign exploration and development spending has gone from 30 percent of the majors' budgets in the early '80s to 45 percent today, and it will rise much higher. The best remaining virgin U.S. properties are all in wildlife refuges or on the continental shelf. They are not going to be drilled in today's political environment.

As a result lots of good small properties are available, cheap, to small- and medium-sized outfits that can use them; and the huge numbers of laid-off oil workers provide a large pool of quality labor from which the juniors can pick.

Another advantage of the juniors, from the individual investor's point of view, is that unlike the majors, they are not heavily owned, or even followed, by the institutions. They tend, consequently, to be underpriced. And if I'm right about the fate of mutual funds in the near future, you do not want a stock they own anyway. If, however, a small company expands enough to reach critical mass, it is then eligible for, and will likely receive, institutional attention.

The junior companies are owned almost exclusively by the public, which is not active in the oil stock market right now; there is little trading in junior oils. The last time the public aggressively bought small oil companies, in 1979, a dozen new stocks were being underwritten every week, and they generally doubled or quadrupled from the offering price. As with all resource bull markets, however, it became a frenzy and latecomers took big losses. So, while these little companies are mostly owned by small investors, those investors have been replacing their oil positions with holdings such as junk bond mutual funds.

In any event, for the last decade, the junior oils have been about the worst place to invest your money. Indeed, many trade at lower prices now than they did when oil hit bottom in 1986. Like oil, gold also fared badly through the '80s, but gold stocks had two 1,000 percent runups along the way from intermediate bottoms reached in 1982 and 1985. The junior oils haven't even had the proverbial dead-cat bounce. They are truly depressed.

That's bad news for those who have been long; but it is good news for you, since we are arguably looking at a once-in-a-decade buying opportunity.

WHICH COMPANIES?

There are two ways to play the junior oils: their common and their convertibles. The convertibles are extremely attractive but, unfortunately, not many companies offer them. None of the twenty juniors shown in Table 23-1 do. These companies all have low debt, experienced management, good current cash flow, and lots of reserves. They will do well if oil prices go nowhere. If they rise for any length of time, the list is full of ten-for-one shots—at least from the prices listed below. But conditions are always changing; conduct your own investigation before taking a position.

Questions and Answers

Q: *Is there any way of predicting oil prices, perhaps by watching other commodities?*

A: In percentage terms crude has paralleled gold throughout the '70s and the '80s. In part for that reason, many pundits have tried to make a case that oil moves with gold. That's true enough, of course. But all the commodities tend to move together for monetary reasons.

There is no special correlation between gold and oil any more than between silver and soybeans, another mystical fallacy. In fact, there's no more relationship between gold and oil than there is between oil and any other commodity, and a lot less correlation than exists between commodities like hogs and corn, or wheat and oats.

There is, however, a journalistic law that says most writers must pretend to expertise beyond the ken of the presumed reader. As someone once said: "It's not what people know that does the damage; it's what they think they know that just ain't so."

Q: *What about the prospects for gas?*

A: If the case for oil is good, the case for gas is great, and the future of the U.S. petroleum industry lies not with oil, but with natural gas.

Table 23-1

U.S. Stocks (U.S. $)	Symbol	12/31/92
American National	ANPC	4.88
Arch Petroleum	ARCH	4.13
Bellwether Exploration	BELW	0.56
Coho Resources	COHO	5.25
Columbus Energy	EGY	7.13
Convest	COV	7.13
CREDO Petroleum	CRED	1.50
Enex Resources	—	6.75
Maynard Oil	MOIL	4.63
Nahama & Weagant	NAWE	4.63
Panhandle Royalty	PANRA	12.25
Questa Oil	QUES	2.00
Southern Mineral	SMIN	3.13
Swift Energy	SFY	9.13
Torreador Royalty	—	2.13
Unit Corp.	UNT	1.75
Canadian Stocks (Can $)		
Benson Petroleum	—	.85
Czar Resources	—	.94
Excel Energy	—	2.43
Jordon Petroleum	—	3.60
Paragon Petroleum	—	3.05
Talisman	—	15.00

The industry has never made an effort to search for gas in the United States because gas has always been "too cheap" relative to oil. Six thousand cubic feet (MCF), the standard measure of quantity of gas, contains the same number of British Thermal Units (BTU), the standard measure of heat content, as a barrel of oil but has typically been worth only half as much, mainly because of inadequate pipeline capacity for delivering gas to the end-user. After all, if you can't get product to the consumer reliably, that reduces demand. And price is solely a function of supply and demand. The pipeline business is highly capital- and regulation-intensive, and has taken years to prepare to exploit the available supplies. The infrastructure problems are being eliminated, however, with the construction of some major pipelines to move Alberta gas to expanding markets in eastern Canada, New England, the Midwest, and California.

Demand for gas will increase more rapidly than demand for oil. Because of environmental concerns and its low cost, natural gas is now the first choice for home heating; 60 percent of new homes built today have gas heat, and many homeowners are converting to gas. Gas will power fleet vehicles. Gas turbines will increasingly allow utilities to use gas for power generation. It will also be used as feedstock for petrochemicals like plastics.

Finally, most winters in the '80s were much warmer than normal, which added to the global warming hysteria, and reduced the income of those in the gas business. Gas consumption tends to be seasonal; it is highest in the winter as it is primarily used for heating. History suggests that we are in for some colder winters soon.

Most of the junior oils are really gas plays. On average, their reserve bases are comprised of nearly two-thirds gas and one-third oil.

In addition to the juniors, there are two further groups of natural gas stocks: the major producers and the distributors. As you might expect in any area which has done very poorly, the stock market has long been bored with companies in the field. Stock prices of major companies are very low and yields very high. The producers are analogous to oil companies and amount to a direct and high-yield call on higher gas prices. The distributors, or pipeline companies, are toll bridges, collecting revenues based on retail consumption. These distributions should interest you if you are still enamored of electric utilities. I can see little to recommend one group over the other at the moment. Table 23–2 lists some well-positioned companies.

Q: *OK, oil is very political. But maybe that's a reason not to invest in the U.S. right now. Maybe the U.S. government will start behaving the way Third World countries did in years past?*

A: In oil, as in everything today, it is important to have political-geographical diversification. But the junior oil companies are mostly in North America, and it is the juniors who have value. The majors are international, but their shares are not as underpriced. I suspect some juniors will start moving abroad much as the junior golds are doing.

There is plenty of oil waiting to be discovered around the world, but most of it is located inconveniently, either geographically or politically, in places like Libya, Ethiopia, Somalia, Vietnam, and Yemen. Going to those places might intimidate conventional thinkers, but it makes tremendous sense.

First, in politically troubled countries the price is right. It's still possible for a junior to compete with a major.

Second, the majors tend to be conservative, and currently seem even less likely to look in high-risk areas than has been the case in the past. And U.S. majors, in particular, are handcuffed in dealing with the universally corrupt governments that preside in Third World countries.

Third, as I've indicated in chapter 27 on politically distressed foreign real estate, these governments come and go. It makes sense to buy cheaply when unfriendly thugs are in power, in anticipation of their replacement.

Q: *Is the price of oil manipulated?*

A: Conspiratorial types like to believe that "the big boys" can set the price of oil as well as that of almost anything else. I find it difficult to believe that somebody can manipulate the price of a commodity that is an essential raw material for scores of

Table 23-2

Name	Symbol	Price $	Yield
Laclede Gas	LG	41.00	5.9%
MCN Corporation	MCN	30.25	5.5%
NUI Corporation	NUI	27.00	5.9%
New Jersey	NJR	26.50	5.7%
Pacific Enterprises	PET	21.00	—
Washington Gas	WGL	39.75	5.4%

basic industries, has millions of users, and whose new production is worth more than a billion dollars a day. If the price of oil could be manipulated, what were the "big boys" doing throughout the '50s and '60s, when a barrel of oil cost less than a bottle of Perrier today?

If it was really possible to enforce a price over the long-term, then the U.S. government would have maintained the price of gold at $35 to this day. To some degree, of course, temporary manipulation is possible. The Fed manipulates interest rates and the money supply a number of ways and, as a result, moves not only all the financial markets, but the whole economy as well. Brokers and promoters often manage for a while to support artificially high markets for their stocks. And cartels can have a temporary, though ultimately self-defeating, effect of keeping a price above where it would otherwise go. The tin cartel, for instance, kept that metal's price so high, for so long, that consumers switched completely to aluminum, glass, and plastic. Now tin prices are lower, because of lost market share and expanded production, than would otherwise be the case. The oil cartel did the same by simultaneously stimulating energy conservation and new oil production. Ultimately, cartels are self-defeating.

24

The Problem with Real Estate

In the United States there is more space where nobody is than where anybody is. That is what makes America what it is.

Gertrude Stein

On January 3, 1930, the following ad ran in the town paper of Greenwich, Connecticut, a fashionable suburb that had long been favored by the well-to-do: "Invest in Greenwich Real Estate Instead of Stocks: The Town of Greenwich 'market' never hits the toboggan. In 50 years, there has never been a decrease in value, but in 50 years total assessed value has increased 50-fold."

Of course, that was still early enough in the last depression for people to believe optimism would support the market. As it turned out, some estates that had sold for $1 million in 1929 subsequently sold for as little as $75,000 in the '30s. Greenwich was considered as recession-proof then as California was late in the '80s. New York was still expanding and Greenwich was where a lot of the rich folks went to live.

Today, much of the U.S. real estate market still looks like Greenwich in 1930. The average person, conditioned by a lifetime of increases in value, is probably still looking at the price history of real estate, not at the fundamentals.

Most people will ride property down in a long-term bear market, simply from inertia. The people who think about it will probably decide it is just another shake-out, like all the recessions we have seen over the last thirty years. Maybe they will be right; the future can never be certain. But there are plenty of reasons to believe that the '90s could be very different from previous decades.

Most people do not want to hear the bearish argument for real estate, since by far their largest asset is their house. For the average American family a house is much more than a home; it's a combination investment, savings program, tax shelter, and retirement program. A crash in housing prices would be more devastating than a stock market crash, not only financially but psychologically. A home is something you make a part of yourself and perhaps pass on to your children; a stock certificate is just something you buy and sell. It pushes a psychological hot button in most people to be told that the one asset they have been counting on to bail them out of all their other financial problems isn't going to make it. Home ownership is more the stuff of the American middle class than motherhood, baseball, and apple pie put together; a real price collapse could be the stuff of political revolution.

But social consequences aside, real estate is a market like any other. No bull market goes on forever, and bull markets are inevitably followed by bear markets; but no one knows how long it might be before the inevitable occurs. And, oddly, the longer a bull market continues, the more certain people are that it will continue even further. At the beginning of a bull market when values are great, buyers are timid and increases in price are viewed as selling opportunities. By the end of a bull market, buyers are confident and bold, and higher prices are seen as further confirmation of a well-established trend, a harbinger of even bigger gains. The longer a trend continues, the less likely it is to be considered just another trend, subject to change. If it goes on long enough it's viewed as something that you can plan your life around.

In 1989, a private study was done on the price history of single-family homes in San Diego. It turns out that real estate fluctuates at least as much as the stock market, both up and down (see Table 24–1).

You'll notice that, on average, the bear markets last about half as long as the bull markets and that the typical drop is well over 50 percent. These numbers are especially interesting because they show that, despite southern California's place as the quintessential growth market in this country, prices still fell off a cliff at the end of every previous boom. But even with the huge drops along the way, a San Diego property purchased in 1867 for a hypothetical $1,000 would have appreciated to more than $450,000, not counting rental income, by 1989—a spectacular gain, even with the decline in the value of the dollar.

Table 24-1 Single Family Homes in San Diego.

Gain or Loss From Previous Period	
1867–1873	+ 1,000%
1873–1877	− 84%
1877–1888	+ 1,500%
1888–1895	− 79%
1895–1913	+ 960%
1913–1917	− 46%
1917–1926	+ 190%
1926–1934	− 57%
1963–1989	+ 970%
1989–????	− ??%

I do not doubt that the long-term trend in property prices will continue to go up; even when the world population levels off wealth will continue compounding. But the point has to be made that if anyone bought at the wrong time in this long uptrend (i.e., 1873, 1888, 1913, 1926, or, quite arguably, 1989), he would have spent a good part of the rest of his life waiting to get even. Timing is critical, regardless of the trend.

A NIGHTMARE ON ELM STREET

The largest percentage of people's net worth is in their homes, although as real estate prices are down from the top of the market in 1989, the percentage is now lower than it was. Prices have dropped at least 10 percent to 20 percent in most areas, and as much as 50 percent for multimillion dollar homes on the West and East coasts. And the market is probably even weaker. Since there is no ticker tape for houses, it takes some months for market information to become widely known. In other words, most homeowners are aware that their houses aren't worth what they were at the peak, but they are only mildly concerned and disappointed that they didn't "toptick" the market. Homeowners are still confident that the approximately half-century old real estate bull market is just taking a breather, as it has done many times in the past.

Of course they may be right. It's both hard and dangerous to pick the ultimate tops and bottoms in any market. After all, why should 1993 be any different from 1981, or 1974, or 1970—all of which were bad years for property, all followed by a resumption of the gigantic bull market that's made everyone in real estate so wealthy?

There are several reasons this decline could be very different. Some—like debt, taxes, illiquidity, and a volatile monetary environment—were present to lesser degrees in past downturns. Demographics, however, are a factor unique to this market, and they have turned quite negative. And the chances are better than ever that the economy could experience a wholesale 1929-style deflation.

DEFLATION

The crisis we face now is likely to result in either a nasty deflation, in something approaching hyperinflation, or in alternating deflation and hyperinflation by the end of the decade. Those alternatives rule out gentle inflation, gentle deflation, or stable prosperity. Unless we have entered a long-awaited New Era, something both different and unpalatable is just around the corner.

A deflation, a drop in the money supply that, in turn, results in a drop in the general price level, could either cause a collapse in real estate or be caused by it. If the Fed contracted the money supply by adopting excessively restrictive policies, or if people and companies decided to pay off and scale back debt, it could cause widespread failures and decreased prices.

On the other hand, a collapse in real estate could bring on a deflation. S&Ls

are almost exclusively, and banks very heavily, into real estate loans. If the market continues its decline, simply because it's overpriced relative to other assets, many more of those loans could go bad. Bad real estate loans and property repossessions could be the straws that break the back of the overextended banking system. Neither the banks nor the Resolution Trust Corporation can sit on repossessions; they have to sell them. That drives the market down even further, causing more loans to go bad. The decline can cascade down, just as higher prices allowed larger loans, leading to even higher prices on the way up.

Deflation is a real possibility, and the prospects for deflation are intertwined with the amount of outstanding debt.

DEBT

Leverage, debt, and the burden of compound interest borrowers must pay could have collapsed the property market any time in the last ten years. It's not inevitable, anymore than it was in 1982, but it's more likely now than ever before. Figure 24-1 tracks the growing role of mortgage money in the market.

Charts like Figure 24–1 cannot call a market top; for all anyone knows, mortgage debt could eventually grow to several times its current percentage of GNP. But, the more margin debt there is in stocks, or mortgage debt in real estate, the less the upside, the greater the downside, and the more unstable the situation.

Real estate has traditionally been the most debt-leveraged of all markets. In the United States, few people can buy real estate, and few people can sell, without borrowing money. Getting a mortgage has always been integral to buying a house except for the very rich. The easy availability of cheap mortgages is the most important single reason that real estate prices increased faster than consumer prices from the '50s through the '70s. U.S. real estate prices are built on a pyramid of long-term mortgage money. But that mortgage money will be increasingly hard to come by as the '90s progress, for several reasons.

One reason is the overwhelming size of the federal deficits. The government

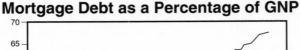

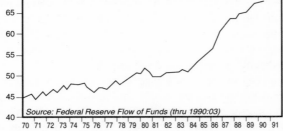

Figure 24-1

has made cheap mortgage money available through agencies like the Veterans Administration (VA), the FHA and HUD. These cost the taxpayers money; and all of them are going to come under major pressures to reduce their subsidies as the government's bankruptcy becomes ever more apparent.

Another major support under the post–WW II property boom was the large number of banks and S&Ls in existence. They created a surplus in the supply of mortgage money, a competitive environment where depositors received more and borrowers paid less than would otherwise have been true. Banks had to work on a narrow spread. But the number of banks has fallen from 14,434 in 1980 to 11,920 in 1991, and S&Ls are going out of business all over the country. With thrifts and banks fighting to stay alive, mortgage money will become scarcer. The existence of fewer lenders will make it tougher for potential homeowners to get a loan.

At the same time, people aren't going to be as anxious to borrow. When the economy is in turmoil, unemployment rolls are growing, real estate prices are dropping, and the general standard of living is declining, it is the rare person who is anxious to go into debt.

Someone with $20,000 or less could almost always buy a $100,000 house; likewise, a person with a $100,000 house could sell to a person with only $20,000, because an institution would provide the other $80,000. In the future, cash will increasingly call the tune on both sides of the transaction, and that means prices are going to plunge toward whatever buyers can afford in cash.

Federal Reserve figures show that mortgage debt is currently about 48 percent of the value of owner-occupied property; it was only 36 percent in 1982 and only 25 percent in 1952. But wealthy people typically pay cash for their homes, and that skews the figures. I suspect the mortgage debt is concentrated among the middle class and that 90 percent of families have one, which equals about 75 percent of resale value.

Mortgage availability has enabled a lot of people to live above their means. A house, after all, is just a consumer good. If you live in a $500,000 house, then you can also afford to wear $1,000 silk suits and drive a $100,000 Ferarri. If you can't afford those things, then perhaps you should consider whether you are inadvertently residing in a home that you wouldn't buy if you had to do it at today's prices.

Of course, in the past inflation has always been on hand to ease the burden of carrying a mortgage, and has been a powerful reason to leverage and buy the most expensive real estate possible. Another massive round of inflation is definitely in the cards. But its effects won't be what they once were.

INFLATION AND INTEREST RATES

The return of inflation could prove to be the worst thing that could happen to property. This may not make sense at first glance, because all forms of tangible wealth, all non-paper assets, tend to benefit from inflation. Mild, relatively predictable inflation proved good for real estate because it drove money into land as a hedge, but still allowed long-term fixed rate money to finance property purchases. Higher inflation will drive even more money into land, but will eliminate the source of financing most people need to buy. And, inflation, before or after a deflation, seems like an inevitability.

Since real estate depends, far more than any other asset, on the availability of borrowed money, we could see a paradox in the next few years: a drop in real estate prices in the midst of high inflation. That would be part of the Banana Republicization of America; chronically high inflation in South America has not resulted in high real estate prices.

A comeback of inflation, especially when the government is approaching bankruptcy, and when the economy is at a major turning point, will spell the end of the 30 year fixed-rate mortgage. This almost happened in the early '80s. The long-term, fixed-rate mortgage has always been unique to the United States and a boon to the homeowner. If rates go up, the homeowner is locked in at the old level, and the lender suffers the loss. If rates go down, the homeowner can refinance at a lower level, which deprives the lender of the higher profit. Why do lenders put themselves in this position? Because they do not hold the paper, but bundle up similar mortgages and sell them into the financial markets.

The main and perhaps only product lenders are likely to offer in the future will be an Annually Renewable Mortgage (ARM), with an annually adjustable interest rate. The future may also see a balloon provision at the end of every five years so the lender can determine whether the loan/equity ratio still favors him. You should also expect the end of the "nonrecourse" provision of most mortgages, which basically allows a homeowner to walk away if his home's value falls below the amount he still owes.

Those changes will shock Americans, but if you want a mortgage in almost any other country in the world, the ARM is the only type available because it makes economic sense. As the United States becomes just another one of the world's 200 countries, rather than a world unto itself, its financial products will resemble those of other places.

It is surprising that the ARM is exactly the kind of mortgage many homebuyers choose, because it offers lower monthly payments in the short run. People have seen rates come down consistently from 1982 to 1992, and they are convinced, based upon that eleven-year history, that the future holds more of the same. But for the reasons I discussed earlier, high inflation among them, interest rates are likely to rise, eventually exceeding the levels of 1982. That will at least double the monthly payment of the typical homeowner. High interest rates will put a lot more pressure on housing prices, which are already weak even with low rates.

What is likely to happen when rates go back up? There will be many more defaults and repossessions.

Of course, there is the prospect of hyperinflation, which would wipe out mortgages, and the dollar, completely. If that happens, it will not happen overnight; people might think it was just a temporary aberration, like the high inflation levels of 1974 and 1980. If so, a lot of property will hit the market, if only because the owner wants to be a millionaire. A pity the money his home brings won't be worth much. Many landowners in Germany in the early 1920s lost all their money that way. They sold out at the beginning of that country's hyperinflation for what seemed like a lot of money at the time.

Meanwhile, with lower marginal tax rates, deductions for interest and depreciation are not what they used to be. The tax laws have always been a major support under the U.S. real estate market.

TAXES

You can't hide real estate, which makes it the most taxable of all investments. Many local governments are in deep financial trouble, and property taxes are excellent candidates for "revenue enhancement." Property levies also suit the envy-driven, tax-the-rich hysteria that is likely to grow as the average person's standard of living declines. This is why, in many countries around the world, the rich may have large, but not ostentatious houses, unlike the mansions so popular in the '80s among the nouveaux riches.

In the past, local property taxes have historically been quite low, in keeping with the small size of local governments. But local taxes are increasingly a major consideration. And they're likely to go a lot higher, due to the poor financial condition of most governments. If you do not pay your property taxes, you will soon find out who really owns the home.

While local taxes were usually too small to hurt real estate in the past, federal income tax policy has always been a positive boost for real estate, causing huge amounts of capital to be directed into property that would otherwise not have been invested there. Since 1986 this is no longer true with the changes in depreciation schedules, the increase in capital gains rates, and the limits on the deductibility of mortgage interest. Even the reduction of the maximum tax from 50 percent to 28 percent was a negative for real estate (although the decrease was a huge boost for the country as a whole), since it made tax benefits a less important consideration for property investment.

Taxes, like every form of government action, cause distortions and misallocations of capital. Taxes induce people to act in ways they otherwise would not. And, in what will become a desperate quest for revenue, the government will unwind the tax breaks that have favored real estate over many decades. As a result the distortions those breaks caused will also come apart. Artificially high property prices will tumble

Another effect of recent changes in the tax law is that, since consumer debt can no longer be deducted, many people have taken out home loans to finance other purchases. They might have borrowed that money anyway, but the fact that they borrowed it on their houses will burden that part of their balance sheets and eventually result in more distress sales into an illiquid market.

ILLIQUIDITY

Real estate is the most illiquid investment. To find a buyer for a piece of property almost always requires an active, and sometimes prolonged, effort. That can be a plus when prices are rising, but in a down market it's a nightmare. And when the market goes sour, the spread between the bid and the asking price can resemble that on a penny stock.

If a significant number of owners become overextended and have to sell, they can break the market, even if most holders are financially sound. Because each piece of property is unique, prices are determined by "comparables." Prices are not set by the majority of the inventory, prices are determined at the margin. Even in the liquid stock market, it's not unusual to have only 2 percent to 4 percent of the shares change hands in a given month, but to see the price move by 20 percent to 30 percent as a result. The attitude of 98 percent of the shareholders has minimal effect on the market price of their asset, because they are neither buyers nor sellers at a given time. Instead, it is what the marginal, but active, 2 percent are doing that determines prices.

This effect is even more pronounced with real estate because of its illiquidity. At least you know what your stock is "worth" based on trading by several percent of the owners each month. But you know the value of your home only from what the guy down the block got for his property last year. This problem was illustrated for farmers in the mid-'80s, when farmland had declined over 50 percent from its peak prices of the early '80s. All farmers were not in trouble, but 15 percent to 20 percent of them were. That marginal number determined market values, despite what the majority thought the dirt was "really" worth.

The same thing has happened more recently with office buildings, and could affect residential properties. When a market is slow or depressed, prices are set by those who have to sell. It is pretty rare that someone has to buy; unlike selling, buying is a purely discretionary activity. The next decade is likely to bring many more forced sellers, and far fewer discretionary buyers. Those who shop for residential property are likely to look at houses in light of their economic values, not their speculative appeal.

THE ECONOMIC VALUE OF A HOUSE

The price of a house, like other goods, is determined by what somebody else is willing to pay for it. But, apart from the speculative psychology that leads people to expect a greater fool to come along, what is a house really worth? The best indicator is what it will rent for. The present value of any investment basically equals the discounted value of the income stream it can generate. When real estate was a sound value, before the 1970s, the rule of thumb for property rentals was 1 percent of market value per month. And then both taxes and interest rates were lower.

At that time rental yields were greater than on competitive investments, like bonds, because people felt the risks were greater. As late as the '60s, most people still remembered the debacle of the '30s when houses did not gain, but lost, value yearly. They required a large yield to compensate them for the perceived risk.

If you consider your house a major economic asset consider selling it and renting instead. At the top of the housing mania in California in 1989, one friend in Santa Barbara thought his house was worth $1,000,000, although its rental value was only about $2,500 per month. I suggested he "hit the bid," invest the proceeds, and rent. He would no longer have had real estate taxes to pay, and much less upkeep, plus a positive cash flow of more than $5,000 per month. He didn't do it. The house is now worth $500,000 and is on its way to $250,000, or about its correct value, based on what it will rent for.

The median-priced house in California is worth about $185,000. But only 20 percent of California households earn the minimum of $61,000 needed to qualify for conventional financing. It must be especially tough for people in the San Francisco area, where the median price is $265,700, the most expensive in the country. People there are buying houses that cost five or six years of before-tax income.

The Census Bureau estimates that 57 percent of all U.S. households can not afford a median-priced house in their area, even if financing with only 5 percent down were available, and even with interest rates at artificially low levels. And today, unlike the '50s and '60s, that generally already assumes a two-income family (see Figure 24-2).

Property had investment potential when most Americans could afford it and when it was bought for its utility, not investment, value. But when people started to

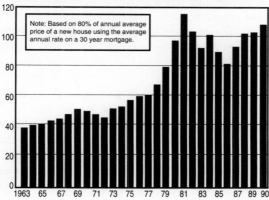

Figure 24-2

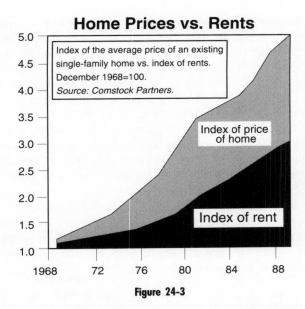

Home Prices vs. Rents

Index of the average price of an existing single-family home vs. index of rents. December 1968=100. *Source: Comstock Partners.*

Index of price of home

Index of rent

Figure 24-3

buy property primarily as an investment, prices rose, property is now a poor investment. Markets typically have the greatest capital gain potential when they offer high current yield. (see Figure 24-3).

How many houses do you know that can be purchased and then rented for positive cash flow today? Also ask yourself before buying, even with a bargain-rate 8 percent mortgage: Is this property really going to appreciate by at least 8 percent per year for the foreseeable future? The average house today rents or earns only about 5 percent per annum of its market value, roughly equivalent to a stock selling at a 20 to 1 P/E ratio, which is pretty steep. And the company represented by the stock should grow in earnings and assets each year, net of depreciation, and the stock is liquid. Few people seem to remember that a house is just an expensive consumer item, like a suit or a car; each has a service life, after which it must be scrapped. The houses built today become total write-offs in thirty to forty years. Any residual value is strictly in the land. A 20-to-1 P/E is excessive for what is essentially a wasting asset.

Of course most people do not see it that way. They still have fond, recent memories of a house being a "no-lose" investment. But now the character of "most people," the demographics that have supported this market, are changing as well.

DEMOGRAPHICS

Baby boomers, the roughly 75 million people born from the early '40s to the early '60s, constitute the largest segment of the U.S. population. They have had a large influence on housing prices. During the '70s and especially the '80s, the boomers started settling down and bought a lot of housing. Housing had been appreciating as long as the boomers had been alive. Indeed, demographics have "always" been on the side of real estate, since the U.S. population has always expanded. The property market started to reflect the impact of demographics in the late '60s when the first cohorts of the boomer generation began to buy houses in earnest.

The natural desire of millions of people moving into middle age is to own their own homes. Along with booming financial markets, their buying kept property prices from falling during the '80s. In other words, the demographic fundamentals overcame what were already negative economic fundamentals. But now, in the '90s most people likely to buy a house have already done so.

The great American bull market in houses actually ended about 1980, the same time gold, oil, commodities, and many other inflation hedges peaked. The nominal price of the median "used house" has gone up by a factor of about four and one-half times since 1968; it was an excellent investment until the '80s. Since then, the inflation-adjusted numbers tell another story entirely. With a whole generation buying, why didn't prices go way up in real terms?

The high real level of interest rates in the '80s was a major reason. Surging demand for capital and a low savings rate resulted in high real rates of interest. Previous generations saw double-digit appreciation financed by single-digit mortgages, but during most of the '80s, a double-digit mortgage rate and a single-digit appreciation were more typical. Meanwhile, inflation declined, eliminating a subsidy that previously favored borrowers. This is a serious turn of affairs, since people are more indebted now than ever before.

Another reason was new construction. Although the entire baby boom generation seemed to be house hunting, those millions of buyers weren't competing for a limited supply. The housing supply can best be compared to the supply of securities in the stock market. When demand exists, thousands of new issues and secondary offerings appear. In a free market, supply always rises to meet demand.

The U.S. population increased from 203.3 million to 226.5 million during the 1970s, a total increase of 23.2 million. During that time 17.676 million new houses were created, almost one for every person. The demographic bulge created by the baby boomers, combined with their lifelong psychological conditioning on the merits of real estate, guaranteed a huge demand. But the demand was met with tremendous new supply. During the '80s there were 14.323 million new housing starts while the population grew by 22.2 million. Since most houses hold two, three or more people, you could argue that there were perhaps two or three times as many houses as were "needed." The feeding frenzy was so strong that prices went up despite the negative fundamentals. As Figure 24-4 shows, the supply of people of home-buying age is going to drop, not just relatively, but in absolute numbers.

What will happen when the baby boom bulge moves on, which is now happening, and the no-lose psychology with it? Houses will be a glut on the market.

The yuppie-based boom in houses was geographically concentrated, mainly in urban California and the Boston-Washington corridor where the young urban

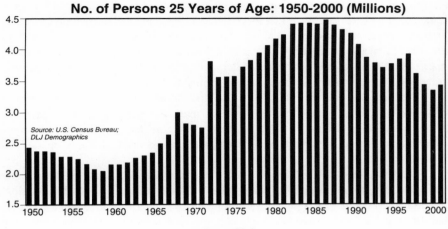

No. of Persons 25 Years of Age: 1950-2000 (Millions)

Source: U.S. Census Bureau;
DLJ Demographics

Figure 24-4

professionals congregated. Those places are also where the media, the financial community and the federal government reside so it is not hard to see how those areas were mistaken for the country as a whole. Most property in the hinterlands, such as Alabama, Maine, Texas, and Kansas, sells for no more than it did ten years ago. And the dollars are worth much less.

The time to buy anything (stocks, collectibles, houses, you-name-it) is before people and dollars start chasing it. It's obvious that the early '50s was the perfect time to buy real estate. The game was on in earnest during the '70s, but since the start of the '80s it has become obvious that the supply of people and the ability to carry debt had to peak soon. The situation is once again analogous to every other market: Now that everyone who could conceivably buy has done so, to whom do all those people sell? Buyers will eventually appear, of course, but not at today's prices. Housing started its downtrend—in real terms—during the '80s (see Figure 24-5).

Figure 24-6 shows mortgage rates rising to a peak in 1981 and falling ever since.

Rates are now at their lowest level in those twenty years. What will happen when they turn up again and drive mortgage payments higher? Housing prices will sink further, accelerating the trend shown in Figure 24-7.

Who will support the market, now that the yuppies are history? Not the Bart Simpson generation born from the early '60s to the early '80s; they're small in number and are suffering from a declining standard of living. Many are moving in with their parents. The sixty-five-and-over age group is the fastest-growing portion of the population; many of those oldsters are looking to cash in and will add to the selling pressure. But there just aren't enough warm bodies to fill the space.

Baby boomers, as a generation, have delayed marriage far longer than any of their predecessors; many men (and women) bought houses while single, another

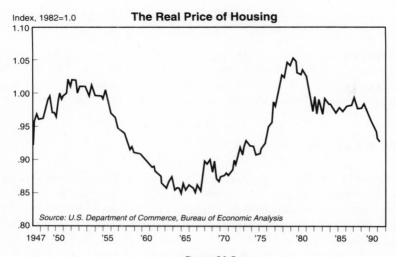

The Real Price of Housing

Index, 1982=1.0

Source: U.S. Department of Commerce, Bureau of Economic Analysis

Figure 24-5

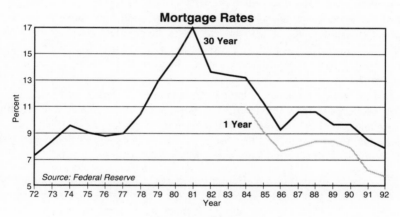

Mortgage Rates

30 Year

1 Year

Percent

Source: Federal Reserve

Year

Figure 24-6

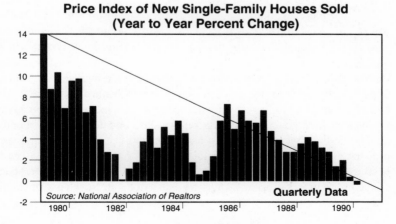

**Price Index of New Single-Family Houses Sold
(Year to Year Percent Change)**

Source: National Association of Realtors

Quarterly Data

Figure 24-7

new phenomenon. As they pair off, what will become of the several million spare houses? They'll come onto the market with predictable results. Moreover, many people, flush with the affluence of the '80s, bought second or even third houses. How many of those houses will hit the market as distress sales in the next few years?

PICKING THE BOTTOM

Property has been good to most people over many years, and you are understandably loathe to part with it. You do not want to pay a huge capital gains tax. You are unable to decide what you should do with the proceeds; maybe it would wind up in an even riskier place. These are real and valid considerations, and there aren't any easy answers.

But consider the real possibility, the strong probability, that after coasting slowly downward for some years, property is now at the lip of a precipice. Real prices have been flat to down during a decade of boom, and now the economy is about to deteriorate badly. If you have to sell in the next few years you may not find a buyer. With very few exceptions, real estate could become the financial graveyard of the average household. Instead, you might want to sell now and beat the last-minute rush.

Just as real estate boosters have been saying for decades, you can't go wrong buying property at the right price. The population will expand, real wealth will increase and wealthy foreigners will continue to prefer the United States as a playground. But I suspect the time to buy most property won't come until the late '90s. While you're waiting, here are a few points to keep in mind.

1. Stay away from urban and suburban areas. (This is a mirror image of the reasons why you should concentrate on the type of properties to be discussed in chapter 25.) With the continuing advances in telecommunications—satellites, High Definition TV, cellular telephones, fax, personal computers, and fiber optics, to name just a few—it will become less important to have your body in a particular place to conduct business. Traffic congestion makes it hard to get where you need to go anyway. The city will fade as an economic center of activity, and wealthy, productive people will increasingly abandon it to the masses.
2. Get out of high-tax areas. Someone who earns a good income in California has to pay a hefty price for the privilege; a move to Nevada automatically means a higher standard of living if you can maintain your income. Lower taxes also mean a smaller government, less regulations, and fewer nosy bureaucrats.
3. Sell properties that have gone up a lot over the last few decades. Expensive property has a lot further to fall than property that reflects quality but hasn't been the object of the market's adoration. In other words, you are better off, with a house in Arkansas or Oklahoma than a home in New York or California.

4.   The return on the property, should you choose to rent it, should, after all costs, be significantly above your bank deposit yield, at least 6 percent per year in real terms. In the late 1960s, before the great boom got under way in earnest, 12 percent was normal cash-on-cash return.

5.   A house, or a building, shouldn't be considered a bargain in today's environment unless it is available considerably below replacement costs. Fifty cents on the dollar is a good working figure; that number was typical of what properties went for after Texas, Oklahoma, and Colorado experienced regional depressions in the mid- to late-'80s. The market for property shouldn't be just "soft" but in such poor condition that you would expect *Business Week* to run a "Death of Real Estate" cover.

6.   Closely watch the value of U.S. real estate relative to comparable foreign markets. That may prove the best, and perhaps the least-observed, indicator of value in the years to come. Keeping informed here will be worth a lot more than just entertainment value at cocktail parties (see chapter 27).

The best argument I can make for U.S. real estate at the moment is that America is the cheapest non–Third World country, with the exception of South Africa. If you want to buy property or live cheaply and well, stay right here in the U.S.A. A dollar goes a lot further here than 125 yen in Japan or 1.7 DMs in Germany.

7.   Everything else being equal, try to restrict your interest to only the most unique and upmarket properties. This has traditionally been good advice ("location, location, location"). But I suspect it's going to become even more important in the future, as American society increasingly divides into the haves and the have-nots. The surest and largest profits will be made by owning something that the truly rich are likely to want. In other words, you don't want the kind of property the "average" American is likely to buy, because the average guy's likely to be losing what he's got, not buying more. Monetary and economic turbulence have always tended to destroy the middle class and to create small upper and large lower stratas. You definitely want to look upmarket, especially in the kind of areas covered in the next chapter.

Questions and Answers

Q. *Can the government turn the real estate market around? Their fiscal and monetary policies have gotten the economy in general, and real estate in particular, out of every past slump in the last forty years.*

A. No. Let's take a somewhat extreme case. Suppose they doubled the money supply tomorrow morning. Property prices would double, but so would everything else. Initially, property prices might actually more than double as people, fearing rapid inflation, panicked out of cash and into something tangible. But that would be more than offset by a total lack of financing resulting from massive inflation. Only the rich are in a position to buy or sell property without borrowed money. Real increases in price are caused by real pressures; increases in wealth and population. Phony money results in phony price increases.

The government is not only incapable of turning the market around, it can only further depress real estate values. The Resolution Trust Corporation, for instance, is loaded with properties and obtaining more all the time. Some argue that since most of this property turns out to be junk, this inventory will not compete with quality property and so will not affect it. That is nonsense. It is like saying that the price of corn doesn't affect the price of soybeans. There is always room for substitution at the margin, and the margins are where prices are set. As hundreds of additional banks and S&Ls go under, joined by increasing numbers of insurance companies, much more property will go on the market, and less capital will be available to finance purchases.

Millions of average Americans may find themselves unable to make their mortgage or rent payments. Meanwhile, local governments will do their share by raising property taxes to stave off their own bankruptcy. First-class real estate will be the only segment left for which a market will exist.

The decline in prices could be the 1990s equivalent of the collapse of the 1930s stock market. We may find out, hopefully to only a limited degree, how Argentines have felt for many decades. In Argentina, as will be the case in the United States, the government not only couldn't solve the problem, it was the exclusive cause of it.

Q. *Does it make any sense to have a mortgage today if prices are really going to drop?*

A. On the one hand, the only way you can go bankrupt is by owing money, which argues against a mortgage. On the other hand, the ultimate fate of the dollar is to approach its intrinsic value, which is, arguably, zero. And that makes a long-term, fixed interest mortgage smart.

It's one thing to arrive at a conclusion that U.S. property has entered on a long-term bear market. But it is priced in dollars, and it seems an even surer bet that dollars are eventually going to zero. Instead of seeing the mortgage as a means to buy property, it might be a better idea to view a mortgage as a way to shortsell the dollar. It's convenient for borrowers, therefore, that the fixed rate mortgage is still available.

I don't like the idea of paying interest. I would rather collect it. Nor do I like the idea of being in debt; it limits your options and puts you at risk. But fixed-interest debt remains an excellent defense against a collapsing currency.

Take this opportunity to do the opposite of what has put the banking system in its current mess: borrow long at low rates, but lend short at high rates. In other words, take the $100,000 you get on your house at 8 percent for fifteen years and redeploy it in some of the propositions this book lists. If the good times of decades past somehow return, your house will appreciate enough to cover the debt, no matter what you do with it. If we face the kind of problems I anticipate, not only would the money you borrow be trivialized by inflation, but the countercyclical investments you make with it could gain many times in value. But borrow no more than you can comfortably service in the meantime.

An even more conservative strategy might be to keep the proceeds in cash. It is true that you will suffer a negative interest rate spread for a period of time, but you will have the liquid cash, which few others will possess. And when rates go higher, you will be in a position to lock in a very high yield, possibly for years. If rates for a 10-year government bond go back to the levels of the early '80s, you should be able to invest the money you've borrowed (at 8 percent) for 15 percent, collecting the difference for another decade. If rates go lower, your worst case is simply paying off the mortgage. In the meantime, you insulate yourself from a collapse of the dollar and a collapse of the real estate market.

Q. *What about the effect of the conservation movement on prices?*

A. The governments of at least six eastern states (Connecticut, Maryland, Massachusetts, New Hampshire, New Jersey, and Rhode Island) have programs under which they will pay you what can amount to almost the entire fair market value of your farmland in exchange for relinquishing your right to develop the property. Local authorities in many other areas have similar programs. Their rationale is to maintain the rural character of their jurisdictions. In other words, you can run horses, grow crops, or just keep your land wild for aesthetics and privacy, while taxpayers reduce your cost basis to near-zero. Like much government economic intervention, it amounts to a welfare program for rich people, funded by the average taxpayer.

These programs merit serious consideration, since I expect little subdivision or development will take place almost anywhere for the next decade. Consequently under some programs you give up little in exchange for a lot of money. Rural property will hold its value much better than urban or suburban real estate. Call your state capitol and ask for information about their Farmland Preservation Program.

One might question the ethics of accepting government largesse, which is always at the expense of your fellow citizens, but all government action inevitably leads to such choices and winds up putting everyone in a *sauve qui peut** environment.

---

*Every man for himself.

25

Property That's Going Up

In every society where property exists there will ever be a struggle between rich and poor. Mixed in one assembly, equal laws can never be expected; they will either be made by the members to plunder the few who are rich, or by the influential to fleece the many who are poor.

John Adams

It may not make much intuitive sense to buy anything during a bear market. But just as there are always some stocks going up when the Standard and Poor's Index might be collapsing, the same is true of property. And since the economic situation could quickly change from deflationary to highly inflationary, it makes sense to diversify. Some types of real estate should do very well in the '90s, paradoxically because of the overall economy.

But even the best areas of the real estate market are no longer the low-risk/ high-reward propositions they were years ago. It is necessary to be highly selective. And in any event, the main reason to own real estate right now is because you enjoy it and do not particularly care about its economics. The market has favored the renter for the last decade, and I expect that will remain the case for some time, as I explained in chapter 24.

Now let's examine the prospects for certain types of resort property.

A NEW MEGATREND IN PROPERTY

During the monetary crisis of the early '70s, controversy erupted on the advantages of having a "survival retreat." Harry Browne was perhaps the first to make the argument that if you wanted to own real estate, it should be in a rural area, in case the going got tough in the big cities. He reasoned that if the economy held together, it might turn out to be a good investment, but if not it would still have a lot of utility value. The argument is still valid today, although with qualifications.

Properly chosen real estate away from major urban areas will do well, not just in spite of, but actually because of, the continuing bear market in the cities and suburbs, the problems of which will drive people to rural areas. For example, the 1992 Los Angeles riots acted as a catalyst; people who were idly considering leaving major metropolitan areas, in general, and California, in particular, suddenly decided they had had enough. For the first time in history, California is losing people. Most of them are going to places like Oregon, Washington, Nevada, Utah, Arizona, Colorado, Montana, and Wyoming.

From the '50s through the '70s the key to making money in real estate was simply to buy in the path of growth and wait. At that time the "megatrend" was for people to flow into suburbs, both from the city centers and rural areas, which suffered absolute as well as relative declines in population. It was a winning formula; many thousands of people who did nothing but own some land in the right place became multimillionaires through no fault of their own. As of 1990, the suburbs contain over 50 percent of the U.S. population and have become what can be termed "fringe cities."

THE END OF THE SUBURB

Suburbs now have developed most of the same problems of the old downtown areas: crime, pollution, and high taxes, plus some new ones of their own—the need to drive a car to get anywhere, crowded roads, and round-trip commutes of up to two or three hours. In fact, suburbs are planned around the automobile. This will become a major problem as governments increase taxes on cars and fuel, to both raise money and "save the environment." The suburbs have actually become the worst of all worlds, offering the disadvantages of both country and city and the advantages of neither.

The suburbs arose in mid-century, with mid-century technology for mid-century needs. Now they are full of 10- to 40-year-old houses that were originally built to last from 20 to 50 years. After a certain point, extending a house's life becomes uneconomic. Along with a combination of laws and demographic pressures, this fact helped create the center city slums. Exactly the same pressures will abet the creation of slums in the fringe cities.

Trends in housing and property are much like trends in any other investment market: they begin, they accelerate, they reverse and then disappear. Often, the vital statistics of property, commodities and stocks can mirror each other. That has been true of property in the suburbs and of the auto industry. For decades it was smart to own GM and its mates because the number of autos and the roads to drive them on were expanding rapidly. People can see that trend has ended, but haven't extended the effects to the suburb, which is a creature of the car.

The suburbs also cater to a social structure that is on its way out, a middle America that no longer exists. The idea of Ozzie Nelson and Ward Cleaver mailing their keys to the bank and walking away from the old homestead is a sad one, but we're no longer living in the 1950s.

The decline of the suburb doesn't mean that the city is going to make a comeback soon. Poor minorities, many of whom have family traditions of living on welfare, are increasingly concentrated in the cities, whose governments are heavily indebted and teetering on bankruptcy, even while their tax base shrinks.

If the economy does as badly as I expect, large cities will become far worse off in the next decade. You will see more migration from the cities, and the start of massive migration out of the suburbs. Where will they go? Not to farming areas. Someone who is used to the amenities of town isn't likely to head for rural Kansas, Nebraska, Texas, or South Dakota. Those areas will remain places to grow food for the indefinite future, and property prices will fluctuate accordingly.

Some suburbanites and city dwellers who can afford it will move to small and mid-sized towns, halting and reversing their long decline. They will improve markedly, but they're not the stuff of high potential investment. The majority of the well-to-do migrants will pile into resort communities. Schools there are generally excellent, reflecting the high average wealth and educational standards of their residents. They have no permanent underclass. Although local politicians tend to lean to the left, they are subject to peer pressure from neighbors they see daily; they are generally not the hardened types who populate the governments of the big cities. Crime and crowded highways are not a problem. The quality of life is right.

Much of this is true of small towns in general, of course. But most small towns lack the cosmopolitan flavor of resort towns that appeals to city folk. It is a question, therefore, of leverage and of anticipating the flow of funds. The type of property I'm talking about can be much more than just a speculation or a change in where you live; it can be part of a change in the way you live. An examination of Aspen, Colorado, an archetypal resort town, will point to the shape of things to come.

THE ASPEN IDEA

Until recently, most people didn't seriously consider a resort town as a full-time residence. Their business activities were elsewhere, and resort towns more or less shut down during the off-seasons. But the new class of multimillionaires who arose in the 1980s want to enjoy the lifestyle their money can buy as they move into their middle and later years. And the computer, the cellular telephone, the fax, and Federal Express make it possible to do so.

Aspen is the perfect case study to illustrate where they are moving. It is a town of 6,000 people, at the end of a small state highway on the way to nowhere. Yet it is internationally famous, constantly making the pages of *People* Magazine and *The New York Times*. Thatcher and Bush picked it for a conference in 1991, as do scores of intellectually or spiritually oriented groups each year. Dozens of Hollywood megastars live there, as do about 300 of the Forbes 400. Everyone may not view these points as recommendations, but it is still indicative of Aspen's increasing, and surprising, appeal.

In good part because of the people it attracts, prices in Aspen are high. The average house in 1992 cost over $1,000,000, and many are in the $5–$10 million plus range. Nevertheless, Aspen remains a liquid market because potential buyers need not look at the right side of the menu much. Further, the homes in those upper reaches are paid for in cash, making the market quite stable. People don't have to scramble to pay the monthly mortgage, and few sales are contingent on financing or the sale of a previous residence.

During the '80s the rich have gotten richer, both relatively and absolutely. The United States is not the true middle-class society it once was; crime is on the rise, and class warfare is becoming a reality. Conditions in the big cities are coming to resemble those in the Third World. You do not drive around in Bogota or Rio with a gold watch on your wrist, because someone may try to cut off your arm to liberate it; life is moving in that direction in New York and Los Angeles.

It is understandable that people with money want to insulate themselves from the problems that surround them. This isn't a new phenomenon; the rich have always had enclaves, like Beverly Hills and Palm Beach. As more simmering problems come to a boil in the '90s, more rich people's ghettos will materialize. Those who can afford to do so will pay a premium to move to areas that are at once beautiful, mellow, cultured and safe.

That brings us back to Aspen. Why is it different from East Podunk, Iowa, and thousands of other similar-sized small towns? There are a number of reasons which you should keep in mind when considering residential real estate for the next decade.

1. **Natural Beauty.** This is why people go to the Rockies, instead of Newark for their vacations. Pretty scenery burns itself into the imagination, and cannot be overrated as a factor when a person decides where to move. It is part of the overall trend toward environmental consciousness.

2. **Ambiance.** Scenery is not enough; there has to be something to do, such as festivals, conferences, cultural activities, athletic events, and plenty of corner cafés. Once a place becomes chic with a few of the rich and famous, they tend to bring their friends. Like ordinary people, these people like to hang out with their peers in places where they are pampered but not mobbed. That is why Beverly Hills became a special place. Ambiance and natural beauty are the major reasons you want to think resort towns; most small towns are boring and provincial.

3. **Facilities.** For a community to be a contender, it must have at least one first-class health club, a great hotel, local Federal Express deliveries, several movie theaters, and good stores. People may want the advantages of small towns, but they do not want to give up the advantages of the cities they are deserting.

4. **Isolation.** It's important to be physically away from it all, to be able to walk 100 yards in any direction and be out in the wilderness; otherwise why not just stay in a suburb? This is the problem with a town such as Vail, which otherwise has most of the required features; it's located right on an interstate and only a two-hour drive from the major population center of Denver.

The four factors above almost always characterize ski resorts, and it's no coincidence that Aspen is also one of the world's leaders in that area. But ski towns have other unique advantages in their favor.

1. **Year-round Activities.** The summer is rarely a problem anywhere, but people usually try to escape winter. Ski resorts offer an incentive for people to stay year-round.
2. **Geographic Limits.** Here is another advantage of ski resorts, which tend to be located in small valleys. A natural limit to the supply of land tends to increase the price of what's available. Mountain towns, and this is a mixed blessing, also tend to attract a lot of "granolas" who, once they are ensconced, are prone to slam the door on the rest of the world through restrictive zoning. That creates an artificial scarcity to buttress the natural one.

   The effect resembles a popular stock with a tiny market capitalization. The price can move explosively and to levels no one would have anticipated with conventional analysis. The West is ideally structured for this effect, since 50 percent to 90 percent of it is owned by various governments, but locals have the benefits offered by the resulting open land. Population density is light except in a few pockets.
3. **Regulatory Limits.** If the land in individual ski areas is restricted, so are the number of areas. The environmentalist juggernaut is making it virtually impossible to open new ski areas or expand existing ones, because they scare wildlife and bring in development. Building up a new area can be as time- and legal-fee–intensive as putting in a strip mine. Of necessity all the demand is directed to the few existing developed resorts.
4. **Exclusivity.** Skiing is a rich man's sport. That tends to keep the riffraff out of town, and rich people like it that way, even if it's politically incorrect even to countenance such an undemocratic thought.

BANKING ON THE INEVITABLE

Can anything go wrong with this scenario? Many places are destroyed by their own success; a place that may be ideal with 5,000 people changes character when it grows to 10,000 or 50,000. This is a regrettable but inevitable fact. Just as the trend from the countryside to the cities ended in the mid-'40s and the trend to the suburbs ended in the early '80s, the trend to resorts will have a finite lifespan.

Regulators have frequently in the past fought trends. For example, huge subsidies were granted to preserve the mythic "family farm." At other times, they have aggravated trends by building gigantic welfare projects to accommodate those people migrating to the cities. They are likely to affect the trend to resort towns as well. They will almost certainly try to keep people out. That's one reason to act now, before their barricades are in place. But the populations of resort areas will expand greatly, regardless.

The best way to insulate yourself from eventual population pressures, or profit from them, is to acquire a good-sized block of land. In the long run, what separates the haves from the have-nots, and the upper from the lower classes, is the ownership of tangible assets. No matter how devastated the economy is, prime property will continue to have value, something that is not likely to be true of currency. And it is hard to go wrong when you have a major social trend on your side, regardless of the economic climate.

WHAT AND WHERE

The argument can be made that Aspen has already "happened," or that it is beyond the reach of most people. Certainly, even though the trend has a way to go, it is no longer in its early stages. The key for most people, therefore, is to find something resembling Aspen, that shares the town's essential characteristics, but that has not been discovered as yet by the market at large. If you buy my basic reasoning, there is no alternative to taking several weeks off and investigating the situation first hand. It's unwise to buy property long distance.

If you're thinking of a move to a small town, and millions of your friends and neighbors and countrymen certainly are or shortly will be, you want to choose one that will benefit from the trend, one where your property will appreciate most. Towns to look at include Aspen, Telluride, Crested Butte, Steamboat Springs, Jackson Hole, Sun Valley, Stowe, Taos, Santa Fe, and Sedona. All but the last two are ski resorts. All fit the parameters spelled out above. It's not an inclusive list, but those are towns that qualify. It is critical to stay with upmarket towns, or those that clearly are moving in that direction. The second-raters could stay second-rate for a long time.

The best advice on the type of property to buy was offered by Frank Lloyd Wright fifty years ago. His view was that no matter how far out you're thinking of going, you should go twice as far. Growth will catch up to you. Of course, in these areas there isn't room to expand forever, as did Chicago and Los Angeles. So the available land will become very valuable.

The small amounts of land available also change the time scales people think in. While an hour's drive in Los Angeles seems like nothing, fifteen minutes in Aspen is forever. It is all relative. You drive twenty minutes away, and land prices drop radically.

For those reasons, land twenty minutes from town is what you want to buy, and at least 10 acres, better yet 100, or 1,000 acres. Something that a rich city slicker can make into a "statement" if you decide to sell it. But you won't want to. That's why this property will become much more expensive. With transportation, communications, computers, and technology in general always improving, it is less and less important to be near a major population center. That is especially true for the wealthy, who do not need to be near a "job." And if I'm right about the Greater Depression, they will not want to be near the cities, either. That doesn't augur well for most commercial property.

26

Commercial Property

The problems with real estate go far beyond houses, even though housing affects the average American the most. Office buildings, hotels, and retail space have always been more volatile than housing. And even though in some cases their value has dropped 50 percent or more from peak prices, they still have a long way to fall. For many years commercial property will continue to be a problem for the banks and insurers that provided the capital to build them.

One interesting feature of the last recession, from 1980 to 1982, is that commercial vacancy rates were quite low and subsequently rose while the economy recovered. Normally, and intuitively, vacancies will be highest at the bottom of a recession, and will fall during a recovery as businesses expand and workers go back to the job (see Figure 26-1).

Between 1979 and 1992, vacancies rose from less than 4 percent to nearly 20 percent. Such a huge amount of new space was added during the '80s that it outpaced even the expansion of the economy from a very deep recession. And now, even at the end of the longest boom in history, vacancies are already at historic highs. The country is going into what should be the sideshow of the century.

The national average office vacancy rate for 49 downtown areas was 16.7 percent as of March 1992; it was higher in the suburbs. Vacancies run 22.7 percent in St. Louis, 22.1 percent in Dallas, 23.9 percent in Denver, 26.1 percent in

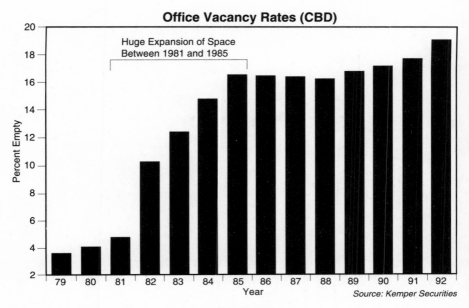

Figure 26-1

Phoenix, 26.9 percent in Miami, and an amazing 33.2 percent in Oklahoma City. Those numbers aren't likely to improve for years.

I feel a hollow satisfaction that many properties have lost 50 percent of their value. Over the last decade I've been one of the world's foremost real estate bears. But the victory is intellectual only, since you cannot really shortsell property.

The question is whether real estate has hit bottom yet. And picking the bottom of the market is as tough as calling the top, and just as dangerous. Trying to call the bottom on the U.S. property market can put you in the position of the guy who saw a safe full of money falling off the top of a 60-story building. He stuck his arms out of a window and tried to catch it, with predictable results. A better idea would have been to wait until it crashed into the sidewalk; then he would not only have kept his arms but would have found the safe broken open for the taking.

Actually, Figure 26-2, showing the returns on commercial property investments since 1979, does resemble the flight path of a safe falling from a penthouse, or at least a flat iron dropped from an airplane.

The real estate sector has seen plenty of bankruptcies so far, but the grand climax has not yet occurred, despite the collapse of the gigantic Olympia and York empire in 1992. One reason is that interest rates are headed back up. As of 1993 interest rates appear to have hit bottom. And the situation is worse than it looks, because the government's Resolution Trust Corporation has only begun to liquidate the properties it acquired from bankrupt savings institutions. As vacancies rise, more loans will go bad and more property will have to be sold. The RTC will

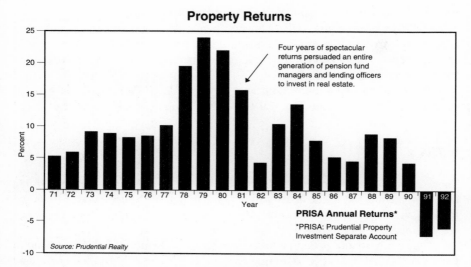

Figure 26-2

acquire even more property as many hundreds of additional banks and S&Ls collapse. Many insurance companies, which have always been huge players in the real estate business, from both the lending and equity sides, will get into a world of trouble as well.

Figure it out. If vacancies were at an all-time high at the peak of the longest boom in modern history, what is likely to happen when the bust climaxes? Probably the same thing that happened to the Empire State Building, which was constructed during a similar boom in the '20s. It changed hands in the '50s for only one-third of its construction cost of more than twenty years earlier.

One might ask what caused the immense rash of overbuilding. Stupidity on the part of developers and financial institutions controlling billions of dollars? No. They are victims of false signals generated by the government's manipulation of the economy. In particular, most real estate deals have been heavily tax-driven. In a free market, where sheltering income from the government would not be a consideration, that much capital would never have flowed into one see-through office tower after another. The misallocations of past decades caused by the tax code will be liquidated through the large-scale bankruptcies of those developers who played this game.

When will the commercial real estate recovery come? It will be slow. And this recovery will be slower and different from those in the past, because there are major new, interrelated factors at work: decentralization, the decline of large organizations, and the telecommunications revolution.

As large corporate dinosaurs downsize and decline, they will not need to occupy whole buildings or even floors of buildings. The smaller organizations that grow will also tend to want smaller buildings, not the megatowers that were typical of the old mass economy. Those towers themselves increasingly fail to reflect population movement patterns, as people disperse from the suburbs into exurbs. Simultaneously, more people are working for themselves out of their homes and have no need of a formal office.

What will happen to all those near-empty buildings? They will find tenants at some price, for some uses. But real prices will continue to drop for years.

HOTELS

There are lots of other commercial accidents waiting to happen, like hotels. In the late '80s, the top end of the hotel market got very hot; it was comparable to the art market, and with many of the same players: the Japanese, and the noveaux riches who wanted a trophy property to match their trophy wives.

Hotels are usually priced in dollars per room, and top properties were sold in the $250,000–$500,000 per room range. The Bel-Air Hotel, which has some land around it but was rather dated the last time I stopped by, went for $1 million per room. The Plaza in New York went for a similar price. The same people also believe a painting is worth $50 million.

A gigantic number of hotel rooms have been built in this country over the last twenty years, catering to rapidly increasing business and consumer travel. The hotel building boom represents a huge distortion in the marketplace, a misallocation of capital about to be liquidated. This downturn in the business cycle, combined with higher fuel costs and improving technology, will empty a lot of hotel rooms and put a real squeeze on the corporations that own them.

Anyone who has done a lot of business travel learns to hate it; that is especially true now that most business people, demographics again, are in their '40s and '50s. As fewer bodies move around to do business, hotels will not be needed in anywhere near their present numbers.

Hotel stocks are worth watching as a short sale possibility, for the indefinite future: Hilton, Marriott, Prime, La Quinta. The stocks look like bargains now, but the market will get much worse before it gets better. When the time comes to buy hotels, the way to do so will be with the convertible bonds most of them offer.

SHOPPING MALLS

Word is just starting to filter out on the next major casualty, the shopping malls. According to MAS Marketing, the average American is visiting his or her local mall only two-thirds as often as ten years ago, stopping in at only half as many stores, and spending only a third as much time in the mall. That is part of the reason why Figure 26-3, showing commercial mortgage foreclosures looks as grim as it does.

Commercial Mortgage Foreclosure

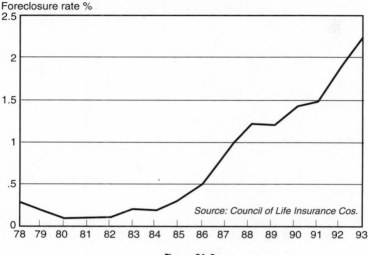

Figure 26-3

I think this trend is going to continue. For one thing, the average person is still deeply in hock and is going to be paying off debt, not taking more on, for years to come. For another, everybody in the baby-boom generation shopped till they dropped in the '80s; it was a mass psychosis, like Saint Vitus' dance in the Middle Ages. T-shirts with the logo "The one who dies with the most toys wins" tell the tale.

Now boomers are surrounded by all this dated junk and are wondering where to get the money to put the kids through school; the "no fun decade" dawns. People are going to be buying less for years. Everyone is purchasing from Wal-Mart, Home Depot, Office Depot, and other discount superstores. These companies and their clones generally stand alone, away from malls, on cheap land. They will grow at the expense of the malls.

Who's going to get hurt worst as more malls default on their loans? The banks haven't seen the end of the decline yet. They perversely lent ever more to mall developers as the market rose after the mid-'80s. Banks have increased real estate loans from 25 percent to 40 percent of their assets.

But it is the insurance companies, who lent the malls almost all their money, who are really going to get tagged. About 20 percent of insurers' assets are in real estate or mortgages, and these investments are not treating them well.

As with any major change in the world, there will be beneficiaries. Two such industries will be mail order and multilevel, or "network marketing."

Mail order will benefit because it allows buyers to avoid sales taxes, which will be crowding 10 percent in many places in the future as governments reach for more revenue. Catalog shopping will be further aided by technologies like interactive

Real Estate Loans/Total Loans*

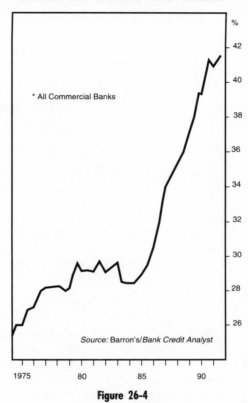

* All Commercial Banks

Source: Barron's/Bank Credit Analyst

1975   80   85   90

Figure 26-4

cable TV. Shipping from a central location will allow retailers better inventory control and lower overhead, even while reaching national markets, not just those folks within driving range. Mail order allows for great specialization of a type a local store cannot support. In any event, people will be less inclined to drive to a store as they move further from population centers and the cost of driving rises. It indicates how poor Sears' management was that they couldn't make money in mail order, even though the company was founded on it.

Multilevel merchants, who distribute products by building pyramid-style sales organizations, will benefit from these same factors, and multilevel will enable the average person looking for extra income, or perhaps just any income, to build a business. Like most new industries, multilevel marketing had its share of scandals and mistakes, but it will mature and grow, because of the delivery system and profit structure it offers, at the expense of conventional retailers and those who rent space to them. Multilevel/network marketing will, perhaps paradoxically, benefit from the trend toward discount superstores as well, since superstores necessarily have limited numbers of salespeople. Multilevel/network marketing is information-intensive with lots of person-to-person contact and service, which, along with the prospects for individuals to build a business, will overcome the disadvantages it may have.

CONCLUSION

This gloomy future will apply mostly to those who are overcommitted to various kinds of commercial property. In any event, it is better to be pessimistic at the beginning of a collapse than at the end. The market will really be depressed in a few years, and that will be the time to look ahead with optimism. Remember that just because a shaky financial structure collapses doesn't mean that the actual buildings it represents collapse. They will do just fine, and the real wealth will remain. It will just change ownership.

27

Finding a Place in the Sun With International Real Estate

To the daring belongs the future.

Emma Goldman, *The Blast*, January 15, 1916

In preindustrial times, only the rare person ever ventured more than a day's walk, perhaps ten miles, from the village where he was born and raised. His horizons, knowledge, and opportunities for improving his status were correspondingly limited. With few exceptions, only those people who ventured achieved wealth, fame, and a degree of self-realization. From the Crusades on, traders made fortunes, but not through real estate acquisition. Their method was to exchange goods and retire to the motherland.

This changed with mass migrations starting in the 1700s and continued into the present. The tired, hungry, huddled masses could leave their homeland penniless, stake out a claim of raw land, and emerge millionaires. The direction of migration is still to North America from the rest of the world. In Orange County, California, in 1991 new homebuyers named Nguyen outnumbered those named Smith two to one. Migration continues to occur for the same reasons: political freedom and economic opportunity. Third Worlders succeed in America because they're willing to work long, hard hours for low pay at jobs most Americans do not want.

Just as foreigners are discovering a land of opportunity in America, Americans can discover opportunities in Third World countries. The prospects are greater than ever, and the risks and costs are lower. Americans, even if they do not have a lot of capital at home, will find that the power of their capital is multiplied many times in poor countries. At the same time, the average American has many skills, connections, and attitudes that, while commonplace and of marginal value at home, are unusual and valuable in Third World countries.

Millions of Third Worlders will immigrate to the United States in the years to come. And smart Americans anxious to better themselves should look to the Third World. It's a question of comparative advantage, which is why bananas are grown in Guatamala and Cadillacs are made in Detroit, and each is exported to the other, to the benefit of all concerned.

For much the same reasons, real estate offers much more upside, with much less risk, in certain foreign countries than in the United States. And Americans are ideally positioned to profit from this.

THE START OF GLOBALIZATION

Inertia is a big factor in dealing with foreign real estate. Foreign securities can be bought and sold in the comfort and privacy of your own home. But real estate demands hands-on investigation and a lot of time on-site. Real estate markets are usually local in nature. Potential buyers probably come from the area. Property generally costs much less in poor countries since local buyers also tend to be relatively poor.

But improved transportation and communications—from the sailing ship, oxcart, and letter through the steamship, train, and telegraph to the airplane, auto, and telephone—have globalized the world economy. And the best is yet to come.

By the late '90s, cellular telephone systems will make it possible to place a call directly by satellite from the middle of the Sahara to the middle of the New Guinea rain forest instantly and cheaply, using only a hand-held unit. Subscription satellite radio and TV will make it possible, on request, to receive the global information these services offer anyplace on the planet's surface. The most recent generation of jets, the 757/767 series, cut costs per seat/mile by about 40 percent from the era of the 727. Hypersonic aircraft will fly by the turn of the century, cutting travel time from New York to Tokyo to about two hours. Further advances in ultralight aircraft will make them practical for anyone now driving a car. Roads, therefore, will be much less important in determining property prices. Solar, and other "soft" technologies, so long awaited and slow in arriving, will eliminate the constraints of bringing in power and other utilities. The world will literally become a global village.

The migration to rural/resort real estate in the United States will extend everywhere on the face of the globe. Primitive countries will benefit the most, and property prices there will reflect the influx of buyers.

The last people to become aware of this global migration will be the rural, unsophisticated locals in those very regions, those who have never ventured more than ten miles, or its modern equivalent, from their home towns. It took the ranchers around Aspen twenty-five years to figure out that their ranches were more valuable as potential subdivisions. Locals in the Andes and the Himalayas will also need time before they realize the value of their property. In both places, the big profits accrue to the person who capitalizes on the trend, not to the original owner of the land.

Most Europeans are well prepared for the global village. They are used to crossing borders, since European countries are small. Most speak several languages and are comfortable in other cultures. Many have relatives who have emigrated in the past, giving them both contacts abroad and a family tradition of internationalism. Americans and Canadians have traditionally been among the most provincial and insular of the technologically and financially advanced nations. Perhaps they thought their countries large enough to offer all the opportunity they needed. Even while multinational corporations have been active abroad, the average investor still has the mind-set of a medieval peasant.

As North American economies and currencies continue their decline in the years to come, the United States and Canada will receive a lot of foreign investment attracted by their relatively "cheap" prices. This new investment will provide liquidity for those who want to sell, and it will bring in needed capital. But it certainly puts the shoe on the other foot, as it were, from the days when a shrewd American could go to Europe or the Orient and buy things at a fraction of their cost at home. That's just another reason for an American to diversify.

DIVERSIFICATION

As a pure investment, there is much to recommend properly chosen foreign property. But there's an even more important factor: diversification. Foreign property can diversify an investor three ways:

1. *Out of the dollar.* The dollar is, almost inevitably, on its way to close to zero, for the reasons detailed earlier. Assets transferred out of dollars are assets sheltered for the long term.
2. *Out of the United States economy.* We can debate whether the United States will hold its own relative to other economies. But it is wise not to have all your eggs in one economic-political basket.
3. *Insulation from foreign exchange controls.* Governments are much more likely to try to control their subjects than themselves. If you do not have assets abroad, out of the direct reach of the U.S. government, you may find it illegal, or very inconvenient and costly, to do so in the future. Real estate is hard to repatriate, unlike money in a bank account that the government can command home.

THE VALUE OF THE DOLLAR

It is important to become less insular and to learn from other countries, especially Third World nations, because our huge deficits will cause the United States to resemble a banana republic. Let's look at what can be learned from two banana republics: Costa Rica and Argentina.

The importance of watching the foreign exchange value of your currency is illustrated by Costa Rica. For many years its currency, the colon, was fixed against the dollar. Then, in 1976, the pressure to devalue because of gigantic foreign trade and government spending deficits became overwhelming, and the currency collapsed overnight by 75 percent.

The little country is self-sufficient in foodstuffs, imports are relatively small because of high tariffs and red tape, and the financial markets are insular and backward. So the domestic effects of the devaluation were not felt quickly, and domestic inflation stayed low for a few months. But prices of everything in the country—from real estate to German cars and French wine—fell by 75 percent for anyone who had hard currency abroad. For several months it was possible to export Mercedes and Dom Perignon from Costa Rica at huge profits, even though a 50 percent to 100 percent duty had been paid on them when they were originally imported. Later, as the implications dawned on the locals, prices went up; they needed to quadruple to get back to pre-devaluation levels in hard currency terms. As a result, fewer Costa Ricans traveled abroad or consumed imported goods.

Similarly, the U.S. dollar is down 50 percent since its peak in early 1985, without much adjustment of local prices. Americans are insulated from the effects of devaluation not by tariffs, but because the domestic economy is so large and self-sufficient. Moreover, the dollar is still the world's reserve currency. But the effects are the same: a loss of ground in real terms and a diminished standard of living.

An even better example is offered by Argentina. In 1989, at the height of one of that country's cyclical currency crises, a friend of mine bought a 10,000-acre parcel about four hours' drive south of Buenos Aires, including several miles of beachfront and excellent buildings, for about US$350,000. I am sure that property had sold for a great deal more in real terms fifty years earlier, when Argentina was still prosperous. Argentinians who earned wages in local currency considered the property quite expensive, even though it looked like a freebie to someone with hard currency. As the Argentine economy turned into a freer market over the next three years, the property revalued to more than a million dollars.

If you believe the United States is in the early stages of the Argentine disease, there are two big lessons to be learned. One, own some property outside the United States, for at least the three reasons listed earlier. Two, maintain cash assets abroad, so that you will be able to buy U.S. property at bargain levels from a ready seller who thinks he is making a score in dollars.

WHERE TO LOOK

Over the long run, U.S. real estate will continue to serve as a good diversification for Americans, just as local real estate served Costa Ricans and Argentines better than did their currency. But it didn't keep them from losing most of their purchasing power relative to foreigners with sound currencies.

There is something to be said for owning property in developed countries, like Switzerland, the United Kingdom, and Germany. I urged investors to do exactly that in 1985, when prices there, and the value of those currencies, were down. That was a matter of timing. The long-term trend suggests directing your attention to Third World countries.

There are three approaches to buying in foreign countries:

1. Buy in countries that are politically distressed and/or have currencies even weaker than the dollar. It is no coincidence that those things usually go together. This amounts to a direct speculation on a turnaround.
2. Buy in countries that are basically sound, or at least more sound than their neighbors in the above category, and are positioned to profit from their neighbors' problems. Buying in such places is not a new technique, even though it is widely overlooked today. It is not unlike what Levi Strauss did during the California gold rush. He found it was much easier and surer to make money selling new "Levi's" to miners than to mine for gold himself. Buying in a Colorado ski resort to capitalize on a meltdown in Los Angeles is a variation on the strategy.
3. Buy in countries that are very sound, have ingrained free-market traditions, and can be counted on to do well despite conditions elsewhere. The United States has been in this category for about a hundred years.

Obviously, there is a lot of overlap among these categories. Hong Kong, for instance, can fall into all three almost simultaneously.

Hong Kong

In the 1960s, when Hong Kong was only an exotic shopping center cum rest-and-relaxation stopover for troops from Vietnam, the steamy seaport was itself as much a bargain as the goods in its shops. And even today, as Hong Kong fills up with some of the world's tallest office buildings, opportunities still appear.

Hong Kong has been "politically distressed" any number of times in the past and is likely to be again. At least as of 1993, its currency is still linked to the U.S. dollar, making currency fluctuations a neutral factor.

The last great buying opportunity was in 1985, during the height of one of the cyclical "China scares." Every few years something happens on the mainland that makes the locals believe that when 1997 comes and the colony is reincorporated into the People's Republic, they will all have their heads displayed on pikes by their poor, envious cousins. Hysteria spreads rapidly, and a lot of people sell for what they can get quickly, figuring it will soon be like Shanghai in 1949.

I happened to be looking at property in Hong Kong in 1985 and was taken aback when some penthouses were selling for less than ground floor apartments in the same building. Why? "When the Chinese take over, they won't fix the elevators." This indicated to me that it was time to buy not only apartments in general but penthouses in particular.

At that time the economics of the place stood up. It was possible to buy a small condo on the top floor of a building right on the harbor, with some of the best views in the world, for $75,000. That price included a total renovation and refurnishing. The equivalent in New York at the time would easily have run $300,000. "Yes," you might say, "but New York was worth more at the time." Not to my way of thinking.

The rents for either the New York apartment or its Hong Kong equivalent were about $1,500 per month. Capitalized, that meant that the Hong Kong apartment was "worth" the same as the New York unit yet sold for a quarter the price. Further, the commission paid to a realtor for renting an apartment in Hong Kong is less than half its New York equivalent, as is the commission for selling it, further enhancing the total return.

Taxes on the New York unit would run about $200 a month, and the condo fee, another $200. In Hong Kong those figures would be about $30 and $30. Taxes, of course, dramatically affect returns. After taxes, commissions, and fees, a landlord nets $900 in New York versus $1,400 in Hong Kong, over 50 percent more.

Federal, state, and local income taxes in the United States can take well over 40 percent of a person's income. In Hong Kong the maximum rate is 18 percent. So your renter has more disposable income, and your own net goes up. Since there are no capital gains taxes in Hong Kong, a seller keeps all the proceeds when he gets out. That serves as an indirect support under the market as well.

Moreover, a quarter of the people on earth live in China, and even in 1985 it was easy to see that the place was developing and changing at warp speed. Beijing's airport facilities were smaller than those of Aspen, so it was a good bet that most of China's development for the foreseeable future would pass through Hong Kong. Only Hong Kong had the transport, communications, accommodations, and available skills to manage incoming business. At the time, I wrote that 5,000 years of Chinese tradition would make the misadventure with Marxism look like nothing more than an aberration, a trivial blip on the screen of China's history.

It was clear that a Hong Kong apartment should be worth substantially more, not less, than its New York equivalent. So why was Hong Kong selling for a fraction of New York at the time, even though it was a better deal? Purely due to the psychology and the relative insularity of the local market. Locals were selling not because they were stupid, but because they realized that the Chinese government sees its people, and their property, as nothing more than a national resource. Locals were prudently diversifying to Europe, Australia, and the Americas; their actions were smart, but their last-minute timing was inappropriate. The bargains were offered in Hong Kong at the time because of a local anomaly. A foreigner with a more disinterested, global view could profit in a way a local would be hard-pressed to do.

It is difficult to assess China's short-run direction; in the long run it will certainly become a true global economic power. But there will be growth pains. As of 1993, the real estate and stock markets in Hong Kong are the hottest in the world. But they will cool off, because the area near Guangzhou (previously Canton) has been transformed in one decade from a backwater farming region to a smaller version of Hong Kong. Guangzhou will steal a lot of Hong Kong's thunder. And there is a strong possibility of a civil conflict between the backward north run by Beijing and the advanced south centered on Guangzhou. The apartment I described earlier is now worth about $300,000. It's time to sell.

A prudent speculator buys when prices are low. He sells when everything looks rosy and reloads for the next suitable opportunity. And there will be more in this region—if not in Hong Kong, then some other part of China.

Canada

It is not necessary to go where blood is running or might run in the streets to find profit. A safe area in a region of conflicts can also present great gains. An investor, like a true economist, is one who doesn't just anticipate the immediate and direct consequences of actions, but also the indirect and delayed ones. How might that have applied to Hong Kong? At the time I asked myself where any refugees from Hong Kong, Taiwan, and other nearby countries would move if things got tough. The answer appeared to be other countries on the Pacific Rim that had stable, common-law cultures, that encouraged immigration, and that had sizable local Chinese communities to act as a nexus for their countrymen. Australia qualified, but Canada was better yet, since it was on the doorstep of the United States.

Canada offers citizenship after only three years of residence; its passport is excellent to carry, since Canada doesn't indulge in the adventures that attract its big neighbor to the south. Canadian real estate was cheap in 1987, even in North American terms, because of the collapse of the Canadian dollar to only US$.71, and because of its depressed, socialistic economy. It was especially cheap by Hong Kong standards.

Toronto seemed like an upmarket version of Detroit or Buffalo. Montreal seemed too politically divisive and ethnic; anyway, the time to have bought in Montreal was during the exodus of English-speaking people during the separatist hysteria in the '70s. Calgary and Edmonton, on the windblown prairie, seemed more a play on oil prices than Chinese immigration. Vancouver was the place to go because it borders the Pacific and has the best weather in Canada. The choice was whether to buy an apartment downtown, a farm out of town, or waterfront property in a good suburb. We decided on waterfront because of its limited availability, because that location puts it at the top of the market, and because most of the Chinese émigrés were quite wealthy. We reasoned that even the poorer immigrants would soon become rich, as well, like overseas Chinese almost everywhere, through their renowned Confucian work ethic. Many Chinese would buy top-end properties themselves, but their population pressure would push existing home-owners farther out, toward the waterfront. That is pretty much what happened, and good waterfront property more than doubled from 1987 to 1991, while the Canadian dollar rose 24 percent to a peak of US$.88.

At this time I would recommend selling, even though Asian immigration is continuing apace. Indeed, most people are unaware that British Columbia will be more than half Asian by the turn of the century. The value of the Canadian dollar also has to be watched closely. It promises to turn into the northern peso over the next few years. Property in Vancouver will probably hold up fairly well, but why try to figure out whether an inrushing wave will overcome the outgoing tide after values have doubled and property is no longer cheap?

Spain

Spain enjoys more tourism than any other country in Europe. Spain is a good analog to California in a number of ways. Southern Spain, at the resort of Marbella, is the most southern point of Europe. It is farther south than Sicily or Greece, and even more southerly than a good deal of North Africa. The climate is identical to San Diego's year round; even the terrain is identical to southern California. But except along the coast, southern Spain, Andalusia, is empty.

With the exception of the weather, Scotland has some similarities to southern Spain in that it's sparsely populated and economically depressed, and some of its property has performed extremely well in recent years. That is especially true of castles, which nobody wanted until recently. The value of these properties probably quintupled in the last decade. The reason, I suspect, is comparable to the reason property in small, exclusive American resorts has exploded: people in advanced countries are abandoning the cities.

Many people in rich countries have reached the level where the additional dollar they can make in the city isn't worth the additional aggravation. They want to escape the cities. That trend will continue in advanced countries, as will migration to the cities in backward countries. If you want to own property as an investment in advanced countries, go for beautiful, relatively unspoilt locations. Poland, inciden-tally, has lots of rundown castles in the countryside for $10,000 or so.

In any event, it is pretty clear what will happen in southern Spain. Costs are about the lowest in Europe, and that fact will draw people from wealthy countries in the north. The weather will draw them, much as California's did in the United States. Another attraction is the lack of crowds, which spurred U.S. migration from the East Coast to the West. And the removal of most political and labor barriers, with the new European Economic Community (EEC), will also help.

The Marbella area went through a boom starting in the early '80s; it experienced huge overbuilding, and prices have since dropped back to the levels, in local currency, of a decade ago. Of course the peseta is now worth over 50 percent more relative to the dollar, but the trend is clear, and this area is the place to be in western Europe. Smart money that buys large tracts of land just back of the coast will do as well as those who bought large tracts of land in southern California in the '50s.

Australia

Most people buy property close to home for the obvious reasons—ease of inspection and maintenance—and they want it to be close enough to get some use out of it. That is why few people have seriously considered Down Under; they can't enjoy their property unless they sit in a flying cattle car for almost a full day to get there. Property has always been cheap in Australia, outside of its main cities, for two reasons: lack of population and long distances. Australia is the size of the continental United States, but has only 15 million inhabitants. And it is literally in the middle of nowhere; even Hong Kong is ten hours away.

That is why if you buy an Australian cattle ranch on the ocean (perhaps 500,000 acres with ten miles of beachfront, houses, paddocks, and a few thousand head of cattle), you might pay only US$500,000, or about $1 per acre, with the improvements thrown in free. In point of fact, though, you are paying for the improvements and getting the land thrown in free. That is hard to understand until you realize that you are a day's drive from the nearest small town, and if the car breaks down along the way, you can forget about calling a mechanic.

Australia always has a few Rhode Island–size parcels on the market for what seem like bargain prices, and it has been that way for decades. Are they really bargains? These country-sized estates have been financial disasters for those who bought them in the past. But I believe things will change radically in the next decade, because of the technologies emerging at present. This freehold land, populated by people who share Western values, will rise from a few cents an acre to the prices now charged for arid land around Phoenix. If you buy now, your children will think you were a genius.

If that's too radical for you but you still like the general idea, look at Tasmania, the big island south of Australia. The climate resembles Seattle's, but with less rain. The scenery is lush and civilized, like the best of the Virginia hunt country. People never lock their doors, and prices are about 30 percent of what you would expect to pay in most places in the United States.

THE THIRD WORLD

The examples above illustrate the characteristics of places where you should buy. But, as I said earlier, the Third World is really the place to look. Currencies fluctuate wildly, and prices fluctuate just as wildly within those currencies. In Brazil, the same apartment on the Copacabana beach can range from $50,000 to $500,000, depending only on the strength of the local currency and the political situation. In the tropical mountains of Bolivia, during their currency collapse of 1986, an elegant house on beautifully landscaped grounds could have been purchased for $50,000; today it's worth $700,000.

Nicaragua provides an example of how fast things can change for the worse. It's probably the prettiest country in Central America, and used to be a favorite hangout of Bianca Jagger's jet-set friends before the Sandinista takeover. In 1980, after the revolution, I found prices there unrealistically high. I decided to pass, reasoning that the country would always be there, but the government wouldn't. I'm tempted to return now; the people are desperately poor, and the market is soft.

My intention, incidentally, is not to be predatory. The speculator provides a public service by offering a bid when otherwise none is available. A speculator simply gives people what they want most at the time. When prices are high and everyone seeks property, he endeavors to keep prices from going even higher by providing a supply. And when prices are low and everyone desperately needs cash, he once again bows to the will of the market. Buying low and selling high is helpful to people when they need cash more than land.

Chile shows dramatically how quickly the market can turn around when governments discard just the most obvious of the stupidities to which they're so partial. When I visited Chile in 1979 I met an arms trader who had become persona non grata during the Allende years. His magnificent house was located in the best part of Santiago, which is itself a beautiful city favored with a climate like that of Santa Barbara. He recounted that in the early '70s, while exiled to Paraguay, he would have sold his elegantly furnished house (with pool, tennis court, and all the accoutrements) for $25,000. He said his neighbors would have been anxious sellers at the same time, for comparable prices and for the same reason: fear of the local government. Today that house is probably worth about $500,000. If it were located in California it would have been worth several million at the top of that market in 1989.

You may be thinking, "Yes, $25,000 was a bargain, but the risk was great." On the contrary. First, relative risk is a function of price. Second, absolute risk in such cases is primarily a question of whether a piece of property will be nationalized or confiscated.

Nationalization was once a real danger in troubled countries with property that could be considered a "means of production"—raw land, mines, or factories. But even in the old days, it was unusual for residential property owned by foreigners to be taken by the government. And now, with the lessons Third World countries have learned from their bout with socialism, nationalization is unlikely anywhere. The residences of citizens who are considered ideologically unsound or politically unreliable may still be in jeopardy, however, which explains their low value in a crisis. But foreigners are almost sacrosanct. Always remember that a crisis presents both danger and opportunity. In these cases, it's mostly the locals' danger and the foreigners' opportunity.

A policy of buying when blood is literally running in the streets might, arguably, have found you buying in Havana in 1960, and then writing off those funds. But one Santiago in 1973 makes up for a score of Havanas.

THE BOTTOM OF THE BARREL

The best buys in the Third World are in the places where few people would think of looking: politically distressed countries.

South America has freed its markets, with resulting stupendous gains in its economies and stock markets. Fewer people know that the same thing is happening in Africa. Zambia, Tanzania, Kenya, and Zaire, among others, are rapidly changing from the regimes of "one man, one vote, one time."

The old formula worked well enough for the people at the top, who were able to loot their countries systematically and salt away the proceeds in Switzerland. That is where all the foreign aid went. Foreign aid might accurately be described as a transfer from poor people in rich countries to rich people in poor countries. The U.S. government still squanders about $20 billion a year this way, and European governments spend proportionally even more. It has all disappeared down a giant rathole.

But with the bankruptcy of the United States and other Western governments, this "aid" will of necessity stop. Any aid the West is still willing to give will be but a drop in the sea of capital necessary to rebuild Eastern Europe. That demand for funds will not leave table scraps for the folks living in the heart of darkness. It will be a nightmare for the mid-level nebbishes in the State Department and the IMF. The tropical gangsters and kleptocrats they have long subsidized will be forced to live off what they have already stolen. Foreign aid has served to prop up incredibly corrupt regimes which, without aid, would have collapsed many years ago, much to the benefit of their subjects. So cutting off aid will be a boon to the common people.

Without further aid Africa will have to set its markets free in order to support itself. Mozambique provides a good example. It was ranked the poorest country in the world by the IMF in 1992.

It is interesting that both rents and prices are extremely high in the capital of Mozambique, the opposite of what you would expect in a war-torn, poverty-stricken nation where a human life isn't worth the price of a meal. They are high for two reasons. First, socialist policies resulted in masses of uninhabitable buildings, just as in the South Bronx, and there was no new construction from 1975 to 1991, so the supply has fallen precipitously. Second, as in most war zones, everyone who could, fled from the countryside to the capital, where life is relatively safe, so demand went way up. You can find opportunity in Maputo, but there is more in the bush and on the beaches.

The dominant impression of a Third World city is conveyed by smell as much as by sight; the diesel fumes and the aroma of garbage ripening in the tropical sun are the same worldwide. Maputo went from being a gem twenty years ago, one of the prettiest, cleanest, and most prosperous colonial cities in the world, to a genuine dump. Under Frelimo* all the stores were shuttered, and none of the electricity or plumbing worked. Meanwhile, a full-scale bush war raged everywhere outside of the capital, making travel hazardous.

Since 1990, the government has backed off from creating a People's Republic, and in just two years the markets again have produce, probably 40 percent of the storefronts are open, and new-car dealerships and factories are being reactivated. The rate of change is unbelievable. With the war ending, the country will again know relative safety and peace, as happened in Zimbabwe after its long civil war. Tourists from Europe will return to throng the beaches and buy $2 lobster dinners.

When going to a place like Mozambique is suggested to most people, their first reaction is they would feel safer in Miami when they want warm weather. But those who buy a dumpy studio apartment in Miami will someday wonder why they didn't go for a large farm on the African coast instead. The reason, of course, is that they are provincial and not very imaginative and probably, alas, belong in Miami.

One South African I met negotiated a fifty-acre plot on the beach just outside Maputo from the government; his cost basis is basically zero. The government gave the property to him because he agreed to develop it for tourists; someday it will have the same value as prime beachfront elsewhere in the world. His resort will be full of Germans and Swedes who have flown to Mozambique to beat the European winter. And there are thousands of miles of pristine, undeveloped, deserted beach on this country's coast. Most nights I slept on the beach, since it was so pleasant; it's strange how you can sleep on the beach safely in a war zone, but you wouldn't dare do so anywhere near a U.S. city.

One bright side to this country—and almost every other nation in Africa—is that the reefs thrive with waterlife since none of the locals have motorboats or sophisticated fishing gear. Of course, after they get modern equipment, the reefs will probably look like they've been vacuum-cleaned. As government property, they'll be treated as if they belonged to no one. Prosperity will destroy their natural beauty, as it has elsewhere in the world; private ownership is the only way to preserve this beauty. That's an excellent ancillary reason to buy tracts of beach-front, and even marine rights.

Another South African I know made his living as a cotton farmer in Swaziland. He sold his spread to take advantage of a Mozambique government grant of 10,000

*Frelimo, Mozambique's Marxist/socialist party.

hectares (25,000 acres) where he will grow cotton. He will employ about 2,000 workers at about $10 per month each, and expects to be immediately profitable, especially since he can import machinery, seed, and other needed materials duty free. Moreover, he was given a three-year tax holiday. By the time he has the operation in production, which should occur as life in Mozambique normalizes, he should be able to sell his holding there for $5 million to $10 million. Not bad.

The country is full of abandoned farms left by the Portuguese when their property was nationalized; some were looted and then deserted. Others, incredibly, are tidy, maintained by loyal workers who await the return of the owners. The government is restoring property to all previous owners, but many will not return to reclaim their houses and land.

How would you like a 1,000-acre dairy farm for $10,000 plus fifteen years' back taxes? Probably another $15,000. This is clearly an opportunity for someone who can find these prior owners and negotiate a sale with them. At the moment, however, it is almost impossible to buy anything in Mozambique in the conventional way since there is no process for transferring title. You can only get long-term leases from the state, which takes lots of palavering with officials, trading of favors, and little envelopes stuffed with cash. But that will change.

CONCLUSION

The situation is much the same all over Africa, parts of South America, and the South Pacific today. The governments of these countries ran them until the wheels fell off, and are turning to free-market economics with a vengeance, not so much the result of ideology, but of necessity. The changes there are real, having been forged by experience.

It is odd to think that the United States, too, is making at least some of the mistakes that so frequently occur in banana republics before it will have its own free-market renaissance.

The next several chapters will examine Japan, Russia, and some other important countries, which are at very different points of evolution.

Questions and Answers

Q. *Doesn't following the advice here really amount to cutting a lot of ties with the United States? And what about citizenship?*

A. Internationalizing your assets is a big step toward insulating yourself from the depredations of government. Increasing numbers of Americans are going even farther and giving up their U.S. citizenship. John Templeton, perhaps the world's most famous fund manager, did so years ago.

Carrying a neutral passport, say Canada's or Ireland's, does not push the "hot buttons" that come with a U.S. passport. And the United States is unique in presuming to tax its subjects on 100 percent of their worldwide income, less an exemption currently set at $75,000—even if they leave the United States and never return. Other countries typically tax only those who spend more than six months within their borders.

Some Americans, who do not need to work in any one location—writers, artists, investors, or inventors—have, therefore, exchanged their U.S. passport for a less restrictive one. If they do not spend more than six months a year in any one country, they can legally live tax-free, even in the United States. It is not a bad deal to spend summers where it is cool and winters where it is warm and be able to afford it on your tax savings.

Of course, if the IRS determines that the major reason for renouncing citizenship is to avoid or reduce taxes, it reserves the right to continue taxing for another ten years. To my knowledge, this rule has never been applied except in the case of Elizabeth Taylor, who renounced and reclaimed her U.S. citizenship several times. Thousands of less-celebrated Americans uneventfully internationalize themselves each year.

For most people, though, if the thought of buying property abroad is academic, then the idea of taking a new citizenship is anathema. But it is wise to remember that everyone in the United States, or their ancestors, left some previous homeland. And *America* is not a set of political rules, and not so much a place, either. It's an idea, an ideal. As such, it transcends geography.

28

The Bubble Bursts in Japan

JAPAN: THE BALLOON IN SEARCH OF A PIN

The Japanese financial markets in the late 1980s became as overpriced as any major markets in history. Morgan Stanley did a study of some of them:

Table 28-1

Bubble	Percentage Rise & Length in Months		Percentage Fall & Length in Months	
Dutch tulips (1634–37)	5900%	(36)	−93%	(10)
French Mississippi shares (1719–21)	6200%	(13)	−99%	(13)
British South Sea shares (1719–20)	1000%	(18)	−84%	(6)
U.S. stocks (1921–32)	497%	(95)	−87%	(33)
Mexican stocks (1978–81)	785%	(30)	−73%	(18)
Silver (1979–82)	710%	(12)	−88%	(24)
Hong Kong stocks (1970–74)	1200%	(28)	−92%	(20)
Taiwanese stocks (1986–90)	1168%	(40)	−80%	(12)
Japanese stocks (1965–?)	3720%	(288)	?	?

A likely response from most Americans might be: "That's interesting, but what's it to me?" The answer is that the world's markets are now so interrelated that it makes a big difference to everyone. The failure of Credit Anstalt in Austria, a bank few Americans knew of, sparked the 1929 depression. And what happens in Japan is far more directly relevant to the United States today than anything that happened in Austria was to the United States sixty years ago. The reason is simple: Japan is one of the world's great financial powers. Twenty of the world's twenty-five biggest banks are Japanese; only one is American. The Japanese stock market, at the 1989 peak of its mania, totaled almost twice the value of America's exchanges.

The top four of the five largest companies in the world in terms of sales are Japanese (C.Itoh, US$118 billion; Mitsui, $113 billion: Marubeni, $106 billion; and Sumitomo, $105 billion). No one needs to be reminded about Japanese cars, electronics, cameras, and computers. Japan's success has created much rancor in America. Instead of celebrating the fact that the Japanese are creating a vast number of high-quality, low-cost goods that increase our choices, spur native industry to compete, and improve our standard of living, many people are urging the government to punish the Japanese for their success. Undoubtedly the same people will be gloating as the Japanese economy falls on hard times. Unfortunately, hard times in Japan will spill over to America. And those same people who found cause to hate the Japanese for improving our standard of living will, in turn, hate them for reducing it.

In any event, the center of gravity of the financial world shifted from New York to Tokyo over the last decade, just as, in the 1920s, it shifted from London to New York. What happens in Tokyo will have a big effect on New York.

JAPANESE STOCKS: THE SHORT OF THE CENTURY

The excessively high valuation of Japanese stocks is exemplified by the recently privatized NTT, the national telephone company. When the company was valued at close to $300 billion in 1989, it was "worth" over twenty times the value of AT&T, and as much as IBM, GE, AT&T, Exxon, and GM all put together. The company had a .2 percent dividend and a P/E of over 200. NTT alone was worth more than the entire German stock market. Somewhat rich for an old, regulated utility.

But even comparing earnings, book value, dividends, and market capitalization doesn't tell the story, because the quality of Japanese earnings and assets is questionable. A considerable part of some companies' earnings is due to successful trading in securities and currency. As you can see in Figure 28-1, prices have risen partly due to an expansion in P/E ratios from a reasonable 10 times earnings in the early '70s to between 30 and 60 times earnings today. When earnings drop, so will investors' enthusiasm. Instead of selling for more than 60 times X, they could easily sell for 10 times $1/4$ X, which amounts to a drop of about 95 percent.

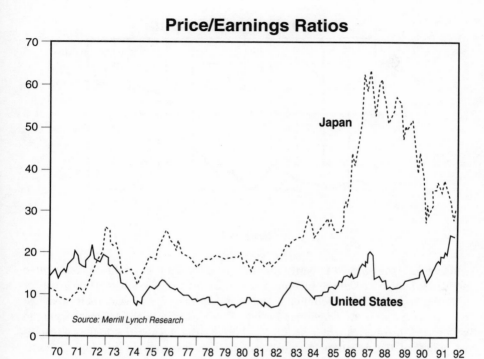

Price/Earnings Ratios

The price-earnings ratio of the Japanese stock market soared to record levels during the late 1980s as a result of easy money and tight supply of free stock.

Figure 28-1

Another indicator that the Nikkei is still overpriced is the boom in the Japanese stock-brokerage industry, which basically means just four firms. Nomura is the biggest, and its profits quintupled between 1983 and 1987; the company has a market capitalization of about $65 billion. Merrill Lynch, the biggest U.S. broker, is worth only about $2.8 billion.

It is always hard to say what a market "should" be worth. Based upon Japan's immense success, its market should sell for a premium to others. But even though it has declined 50 percent from its manic top, Japanese securities still sell for a gigantic premium to the rest of the world's markets. And the other markets are themselves selling for premium prices.

THE TRADE SURPLUS

Japan's huge trade surplus proved a major economic factor in the boom, because those several hundred billions of dollars that come in each year have to go

Japan's Trade Surplus

Source: Economic Planning Agency

Figure 28-2

somewhere. The surplus is partly due to self-sufficiency in quality manufactured goods. It is also due to the incompetence of overseas competitors. (For instance, Chrysler and GM, even assuming a Japanese consumer would want their products, do not make cars with a right-hand drive. That's as silly as the Japanese trying to export cars to America without a left-hand drive.) But it's also due to the mercantilist policy of the government, which emphasizes low imports and high exports.

A strong cultural factor is the immense confidence the Japanese have that their government will take any action necessary to prevent a collapse. The Japanese believe that their government should, can, and does control the economy and the markets. That confidence was reinforced in mid-1992, when the Japanese government earmarked 6 trillion yen ($48 billion) of public funds in an extraordinary effort to prop up business, stocks, and real estate. Like all government intervention, the spending had a temporary, positive effect, which prevented the markets from cleansing themselves and created even more distortions in the system.

Moreover, the Japanese stock market does not have a tradition of valuing stocks based on Graham-Dodd fundamentals, so things like P/Es and book values are traditionally of minor importance. Tokyo stocks were valued more on their prospects, which is to say "blue sky," than on their financials. Once a market is cut loose from fundamental values, who can say what it is worth? Tokyo is like a gigantic version of Vancouver.

Part of the boom could be attributed to the natural tendency to join the fray when everyone else is making money. The Japanese have an old saying: "No one is in danger if we all cross together on a red light," unless, I suppose, the red light is at a railroad crossing. The same psychology also makes everyone scream at a rock concert, applaud a vacuous political speech, or panic when someone yells "Fire!" in a crowded theater. Although that last analogy will be more descriptive after the slide continues into the mid-'90s.

Despite international interest, the largest percentage of Japanese stocks is owned by Japanese. The market is insular and controlled by the local psychology. But the Japanese investor is as arrogant, naive, and spoiled as a California homeowner. He has experienced only one market, a bull market. The one lesson he has learned is that it is a mistake to sell. So he is not terribly frightened at the moment. And markets do not bottom while nobody's scared enough to panic and sell.

What caused the bubble to burst? Perhaps a basically unnatural bull market is just dying a natural death, after everyone who can possibly buy has bought all he can. But a "natural" death for a market is no more pleasant than any other kind, if what happened in 1929 is any indication. Why the boom began and ended is academic, because every mania creates rationalizations why its market should rise to a given level. The autopsy of the Tokyo bubble will be performed by historians. More important, you must determine how far the Japanese market will collapse and how you can insulate yourself from the consequences.

CHANGES

Japan's success is the result of massive exports of manufactured goods. But they are now facing serious problems. Entirely apart from the fact that the world is awash in cars and electronic equipment, lower-cost producers will increasingly manufacture goods to undercut the Japanese. Taiwan, Korea, China, and Brazil are using the latest manufacturing technology in combination with their cheaper labor to do so.

A number of countries, including the United States, will seek to restrict Japanese imports, as well as the products of their new competitors, to protect the interests of inefficient local producers. The creation of several world trading blocks, a silly idea at the best of times, is especially dangerous when a trade war seems to be brewing.

The 100 percent appreciation of the yen, from roughly 260 to 120 to the dollar since 1985, has hurt Japanese competitiveness and squeezed their profit margins, and it has boosted the value to foreign investors of Japanese stocks. It is ironic that, the increased value of the yen and the decrease in profit margins have simultaneously produced conditions that are ripe for a collapse in companies' earnings. If all currencies were redeemable with a fixed amount of gold, a tremendous variable would be taken out of the equation. As it stands, the yen continues to be a greatly overvalued currency, trading at around 120 to the dollar in 1993. On a "purchasing-power parity" basis—the best long-term measure of where a currency "should" be—the yen is overpriced by 40 percent. About 190 to the dollar would be more like it. A strong currency is a plus for the Japanese, not a minus, since it enables them to pay less for imports and to buy foreign assets at what become, in yen terms, bargain prices. But it hurts exports and may not be good for their stock market.

Conditions within Japan that favored their stocks in the past are also changing. The work ethic born of defeat in the war has been eroded over the past two generations. The country's demographics are changing; the population is growing older, and that means fewer workers, higher wages relative to other costs, and an increasing welfare burden.

Industry in Japan is not only growing at a slower rate, it is declining in absolute terms, and that trend is still in motion. The same is true of corporate earnings. Declining retail sales, however, prove that the problem is not due only to a slowdown in the economies of its trading partners. There's trouble at home (see Figures 28-3 through 28-5).

WHERE IS THE BOTTOM?

Despite recent large sell-offs, Japan's stock and property markets are not cheap. Prices continue to reflect the good times of the last few decades. The next few years will probably be grim enough to shake up price perceptions; views ingrained over

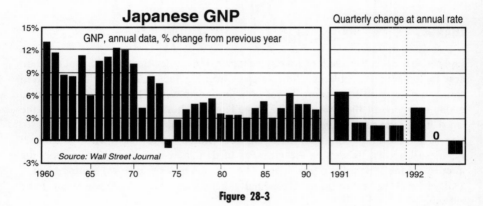

Figure 28-3

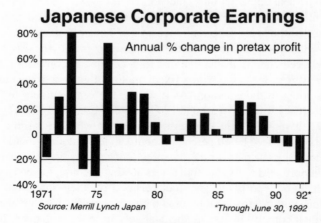

Figure 28-4

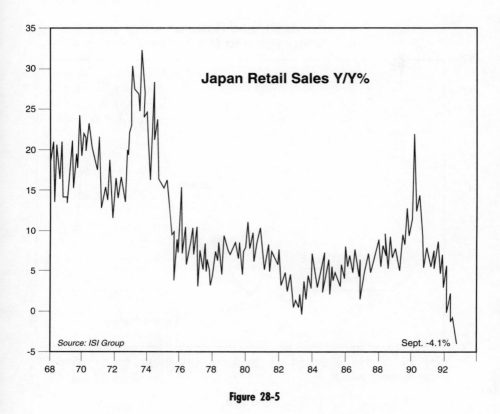

Figure 28-5

many years do not turn on a dime. As with most historic events, Japan's crisis will not bottom out until the collapse of its financial markets is the headline in every magazine and newspaper around the world.

As of 1993, with the Nikkei Dow at 17,000, the Tokyo market is again at historically reasonable, but not cheap, levels. Of the approximately 2,050 public Japanese companies, about 10 percent sold for less than their book value (Fig. 28-6). And the market as a whole sold at price/book value ratios typical of the early '80s.

At some point, probably in the mid-'90s, the Japanese market will present a rare bargain, with opportunities as good as those of decades ago. A number of points should be considered before an investor takes the plunge.

1. At 17,000, the market has only sold off from once-in-a-lifetime manic levels to "reasonable" levels. All the excesses have yet to be washed out of the system, and since the world economic situation will get worse before it improves, we will most likely see once-in-a-lifetime bargain prices before a true uptrend resumes. Buying prematurely could be like buying U.S. stocks in 1930; they were "cheap," but only relative to where they had been in the 1920s.

Japanese Ratio of
Stock Price to Book Value

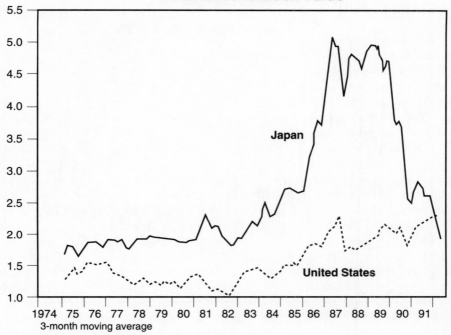

Figure 28-6

2. One can properly question how real Japanese profits are. Much of the profits they show are trading gains realized during the boom years. When more companies have to liquidate, at a loss, shares they bought at the top of the bull market, their earnings and book values could drop dramatically.

The Tokyo Exchange resembles a cartel more than a market. In what is known as the "keiretsu" system, it is traditional for all the big companies to own substantial blocks of other big companies with whom they have relationships. It is estimated that 70 percent of Tokyo stocks are locked up in the hands of "friends." With most of the stock tightly held, a little bit of buying had an inordinate effect, just as with Vancouver penny stocks. All the holders had profits, so they felt confident in buying more, which took prices higher yet, resulting in P/E ratios of over 100 in many cases.

This effect was amplified because 80 percent of Tokyo's volume is produced by just the four big brokers, and only a couple of dozen big institutions dominate the market for the float. It is a tight "good ol' boys" market, with only a small percentage (3 percent–8 percent) owned by unpredictable, uncontrollable foreigners. Now the paper profits are almost gone, and it is serious business. For the first time, corporations are beginning to sell each other's stock into the market. The process will feed on itself as the market declines, just as it did when it rose. Like a pendulum, the further it swings to one side, the further it's likely to swing to the other.

3. Bottom picking is a delicate art because stock prices often turn before fundamentals. In any event, the trend is still down, for both earnings and share prices, as shown in Figure 28-4, above, and Figure 28-7, below. It is a mistake to fight the tape. Sometimes a 90 percent stock market collapse takes place over a short time, as in the United States from 1929 to 1933 and in Hong Kong from 1973 to 1974. In other instances it stretches over decades. The Italian market also dropped over 90 percent—in real terms—from 1961 to 1978.

4. Another way of putting Figure 28-7 in perspective is to compare stock prices to GNP. Except during a manic peak in 1972, at 52 percent of GNP, just before the Japanese market crashed, the ratio of the total value of Japanese stocks to the country's GNP throughout the 1960s and 1970s was consistently between 20 percent and 34 percent. This ratio reached above 153 percent in 1989. Right now it is still about 70 percent. If the ratio drops to historic levels, we can expect about 8,000 on the Nikkei. That would be a "normal," not panic, level. But manias are usually followed by panics; 4,000 on the Nikkei isn't out of the question.

5. A great deal of capital, about 15 trillion yen, was raised in the '80s in the form of convertible bonds. That is approximately US$130 billion that will have to be redeemed, or rolled over at much higher interest rates, in 1993 and 1994. Those redemptions or increased payments will squeeze both corporate earnings and stock prices.

6. The Japanese use debt much more aggressively than the Americans, which is a disturbing thought. At some point their banks, which as previously noted

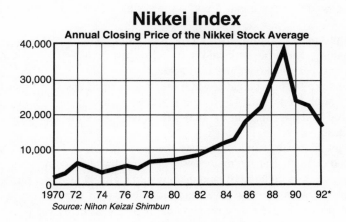

Figure 28-7

include nine of the ten largest in the world, will likely have large defaults on their corporate and especially their real estate loans.

Bank debt remains at record levels, about 1.05 times GNP in 1992. That's down from a peak of 1.11 times GNP in 1989, but way above the .55 to .75 of GNP that was typical during Japan's steady growth years from 1960 to 1980. The more you leverage on the way up, the steeper the drop when the cycle reverses, which it has. Japanese banks are in trouble.

This high Japanese debt leverage makes it tough to say how bad it will get. The banks extended almost all of the debt, which makes the health of the banks even more critical in Japan than is the case in the United States. Worse yet, roughly 60 percent of the Japanese banks' capital and surplus is in the form of equity in their client companies, so the banks' health and stability are tied directly to the level of the stock market, unlike the United States or Britain, where shareholdings equal only about 3 percent of the banks' capital. As the Japanese market went up, the banks' capital strength grew, and they were able to lend ever more, which helped the markets rise even further. Now that the market has turned and is falling, basically of its own weight, the process is in reverse. The keiretsu system was especially strong among bank stocks, some of which had only 8–10 percent of their shares floating in the open market.

With the Nikkei at 17,000, most Japanese banks are right at the 8 percent line drawn by the Bank for International Settlements (the BIS) for capital-to-loan ratios. If the market falls further, they will have to call in loans, much as U.S. banks have been doing. This will exacerbate the decline in property prices, further weakening their capital-to-loan ratios.

7. Dividend yields are excellent indicators of value in all stock markets. The Japanese market yielded about 3 percent in dividends at the bottom in 1973. Current yields have recently doubled from 0.5 percent to 1 percent as a result of the market's 50 percent drop. Depending on local interest rates at the time, 3 percent is a fair target. That would imply about 5,000 on the Nikkei Dow, everything else being equal.

Trying to pick a bottom when all the indicators say a market is at an all-time low is one thing. But arbitrarily calling for a low just because it's down 50 percent from a lunatic peak is something else again.

Markets are historic bargains when they sell for perhaps five times earnings, one-half of book value, and 12 percent dividend yields. Hong Kong, Spain, and Belgium sold at those levels in the mid-'80s when I recommended them. Japan is nowhere close.

A major recession would devastate the stock prices of Japanese companies, which is bad enough. But the major asset of many Japanese companies is the real estate they own, so a collapse of land there would logically lead to a further decline in stock prices. Many stocks have made runs based on their real estate values, because the price of some Tokyo property has tripled in as many years, and risen up to 1,000 times in the last twenty; insane real estate prices have been used to justify manic stock prices. As in the United States, a Japanese real estate crash could prove far more devastating than a stock market crash.

JAPANESE REAL ESTATE

The U.S. real estate market is in the midst of a major meltdown. But our problems are trivial compared to Japan's. A few facts will illustrate how crazy the market has become at its peak.

- An ordinary, tiny 800-square-foot apartment located two hours commute from central Tokyo went for almost $500,000.

- A detached single-family home within Tokyo city limits could fetch $30 to $40 million.

- A 450-square-foot noodle shop in downtown Tokyo is rumored to have sold for $14 million.

- The three central districts of Tokyo quintupled in value from 1985 to 1989.

- In 1990, at then-current property prices and rents, it would take more than one hundred years for a central Tokyo office building to pay for itself.

- Many Japanese couples have taken mortgages of six to ten times their annual incomes in order to acquire an apartment.

- Golf course memberships are traded, with prices published daily; the average membership costs $500,000. The membership doesn't represent a claim on any assets, nor can it be redeemed for anything. It is good only for getting on the course, sometimes after making a reservation up to six months in advance, in addition to paying a $150+ per-round greens fee.

- The director general of the Economic Research Institute of the Japanese government's Economic Planning Agency said the following in 1987 (I'm quoting him verbatim). "We have calculated land value in two places in central Tokyo close to the Imperial Palace, Ohtemachi and Toranomon. We found that if we sold all the land in those areas, we could buy all of Canada, or all of California. We thought at first we had made a one-digit or two-digit mistake, but we checked it, and it's crazy, but that's the reality."

- The Japanese Association of Real Estate found that, as of January 1, 1990, which was roughly the peak, residential land prices in Tokyo were 89 times greater than for comparable properties in New York, 33 times greater than in London, 23 times greater than in Paris, 6 times greater than in Hong Kong and 13 times greater than in Singapore. It is true that prices have dropped by more than 20 percent since then, but they still have a long way to fall. As Figure 28-8 indicates, the downtrend shows no sign of bottoming.

Despite the fact it's come down considerably from its peak in 1990, the Japanese real estate market is clearly a giant balloon in search of a pin, and when it

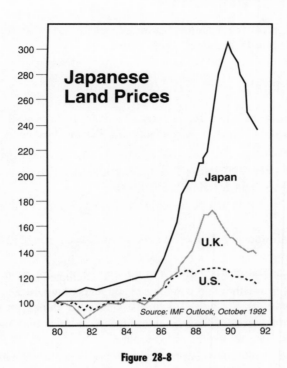

Figure 28-8

pops it could bring down the financial structure of the whole world. This is the kind of stuff Charles McKay wrote about in *Extraordinary Delusions and the Madness of Crowds*.

WHY?

Why did Japanese real estate reach such lunatic levels? It was a confluence of a number of reasons: political, economic, financial, cultural, and psychological. They tie together and compound one another. Of these, politics has been by far the biggest factor in creating Japan's "bubble economy."

Japanese land-use policies constricted supply and artificially increased demand. Every arbitrary and outmoded zoning restriction that can be found in the United States is evident in Japan. But their detrimental effect is much greater in Japan because a population half that of the United States is crowded into a land area the size of California, but with much less habitable land than California.

Strict building height requirements are enforced in many areas, which, more than technical or cultural reasons, forced Tokyo to spread over hundreds of square miles. A strong central government made it important to locate in Tokyo to be a player; it is as if New York, Los Angeles, Chicago, and Washington were all one city. That made Tokyo both inordinately important and extraordinarily expensive.

For decades, the Japanese government has encouraged people to save rather than consume. The immediate and direct effect was a high savings rate, which boosted economic development. But one of the indirect and delayed effects was a country of wealthy people living in what most people of similar means in the rest of the world would consider substandard housing. The high savings rate kept interest rates down and helped make available the mortgage money driving prices so high.

Government policy also created a major incentive to take on large mortgages, with a land sales tax of up to 80 percent. It made no sense to sell the property and pay the tax when it was possible to simply borrow against the property at 3 to 4 percent interest rates made possible by the high savings rate and the flood of capital available from the trade surplus. By discouraging sales, the high tax rate further restricted supply. As in the United States, farmers are heavily subsidized on the one hand, but barred from rezoning farmland close to the city for development.

The excessive use of credit has been at the root of most financial debacles throughout history. One-hundred-percent mortgage loans were the norm in Tokyo for most of the '80s, so the market is extraordinarily leveraged.

As the market soared out of control, the solons attempted to cool it, encouraging people to consume rather than save, changing the tax laws, allowing farmers to rezone land, and reviewing height limits, among other things. Of course their timing proved as perverse as the original regulations, accelerating a slide that was already underway. The situation is reminiscent of Gerry Ford's WIN (Whip Inflation Now) button campaign, which started after inflation was already declining back in 1975. Governments, predictably, wind up fighting the last war.

THE CONSEQUENCES

The consequences of the collapse of Tokyo's stock and real estate markets are also hard to quantify. At its peak, the Japanese stock market was worth $4,100 billion and the Tokyo property market $6,000 billion.

A Japanese market meltdown could be more serious for the world than a plunge in the roughly equal-sized U.S. markets. This is true despite the fact the Japanese economy is, surprisingly to many, less than 40 percent the size of that of the United States. The depth of a crash in Japan is likely to be far greater than will be the case in the United States, not only because of Tokyo's more extreme overvaluation, but because the market is so thin. And since shortselling isn't allowed, there will be no support on the way down from shorts buying to cover their profitable positions; at least, if a crash occurred in New York, people would have some way to hedge against it, or even profit from it, thereby mitigating the effect of the disaster.

Japan is a net capital exporter, not a borrower, as the United States now is. When things get tough enough, it is a cinch the Japanese will not only cease new investments abroad but will bring home what they already have invested elsewhere. They have become significant players in recent years, and the world's economies and markets are much more interlinked today. Japan will be repatriating the capital that has helped fuel the boom in the rest of the world. Lack of new investment, and the wave of selling that would hit the U.S. stock, bond, and real estate markets, would send them into a tailspin.

A collapse in Tokyo, therefore, wouldn't just be a story on the evening news; it could be the signal for a worldwide financial and economic catastrophe. There's no rule that says a depression in America has to be made here; everything is imported these days.

Maybe the wholesale debacle that could potentially start in the Japanese financial markets can be papered over or crisis managed. We muddled through the oil crisis, which roughly coincided with the last two recessions, and I certainly hope we can do so again. But the Japanese wild card is only one of dozens in the deck.

The Nikkei is still grossly overpriced and a downtrend is in motion. Do not try to pick the ultimate bottom. I suspect the ultimate bottom will be much lower than anyone now thinks "reasonable," just as the ultimate top was far higher than anyone thought possible. Many stock markets have lost 90 percent or more of their value in the past, and it is certain to happen again.

When Japan goes, it's likely to be the greatest crash in history, even worse than 1929 in the United States. You may be able to buy AAA Japanese corporations for 10 percent dividend yields in a few years, if you have the cash and the courage—and if the U.S. government hasn't imposed foreign exchange controls that preclude investment abroad. I think it will be the sideshow of the century.

Questions and Answers

Q. *Perhaps the United States has been too liberal in its dealing with Japan. Maybe it's time to look out for number one by placing tariffs and quotas on their goods that cost American jobs and profits?*

A. One of the major causes for the severity of the 1930s depression was the Smoot-Hawley Tariff Act, a knee-jerk reaction of the U.S. Congress intended to protect American business and workers. It had the effect of collapsing world trade. It not only denied American consumers foreign goods that they might have preferred, but it caused widespread failures and unemployment abroad; foreigners then lacked the means to buy American products, and a spiral of even more American failures and unemployment resulted.

It has become fashionable among jingoists, including many Washington and media opinion leaders, to blame any real or perceived problem on an external force. During the OPEC oil crisis days, busybodies nationwide fretted about the Arabs buying up America. Memories are short. During the 1960s, xenophobic Europeans were trying to pass laws preventing America from buying up Europe, because they didn't think they could meet what was then called "The American Challenge." That quaint notion is mostly good for a laugh today.

As Roseanne Rosannadanna of "Saturday Night Live" was fond of saying, "If it's not one thing, it's something else. It's always something." The Greeks had their day, as did the Persians, Romans, Spanish, French, British, and Germans. The Japanese are enjoying the last few hours of their day in the sun, and then it will be the Chinese or the Mexicans or the Indians.

In any event, the nationality of the currently ascendant group is a nonproblem; individuals rise and fall to their own level based on their own actions. Trying to make laws to protect the country from others' success denies Americans the benefits of work by other people; applying protectionist logic widely would transform this country into an oversized Albania.

Q: *After this financial drama sorts itself out, will the United States and Japan achieve a new, mutually beneficial relationship?*

A: Probably not. Every nation is insufferably nationalistic. Unfortunately, the Japanese and the Americans are two of the worst offenders and believe that anyone who is not one of them is genetically disadvantaged. Moreover, they are radically different cultures, leaving plenty of room for miscommunication, or worse.

After a forty-year time lag, a lot of Japanese still feel very bitter about the bombing of Hiroshima and Nagasaki. Perhaps Japan has been easy to get along with over the past decades due to its defeat and because it was not very powerful; but things change. In recent years many Japanese executives have made deprecating comments about U.S. industry: "If we'd made the shuttle, the heat deflecting tiles would never have fallen off," and "The Americans are very good farmers. They should stick to that and not try to make cars." Such comments would have been unthinkable in the past. A lot of mutual resentment seems to be building.

Japan has a very old martial culture, and military power is a logical offshoot of economic power. In a few years, when the time comes to invest in Japanese stocks at a 75 percent to 90 percent discount, hopefully at about the same time we can sell gold stocks for many hundreds of percent premiums, the Japanese defense industry will prove most interesting. The weapons business is the biggest in the world, bigger even than illegal drugs, and the Japanese have almost no participation there. With their tremendous abilities to produce to high standards and innovate, the Japanese should surpass the American, Russian, British, French, and other arms manufacturers as easily as they did the automakers. Arms will, before the end of the decade, be a perfect area to pick up the slack created by dropping consumer goods exports.

Japanese entry into the military arena, I suspect, will further raise American resentment. That is likely to be even more true if the United States continues to act like a great imperial power, trying to "strategically" police the world. U.S. foreign policy makes the country seem like a star that's gone supernova: great expansion, lots of heat and light; dangerous, but on the point of collapsing into a black hole after having dissipated all its energy. Large property purchases by the Japanese have been the cause of some U.S.-Japanese friction. This is a real nonproblem and a positive boon to property owners. Unfortunately, the envious get a lot of mileage out of viewing other people's property as "our" property. But the Japanese may forgo buying U.S. government debt in the future, or even start selling it; and that would certainly raise jingoistic cries of economic sabotage.

FINAL THOUGHT

As I said, some values are starting to appear in the Tokyo stock market. Peter Cavelti a Swiss/Canadian money manager has zeroed in on six major companies that bear watching (see Table 28–2). You can follow their prices in the foreign markets section of the daily *Wall Street Journal*.

You will note that the price-to-earnings ratios (P/Es) and price-to-cash-flow ratios (P/CFs) are generally less than those of comparable New York stocks, and the price to book values (P/BVs) are considerably lower (the P/BV on the Dow is 2.5). Further, they all have lots of cash. But take your time. They'll get much cheaper.

Table 28-2

Company	Price	P/E	P/CF	P/BV
Canon	¥ 1460	21.3	7.8	1.6
Fuji Photo	¥ 2980	16	8.5	1.5
Hitachi	¥ 870	16	4.9	1.2
Matsushita	¥ 1430	15.8	4.9	1.1
Sony	¥ 4480	14.6	5.1	1.2
Toyota	¥ 1500	14.7	7.2	1.3

Part III

What's Going to Happen Next?

29

The Ex-Soviet Union, the Next Yugoslavia

This island is almost made of coal and surrounded by fish. Only an organizing genius could produce a shortage of coal and fish in Great Britain at the same time.

> Aneurin Bevan
> (Bevan's statement regarding a socialist
> Britain could serve as a motto for Russia.)

Today, the State has succeeded in meddling in every aspect of our lives. From the cradle to the tomb, it strangles us in its arms. Sometimes as the central government, sometimes as the provincial or local State, now as the commune-State, it pursues us at each step, it appears at every street corner, it imposes on us, holds us, harasses us.

It regulates all our actions. It accumulates mountains of laws and ordinances in which the shrewdest lawyer is lost. Each day it creates new gears to awkwardly patch up the broken old watch, and it comes to create a machine so complex, so inferior, so obstructive, that it revolts even those who are charged with running it.

It creates an army of employees, spiders with hooked fingers, who know the universe only through the dirty windows of their offices, or by their obscure, absurd, illegible old papers, an evil band who have only one religion, that of the buck; only one care, that of hooking up with any party whatever in order to be guaranteed maximum political appointments for a minimum of work.
The results we know only too well.

> Peter Kropotkin, *Words of a Rebel*

Those three republics have no right to declare the Soviet Union nonexistent. What do they mean there's no such country as the U.S.S.R.?

> Mikhail Gorbachev

I first visited the Soviet Union in 1977. I went in April, a time when only the German army should think of visiting. Moscow was like Pittsburgh in 1932, without the charm. Shopping in GUM was reminiscent of an especially bad branch

339

of the U.S. Postal Service. The food was mediocre, and people were universally uncouth, impolite, and suspicious. The domestic airliners were converted bombers, none of the cars had windshield wipers, and labor details of grandmothers were cleaning the streets of the Workers' Paradise.

On the other hand, the after-hours bars were among the best I have seen. I was approached by people who wanted to trade Red Army belt buckles, one of the few items of any value to someone from an advanced country, for my jeans, nylon windbreaker, chewing gum, or Yankee cigarettes. Even in 1977 prices were dirt cheap; the only problem was the almost total lack of anything to buy, except incredibly shoddy Corfam shoes.

I took one of those standard Intourist package deals that visited musty old art museums. I found better entertainment, however, since most of the other tourists turned out to be hard-core American leftists. They spent their time earnestly reassuring each other of the progress the workers and peasants were making and expressing solidarity with the masses for opposing the powers of darkness to the West. On our first evening in the Motherland, I was seated at dinner with five tourists whose conversation turned to the fact that most of us had only dollars, since the GosBank stayed open only for about two hours a day. One guy had, however, lined up for rubles, and he offered to make change for the rest of us.

Clearly, this was an opportunity. When I had completed my transaction, I stood up, flashed some ID in my wallet, and announced, with a change in my accent and a serious but smug expression: "Yuri Bursukov,* Soviet People's Secret Police. You are all under arrest for crimes against the national currency. You will please remain at this table until the arrival of my uniformed comrades." I looked around the table for about five seconds, a long time under such a circumstance; they looked physically ill, and it wasn't just because of the greasy soup. Then I sat down, chortled, and said: "Just kidding." Who says there weren't any laughs in the U.S.S.R.?"

But that was the good old days. The future holds fewer laughs.

THE U.S.S.R. AS A TRENDSETTER

Economist Ludwig von Mises explained that the collapse of socialism was inevitable, because without free markets the system is unable to calculate workable prices, and with politically assigned prices, efficient production is impossible. *Will the Soviet Union Survive Until 1984?* written by Andre Amalrik in the '60s held that the U.S.S.R., a modern version of the old Russian empire assembled and maintained by pure force, would be torn apart by dissension among its numerous nationalities. They were both correct.

*I chose that name because Yuri was the head of *Izvestia* in Washington when I lived there. Over dinner we had amiable debates about philosophy, which I always won, but he never defected. Those KGB guys were no pushovers.

Technology, however, was the straw that broke the Soviet camel's back. The computer-telecommunications revolution made strict control impossible, since it necessarily provided access to all the information in the world and a printing press to boot. International television coverage exposes people to life outside their own arbitrary political borders, as does modern tourism. Gorbachev didn't formulate glasnost and perestroika because he was enlightened, but because he had a choice of becoming more like Albania or more like the West—it really wasn't much of a choice. Politics was the problem, and technology was the cure.

Will the reforms underway in the old Soviet republics succeed? Only total reform will succeed, and reality will speed its implementation. "Scientific socialism" will pass, like hundreds of other unworkable and destructive ideas before it, leaving the world bruised, but largely intact. Despite a long tradition of state oppression, I suspect the average Russian will eagerly accept the benefits a Western system of government has to offer.

THE FUTURE

There is a chance that the former Soviet Republics will savor the collapse of communism and quietly rebuild their lives. But that would be a break with tradition. More likely, prolonged power struggles will take place.

The timing of any upheaval is uncertain, but revolutions tend to get underway in the spring, when hormones are rising and when people can conveniently form mobs in good weather after a winter of hardship and plotting. The next few years will prove very grim economically. The Russians are used to subsistence living, but now that they are exposed to the wealth of the West, they may become embittered that they were subjected to a gigantic swindle over the last seventy years. A violent upheaval could occur, with almost anyone seizing the reins of power.

The best historical comparison might be France in 1790. The French Revolution started out with fraternity, liberty, and equality, and then it turned into the Terror. After that, you might have thought the place was too devastated by the likes of Robespierre to be much of a threat to anyone outside its own borders. But then Napoleon appeared on the scene, practically from out of nowhere, and proceeded to take his armies, like a giant outlaw motorcycle gang, on a fifteen-year rampage across Europe. Who could have guessed? Chaotic environments frequently attract single-minded megalomaniacs.

There are only two ways to get what you want in the material world: production and trade, or theft. It is unfortunate that the old Soviet bloc has a weak tradition of production and trade but a distinguished tradition of plunder dating back to Genghis Khan. It is likely some strongman will arise in the next few years and decide to take the traditional way out. The new leadership in all the Eastern bloc countries are only non-Stalinists, not necessarily lovers of individual liberty. They will likely try to find a middle path, the old socialism with a human face. They'll find, however, that if socialism has a human face, it looks like Charles Manson or at best a malevolent version of Alfred E. Neuman.

THE SOVIET TIME BOMB

There's a lot of optimism about the economic benefits stemming from the collapse of the Soviet empire; many commentators seem to equate the absence of communism with the presence of free markets. That is far from the case. Five hundred million impoverished and disgruntled people do not constitute an engine to pull the rest of the world out of an economic swamp as some pundits predict. More likely the old Soviet republics will sink back into some form of socialism.

The flow of goods and capital will remain a one-way street—West to East—for some years to come. Actually that is no big change, since the $60 billion in credits advanced the Soviets over past decades are all that kept their economies from collapsing earlier. Their industrial capability is extremely weak.

The place is a time bomb, charged with 25,000 nuclear weapons, managed by millions of sociopathic ex-party hacks, and populated by scores of millions of desperate people, without hope or adequate food. It is natural that the thugs who worked for the Communist party will get into organized crime, running any number of nasty, informal little governments. That type of activity will set the ethical tone of the new Russia. Chaos will likely ensue as not just the fifteen ex-republics but the approximately 125 nationalities start going for each other's throats. There's an excellent chance we'll see the rise of warlords, as happened in China during the '20s and '30s and in Somalia today.

Once the U.S.S.R. goes the way of Yugoslavia, as I think is likely, lenders can write off the $60 billion in credits they have advanced. That will be another major hit to what's left of the big banks' balance sheets, although the lending was largely done by European—mostly German—institutions.

In the meantime, the U.S. government is doing its best to prop up what remains of Russia with billions of taxpayers' dollars, antagonizing the people of breakaway republics.

HYPERINFLATION

One reason for gold's weakness during all this drama is the fact that the Soviets have unloaded their above-ground supplies of gold to keep their economy functioning. Stories from Russia indicate that if they have any more gold, nobody knows where it is. This means that what has always been considered a huge overhang, tens of millions of ounces, has already depressed the gold market. Nor will there be any significant future sales as Soviet gold production declines and what gold remains, one hopes, is used to back a convertible ruble.

I say "hopes" not because of any concern about the gold market, but because of what will happen when the ruble loses all its value. Runaway inflation is a great catalyst for violent upheaval, since it destroys the future. Those stashed rubles were intended to buy an extra coat during a cold winter, or some small luxury, or maybe just some peace of mind. Soon they will have absolutely no value. It is arguable the result will be far worse in the Soviet republics than it was in the France of 1789, the Confederacy of 1865, Germany of 1923, or any of the Third World countries where such disasters occur with some frequency.

In all those other countries, most people at least owned property. Many had a farm or a shop, owned some shares, or had some gold coins and jewelry tucked away. If not, they had friends or relatives who did, or some connections abroad who would help them. As bad as things were in the United States in the '30s, people still had businesses, savings, and farms—incentives to rebuild. And the system allowed them to start anew. The Russians have none of that. They own little; the state owns everything. And since the state already owns everything, it has nothing to tax. When the ruble becomes totally worthless, they'll have nothing with which to induce workers to work for the state, or farmers to farm for the state. They will stop printing ruble notes only to conserve the paper. All economic activity will take place outside the system. It promises to be the biggest economic/political catastrophe in history, after communism itself.

The only possible solution is to back the ruble with the remaining gold to give it some value. Simultaneously, all state property must be distributed, directly or in the form of stock shares, to the people. True, that property has little value—what good is a fifty-year-old steel mill?—but it is something.

The liberation of the Eastern bloc is a huge plus for the future, but the future will be a long while coming. In the meantime, the world-class problems left by seventy-five years of socialism are going to linger, fester, and mutate. And having the apparatchiks from the IMF and the U.S. government try to advise them is like having the blind lead the doubly dismembered.

THE SOLUTION

Some people believe that the problems in Eastern Europe can be overcome with something like a new Marshall Plan. But the billions transferred under the Marshall Plan to European governments after the war were extracted from the savings and investments of U.S. citizens. Lots of that money did rebuild factories, mines, and roads, but not very efficiently. If the same money had been left in the hands of U.S. investors, they would have directed it to the areas of highest return, and both parties would have been far richer as a result. As it stands, the Marshall Plan fattened government payrolls on both sides of the Atlantic, with a little trickle-down of goods and a tidal wave of self-serving propaganda.

The only way the East will prosper is to open up its markets to private capital, on any available terms. The worst response would be a new Marshall Plan—even if the U.S. government were not itself on the way to bankruptcy.

In every crisis both danger and opportunity abound. The danger is the precipitous and violent collapse of socialist states around the world; the opportunity is to transform these societies into bigger versions of Hong Kong. If they were not so experienced in the practical workings of socialism, they would be too complacent to want to try a completely free market. And that's exactly the problem with the United States. People are so complacent we're likely to go the way of the Soviets, while the rest of the world heads toward a free market. The relative decline of the United States is likely to continue, for that reason if no other.

PROFITING FROM THE COLLAPSE OF SOCIALISM

A word to the risk-takers. Be as cautious about schemes to get rich from the liberalization of Eastern Europe as one should have been regarding China ten years ago. The rules in this arena are similar to the rough-and-tumble world of start-up penny stocks: unless you are a pro who can hit and run very quickly, stay away until you can tell what you are dealing with and can see that it has managed to launch itself successfully. The pioneers get arrows in their backs.

The old U.S.S.R. is not now, nor will it be for the near-term future, a place for solid investment. But that's not to say a lot of money cannot be made there, perhaps more than later when life settles. And investing now will form the basis of long-term relationships that will pay dividends in the future. That strategy was a key to Armand Hammer's success in the Soviet Union in 1917.

The problem for the average Western investor is transaction costs. You essentially have to make it a full-time business. Are there many opportunities? Yes, but very high-risk ones. Property rights are only marginally established legally and little appreciated philosophically. That limits the entrepreneur to quick-turnaround, cash-on-the-barrelhead, import-export schemes. Importing is problematical because the locals lack hard currency, and little is produced that anyone abroad would want. Artwork and caviar are the exceptions.

In the pre-perestroika days, a Soviet artist had to belong to the Writers and Artists Union to sell his work officially. As a result, artists there are of two kinds: union members, who may be excellent or who are as often politically connected hacks; and nonmembers, who may actually have the fire and imagination that sometimes makes for great art.

The value of good contemporary paintings has risen substantially since perestroika. Needless to say, professional dealers from the West have known about Russian art for some time. A quality painting that would sell for $50 to $500 in Russia would fetch $5,000 in the United States. Values inside Russia are very cheap, after all, McDonald's has fifty applicants for every job, at a wage equivalent to twenty-five cents an hour.

NEW BORDERS

Splitting the U.S.S.R. into its components brings up the questions of whether dismemberment will become the wave of the future.

On the one hand, common sense and economic necessity dictate that national borders should evaporate throughout the world. The EEC is the first example, and the United States will likely arrive at a similar arrangement with Canada and Mexico. Economic unity is not achieved through the negotiation of complex treaties, however. It requires nothing more than the absence of barriers, which automatically results in free markets.

On the other hand, political unity usually means continual, covert war, with almost everyone fighting for power to redistribute other people's wealth toward themselves. That is why independence movements still exist, after centuries of unity, in Wales, Scotland, and Northern Ireland in the United Kingdom and among the Galicians and Basques in Spain and the Bretons in France. And I am describing only Western Europe.

In Eastern Europe, Yugoslavia is the trendsetter. Most former Soviet bloc countries have substantial minorities cut off by an arbitrary border from their ethnic fellows in adjoining lands. The same is true throughout Africa, India, and China. By and large, these people are very dissatisfied; it is the nature of politics that people are divided into the exploiters and the exploited.

Put another way, the world itself, not only the Soviet Union and Eastern Europe, is highly unstable. Think of Pakistan, Iran, Turkey, Egypt, and many others. In the world we grew up in, it didn't really matter who these people were or what they thought or did; it was grist for *National Geographic* but otherwise of little importance. Now the world is a much smaller place, and it can matter a lot. Most people, for instance, had never even heard of Iraq until 1990.

Although it seems like a paradox, the way to unite the world and ensure peace is not by creating world government, but by abolishing the outmoded institution of government. That's likely to happen in the next century. But in the meantime, we will see many borders evaporating and changing. As the Al Stewart song "On The Border" says: "On the wall, the colors of the map are running." Unfortunately, it is unlikely to be an entirely peaceful process.

RUSSIA AND THE WEST

A serious turn for the worse in Russia could reactivate the bomb-shelter mentality of the early '70s. You remember: buy gold, buy silver, buy Swiss francs, and keep freeze-dried food in your rural cabin. That's a far cry from the glitz and ostentation of the '80s, but things do change.

In any event, I'm betting on seeing some of the most interesting times in world history over the next decade. The only absolute certainty for investments is extreme volatility. And that will make it harder to keep what you have than at any other time in this century. Just hope that nothing untoward happens to any of the more than 25,000 nuclear weapons the Russian and sister republics currently control. Russia is a Third World country with a First World military, and one cannot predict who might gain control of some of that hardware.

And hope also that an increasingly adventurist U.S. government doesn't decide to become actively involved, and that we do not use foreign chaos as an excuse to quash even more civil liberties. Those topics are the subjects of the next chapters.

30

Third World Wars

War, like any other racket, pays high dividends to the very few . . . The cost of operations is always transferred to the people who do not profit.

Gen. Smedley Butler

War is the health of the state

Randolph Bourne

There's no difference between one's killing and making decisions that will send others to kill. It's exactly the same thing, or even worse.

Golda Meir

Ever since States came into existence, the political world has always been and still continues to be the stage for high knavery and unsurpassed brigandage— brigandage and knavery which are held in high honor, since they are ordained by patriotism, by transcendent morality, and by the supreme interest of the State. This explains to us why all the history of ancient and modern States is nothing more than a series of revolting crimes; why present and past kings and ministers of all times and all countries—statesman, diplomats, bureaucrats, and warriors—if judged from the point of view of simple morality and human justice, deserve a thousand times the gallows or penal servitude.

For there is no terror, cruelty, sacrilege, perjury, imposture, infamous transaction, cynical theft, brazen robbery, or foul treason which has not been and is not still being committed daily by representatives of the State.

Michael Bakunin

RISE AND FALL

Between the Renaissance and the present, European peoples and ideas have dominated world events. This is true for a number of reasons, but the main one is the superior technologies invented in the West. For most of the last 500 years, the outcome of a military conflict was a foregone conclusion: victory by white Westerners over the less technologically advanced heathen.

Starting late in the nineteenth century, however, a few surprises occurred at disparate places like Little Big Horn, Ishandlwana, and the Sudan, when the natives managed to get hold of European weapons or just caught Westerners unprepared. But those battles were written off as flukes, as bad management by local commanders. When the Russians were beaten by the Japanese in 1905, historical eyebrows were raised around the world, since it was the first time Europeans had lost, not just a battle, but a whole war to a people viewed as primitive. A disturbing development, especially when viewed through the long-term lens that Oswald Spengler and Arnold Toynbee used. They would both see subsequent events, militarily, economically, politically, and socially, as evidence of a declining culture heading to a major crisis.

In any event, Western empire building proceeded, albeit with less momentum, in Asia, Africa, and the Pacific until World War II. Since then, even economically backward Third World countries have acquired sufficient modern firepower to overturn the colonial holdovers that governed their countries. A major sea change has been under way, and within the memory of most people alive today. Armies of advanced countries have been defeated by sandal-clad natives the world over.

Now that the Soviet empire, the last of the great nineteenth-century colonial powers, has collapsed, it is clear that the shape of things to come will differ radically from what we have been used to. For close to 50 years when we thought of "war," it meant conflict between the U.S. and the U.S.S.R. or one of their proxies. The regional China-India, China-Vietnam, China-Taiwan, India-Pakistan, and Ethiopia-Somalia conflicts were newsworthy but were seen as sideshows as long as they did not directly involve the major powers.

The Iran-Iraq war received more attention because of its oil component, American hopes that Saddam Hussein would depose the Ayatollah, and a fascination with the ability of two Third World countries to fight a prolonged war with modern weapons and hundreds of thousands of deaths. The Israel-Arab conflict's huge tank battles and potential for involving the United States also demanded more notice. These events were not tribal scuffles settled with small arms, of interest primarily to anthropologists. These wars were serious business on a scale meaningful to advanced countries.

It has not even today sunk in that there are dozens of countries around capable of deploying armies of meaningful size and far reaching offensive ability. And in a shrinking world, it is not likely they will confine their attention to the next-door neighbor alone.

A NONBIPOLAR INTERREGNUM

The economic collapse of the U.S.S.R. was long predicted by Von Mises and other Austrian-school economists; its political disintegration was presaged by the earlier collapse of the Spanish, Portuguese, Dutch, British, and French empires. Only the timing was in doubt.

The U.S.S.R. was never more than a Third World country with a First World military, but its military gave it the kind of power that other Third World countries could understand. Even if, because of the examples set by Hong Kong, Singapore, Korea, and Taiwan, they realize that capitalism is necessary to advance economically, a good chance exists that many will see economic advancement as a means to an end as much as an end in itself.

The cause of war, which is the institution of the state itself, has not disappeared. An increasing number of powerful governments are in existence today. They are all politically driven. And, as Clausewitz said, war is the continuation of politics by other means. When economies slow down, or when political groups within countries become restive, or when another country appears threatening or tempting, or just when sociopathic leaders come to power, they will resort to military solutions. Many leaders will always believe what Napoleon is supposed to have said: "The only thing we can't do with bayonets is sit on them."

There are, after all, only two practical ways individuals or nations can get what they want: production and trade, or theft. Societies dominated by socialist thinking are largely incapable of the former, so war is a logical and likely alternative. It is an excellent bet that a number of these armed Third World countries, of which the average person isn't even aware, will try to play the kind of aggrandizing game Iraq did in 1990.

A huge spate of apocalyptic books and movies in the '80s predicted World War III. It could have happened. Fortunately, the U.S.S.R. suffered domestic collapse before it found a suitable military opening. Although it was not the best, and certainly not the least risky, way to accomplish the objective, Reagan's gigantic defense build-up was an important element in both bankrupting the Soviets and keeping them at bay. So far, so good.

Now there are a dozen little satrapies within the old Soviet borders. And there are scores of conventional Third World countries. It is arguable that they will obtain their own or some of the U.S.S.R.'s 25,000 nuclear weapons while retaining their historical hatreds.

BE THE FIRST ON YOUR BLOCK

Nuclear weapons won't just go away. They do present some unique advantages. They are very cheap, especially in relation to the amount of damage they can do. The extent of their destructive power is unmatched. They are small and surprisingly easy to make.

Irwin Strauss wrote a book entitled *Basement Nukes* in the '70s. In it he described for the layman the manufacturing of a nuclear weapon from scratch, using basic machine-shop tools. Homemade nuclear weapons are already within the technical and financial reach of a middle-class American family, as it were. The major construction difficulty would be the availability of fissionable material, which, if an enterprising Tom Swift-type couldn't steal from it some nuclear facility, he could manufacture himself.

The project isn't as intimidating as you might think. After all, yellowcake, U_3O_8, is simple enough to extract from raw uranium ore found throughout the world. Pure uranium can easily be refined chemically from that compound. The tough part is to separate and concentrate the isotopes of the uranium metal, U_{235} and U_{238}, but it can be done by a layman. Assume you wanted to fabricate a gun from scratch. You could buy steel, but if none were available, you need only find an iron ore deposit and refine enough to suit your purposes. It would take longer, cost more, and result in a lower-quality product, but you could do the job.

Nearly fifty years have passed since the Manhattan Project designed and constructed the first A-bomb. The advances in theoretical and practical knowledge since then have been stupendous. Many hundreds of papers have been produced on the subject and are part of the public domain. The power of your home computer is many orders of magnitude beyond what scientists then had. All manner of materials are better, cheaper, and more readily available. And we know the project is technically feasible, which Oppenheimer's team did not.

There are a myriad of historical analogies. Daimler and Benz had to be geniuses to design the first motorcar; now any teenager can make a vastly superior hot rod in his garage. Building the ENIAC, the world's first electronic computer, took world-class brains and capital; the Apple PC was the part-time project of a couple of ex-hippies.

The United States and Russians each have enough nuclear weapons for mistakes to happen. It actually makes little sense for someone who wants to be a nuclear power to make a bomb, since bribing a corrupt ex-Soviet general to part with a few small devices would be much cheaper, faster, and easier. Britain, France, China, and India have had nuclear weapons for decades. Israel, South Africa, and Pakistan almost certainly have them. Within the next decade any country or group that wants nuclear weapons will certainly have them, if sufficiently motivated. Delivery systems are even less of a problem. Why use unwieldy missiles when a car, a boat, a Cessna, or even a generous backpack will do the job?

Until now, it was a fun, macho game for a big country to dare a little country to knock the chip off its shoulder. But cheap technology has done for governments what the Colt revolver did for individuals more than a century ago: size no longer makes you stronger, just a bigger target.

THE UNITED STATES AGAINST THE WORLD

Since about the time of the Vietnam War, it has become almost a cottage industry among amateur historians to compare today's America with the Roman Empire in its final days. It is certainly a tempting and ever more apt analogy. Indeed, it would be somewhat surprising, at least based on the work of Spengler and Toynbee, if the United States did not go the way of Rome and every other "great power" of the past. Much like a star going nova, countries often exhibit their greatest expansion and throw off the most light and heat, with the greatest danger to their neighbors, just before the implosion that their expansion made inevitable. The U.S.S.R. followed the pattern.

Once the United States was well loved and respected. American tourists in the '60s—and I'm assured it was even better in the '50s—became objects of adoration, not because they had done anything to deserve it, but simply because they carried the right passport.

The change started as the Vietnam conflict gained momentum; people in distant parts of the world began to view Americans the way Latin Americans had for a century, as aggressive interlopers anxious to manufacture an excuse to send in the marines. Americans always thought of themselves as the good guys, but the locals liked U.S. soldiers strutting around their hometowns about as much as we would want an army of Chinese reordering our lives. Even if they passed out chocolate, nylons, and cigarettes.

A couple of rules seem to apply. One: the more alien the intruder, the more serious the affront. That is why you do not hold it against your brother if he beats you up, but you bear a grudge against a youngster from across town. Americans do not resent Brits, despite the events of 1776 and 1812. Even Germans do not resent Americans, because they share the same basic culture. But people tend to fear and dislike those who are different. Understanding is possible only when you like someone, share their views on reality, and are able to communicate with them. That gets harder as the differences in culture become greater.

Enforcing a new world order on weaker countries, even if we were "right," or only maintaining order, isn't a formula for good relations. It can easily be viewed as taking advantage of or beating up on someone with a different culture and values; it could later prove dangerous when they, too, acquire nuclear or cheaper, more efficient biological weapons. Since, however mistakenly, most people equate their government with their country, they will not sympathize with the argument that they should not take an invasion or bombing personally because we only wanted to change their leadership. Instead they are likely to take such an attack very personally indeed.

Another rule: the more "primitive" a society—tribal, unindustrialized, religious, and traditional—the deeper the wound. In the West we are individuals first and foremost, and only in America is "class" a permeable barrier. Membership in some group because of an accident of birth isn't nearly as important as self-realization. But in most Third World countries, which have static and stratified societies, a person's identity is his group, hence the caste system, tribalism, nationalism, and collectivism. That is why Arabs hate Israelis, Armenians hate Azeris, and Serbs hate Bosnians. These feuds, like that of the Hatfields and McCoys, carry on for generations after everybody has forgotten why.

Americans in general do not adopt the enmity of their parents toward their enemies. Our parents have their own lives and live in separate houses; a telephone call is sometimes considered adequate communication. In the Third World, however, the extended family means that the sins, beliefs, and obligations of parents devolve upon their children. Drop a bomb on Iraq today and in fifty years some victim's grandchild will still be looking for revenge.

It was one thing for the marines to teach manners to offensive foreigners in the nineteenth-century. But it is very dangerous to do the same thing to foreigners who have twentieth-century technology. The West's edge in weapons is likely to be inadequate against enemies with huge numerical superiority, unless they are blatantly stupid. And having all manner of high-tech weapons is of no use if the enemy has weapons of mass destruction and the will to use them.

THE GULF WAR

Purely conventional warfare has become too expensive to be practical, a fact that will be one of the major insights of the Gulf War. Iraq has only 17 million people, and even so the war proved immensely expensive in money and material, especially since the U.S. government had to borrow every penny it spent, despite grudging contributions from allies.

Nobody seems to have precise figures on the costs or the number of Iraqi casualties, but $50 billion and 100,000 dead seem to be good working numbers. That's about $500,000 per person. In Vietnam, by contrast, it took only about $160 billion to kill about one million locals, or approximately $16,000 a person; relatively speaking, Vietnam was a "better deal." Who would have ever guessed Vietnam would turn out to be cost/benefit effective in any way?

During the late '70s, some observed that it would have been cheaper and more effective to bribe the VC and NVA into deserting by offering them free airfare to America and a house and a car when they arrived. Things are a lot more expensive today, in no small measure because of Vietnam. But even at today's prices, the $500,000 spent for each dead Iraqi goes a long way, especially when you consider that the average net worth of even those in the top 20 percent of the U.S. population is only $111,000. Perhaps we should have simply given each man, woman, and child in Iraq about $3,000, or about 150 percent of their per capita GNP, and induced the entire country to desert.

We're still paying for the Vietnam War, since it was fought with 100 percent borrowed money. $160 billion over about twenty years at about 8 percent compounded is already $640 billion, and growing at about $50 billion a year. The bill for the instant gratification in Iraq will also grow for years. I'm not sure how to compute the interest on "collateral damage" in its myriad forms.

The Gulf War was the opening gambit in the war games of the '90s, and very important for that reason. Saddam couldn't help but win even when he lost, because scores of millions of Arabs, hundreds of millions of Muslims, and possibly billions of Third Worlders may eventually see him as a hero, however flawed, who stood fearlessly against fantastic odds. But Saddam is just a typical Third World dictator, albeit with more resources than most. Not long ago he was seen as an ally in the mold of Batista, Somoza, Diem, Mobutu, and scores of other sociopaths whom the U.S. government has supported with no regard for principles.

The big X-factor in the adventure is its religious overtones. It's hard to see how dropping thousands of tons of high explosives on Baghdad and killing thousands of Iraqis made us a lot of friends. It is cultural. The Muslims have felt abused by the West since the Crusades, and they view the Gulf War as a continuation of those conflicts.

The war was altruistically couched in terms of defending the underdog and promoting democracy, but most people in the Third World probably saw it as a demonstration of realpolitik, with economic motives. It involved the West using its superior firepower to ensure the supply of "our" oil, which the locals see as their property. U.S. Senator Robert Dole was amazingly candid when he remarked: "We are there for three letters: o-i-l. That is why we are in the Gulf. We are not there to save democracy. Saudi Arabia is not a democracy. Neither is Kuwait."

The West lost even as it won against Iraq, because it was obvious that all its strength was needed to handle a small country. What do we do when and if China, India, Pakistan, Indonesia, Mexico, Brazil, or Turkey try the same stunt? Especially if the offending regime had wide popular support, sending in the marines would be a nineteenth-century solution to a twenty-first-century problem.

The vast majority of Americans seemed to be in support of the Gulf War, for whatever reason. But war is always bad for the economy, even if it is the health of the state. The United States has recently shown a disturbing trend to use the military with little provocation: Grenada in 1983, Libya in 1986, Panama in 1989, Kuwait, and most lately Somalia. These incursions were all for what Americans saw as good reasons, but many foreigners saw only an aggressive power that sends its troops into other countries when it seems expedient. Perhaps Serbia will be next, and then parts of the old U.S.S.R.; there are plenty of places where a "need" can be argued.

Military prowess is a poor substitute for the real roots of greatness, or even for economic power, as the Russians have just discovered and as the Germans and Japanese learned in World War II or the Romans found in the late empire. War is the most unpredictable of human activities, has unintended consequences, and can take on a life of its own.

THE BIGGER PICTURE

As the U.S. government indulges in adventures around the globe it will step on land mines. How should we respond? The first question to answer is: "Who is 'we'?" If "we" is the people of the United States, it would be difficult to get a consensus from 250 million individuals of varying ethnic backgrounds, often antagonistic religious and philosophical beliefs, and vastly different financial circumstances. What usually happens in wartime is that those in leadership whip up a "patriotic" hysteria.

The average person (who often cannot find the enemy country on a map and knows nothing of its language, culture, or traditions) goes along mainly out of inarticulate jingoism ("That will show the world America is still number one"), ignorance ("The president knows what he's doing"), righteousness ("God's on our side"), groupthink, or a misplaced sense of adventure spawned by Rambo movies. Once these forces begin to roll, they can easily overwhelm those who might oppose the adventure.

In fact, "we" often means only the individuals in the government acting out their personal ambitions and fears. It doesn't matter if they are intelligent or well informed; it becomes an emotional, not a rational, issue. Unfortunately, we are saddled with the consequences of their actions, whether we approve of them or not.

With that caveat about who "we" are, I suggest we act more like the America that the Founding Fathers had in mind and that the world once loved. I remember a poignant comment that appeared in the *Wall Street Journal* a few years ago. A poor Egyptian said: "I no understand you Americans. You have nice cars, rock and roll music, California girls. Why you want hurt us, make war?" If the present trend continues, the United States in particular, although some of its allies in Europe should be included, may find they have a tiger by the tail. It is very much like combining the correct portions of sulfur, charcoal, and saltpeter in a dry place: they blow up. But just because the outcome is predictable doesn't mean it's imminent. Just because it's likely to happen doesn't mean it's likely to happen immediately. Something that is likely to happen often takes longer than you would imagine, but once underway it usually happens quickly.

In retrospect many events seem inevitable. The American Civil War and both world wars had a strong element of inevitability. I suspect that increased Third World conflicts will someday also be viewed as having been inevitable.

FOREIGN ADVENTURE

Who knows which country will be next on the U.S. military's dance card? Perhaps Bosnia, after Somalia, and then maybe Liberia, Haiti, the old U.S.S.R., Iran, or a dozen other candidates, for a score of different reasons. The '70s T-shirt "Join the army. Visit strange, exotic places. Meet interesting, unusual people. And kill them," is gaining new currency.

Will this trend continue? It seems to be gaining momentum. I can't see a logical reason why massive numbers of U.S. troops are going all over the world. In Somalia, the situation will likely return to the status quo ante as soon as the Americans leave. It is also a mystery why any outsiders, but particularly Americans, would become involved in Bosnia with its Muslim vs. Christian overtones. Where will it end? And why is the U.S. government spending billions on these arbitrary and very dangerous adventures when it can scarcely pay the interest on its own debt?

It is as if the government were using the script from *Apocalypse Now* as a model for its long-term planning. And like those of Colonel Kurtz, its methods are increasingly "unsound." In fact, it's increasingly hard to see any method. And now President Clinton seems anxious to pick up the ball. "The horror, the horror."

The average person can do little to change this trend. But it may be possible to insulate yourself from some of its financial consequences.

WAR PROFITEERING

If that's the way the international situation seems to be shaping up over the next decade, what are its investment implications for defense stocks in particular? All things have their season.

On first blush, the shares of stocks representing the military-industrial complex have a lot of potential, since war is their business and business looks good. As is usually the case, however, there are conflicting signals. On the one hand, even if there are a lot of Third World wars, police actions, and such, the dollar volume of defense spending is still unlikely to rival the monstrous amounts that went into the late cold war. On the other hand, the stocks are down considerably from the highs they reached at the peak of the spending boom.

Much depends on the nature of the military spending in the future. My guess is that our future Third World wars will be much more manpower- than equipment-intensive, with the exception of electronics, for several reasons.

First, despite all we hear about the value of a single human life, politicians understand that you can afford to lose 1,000 grunts a lot sooner than even one B-2 at $500 million a plane. And the United States just cannot afford that kind of hardware anymore, for the reasons spelled out earlier in this book.

Second, one of the lessons of Vietnam was that human capital, which Third World countries have in huge abundance, will triumph over hardware every time; even if our soldiers have a kill ratio of 10 to one, we will run out of money before they run out of people. The war in Iraq seemed to teach a different lesson, but that was an anomaly, if only because of the desert terrain. The enemy learned lessons from the experience and will not make the same mistakes.

Third, whether they want to spend the money on guns or not, there will not be enough of it to lavish on exotic military hardware; that helped bankrupt the Soviets, like the British and the French before them, as well as the Spanish and the Romans. The same can happen to the Americans if we continue to act as the world's self-appointed policemen. In the end, global adventures will prove as profitless for defense contractors as they will surely be for citizens.

THE ARMS BUSINESS

Even if the United States remains prosperous, I have reservations about the defense contractors. The arms business is one of the most corrupt in the world, which is a natural consequence of several things.

First, selling instruments of death and destruction cannot help but distort one's view of humanity. The normal constraints of peer pressure and moral opprobrium do not ensure ethical conduct in this business. Second, these companies do almost all their business with governments. Most foreign governments are even more unfettered than our own, and their military and intelligence departments are where all the really bad hombres gravitate. Third, most defense executives are ex-government bureaucrats, many of whom now have cushy jobs with the contractors as an indirect reward for favors they conferred while supposedly working for the U.S. taxpayer.

It has always been true that contracts do not necessarily go to the companies with the best product, but to those with the best political connections and the subtle ability to bribe. Most large defense companies receive 75 percent or more of their revenues from the U.S. or foreign governments. Profits are often the result not of innovation and cost control but of goldplating and cost inflation. Especially in big companies, the engineers take a remote back seat to the glad-handing, memo-writing executives.

These companies weren't always that way. They all started as entrepreneurial enterprises selling commercial planes and were run by engineers with a flair for business, like Glenn Curtiss. As late as World War II, military aircraft were built "on spec" rather than on a cost-plus basis. That explains how the P-51, the finest fighter of that conflict, went from concept to production in just 117 days, at a cost of $50,000 per plane. Of course, today's planes are larger and more complex, but that doesn't account for the P-51's successors, like the F-14 and the F-22, increasing literally 1,000 times in price and taking so long to develop that they are obsolescent by the time they are ready for service. We have seen tremendous advances in computers, materials, and engineering techniques to increase efficiency and decrease real costs. The expense is caused by the red tape that entwines these companies.

WHICH COMPANIES

Still, some defense stocks may provide a hedge against the inclination of a fair minority of the world's roughly 200 governments to lavish their citizens' wealth on toys for the generals.

I prefer to invest in a small company with a unique proprietary product that could provide tremendous leverage if it found favor: ideally, a boutique run by its founder with proven success in the commercial market, like the aviation companies of the '20s, '30s, and '40s. I'm unaware of any that fit the bill at present, but anyone who follows the aviation industry can't help but be impressed with two men: Paul Macready (inventor of the *Gossamer Albatross* and the *SunRacer*), who runs a small company called Aerovironment, and Burt Rutan (inventor of the globe-circling *Voyager*), who runs Composite Scales. If either of their companies ever goes public, I will be an eager buyer if the price is at all reasonable.

In small companies, management is typically the biggest shareholder, with most of their personal net wealth invested in it. That does not guarantee that they will do the right thing by shareholders, but it helps.

That brings us to the big contractors. I find little to choose among them except for the degree to which they depend on government contracts as opposed to commercial orders. The big companies are subject to intense scrutiny and public pressure; regardless of how much their managements try to pad the bill, it is not politically feasible for them to show a lot of earnings. Nor is it socially acceptable for any large company to show obscene profits, least of all the defense companies, since they feed directly at the public trough and are in an unsavory business. My guess is that managements solve this problem by bleeding off substantial share-holder funds to "consulting" companies located in tax havens, where they dis-creetly accrue to the benefit of insiders.

This is why, in my opinion, most of the big defense contractors typically sell at what appear to be bargain levels relative to other stocks. Defense companies as a group are off more than 50 percent from their peaks; any time a whole industry declined that much it deserves a speculator's attention. Any individual company's stock may fall because it is doing poorly, and you may not want it at any price. While some discount may be appropriate, it is likely defense issues are as low as they are partly because of market fashion. The defense industry isn't going away.

Most large defense contractors reached their peaks, in inflation-adjusted dol-lars, in 1983 when the Reagan armaments build-up was in full swing. This was after a prolonged collapse starting in 1973, when a major bear market coincided with a wind-down of the Vietnam War. The way I see it, our present situation is analogous to that of the early '70s, since we're coming off a major defense spending binge and simultaneously entering a bear market.

How cheap are the defense and aerospace stocks? Should you hold those you now own? When should you look to buy them? Bottom-picking is a dangerous occupation in any event, and I believe it is still too early to try it with these stocks. Sure, most are already down a lot from their peaks. Many sell for 50 percent or less of book, which is at bear market levels.

You can count on a lot of Third World wars to direct capital to these companies, but it will not be the same as during the Reagan era. Megacost weapons like the B-1 (a $250-million turkey), the B-2, the F-22, aircraft carriers, and submarines will be casualities along with the stocks of the outfits that make them. What is the sense of producing billion-dollar ships that can and will be sunk by million-dollar Exocet missiles? What is the sense of multimillion-dollar tanks that can be destroyed by shoulder-launched missiles costing only a few thousand dollars?

For these reasons I am negative on companies like General Dynamics, Grumman, Lockheed, McDonnell-Douglas, and Northrop. I expect outfits like Logicon, which provides training and electronic services, and Nichols Research, basically a think tank, will do better. Companies selling software and intangibles like brainpower can control their costs and fix their prices far more effectively than those who have to rely on $200 hammers and $600 toilet seats for revenues. The smaller companies fitting this description have a consistent history of growing earnings and dividends, which is completely untrue of the large contractors. Insiders own a significant share of both companies, as well.

United Industrial is a company competing to replace the Army's M-16 rifle. I wouldn't buy it, but I have looked at some of their submissions; exotic hi-tech in the form of caseless cartridges (possibly a good idea, although fraught with potential problems) and flechettes (tiny darts replacing the traditional bullet, which is almost certainly a disastrous idea) seem quite the fashion. This is typical of the whole procurement process. Instead of buying something cheap, proven, unbreakable, soldier-proof, and effective, the Pentagon prefers incredibly complex novelties that cost a fortune in overruns to develop. Assuming the soldiers can even figure out how to deploy these fancy new weapons, they break or jam in short order. After being stuck with the expensive and unreliable M-16 for twenty-five years, American soldiers are now likely to be saddled with something even worse. What they should have is a homegrown version of the ultrareliable and indestructible AK-47. But that's neither here nor there, and it's peanuts by comparison to boondoggles like the Acquila and the Sergeant York. *C'est la guerre.*

THE PREMIER AEROSPACE COMPANY

Boeing is the premier aerospace company and will likely remain so. It generates only 26 percent of sales to government and will likely expand its market share in defense.

This company will be a smart investment when the market as a whole returns to reasonable levels, since most of the world's commercial air fleet is going to need replacement. Older planes need lots of maintenance, require more crew, and burn a lot more fuel. In addition, passengers prefer to fly a carrier with new equipment if they have a choice. Boeing's order backlog, an amazing $100 billion, is the greatest in history. That backlog will likely suffer a lot of attrition as the current downturn accelerates, but the longer airlines delay purchases, the more explosive the rebound will be.

Incidentally, the same is true of the market for light commercial aircraft, which has already been completely devastated; shipments of piston aircraft, small Pipers, Cessnas, and the like are down an incredible 96 percent, and jets and propjets are down 50 percent. In the case of the light aircraft, product liability laws are the main culprit, but the economy will drive another nail in the industry's coffin. Unfortunately, the producers are owned by conglomerates, so there's no direct play on a recovery. But that is where outfits like Macready's and Rutan's will make their marks.

Boeing sold for 6.5 percent in dividends and about book value at the bottom of the 1982 recession. That might mean the stock could be available for as little as $20 to $25 in the near future.

31

The New Class in the No-Fun Nineties

The liberals can understand everything but people who don't understand them.
Lenny Bruce

Every State, even the most republican and the most democratic State—even the would-be people's State conceived by Marx—is in its essence only a machine governing the masses from above, through an intelligent and therefore privileged minority, allegedly knowing the genuine interests of the people better than the people themselves.
Michael Bakunin, *Statism and Anarchy*, 1873

The instinctive aims of those who govern—of those who frame the laws of the country as well as of those who exercise the executive power—are, because of their exceptional position, diametrically opposed to the instinctive popular aspirations. Whatever their democratic sentiments and intentions may be, viewing society from the high position in which they find themselves, they cannot consider this society in any other way but that in which a schoolmaster views his pupils. And there can be no equality between schoolmaster and pupils.
Michael Bakunin, *The Bear of Berne and the Bear of St. Petersburg*, 1870

The prospect of Third World wars brings up the question of what comes next for the nation. What will America in the '90s be like? The attitudes of the Clinton administration will be as important in the next four years as interest rates, the business cycle, taxes, inflation, or anything else. Let's first see where we've been.

Most recent epochs can be summed up with a few key images: the Roaring '20s with speakeasies, flappers, and a booming stock market; the '30s with breadlines and *The Grapes of Wrath*; the '40s with World War II.

The '50s, notwithstanding poodle skirts, big-finned cars, and Levittown housing, were widely expected to involve a return of the Great Depression, but instead were a time of broadly based, real prosperity. The '60s represented the peak of American prosperity. Vietnam and hippies were luxuries that seemed easily afford-

able. Any apprehensions that the '70s might not continue the trend were easy to
drown out with rock 'n' roll.

But the '70s turned out to be a miserable decade. Oil crises, high inflation,
Watergate, military retreat, clunky cars, and disco music were appropriate tokens
for the start of either the Greater Depression or the Epoque de Malaise discussed in
chapter 1. By the end of the '70s, it was hard to imagine things getting much worse,
but that clearly seemed to be the trend.

Then came the '80s, which demonstrated how rapidly the zeitgeist can change.
The financial markets boomed. Reagan was a wise and kindly, if somewhat
bumbling, grandfather who could kiss the world political situation and make it
better. And the U.S. military, kitted out in neat-looking cammies and Wehrmacht-
style kevlar helmets, started taking names and kicking tails the world over: Grenada, Panama, Lebanon. America was riding high, at least militarily.

As much fun as they were at the time, none of these eras went on forever, and
the '80s ended roughly on schedule. All these eras were psychological rather than
chronological decades. The '60s, for instance, really began in November 1963 with
Kennedy's assassination and ended in 1973 with the Vietnam War.

The '90s will be different economically and financially, of course. There is not
much an individual can do to change the economy, but he can do a lot to profit from
it by observing the political environment that shapes the economy.

Politics has a huge influence on American life, far more than ever before. The
government allocates a much larger portion of America's wealth, and has far more
laws to enforce, than has ever been the case. The '90s will provide as much drama
as we have seen in other times and places. You should not plan your life around the
assumption that the next ten years will prove to be particularly mellow.

Two phenomena will affect the way the world is going to work: the rise of the
New Class, and the coming of age of the baby boomers. They are both signaled by
the election of Bill Clinton and Al Gore.

THE "NEW CLASS" TAKES CONTROL

Notwithstanding that 57 percent of the electorate voted against him, Bill Clinton
will set the tone for America, at least until 1997. His policies may not have massive
support, but this will not lessen his influence on the direction of the country.

Woodrow Wilson was also elected narrowly in 1912, and that didn't stop him
from siring both the income tax and the Federal Reserve System in 1913. He was
even reelected in time to join the slaughter of World War I. I'm not really sure
whether leaders create their times or are just products of them. But a particular
leader can have a vast influence. So let's look at what the Clinton administration is
likely to have in store for us.

It's difficult to determine what Clinton's personal beliefs are. My suspicion is that he primarily has a very strong belief that he knows best. That's one of the most dangerous beliefs anyone can have, because it means he is likely to be completely opportunistic. It also means he is not likely to be market-oriented, because the market may want things at odds with what he "knows" is right.

Neither Clinton nor Al Gore has ever had a real job. They've spent their whole lives on the public payroll, in pursuit of political power. Whatever Clinton does is likely to be cloaked as realism or pragmatism. "Realism" is an abnegation of philosophy, or of any belief at all. It will appeal to those who supported George Bush. "Pragmatism" is a nonphilosophy of getting done what "needs to be done," that is, whatever seems like a good idea at the time, by whatever means necessary. It will win the approval of many Ross Perot fans.

But what does Bill Clinton feel needs to be done? His personal writings are exhortatory and short on specifics. But we can look at what some of his close advisors have said and at the character of his peer group. Politicians are adept at bending with the wind, but the beliefs of a peer group take time to turn around, like the direction of a large ship. Bill and his colleagues are all, without exception, members of what has been called the "New Class." They are an extraordinary group.

THE NEW CLASS

The New Class is less a political than a socioeconomic grouping. The term was originated by Milovan Djilas, a renegade Yugoslav Communist, but has been best described in the United States by Irving Kristol, B. Bruce-Biggs, and Herman Kahn. Robert Reich, Clinton's chief economic advisor, calls them "symbolists" or "symbolic analysts." They are concerned with what Marx termed the "means of production," but they do not deal with them directly. You will not find members of the New Class farming, mining, manufacturing, inventing, or working with their hands. In other words, they are less interested in experimenting with nature, tinkering with technology, or manipulating physical reality than in experimenting with human nature, tinkering with politics, and manipulating society.

These people trade in symbols, words, and concepts. Typically they are writers, editors, producers, media people, mid- to upper-level bureaucrats, academics, entertainers, lobbyists, lawyers, planners, artists, analysts, consultants, and employees of charitable organizations. They are the direct descendants of scribes and priests.

The New Class tends to be well educated and earn enough to have the leisure to ponder the "important" things in life. It's a safe bet that if Woody Allen had to log twelve hours a day in a coal mine, he would be short on the time and energy it takes to cultivate sixteen tons of angst. Although the New Class makes much of "caring" for those who aren't economically privileged, they usually have little direct contact with the working classes. They tend to see the hands-on production that proletarians engage in as somewhat degrading, although they are too politically correct to voice such an insensitive sentiment. All the brouhaha during the '80s about America becoming a nation of "hamburger-flippers" was largely a result of their distaste for manual labor. The fact that entry-level jobs are educational and build the skills and attitudes for higher positions is lost on them.

Even if they do not always have substantial net worth, the New Class always affects upper-middle-class values. They feel that economic plenty and material comfort are their birthright, but they have little real understanding of how those conditions are created. They feel that the government creates wealth and commercial interests unfairly exploit it. Like European and British aristocrats, they believe money is something that proper ladies and gentlemen simply have. Only members of the trade need abase themselves in catering to the needs of others. Newly made fortunes are not viewed as proof of having successfully provided other people with what they want, so much as proof of probably having done something unethical.

Like any elite, they enjoy their positions on top and want to maintain them. That is why they tend—like nearly every elite—to be against free markets, although they are for political democracy, mainly because they feel—correctly—they're able to manipulate the attitudes of many voters. Because economic progress tends to raise those on the bottom into the middle and upper-middle classes, the upwardly mobile people dilute the power and influence of those who have already arrived. A stagnant economy, on the other hand, tends to cement people in their current status.

After all, if the average proletarian were to double his standard of living, it would be that much harder to get a table at Spago or Elaine's; the beaches at chichi Caribbean resorts and the slopes of Aspen would be more crowded and less exclusive. You will not hear those sentiments stated publicly, but you will hear them at private parties in New York, Washington, and San Francisco. What you will hear in public are proposals that access to national parks and wilderness areas be restricted, since doing so can be justified in the name of the environment. These views are, of course, alien to what has been traditionally American. New Class values are much closer to traditional European values, which are aristocratic in outlook.

The New Class tends to be suspicious of both technology and capitalism, not despite the fact that they have elevated the average person to a high standard of living, but because of it. Technology and capitalism are held responsible for a litany of supposed ills: too many cars, parking lots, strip shopping centers, and suburbs; too few snail darters and spotted owls. In the view of the New Class, the problem boils down to too many people, other than themselves, living too well and thereby having too much of an effect on the planet. A reasonable person can certainly see that economic growth creates serious problems and that there is room for improvement. The trouble is that the New Class thinks it knows best and is anxious to impose its solutions on everyone else. Not surprisingly, they share pretty much the same solutions.

When it comes to solutions for the ills of society, the New Class is righteous, taking on the tone of moral crusaders, with correspondingly uncompromising attitudes. Since they control the news, entertainment, educational, and literary media, and since they socialize and work mainly with each other, they think everyone shares their beliefs. And they're not completely incorrect in that assumption. Since they're in a position to set the parameters of a debate, "Should there be government welfare?" is never asked, but "Who should get how much, and who should decide?" is open for discussion. Consequently, they limit the views they expose themselves to.

CLINTON'S ADVISER

New Class ideas are extensively discussed in Secretary of Labor Robert Reich's most recent book, *The Work of Nations*, in which he spells out his description of the way the world works and a few elements of his prescription for making it work more to his liking. Some of Reich's observations are quite astute. He openly acknowledges, for instance, the extreme unlikelihood of any baby boomers collecting Social Security. It is also apparent he has been exposed to the arguments for laissez-faire government, and even if he does not exactly favor them, he at least understands them. His main thesis is the inevitable dominance of "symbolic analysts," as he prefers to call the New Class.

There are lots of ways to pigeonhole people economically. Marx said they were members of either the proletariat or the bourgeoisie. Mao emphasized the workers and peasants. More recent observers refer to service workers and information workers. All these distinctions are useful, or at least were, in their time and place. Reich makes a distinction between routine workers, in-person service workers, and symbolic analysts. It's a worthwhile set of distinctions that leads to interesting conclusions.

Routine workers are those who labor in manufacturing, farming, or extractive industries. Reich recognizes that in America these workers are in trouble because consumers do not care if a widget is made, rice is grown, or iron is mined in Brazil or the continental United States. Consumers want the widget, rice, or iron for the best price. So why would any manufacturer in his right mind pay an American, and arguably one with marginal work habits, $20 an hour to do work a Brazilian would kill to get at $1 an hour? Additional advantages include tax benefits, regulatory relief, and lower costs of operating in less-developed countries. Routine-type work of all descriptions will migrate to low-cost countries. Reich points out that if someone earns his living in that type of business, his personal ship is sinking. The collapse in union membership in the last twenty years is evidence enough.

In-person service workers are retail salespeople, health-care providers, auto mechanics, waiters, secretaries, and the like. These people are insulated from foreign competition by the fact the service must be performed on the spot. This field will grow, but much of the growth will be absorbed by immigrants to America from low-wage countries. Reich expects the personal ships of American in-person service workers to take on some water. How much money can you earn, after all, doing piecework?

The future lies with symbolic analysts, those holding the occupations of the New Class who can trade their skills on the international market. If they do not like political-social-economic conditions in one country, they can and will move to another. Reich correctly states that these people have more allegiance to their class than to their place of birth. An American symbolic analyst has more in common with a colleague from a foreign country than he does with a routine worker from Des Moines.

Reich sees, therefore, the futility of putting up tariff and other barriers to save sunset industries. He is well aware of how taxes and welfare can draw in, or scare away, different classes of people. He accepts that it is increasingly impossible to say whether a certain car is Japanese or American. Hondas are made in the United States, Fords in Mexico; both use parts imported from a half-dozen other countries. It is also impossible to identify a corporation's nationality. For example, most of IBM's profits and about half its employees are already abroad. Would IBM still be a U.S. corporation if it moved its headquarters to Switzerland and elected a Korean as chairman and a Swede as CEO? If Americans owned most of the stock of, say, Northern Telecom, a Canadian corporation, should they buy from it or from an "American" company in which Europeans may own most of the stock? Reich builds an excellent argument that borders are ceasing to exist, de facto if not de jure. And he's absolutely right.

So what does Reich, and presumably President Clinton, suggest be done? Reich can see what amounts to the handwriting on the wall: If government tries to change those trends, it will be overwhelmed. You might think his conclusion would be something like: "It's pretty obvious that government taxes and regulations are increasingly a hindrance to these changes. Perhaps we should try to wind the institution down slowly and let the people of the world go about their business in peace."

But he comes to a different conclusion. He says, after sounding like a laissez-faire citizen of the world: "This position is not that of a laissez-faire cosmopolitan because it rests on a sense of national purpose—of principled cultural and historic connection to a common political endeavor. It seeks to encourage new learning within the nation, to smooth the transition of the nation's workforce from older industries, to educate and train the nation's workers, to improve the nation's infrastructure and to create international rules of fair play." He expands these remarks to include pre- and postnatal care and access to college regardless of financial capability. That is exactly what Clinton has promised. Reich winds up making a lot of good arguments for a free market but then says he really doesn't believe them.

An intellectual appreciation of where the free market takes the world is one thing. But advising the government—especially when it's going to make him rich, famous, and powerful—requires finding something for it to do. And Reich, like Clinton, is thoroughly imbued with New Class values, which fairly beg for government action.

NEW CLASS VALUES

At least eight themes unify and define the thinking of the New Class. In most cases they've taken something that either is, or has the potential of becoming, a real problem and blown it totally out of proportion. It is analogous to a campfire being a good thing, but a forest fire being too much of a good thing.

1. **Technology.** The New Class is deeply suspicious of technology. Few of them have had any real scientific training, and almost none has had any exposure to engineering, so very few have a practical understanding of technology per se. People naturally fear anything they do not really understand. They want to control scientists and engineers who, they are convinced, do not have the wisdom, which mostly resides in the New Class, to employ their powers appropriately.

The New Class thinks that technology mostly leads to bad results. Their tendency is to decrease automotive pollution by decreasing driving 50 percent through punitive regulations rather than to encourage installation of a new device to cut pollution by 99 percent. Since they mistrust mankind, they do not want them to have much power over the environment, hence the technophobia that accompanies the "back to the earth" movement. And that, of course, is another major theme.

2. **Ecology/Environment.** Greenism is becoming a new religion, where "ecology" is a deity to whom worshipers must offer sacrifice. Religion offers a pretty good analogy, and not just because it's also historically antitechnology. Greenism could replace traditional religion for a large portion of the population in the decades to come, even though its views are at odds with the Jewish, Christian, and Muslim doctrines that give mankind direct dominion over the world.

I find this an interesting subtheme, if only because I have always been sympathetic with the Nordic and Celtic cultures that prevailed in pre-Roman, pre-Christian Europe. They were probably the most libertarian cultures in the history of the world, with strong emphasis on personal privacy and property rights and a respect for nature. But only their nature-worship aspects seem to be emphasized in New Class circles.

Despite a generally antiscientific bent, the New Class will cite science when convenient, often out of context. In any event, science takes a backseat to the hysteria that is socially acceptable when it comes to environmental issues. Even the most remote possibilities of disaster are taken seriously and arouse calls for instant government action that are often based on inadequate data, poorly thought through, and often counterproductive. Cost-benefit calculations are rarely done and are imprecise when they are done. Instead, the New Class tends to believe that the ends justify the means, no matter what the means may cost.

3. **Health and Safety.** The New Class believes man incapable of making a rational or informed judgment about what risks he accepts. Like many who enjoy privileged lifestyles, the New Class tends to be afraid of risk or change. As a result, even the normal risks of living are blown out of all proportion.

Since the New Class is better educated and more sophisticated than the population at large, it tends to believe it knows what is best for the masses. The end product, of course, is a busybody mentality, which is only natural, since social workers, politicians, and pundits are really only professional busybodies; their job descriptions are to set standards for others and then make sure those others conform to their standards.

And, after all, if "society" is going to pay the costs of an individual's sickness or injury, it follows that society's New Class guardians should ensure that the individual behaves appropriately, whether or not those who have to obey the rules and pay taxes for the privilege really like them.

4. **Social justice.** The New Class translates social justice as not just equality before the law or equality of opportunity, but as equality of income and standing. In their calculation two wrongs can make a right, which is what "affirmative action" is all about. As a result, people are treated not so much as individuals, but as members of racial, religious, or other groups. This serves to entrench the problem the New Class claims to want to solve, and as a bonus sets up an atmosphere for class warfare.

5. **Economic development.** Much emphasis was placed on "jobs" during the 1992 elections, although exactly what that meant wasn't made clear. A process of elimination is helpful. We know jobs in fast-food restaurants aren't socially acceptable, and factory and other repetitive work is behind the power curve. But the world is not yet ready for everyone to be a TV producer, lawyer, lobbyist, consultant, or some other kind of symbolic analyst. What kind of job might the candidates have meant? It's tough to create productive work for people when you do not let the market tell you what it wants. But the New Class will tell the market what it *should* want. That is called an "industrial policy."

Of course the government can create jobs by hiring people for public works projects, shoring up the country's deteriorating infrastructure. (The paradox of why the government-owned infrastructure is collapsing, but privately owned buildings are well maintained, is never addressed.)

Another alternative brought forward by those who believe in an industrial policy is to make large grants to large companies to employ large numbers of workers. One alternative not likely to get wide attention is the firing of government employees and the elimination of taxes and regulations to get the economy moving.

The peer pressure, social opprobrium, and moral approbation—and overt regulations—arising from New Class values result in the fact that people tend to work less hard, take fewer risks, and seek more leisure. Obviously, everyone makes these choices for themselves, but if the Wright brothers had to develop an airplane in today's environment, they likely would have become discouraged before they succeeded.

6. **Free markets.** Since the manifest bankruptcy of socialist systems around the world, it has become less fashionable or credible to deny the benefits of a free market. Instead the emphasis has changed to "perfecting" the markets through a government–private "partnership" of "national industrial policy," "targeted spending," and other euphemisms for planning, directing, and controlling the economy.

The trouble with the market's "invisible hand" is that it moves too slowly to suit people who want results while they are in office. Although the results may be what the market—that is, most people—wants, the New Class believes the majority of people do not know what is in their best interests. The New Class will grudgingly acknowledge that free markets and capitalism can be "efficient," but then claim they aren't adequately "moral," i.e., in tune with the values of planners. Regulation is likely to increase, not decrease.

7. **Entrepreneurialism**. Entrepreneurs and businessmen in general are held in low esteem by the New Class. Businessmen employ workers, which leads to the presumption that they also exploit them. They advertise, which means they "induce" people to buy things they don't really "need." They make a lot of money, so they are expanding the gap between rich and poor. New Class attitudes toward business are similar to the attitude of European aristocrats toward work in general: it is best left to the lower classes and those who haven't found a way to rise above it.

The fact that businessmen are typically "doers" leads the New Class, who see themselves as "thinkers," to look down on them. It's a culture clash, and businessmen are viewed suspiciously, unless they can prove their social value in some way other than just making a profit. Someone who makes a million dollars producing a new razor or a cancer cure is looked upon as if he alone, and not all of society, were the beneficiary.

8. **Traditional values.** Boy Scout virtues are out and radical chic is in. Nineteenth-century values (courage, perseverance, responsibility, and achievement) are out. John Wayne is unhip; Alan Alda is a more acceptable male role model. Some lip service will be paid to traditional values to appease the silent majority. But these traditional values are pretty much held in contempt by the New Class. "Alternative lifestyles" will likely meet with tacit approval, if not encouragement.

That's not to be confused with the get-along-go-along tolerance for, and encouragement of, diversity typical of libertarians. The New Class harbors an active dislike for "middle-class values" and a desire to create a new set of values. In the process it may create the conditions for active class warfare.

HOW RAPID THE CHANGE

One of the favorable consequences of the Reagan years was that, due to his middlebrow views, few of his appointees and staffers were New Class. They were much more representative of Middle America and Main Street, salted with people from the New Right. Clinton is too much of a politician to make radical policy changes himself. But since he surrounds himself with members of the New Class, it will be the little folks behind the scenes in the Clinton administration who will really make a difference.

And this, far more than Clinton and Gore themselves being New Class, will change the way things work. A new president appoints about 3,000 people to positions that are important but below the level of Senate confirmation. You can absolutely plan on it that every one of them will try to spray-paint some New Class values on the side of your house.

The change will not be as radical as they might like. Because well over half of all government spending is already designated and another quarter is needed for interest payments, there is relatively little left. Since the economy will continue to stagger along for the reasons outlined earlier, they will be forced to be more realistic and pragmatic than if the national piggy bank were full.

Stocks positioned to capitalize on the type of spending Reich has outlined (in *The Work of Nations*) will not be given the boost some people hope will happen. With the market at a ridiculous peak, second-guessing Clinton stocks will likely prove disappointing.

THE BEGINNINGS, AND END, OF THE NEW CLASS

It's not that individual members of the New Class necessarily think their values are intellectually defensible. But they will tend to defend their positions much the way many ex-Catholics still argue Church dogma with Protestants. Being a member of a peer group is an emotional thing, rousing atavistic responses. It's like patriotism; most everyone feels it, even though it makes little rational sense.

Economist Joseph Schumpeter anticipated the rise of the New Class early in this century, recognizing it as part of a phenomenon that tends to cause capitalistic societies to self-destruct. His argument was that capitalism tends to breed anti-capitalistic mentalities not because it doesn't produce wealth, but because capitalism succeeds so very well.

Children of well-off parents tend to accept wealth as a given and so do not usually have the drive it takes, or the compelling needs their parents had, to create their own fortunes. Their parents were surrounded by at least relative poverty and rose above it through innovation, hard work, and savings. The children, however, grow up with the luxury to disdain abundance, especially since there are a lot of seemingly deserving people, whether they're across town, or in Somalia, who must do without. This is most true when children carry guilt about their wealth, which is common since the children have done nothing to create it or "deserve" it. As a result, they develop false solutions to their perceived problem. That often means alcohol, drugs, or general dissipation; psychologically and intellectually it usually means adopting New Class values.

So most children of affluent parents hit upon counterproductive and innately hypocritical solutions to the problems they perceive with the wealth around them. The New Class values they embrace are anti wealth and anti capitalist, and some feel a sense of cognitive dissonance. Not everyone is taken in; some eventually reason their way out of what can easily become a slough of despond. Probably the greatest and most lasting contribution of Ayn Rand to philosophy and economics is that she established a moral and ethical basis for capitalism and free markets. Previously both had been defended on the basis that they were natural or efficient or the best way to help the poor. Rand is a bête noir of the New Class. But her work is due for a revival.

The New Class is correct that basic industries—agriculture, mining, and manufacturing—will become less significant in terms of the number of people engaged in them, even though their products will be more important than ever. Progress will continue in stops and starts. As the New Class grows in number and influence, which it will over the next four years, their more otherworldly ideas will slow progress and cause a reaction. But, as Marx would have said, the "historical imperative" is on their side. The world is going to get wealthier, most people will join the leisure class, and New Class ideas will gain more dominance.

My guess is that many of the New Class's current ideas, starting with the most extreme, will eventually fall by the wayside. After all, as its numbers grow to include the majority of people, the New Class will have the greatest interest in eliminating the income tax, since they will earn the most. They have the skills to start new businesses, so they will be frustrated by their own regulations. They are in the best position to accumulate capital, so they should be interested in a sound money system. The fact that the New Class is well educated and has time to think means that an increasing number of them will eventually be intellectually convinced of the merits of a free market system.

Marx would probably have noted that the New Class values are fraught with "internal contradictions" and are sure to change. It is probably a lot like the evolution of the working class. They used to want to smash machines and string up the owners. Now they want more machines because they have come to understand that machines allow high wages, and they would like to become the owners.

Science fiction is as good a predictor of where it's all going to end as anything else. Maybe we will have a kinder and gentler version of *1984* in the next century. Maybe it will resemble Huxley's *Brave New World*. Maybe it will be more like the movie *Zardoz* or David Brin's recent book, *Earth*, or Paul Theroux's *The O-Zone*. The possibilities are too numerous to appraise realistically. I tend to take an optimistic view, certainly for the long term.

The fifty years since World War II have been unlike any other five decades in human history. World population has grown from 2.5 billion to 5.5 billion, world GNP from $2 trillion to about $16 trillion. People around the world have gone from mostly preliterate to fairly educated, rural to urban, and preindustrial to relatively industrial. And the rate of change is still accelerating, although the New Class will slow things down, for a while anyway.

But don't worry. It's just a stage they are going through. They are mostly baby boomers. And baby boomers have gone through several stages already. Their current embrace of New Class values is just their newest and most important stage.

BABY BOOMERS AND NEW PURITANISM IN THE NO-FUN '90S.

Clinton, Gore, and their wives are not only members of the New Class, they are also post–World War II baby boomers. Not all boomers are members of the New Class, of course. But people of the same generation have shared experiences that mold their characters in similar ways. Boomers have so far gone through three stages, and they are about to enter a fourth.

As youngsters in the '50s, boomers were typified by Beaver Cleaver and the Mouseketeers. They grew up when America led the world in every endeavor of any importance. Boomers were coddled and sheltered by a civic-minded generation that had experienced the Great Depression, fought World War II, and believed in Roosevelt's sense of national purpose. This generation almost universally tried to give their children a better life than theirs had been, and they pretty much succeeded.

Beaver and the Mouseketeers evolved into the counterculture of the '60s and '70s. Whether or not everyone became a hippie, wore bell-bottoms, took drugs, and generally did their thing in the '60s and '70s, they were all influenced by the prevailing ethos. Maybe the sexual revolution could have been predicted because of the pill and penicillin, but it wasn't. It outraged older generations who grew up in the afterglow of the Victorian era. The sea change in attitudes and lifestyles was so widespread that the "generation gap" became a common concern. It was unthinkable to parents who had lived through World War II that their kids not only didn't support the Vietnam War, they staged mass protests against it.

Next came—again completely unpredicted—the rise of the yuppies, whose main interests were money and serious consumerism. It is interesting that although the values of hippiedom and yuppiedom are almost antithetical, the hippies and the yuppies are the same people. That brings us up to the present. Yuppies are already passé, and the boomers are mutating again. Into what?

The '90s will be as different from the '80s as the '80s were from the '60s and '70s, and those decades from the '50s. I expect the '90s to become known as the "no-fun decade." There are lots of straws in the wind.

Sex is out because of AIDS and also because of the threat of suits over harassment, discrimination, and date rape. Drugs, including alcohol and tobacco, are most definitely out in the face of the current prohibition achieved by the war on drugs. Protesting against foreign adventures, from Grenada to Somalia, is unfashionable; joining the military is even applauded. The money and consumerism of the '80s are now seen as counter to the best interests of Mother Earth. And even if they were not, it has become apparent that the currently maturing generation, born between 1960 and 1980 and who compare to the boomers as little as Bart Simpson does to the Beaver, will not live as well as their elders.

To be more specific, we will encounter an ideologically driven new puritanism. The boomers have always been an inner-directed group. That is natural enough, since the United States *was* the world of the '50s. The '60s emphasized self-realization and getting inside one's head, and the '80s were the "me" generation. The boomers in the '90s, therefore, will disdain consensus, unlike their civic-minded parents or their outer-directed, easy-going older brothers and sisters in the silent generation who came of age in the late '40s through the '50s.

Boomers figure they have seen and done it all. They were the first generation to benefit from the jet plane and to travel widely. Their lifestyles have taken them from Smallville to Woodstock to Wall Street. They think they know good from evil, what with the civil rights movement, Vietnam, and '60s consciousness-raising. They feel they met the challenge of what turned out to be the corrupt and ephemeral financial world in the '80s. And they are not going to hesitate to imprint their wisdom on the rest of society and on the world.

Take note of the stridency in Clinton and Gore, as well as of ex-vice-president Dan Quayle. It is even more evident in all three of their wives. Bill Bennett, the ex-drug czar and cheerleader of the disastrous war on drugs, is also a boomer. All these people are at the leading edge of the boom generation as it moves into its mid-forties, and they are typical of what is to come.

It doesn't matter that some of these people hold differing political opinions. What typifies boomers is their psychological tone, righteousness, and stridency. Many boomers are part of the religious right, for instance, who do not share many of the New Class values that will direct government but are, typically of boomers, probably even more dogmatic in their own beliefs. It is hard to say what they and other conservative groups, comprising people like Quayle, Bennett, and Pat Buchanan, will do now that their New Class peers control not only the media and academe but the government as well. It is likely that the Republican party will serve as a rallying point and swing even more to the right.

One forgets that Jefferson was serious when he said a revolution every twenty years would do the country good. Some of the New Right are capable of bringing that radical point to the public's attention. There are plenty of issues that people on both sides of the barricades might think are worthy of a revolution. My guess is that the earth, ecology, the ozone layer, population control, abortion, welfare rights, animal rights, minority rights, and feminism will be centerpieces in this drama.

The situation is greatly complicated by America's no longer being the only country that really matters, as was the case for some time after the end of World War II. Few people in the Third World in general, and the Muslim portion in particular, share the values of either the New Class or their New Right counterparts. If the boomers' ideological drive is combined with America's newfound enthusiasm for sending in the marines, we could well see a confrontation with these folks.

Since compromise isn't big on the boomer agenda, conflict could be very dangerous. If asked whether they would be willing to burn down the barn to kill the rat, you will be told that it depends on the value you place upon the preservation of the barn as opposed to the destruction of the rat. If sacrificing the barn is perceived as "right" or "good," it will be done. The baby-boomers' generation can be counted on to react the same way as Lincoln's generation, which resulted in the Civil War, or Wilson's, which gave us World War I: no compromise, take no prisoners, and let justice prevail though the heavens fall.

As aggressive and powerful as the United States is, it is likely to be a while before any foreign power flexes its military and economic muscle in earnest. But it will happen again.

32

Saving the Rain Forest
From Ecohysteria

Authoritarian socialism has failed almost everywhere, but you will not find a
single Marxist who will say it has failed because it was wrong or impractical.
He will say it has failed because nobody went far enough with it. So failure
never proves a myth is wrong.

Jean-François Revel

The main spur to trade, or rather to industry and ingenuity, is the exorbitant
appetites of men, which they will take pains to gratifie, and so be disposed to
work, when nothing else will incline them to it; for did men content themselves
with bare necessaries, we should have a poor world.

Sir Dudley North (1641-1691)
Discourses upon Trade

The "green" movement is going to have a huge influence on the economic and
investment climate in the years to come. Already a strong force, it is likely to
become much bigger, and the movement's effect will go far beyond the world of
investments. One straw in the wind is the best-seller status of Al Gore's *Earth in the
Balance* and his emphasis on its themes in his campaign for the vice presidency in
1992.

Green is a popular color in many new books. Of thirty-eight new titles in the
Futurist Bookstore's 1992 catalogue, thirteen were explicitly "green" or at least
positioned to capitalize on "green" concerns. As I write, global warming, the
ozone layer, and the rain forest seem to be the flavors of the day. Global hunger,
resource conservation, saving the whales, and global cooling appear to have taken a
back seat for the moment.

RELIGION AS SCIENCE

The "green" movement should be taken very seriously, but there is room for skepticism about its claims and beliefs. Many of them blur the distinction between religious dogma and scientific theory. So, in the interests of precision, let's use the dictionary.

Webster's Unabridged says religion is "concern over what exists beyond the visible world, differentiated from philosophy in that it operates through faith or intuition rather than reason, and generally including the idea of the existence of a single being, group of beings, an eternal principle, or a transcendental spiritual entity that has created the world, that governs it, that controls its destiny, or that intervenes occasionally in the natural course of its history, as well as the idea that ritual, prayer, spiritual exercises, certain principles of everyday conduct, etc., are expedient, due, or spiritually rewarding, or arise naturally out of an inner need as a human response to the belief in such principle, being, etc."

The same dictionary defines science as "a branch of knowledge or study dealing with a body of facts or truths systematically arranged and showing the operation of general laws." The facts and laws in question are arrived at via the scientific method, which is "a method of research in which the problem is identified, relevant data is gathered, a hypothesis is formulated from these data, and the hypothesis is empirically tested."

It's not unfair, or inaccurate, to say the "green" movement has most, if not all, of the elements of a religion, and only a tenuous relationship with science. Of course, uttering such a heresy will outrage "green" warriors. Mother Nature has again, as in animist times, taken on the aspect of a goddess. She is seen as normally gentle but capable of the vengefulness of Yahweh should mankind in general, and scientists in particular, dare to try fooling her. As Gaia, she's ready to intervene in the course of history. To placate her, devotees recycle and bicycle as principles of everyday conduct. While they have no proof these things have much real effect on the visible world, they do find these actions spiritually rewarding, and paying lip service to ecology does fulfill a human need. Traditional religions place Jehovah, God, or Allah first. Greenism places the earth first.

Like most religions, greenism deals with matters of genuine importance. But just as some religions have proceeded from realism to extreme and arcane practices, so has this one. The greens have combined some intuitive concerns with a smattering of science, arrived at some conclusions, and made them articles of faith. Anyone who questions their usually alarmist projections for the fate of the earth is likely to be ostracized as a moral reprobate or a heretic.

A SECULAR RELIGION

The "green" movement has many structural similarities to Marxism, another secular religion. It assures adherents that history is on their side and rewards them with a sense of belonging and purpose. Both Marxism and greenism have diagnosed the world's problems and offer solutions that are not only psychologically appealing to many people but also seem morally "right." Like Marxism, greenism pretends to science but amounts to dogma.

Now that Marxism has been relegated to the scrap heap of history, its adherents have had to find a new centerpiece for their belief system. And just as the Marxists had a hidden agenda of controlling other people, it is arguable that most of the professional greens do also. After all, at least in the West, they are largely the very same people. Protecting the earth, as important as it unquestionably is, serves as an excellent pretext for almost any controls. This opens the door, as with the Marxists, to an end-justifies-the-means approach: absolutely nothing is more important than saving the earth.

The great mass of greens support the movement because they are concerned about real problems and not aware of any better solutions. In all fairness, therefore, it has to be said that the movement's roots are planted in ignorance as much as malevolence. The same was true of many socialist sympathizers, even after Stalin, Mao, Pol Pot, and scores of lesser children of the night unveiled the true nature of the beast. Especially toward the end, socialist beliefs had only a limited intellectual appeal, since the facts contradicted them everywhere. Their appeal was psychological and spiritual. In other words, religious and not susceptible to reason.

Most greens are nonviolent, but the movement is increasingly strident, and there is also a strain of malevolence and suppressed violence, at least within some branches. Already the equivalent of a Leninist wing has arisen, the followers of Edward Albee, who run around "spiking" trees and "monkey wrenching" bulldozers. The Greenpeace *Green Warrior* has a similar role at sea.

The Marxist agenda succeeded in destroying the economy of half the world and a lot of its environment as a bonus. The green agenda promises to do the same for the environment, with the destruction of the economy as a perverse bonus.

You may be wondering whether I am insensitive to the fate of the earth and its creatures. Far from it. Protecting the earth as a pleasant place to live is critical. And there clearly are real problems that need to be dealt with. But the solutions proposed by almost all of the greens will aggravate the problems. Their books almost uniformly advocate political activism and socialist planning, positing a "kinder and gentler" Eastern Europe. There are much more effective ways to address the problems: more economically effective and more effective scientifically. But not with green science or economics.

GREEN SCIENCE

The commingling of science with politics or religion should always give rise to suspicion. The Church persecuted Galileo for believing the earth revolved around the sun because of the theological implications of his theory. Soviet biology under Lysenko denied the science of genetics because it questioned the possibility of creating the "New Socialist Man." "Creationist geology" is about how the world was created in about 4004 B.C. Green science operates from the premise that the interests of people are mostly at odds with the interests of the planet. Like past applications of religion to science, only data supporting the dogma are accepted, a complete reversal of the scientific method's openness to data that contradicts a theory.

Consumer advocates and related groups have largely been subsumed under a green banner. Many of the issues they address range from half-baked to almost purposefully destructive. A good example of green-consumer-safety science was the Alar scare contrived in 1989 by the National Resources Defense Council. It nearly destroyed the U.S. apple industry. Later tests showed that Alar, which was tipped as "the most potent cancer-causing agent in our food supply," is benign. A daily glass of wine is 4,700 times more risky than an Alar-treated apple. You would have to eat 28,000 pounds of those apples daily for seventy years to reach the Alar level that causes tumors in rats. The Corvair rollover scare of the '60s and the cyclamate sweetener scare of the '70s are two other well-known examples. Although in each case the danger has been debunked, the damage is done.

Asbestos is a more recent example. Although it can be dangerous when loose, it's of no danger after it has been sealed in buildings. Nonetheless, green forces contrived to have it replaced in thousands of buildings, at huge risk and cost, for no useful reason. Since the Environmental Protection Agency (EPA) is staffed by green ideologues, this type of farce will continue. The FDA's permanent ban on all tryptophan supplements in 1990, because of some impurities in one shipment from one factory, is in the same class.

The quality of the science doesn't improve when the issues get bigger, nor do the motivations of the greens change, even though the stakes rise. Global warming, for instance, is proclaimed as a fact and is attributed to the emission of "greenhouse gases" like carbon dioxide by human activity. Although the supposed rise in the earth's temperature is based on limited observations and possibly skewed data collected over only a few decades, it is treated in the popular media as a matter broaching no dissent. In fact, while man's effect on the planet is significant in his own terms, it has a trivial effect on the earth itself.

In the larger scheme of things, the earth's climate has continued to change since the atmosphere first accumulated perhaps three billion years ago. Antarctica was temperate 40 million years ago and Alaska subtropical. Eighty million years ago Greenland was tropical; 5 million years ago it was a temperate forest. Only 17,000 years ago, at the peak of the last major ice age, most of the northern hemisphere was covered with ice thousands of feet thick and looked like Greenland today. Only eight hundred years ago, Viking farmers were growing grain in Greenland, but they were driven out of Greenland as the little Ice Age of 1450–1850 commenced. We have, in effect, had global warming since the end of that ice age. It is part of a cyclical process that has been going on longer than history.

Over the millions of years of the earth's history, the sun, oceans, atmosphere, life forms, and land masses have interacted, in ways that are still only vaguely understood, to change the climate drastically. Man has had nothing to do with it until very recently. Over the last century humans have had an increasing effect.

Especially over the next few decades, as the final gasps of the industrial revolution spew a few billion tons of extra gases into the atmosphere, that effect will be even greater. Most likely it will raise temperatures somewhat. But the gases from volcanos alone have produced much more damage. Mt. Pinatubo in the Philippines, which buried Clark Air Force Base in 1991, is estimated to have emitted more than 30 million tons of sulfur-rich gas in that one year. And scores of volcanoes are active at any one time. Even the billion tons of dirty coal burned annually in China generate only 9 million tons of sulfur dioxide. In any event, the earth has built mountains and submerged continents for millennia, and the process will continue for billions of years into the future.

There's no question that mankind can have a large effect on the planet. But if anything can change the face of the planet for the better, it will be technology, not lobbying and not industrial policy. The real crux of the green argument, however, is not about these relatively tangential issues. Rather, they attempt to address the "real" problem greens object to, namely, too many people.

THE PEOPLE PROBLEM

The driving force behind all the problems the greens perceive really boils down to the number of people in existence. Most people, including myself, are at least somewhat sympathetic to that concern. No one savors the squalid, teeming cities or the sprawling, sterile suburbs that increasingly cover the planet. And who wouldn't like to have the whole earth as a private playground for just himself and a few friends?

But, surprising to some, the high standard of living we enjoy and the immense possibilities for the future mostly came about as the result of the vast number of people who populate the earth. It takes many millions of individuals to produce one Edison, Einstein, Shakespeare, or Milken. It takes a market of hundreds of millions to support the development and production of the vast variety of available consumer goods. And who's to say that New York and Paris don't offer more pleasure than the Grand Canyon? But, at some point, further growth in the human population will result in diminishing returns.

In 1990 the United Nations estimated the world's population at 5.3 billion. As of January 1993 it had grown to over 5.5 billion, an addition almost equal to the population of the United States. If the world's population continues to grow at its present rate, it will double by 2025 and will keep doubling about every twenty-five years, reaching about 352 billion, by 2150, which breaks down into 12,100 people for every square mile of land on the earth's surface. By 2250, the number would be 6 trillion, or about 200 for every acre of space on the planet, including the oceans, deserts, and mountains. As demographer Ansley Cole observed in 1970, even at a much lower rate of compound growth, in a few thousand years our descendants would "form a sphere of flesh whose radius would, neglecting relativity, expand at the speed of light."

That doesn't leave a lot of space for the rain forest, whales, or elegant houses in which to have brie-and-chardonnay parties. At some point world population growth must stop. That has already happened in North America, Western Europe, and Japan. If immigration is subtracted, the population of those regions is shown to be declining. It takes about 2.2 children per couple to maintain a stable population, but most of my friends, and probably yours, have one child, or none. Few have two or more.

That is not true in the Third World. Poor people there have huge numbers of children for the same reasons our own ancestors once did. They expect most to die before maturity, although technology now has changed that. They serve as cheap agricultural labor. They act as a retirement annuity when the parents grow old. And they are a source of pride and comfort. It is hard to prevent their births, even if that were desired. People marry young because it is expected and economically neces-sary, and there's nothing else to do. Some traditional religions encourage large families.

Those reasons will become irrelevant as Third Worlders grow wealthier, just as has been the case in advanced societies. Abundant food, shelter, and medical care ensure that most children reach maturity. Children are a financial liability and have little labor value in a city. In a capitalist system parents are able to save and build assets on their own for old age. In capitalist cities, the patriarch cannot create a clan because children move away to follow careers. Birth control is readily available. There are plenty of alternatives to marriage, and nobody in cities expects much from their neighbors. Finally, traditional religion is a minor factor. The population problem will, in other words, mostly solve itself as Figure 32-1—drawn from a long-term perspective—illustrates.

But since these things do not turn on a dime, the world will likely peak at 10–20 billion people before population growth ceases. And since all these people will consume fuel, create garbage, live on land, and drive cars, they are going to put vastly more pressure on Gaia. A number of consequences will result. One will be a

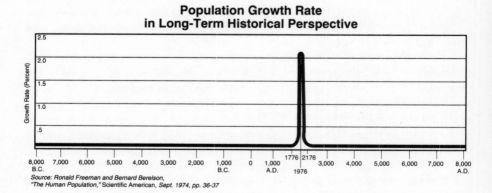

**Population Growth Rate
in Long-Term Historical Perspective**

Source: Ronald Freeman and Bernard Berelson,
"The Human Population," Scientific American, Sept. 1974, pp. 36-37

Figure 32–1

growing resentment on the part of people in Europe, America, and Japan against all those Third Worlders who are "overpopulating" the planet.

For instance, while we realize the stupidity of it now, no one at the time criticized our ancestors when they cut down the forests and wiped out numerous wild animal species as recently as a hundred years ago. But it is not considered acceptable for Third World societies to do the same today. Ecologically sensitive people aren't at all sympathetic with the poor in the Third World who damage "our" planet by their subsistence. The resentment is likely to become mutual.

One can also expect a backlash against Third World immigration to Europe and North America. The culture, economic status, and ethnic makeup of the new immigrants differ considerably from those of current residents—another cause for mutual resentment. Pressures are going to grow considerably. There will be less enthusiasm to prevent starvation in places like Somalia as hordes of poor people are increasingly perceived as a problem, not an opportunity for charity.

The potential for North-South conflict, which was a popular subject of concern in the '70s, is likely to surface again but in a green context. Not all the fallout from the green movement will be bad, however. It should provide the most acceptable excuse for reducing welfare benefits and foreign aid, or at least tying them to family-planning measures. The availability of welfare, especially extra benefits for children, has deprived the recipients of the motivation and responsibility for limiting the size of their families. Future limits will be resented as racism, since it will primarily affect people with brown, black, or yellow skin.

There is no question that the great increase in the number of people will change the quality of life on the planet. Although the worst-case scenario, of the type represented in the movies *Soylent Green* and *Blade Runner* is extremely remote, they are what the greens anticipate as they extrapolate the current trends they choose to look at. As a result, the greens and the New Class (see chapter 31) will face a real dilemma: the fact that they fear and dislike people in general and, in particular, those who do not share their views. Yet they want the moral high ground.

GREEN PROFITEERING

As problematical as the green movement may be, it will grow rapidly for at least the next decade. Two questions arise: What can a concerned person do to improve environmental problems? And how can one profit from the green trend? The answer to both questions is the same. Profits are a natural consequence of providing real solutions to real problems. But an immense number of mostly cosmetic solutions are being directed toward nonproblems.

It might be a good idea to look at a few issues in that light. The approach to the problems of basic food and raw materials have been discussed in earlier chapters, as were the pressures placed on Gaia herself. The best simple way to profit from most green problems will be through the shares of companies that are involved in new technologies.

As I pointed out in chapter 1, it's most plausible that not only will the world's population double or triple, so will its standard of living. That implies at least five to ten times the current demand for luxury items, including nondurables like exotic foods and fine clothing and durables like desirable residential land and fine furniture. Moreover, the prices for items rich people buy are less likely to be regulated than the products needed by poor people, and the well-off are much less price-sensitive.

The price of such luxuries as sushi ingredients, caviar, good wine and beef, exotic fruits and vegetables, tropical hardwoods, silk and good cigars will go through the roof. Owning the means of production of those items will be extremely profitable. It also means that prices of exotic properties, artwork, and collectibles, such as vintage Ferarris, will have a major resurgence after the Greater Depression comes to an end. But let's return to the ecology.

WHO'S REALLY DESTROYING THE RAIN FOREST?

You may wonder why the rain forest is still being destroyed, even though it is widely accepted that it should be saved. The rainforest is being cut down for what appear to be economic reasons, and so its destruction is blamed on the free market, while the proposals to save it are political. That viewpoint stands the problem on its head. In fact, the rain forest is being destroyed for political reasons, and its salvation lies with economics and a completely free market. Government action, in other words, is the main problem, although it's widely perceived as the only workable solution.

There are at least five reasons the rain forest in South America, Africa and Asia is disappearing despite the fact "everyone" deplores its destruction. First, government policies keep rain forest land priced far below its real value in a free market. The statist governments that dominate most tropical lands make it both hard and dangerous for foreigners to invest, even while their policies encourage residents to get their money offshore by any means possible. The result is a chronic lack of capital, resulting in extraordinarily cheap land.

These depressed prices make it economically viable for businessmen to buy forest land, cut and sell a crop of timber, and then graze cattle on it for a year or two before it turns to wasteland. So, because of state policies, land is worth significantly less than a year's crops, the exact opposite of what would make economic sense in a free market. In an open, free market this land would be too expensive for an owner to profit by allowing it to turn to wasteland.

Second, the same governments are always short of foreign exchange and so offer subsidies of one kind or another to encourage exports. Timber and cattle are export commodities that show quick cash returns, and their production is encouraged. Exporting raw commodities is also favored by local businessmen as a great way to get capital offshore and beyond the reach of the local government by using double invoicing and other techniques.

Third, all of this is compounded by the unpredictability of life under statist governments. Political instability inevitably directs everyone's attention to the short term. Property rights are ephemeral and can be compromised by political fiat. Only an idiot would invest for the next generation when his property could be expropriated or its use restricted at any time.

In that environment, it makes far more sense to rape the land for a quick profit and leave the damage for the next guy to worry about. This mind-set—the exact opposite of the ethic that built Western civilization—institutionalizes a culture of poverty. Peasants, who basically have no property, are willing to burn a tree for firewood, even though it might be worth a million times more when transformed into antibiotics. They can see and feel the instant benefit the fire offers.

A fourth reason is that the tax structures and so-called development policies of most of these countries almost always discourage the holding of raw land. The governments are philosophically opposed to "land speculation," which is what holding raw land amounts to. And they want to encourage development and exports, which amounts to clearing the land. So their tax policies further speed the clearing of the rain forest.

They are abetted by international "development" agencies like the World Bank, which loan billions to build uneconomic dams, roads, and steel mills in the middle of nowhere, in other words, in the middle of the rain forest. From that point of view, it is probably a good thing that most foreign aid money winds up being diverted to the rulers' Swiss bank accounts, or the damage would be even greater.

A fifth reason is a desire on the part of the governments to populate virgin land, sometimes in order to defuse urban poverty, for which they're largely responsible, sometimes to prevent their neighbors from impinging, or sometimes for purely ideological reasons. Indonesia, Brazil, and Cambodia are examples.

None of these factors would operate in a free market.

BUY THE RAIN FOREST

The real answer for those who are concerned about the fate of the earth is simply to buy up as much pristine land as they can afford and set it aside in perpetuity. The approximately $500 million raised by environmental groups each year could buy a lot of rain forest.

One acquaintance of mine bought an area the size of Switzerland in Brazil's Rondonia for less than $200,000 in 1982. He sees it as a "development" play. In 1991 an American friend bought a smaller parcel, about 30,000 acres, for about a dollar an acre; the price was much higher than the larger lot at $200,000 but still almost free, in our terms. He purchased it because of ecological concerns, but is forced to view it as a "throwaway" holding, because he can't effectively protect it from squatters.

If vastly more land could be bought—and rights effectively enforced—it would drive up prices of the remainder, making it uneconomic to clear it for cattle raising.

Two groups that do take an effective market approach to preserving nature are the Nature Conservancy, which now owns nearly 2.6 million acres around the world, and Ducks Unlimited, which limits its similar efforts to North America. These are two of the very few that deserve support, if you believe in free-market solutions to the problem. Keep this approach in mind the next time you encounter some uninformed green who wants you to turn off the lights and freeze in the dark in order to solve the world's problems.

Property rights would solve the environmental problems at sea equally well. When nobody owns a patch of ocean, it makes sense to clear everything out before someone else does. If everybody owns something, then nobody owns it, and it is treated that way. But if individuals or corporations had proprietary rights over the seas, they would conserve and improve its resources, just as a farmer conserves and improves his land. Having a state, or the United Nations, allocate rights results in corruption and does little to attack the root of the problem.

In brief, anything worth doing can and should be done for a profit by means of property rights. A profit is evidence, and property rights ensure, that a resource is being used in the most productive way. And you can be sure that with billions of people coming into the world, all resources will be used, one way or the other.

THE GREENS VERSUS THE PLANET AND ITS PEOPLE

The market solution above is simple, direct, cheap, and effective. But it holds little appeal for either ecoNazis, those who are eager to use force to impose their notions of ecological salvation on society, or ecoNinnies, those who go along with the ecoNazis out of guilt, ignorance, fear, desperation, or plain stupidity. Free-market solutions wouldn't fit in with their religious dogma or psychological predispositions.

Such solutions necessarily validate the idea of private property, of which they are deeply suspicious. So, instead of supporting a workable solution, the typical ecoNinny winds up giving money to a bureaucratic green organization, where it all goes to salaries and overhead. The end product is a lobbying effort that, if it succeeds, results in another bureaucracy staffed by self-aggrandizing ecoNazis.

The movements' leaders are quite bold and often do not bother to disguise their feelings. They see people as the problem, not just another, inevitable force for change in the earth's four billion-year evolution. Here are four of the movement's leading lights.

—Dr. Helen Caldicott: "Free enterprise really means rich people get richer. And they have the freedom to exploit and psychologically rape their fellow human beings in the process. . . . Capitalism is destroying the earth. Cuba is a wonderful country. What Castro's done is superb."

—Paul Watson, founder of Greenpeace: "I got the impression that instead of going out to shoot birds, I should go out and shoot the kids who shoot birds."

—David Brower, of Friends of the Earth: "Childbearing [should be] a punishable crime against society, unless the parents hold a government license. . . . All potential parents [should be] required to use contraceptive chemicals, the government issuing antidotes to citizens chosen for childbearing." And again: "I founded Friends of the Earth to make the Sierra Club look reasonable. Earth First! now makes us look reasonable."

—David Foreman, founder of Earth First! has said: "Man is the cancer of nature, and I am the antibody."

I wish the tone and volume of ecohysteria now being cranked out would let me draw a more optimistic conclusion about the shape of things to come. I wish I could say the phenomenon may be peaking because it is so popular. But I think not. More likely, ecohysteria is here to stay for many years.

Once again, it's pretty much a replay of what happened with Marxism. For nearly a century it was promoted as a well-intentioned system that only occasionally went wrong when a misdirected individual, such as every socialist political leader, went a little too far. But even though they have been discredited intellectually, Marxists still hold the high ground by claiming to be moral. It's a religious phenomenon.

The same is true of the so-called war on drugs. It's unbelievably expensive and destructive of civil liberties and is the cause for creating a whole new criminal class. But people have been intimidated into believing it's wrong not to support it. Ditto for almost every government program, from Social Security on down.

In the long run, in addition to the purchase plan mentioned above, the only way to save nature is to increase the economic status of people around the world. It is the poor who are devastating the earth; they have no other way to stay alive. It is the rich, educated classes who are not only concerned but in a position to improve things. The costly and destructive taxes and regulations the greens advocate will serve to ensure the environment and all of us are worse off. Their programs are as counterproductive as those of their kindred spirits in the socialist movement.

It is important to be cautious about whom you support in this area. Do not be intimidated into cutting your own throat. Don't roll over because it seems like the ecoNazis/ecoNinnys and their flavor-of-the-day causes seem well intentioned. Support only groups whose programs and intentions you have thoroughly investigated. The scientific-technological problems of actually improving conditions are trivial by comparison with the philosophical-psychological problems of the members of the green movement.

POLITICALLY CORRECT GREEN INVESTMENTS

Are there other ways of profiting from all of this? Should you, for instance, consider investing in any of the so-called environmentally friendly mutual funds that have sprung up in recent years? I'm of two minds. And when all the indicators fail to point in one direction, I would as soon pass. I can see more market demand for green-oriented companies' products, and I can see more investors wanting to own their stocks, if only for ideological reasons.

Green investors face a problem in finding stocks to buy. There are not that many environmentally friendly and politically correct companies that are also well managed and reasonably priced. Perversely, some of the best plays on the green tide will be some of the very companies greens find most offensive. Many businessmen support environmentalism mainly because it can be used to hurt their competition, which is exactly the reason big business has usually supported regulation. For example, some ranchers support the green movement to preclude competitors from using government range lands. Some miners will support it, to make it harder for potential competitors to develop new mines.

DuPont was receptive to claims that chlorofluorocarbons (CFCs) seriously harm the ozone layer (an unproven and somewhat improbable assertion), since it owns the patent on the only practical substitute for Freon. The spotted-owl controversy hurt the part of the lumber industry that leased government land for cutting. But taking acreage out of production increased the value of the remaining acreage. That, and not the greens' arguments, is probably the real reason why Weyerhaeuser, the largest U.S. private timberland owner, helped finance the green lobbyists who shut down its competitors. And, of course, that government timberland was clear-cut with impunity simply because the lessees didn't own it; they were getting it practically free from the government.

There are plenty of potential problems with green companies. Management may put their own political agendas ahead of investors' profits. Owning faddish, high P/E stocks at the very top of an overextended bull market could prove a very expensive political statement. And a sampling of envirostocks typically shows them to be very pricey relative to the competition.

Take Ben & Jerry's (BJICA, $35), the prototypical stock for tree-hugging environmentalists who like ice cream after their granola. The company is profitable, and its earnings have grown consistently—even though they pay out 7.5 percent of earnings to politically correct causes. I find no fault with their shareholder meetings, usually featuring the Grateful Dead, or the fact no executive can make more than ten times what the lowest-paid gofer takes home. And, in any event, the shareholders actively support the policies.

It certainly has been a formula for success. Baby boomers can assuage their guilt about eating ice cream while people are starving in Ethiopia, or wherever, by buying it from Ben & Jerry's. Not only that, but the premium ice cream game is a good one to be in during hard times, because people who can't afford real luxuries will buy an expensive ice cream to give themselves a taste of the good life. If the feds ever drop subsidies and controls on milk, which cost billions yearly and could go away of necessity as the budget deficit balloons, B&J's profits could soar as the price of milk dropped. In other words, I wouldn't want to be short the stock, even though it sells for a cream-rich 26 times earnings.

But let's do some comparison shopping. The same contrarian inclinations that tell me to pass on Ben & Jerry's tell me to buy Sturm Ruger (RGR, $28), a leading manufacturer of firearms. What business could be less ecosensitive or more unpopular with the politically correct than manufacturing high capacity pistols and rifles? You'd expect it to be a cheap stock, and it is, relatively speaking. RGR sells at 14 times earnings, yields 4.3 percent, with a good pattern of dividend increases (whereas BJICA pays no dividend). RGR carries no debt (unlike BJICA) and has a strong balance sheet.

The fundamentals might be iffy, though. Suppose the feds eventually ban guns and a good part of the market disappears? On the other hand, suppose the feds create a real police state; business could boom in spite of a civilian ban. (I'm only half kidding.)

This is the classic problem that confronts a stock picker. Which parts of the puzzle do you look at, and how much attention should you pay to each? If you're going to be a contrarian, how can you avoid picking tops and bottoms prematurely? The comparison of Ben & Jerry's with Ruger illustrates the problem perfectly. My guess is that even though Ruger is a far better fundamental buy, it likely will go lower and BJICA will go higher. And that generally will prove true of other eco-friendly stocks. Does that mean they should be bought? I think not. As much as eco-consciousness may help BJICA and its fellow travelers, it won't be enough to keep it from going down in a bear market. Perversely, that bear market will be fueled by some of the same sentiments and values that currently favor BJICA.

Green investing is generally perceived as "ethical investing." But ethics aren't at all what they seem when it comes to investing. Ethics have been largely replaced by a form of legislated morality, which is related to the green movement, but has much broader—and much more dangerous—implications.

33

Where Have All the Nazis Gone?

Experience invariably [shows] that laws, however barbarous they may be, have never served to suppress vice or to discourage delinquency. The more severe the penalties imposed on the consumers and traffickers of cocaine, the greater will be the attraction of forbidden fruits and the fascination of the risks incurred by the consumer, and the greater will be the profits made by the speculators, avid for money.

It is useless, therefore, to hope for anything from the law. We must suggest another solution. Make the use and sale of cocaine free from restrictions and open kiosks where it would be sold at cost price or even under cost, And then launch a great propaganda campaign.

Errico Malatesta, *Umanità Nova*, August 10, 1922

The most absurd apology for authority and law is that they serve to diminish crime. Aside from the fact that the State is itself the greatest criminal, breaking every written and natural law, stealing in the form of taxes, killing in the form of war and capital punishment, it has come to an absolute standstill in coping with crime. It has failed utterly to destroy or even minimize the horrible scourge of its own creation.

Emma Goldman, *Anarchism*, 1910

Be it never forgotten that the cure for evil and disorder is *more* liberty, not suppression.

Alexander Berkman, *What Is Communist Anarchism?* 1928

Laws—just laws, natural laws—are not made, they are discovered . . . Government is for slaves; free men govern themselves.

Albert Parsons, on being sentenced to hang, 1886,
for the Haymarket bombing

Views on the ethical character of free markets differ widely. Some people view free markets as morally abhorrent or, at the least, highly suspect. Others, including myself, see them as the only moral way for people to acquire what they want. Regardless of one's viewpoint, markets are a natural phenomenon because there is no other way men can relate freely and without coercion.

People appear to have the same general desires and motivations in every time and place. Technology enables them to change the world in accordance with those desires. But political and legal systems decide how much progress they actually make.

Differences in their political and legal systems are solely responsible for the prosperity of Hong Kong, the mediocrity of Macau, and the dismal poverty, until recently, of China; the people in all three places are otherwise very similar. The same reason explains the difference between the former East Germany and West Germany. To use a less-drastic example, the nature of the law accounts for the difference between the United States and Canada. Despite Canada's greater resource base and more homogeneous population, both of which were considered huge advantages until quite recently, the United States has always had a significantly higher standard of living.

This is equally true of the same country under different governments: Chile, before and after the Allende regime, and Great Britain, before and after it adopted socialist policies after WWI, and before and after Thatcher. This hardly merits serious discussion among reasonable people. What does seem the subject of debate, or at least confusion, is whether the United States is somehow exempt from the experience of every other country in this regard. A reasonable person would have to say it is not, but the government does not behave as if that's the case.

The arguments I've made earlier in this book for various investments assume that the United States legal system will basically remain unchanged. Of course, nothing is static, and the nature of law in the United States is evolving. But there are many indications that it is rapidly heading in a direction that will change its very nature. As Marx observed in his "Law of Transformation," something can change a great deal in degree and still retain its essential character, as does water when cooled from 211 to 33 degrees Fahrenheit. But after the same object crosses a certain threshold, in the case of water, 32 degrees, turning into ice, it is no longer the same thing for practical purposes.

The deterioration of American law has been underway since its inception, but the trend accelerated greatly during the '30s, gained momentum in the '60s, and is now approaching warp speed. And the degeneration of the law could alone—not counting the effects of taxes, inflation, debt, or the business cycle, which go hand-in-hand with that trend—ensure that the '90s become a time of worse than deep malaise, a time of economic depression. Let's look at what the changes in the character of law are likely to do to the nature of investment, not to mention everyday life.

THE LAW AS AN ADVERSARY

The purpose of laws is to make life safer and production easier. But the law has increasingly served to do just the opposite. Like almost all institutions, as the legal system has grown larger and older, it has become more sclerotic and dysfunctional.

The degeneration has become noticeable enough that the explosion of litigation and its tremendous costs to production became a 1992 campaign issue. The number of lawsuits filed in federal district courts has grown rapidly: 1960—89,112; 1970—127,280; 1980—197,710; 1990—279,288 suits.* It is impossible to get into court and, once there, impossible to get out. In any event, lawsuits are an adventure only for the wealthy or for the indigent who can find an ambulance-chaser to take a case on contingency. And since the United States, with only 5 percent of the world's population, has 70 percent of the world's lawyers, there are plenty of takers.

Most people lay the blame on the lawyers' greed and lack of ethics. It's hard to argue with that, but the legions of aggressive lawyers plaguing the country are only a symptom. The disease itself is the myriad laws and the regulations that implement them. They are literally created faster than a single person can read them, even as a full-time job. In 1991 the Federal Register published 67,715 pages of new federal laws and regulations.

And although federal laws have the broadest effect, state and local measures are just as burdensome. One example is a 1991 Oklahoma statute requiring taxpayers to declare everything they own to the tax authorities, including guns, coins, art, furniture, and *clothing*. Failure to comply is countered with a personal visit from a tax assessor. If he isn't allowed into your house, he is authorized to obtain a search warrant. I find it surprising this has not caused a mass exodus from the state. Between 1976 and 1986 alone, state legislatures made 248,000 new laws.†

In a just society, law concerns itself with only two matters: contracts (have you done all that you agreed to do?) and torts (have you encroached upon another's person or property?). These are encompassed by "common law." Common law, determining right and wrong, is based on principles of justice that can be considered universal in societies.

That is vastly different from "legislation" or "political law," which is arbitrarily constructed by officials. Legislation mostly deals with what have come to be known as "victimless crimes." Charles Meachling, Jr., a former Cambridge law professor, described it in the *Brookings Review*.

> In the U.S., the sanctimonious maxim that "Ignorance of the law is no excuse" puts every citizen at risk. That may have been a sound rule in simpler times, when the catalog of punishable offenses was limited to traditional offenses like murder, robbery, rape, and larceny; but it becomes a sinister joke when applied to the five-foot shelf of the U.S. criminal code and the even more voluminous statutes of individual states.
>
> Moreover, in the U.S. a citizen cannot rely on the plain meaning of a statute, or what passes for it. He must retain a lawyer to parse its legislative history and judicial evolution. So many forms of social and economic activity have now been criminalized that the discretionary power of federal and state authorities to pick and choose targets for prosecution has made enforcement utterly arbitrary.
>
> In the case of the tax codes, not one citizen in ten million can tell whether he has committed a trivial error or subjected himself to the risk of a felony conviction. In

Wall Street Journal, August 4, 1991.

†*Wall Street Journal*, January 21, 1987.

addition, by a grotesque inversion of legal principle, the burden is on the taxpayer to prove his innocence.

These laws, and their interpretation by a judiciary that has been schooled to respect them blindly, have resulted in a myriad of cases that can only be described as bizarre. A classic example is provided by the burglar who, while robbing a California high school, fell through a skylight, sued, and won $260,000 in damages plus a $1,200 monthly stipend from the local school board.*

The volumes of new laws and regulations spewed forth by lawmakers means that time and money that would have been spent meeting market demands is instead devoted to complying with encoded political whims. A 1991 survey by the Conference Board, a group of 3,600 organizations in more than fifty nations, reports that for fear of being prosecuted:

- 47 percent of U.S. manufacturers have withdrawn a product from the market.

- 25 percent of U.S. manufacturers have discontinued some forms of product research.

- Approximately 15 percent of U.S. companies have laid off workers as a direct result of product liability experience.[†]

Every regulatory agency seems to have its own separate agenda, completely divorced from, and sometimes at odds with, whatever good intentions might have prompted its creation.

It's not within our scope to look at every area where the law is a detriment to economic activity. Most laws raise costs by wasting and misallocating capital one way or another. But a new class of law is proliferating that makes prosecution almost completely arbitrary and unpredictable and carries incredibly severe penalties.

One well-known example is RICO (the Racketeer Influenced Corrupt Organizations Act), which allows the government to prosecute an individual under a different, and incredibly draconian,[‡] set of laws if an alleged crime is deemed part of a pattern. Related to RICO is the so-called "White Collar Kingpin" act of November 1990, which had its first conviction in December 1992; the law can be used when the accused has engaged in a "series" of crimes against a financial institution. Conviction carries a ten-year minimum sentence and a maximum of life. These laws are enforced especially against legitimate business people who violate other statutes where prosecution is more difficult.

Whether you become a victim of those or of other laws is in some measure a matter of chance, because each year everyone breaks many of the millions of laws on the books, mostly inadvertently. But two sets of statutes are of special interest from a financial perspective because they attack the basic concept of property

---

*U.S. News and World Report, August 19, 1991.

†Wall Street Journal, August 4, 1991.

‡Severe, after the judge Draco.

rights. These are the laws dealing with "money laundering," and the forfeiture laws. Both have their genesis in the war on drugs.

Since the start of the war on drugs, the legal system has dropped all pretense of due process.

MONEY LAUNDERING

The U.N. Convention against Illicit Traffic in Narcotic Drugs defines money laundering as "the concealment or disguise of the true nature, source, disposition, movement, or ownership of proceeds and includes the movement or conversion of proceeds by electronic transmission." The treaty does not specify that the proceeds need be from any illegal activity; the simple act of protecting your financial privacy leaves you open to sanctions. About seventy nations, including the United States since 1990, are signatories to this treaty, and treaties have the effect of law within the United States.

The Money Laundering Control Act of 1986 is one of a continuing series of federal statutes, starting with the perversely named Bank Secrecy Act of 1970, that declare a vast number of seemingly innocent financial transactions to be felonies. The act makes violating, or making any effort to evade, any state or federal reporting or record-keeping laws or regulations the crime of money laundering. It purports to concern itself with the proceeds from any illegal activity and carries a penalty of up to $500,000 and twenty years' imprisonment.

The application of this law in crimes such as kidnapping and fraud is obvious. But the law also makes it a crime to receive funds derived from *suspected* unlawful activities. In debate for the passage of the provision in the House, Rep. Bill McCollum argued: "The corner grocer of a community is aware of the reputation of the local drug trafficker. That person comes to the store and buys five pounds of hamburger. The grocer has to know that what he's coming in to buy groceries with is indeed the money derived from a particular designated crime. I don't have any problem whatsoever in holding the grocer accountable for the crime of money laundering."

And that's just what the law does. In fact it goes further, since it contains specific language stating that *ignorance of the source of the money is no excuse*, to wit (Sec.1957): "The government is not required to prove the defendent knew that the offense from which the criminally derived property was derived was a specified unlawful activity."

The only practical protection for someone like McCollum's grocer, other than the fact there is not yet a Treasury agent at every grocery, might be that transactions under $10,000 are exempt. But if many small transactions add up to that amount, the parties could be prosecuted for the separate crime of "structuring" (Sec. 5324). This crime is arbitrarily defined but can be deemed to be the act of structuring financial activities to avoid reporting requirements. One recent case is described by Mark Nestmann, editor of *Privacy*.

In 1991, a 65-year-old Alabama physician had his life savings seized by the IRS because of alleged structuring in his bank account. Having experienced the Great Depression, the doctor kept his money deposited in several different banks, so the failure of one wouldn't cause the loss of all his wealth. He also kept some cash at home, but paid taxes on this as well as on all his other income.

A long-time friend opened a bank nearby, and the doctor consolidated his savings there, including his cash reserves. The banker, realizing the doctor's funds were legitimately earned, took it upon himself to structure the transactions in order to avoid bringing undue attention to the cash deposits. Consequently, a creative U.S. attorney used section 5324 to seize the entire account. The doctor, now a pauper, still faces five years' imprisonment. When asked if the seizure was fair, the U.S. Attorney replied "It's a tough law."

All cash transactions are suspect, and since the passage of the Deficit Reduction Act of 1984, all merchants, not just financial institutions, are required to file a form 8300 when they receive $10,000 or more in one or more related transactions. Since February 1992, instructions for the form suggest filing the form for transactions less than $10,000 if they seem "suspicious." A failure to file the form properly is punishable by fines of up to $500,000 and imprisonment of up to five years. In 1991, Treasury agents visited over 5,000 stores to check compliance, usually in the form of an impromptu sting operation.

Furthermore, the right of the accused to hire an attorney is compromised in that it may make an attorney a party to the crime by accepting possibly tainted money from a client. It is far easier for prosecutors to convict when they are dealing with a court-appointed attorney.

The money-laundering law is being vigorously applied by the IRS, of course, but all the agencies involved in economic regulation are also using it, since a conviction may be much easier to gain, and with much stiffer penalties, than under the provisions for the underlying alleged crime itself. And it's easy to find potential victims, since the law offers rewards of 25 percent of proceeds up to $150,000 to citizens who turn in someone for money laundering.

FORFEITURES

With the enactment of the Comprehensive Crime Control Act in 1984, the government granted itself a set of powers so draconian that they stretch the bounds of credibility for the average American. The law's primary intent was to aid the war on drugs, but its practical application is much wider. One of its major provisions allows the confiscation and forfeiture of any cash or goods that the police have "probable cause" to believe might either have been bought from the profits of illegal activity or used to facilitate illegal activities. In one case, that included the confiscation of a house, because two phone calls were made from it in an *alleged* drug deal.*

USA Today, May 18, 1992.

The DEA posts a notice of its weekly seizures every Wednesday in the "Life" section of *USA Today*; a minimum of a full page is filled with at least a thousand first, second, and third notices of forfeitures to the U.S. government. The FBI listings are usually found in the Sunday *New York Times*. Once your property is seized, you can go to court to reverse the process, but at your own expense and only after posting a bond of at least 10 percent. In 1991 federal authorities alone attached $644 million under the forfeiture laws, and the number will be over $1.3 billion in 1992, up from $30 million in 1985, the first year the law took effect.

Whose property is being seized? Almost anyone's is vulnerable, and where drugs are believed to be involved, "probable cause" boils down to the vaguest suspicion. The evidence of abuse is largely anecdotal, since I'm unaware of any thorough study. The best monitor of forfeiture activity is a group known as F.E.A.R.,* which assembles and publishes major media stories on the subject several times a year.

Any federal agency can seize property based on no more than suspicion of a violation of law. Many states have enacted their own seizure law based on the federal statute. In New Jersey, for instance, $17 milion has been generated for the state and $66 million for local jurisdictions since their law was enacted in 1986. Most have ostensibly been drug-related, but the many hundreds of confiscations also include a medical student who had all his business equipment confiscated on the grounds that he was practicing psychiatry without a license.† He was offering counseling from his home. States that do not have their own law typically use a procedure known as "federal adoption," which entitles the state or local authority to keep 80–85 percent of the proceeds, with the remainder going to the feds.

There are hundreds of horror stories on record about how this law is applied in practice. It is worth relating a few to give you a flavor of things to come.

WILLY JONES MEETS WILLIAM BENNETT

On April 5, 1992, reporter Steve Kroft of CBS News' *60 Minutes* did a segment on forfeiture laws, dealing with two victims. Kroft introduced the segment by stating:

> If someone were to tell you that, thanks to the forfeiture laws, a law enforcement officer can seize your property, your car, and your money without ever charging you with anything, without arresting you and without ever convicting you of a crime, you'd probably say, "That's not possible—not in America." Well, it is. Just ask Willy Jones.

Willy Jones is a black man who runs a small landscaping business outside Nashville. Once or twice a year he goes out of state to buy shrubbery. In 1991 Jones went to the Nashville airport and paid cash for a round-trip ticket to Houston. A few

---

*Forfeiture Endangers American Rights, PO Box 513, Franklin, NJ 07416, 201-827-2177.

†*New York Times*, September 13, 1992.

minutes later, two Nashville police officers stopped, questioned him, and with Jones's permission, searched him, finding $9,000 in his money belt. Jones insisted the money was for shrubbery, since he got a better deal when he paid cash. The police didn't believe him and seized the money, using the forfeiture law.

Kroft says: "Jones has never been charged with a crime, nor is there any indication he ever will be. The way the forfeiture law works, the police officers didn't have to arrest Willy Jones or, for that matter, prove he was a drug courier. In effect, what they did was arrest his money; all they needed was probable cause that the money was somehow drug-related."

Why did the cops zero in on Jones? Because the agent who sold him his ticket called them. Drug interdiction units at airports throughout the country pay airline employees for tips on people who might be carrying money or drugs. Kroft wanted to find out how easily it could happen, so he sent a reporter to buy a ticket to Houston with cash; within 15 minutes, the reporter was accosted by two officers who proceeded to interrogate him. It was clear that the reporter's cash was going the way of Willy Jones's until he identified himself as being with *60 Minutes*.

Kroft interviewed the DEA's administrative law judge Robert Bonner, who was handling Jones's case. The conversation was nothing short of an outrage, as the man explained that probable cause was all the grounds necessary for seizure; that Jones could get his money back if he proved it wasn't drug money by presenting his case to a federal judge or a jury. The situation is similar to that under the tax laws, where the citizen can be considered guilty until he proves his innocence.

Jones's lawyer, Bo Edwards, commented: "If the government takes your property and you get your day in court, you must prove to the government and the court that the property was not involved in a drug transaction and that you didn't intend for it to be involved in a drug transaction. The Bill of Rights applies to criminal cases. For example, the right to have a lawyer, the right to a trial by jury, that the government must prove its case beyond a reasonable doubt. None of those rights apply in a civil case where the government is bringing a civil forfeiture case against your property."

In fact, where seizures involve real estate or items likely to be contested, the cases have names like *U.S.* v. *$150,660.00* and *U.S.* v. *Approximately 2,538.85 Shares*.

60 Minutes then looked at the case of Billy Munnerlyn, who ran a successful air charter business. In October 1989 he flew a man named Albert Wright from Little Rock, Arkansas, to Ontario, California, where they were met by a group of DEA agents. The agents confiscated Wright's locked baggage, containing $2.7 million in cash, suspected of being drug money. Wright and Munnerlyn were both arrested, although charges against Munnerlyn were dropped for lack of evidence. Munnerlyn thought the episode was over until the government confiscated his plane, calling the action *U.S.* v. *One 1969 Gates Lear Jet*, because the plane broke the law by transporting cash that may have been drug-related.

As it turned out, the government decided not to prosecute Wright, who was released. The Lear Jet sat in the government's possession, deteriorating, while

Munnerlyn spent $85,000 in legal fees in an attempt to get it back. In 1991, a Los Angeles jury ruled in his favor, but a judge overruled the verdict and ordered another trial, which Munnerlyn could not afford.

These two examples are specially worth noting, because *60 Minutes* is widely viewed. Hundreds of examples of this type of outrage are documented yearly. But the public's attention span is short, people forget, and they eventually become inured to any state of affairs. In any event, there appears to be widespread support for the drug laws, as a part of the new puritanism discussed in chapter 31.

REVENUE ENHANCEMENT BY SEIZURE

You may believe that these laws are so onerous, and such an affront to the concept of America itself, that they will be overturned. The opposite is more likely because government at all levels is financially strapped and the laws are an excellent vehicle for "revenue enhancement."

On the local level, hundreds of millions of dollars are now retained by local police annually. They like the extra income, which they use to pay themselves overtime, finance college degrees, and buy exotic police toys and other items to enhance law enforcement. Local police have a high incentive to pursue forfeitures vigorously.

Further, the victims are not a coherent group, like widget manufacturers or even taxpayers in general; they are disparate, have no common bond, and often have no assets after the seizure. The public broadly approves of actions taken in the war on drugs, and those who do not are loathe to comment. (I suspect, for the same reason that few spoke up at the Salem witch trials.)

The original intent of forfeiture laws was to discourage crime by seizing the profits it generates. But strong evidence suggests that the income forfeitures can generate will become a bigger motive for applying these laws as time goes by. The fact that the majority of seizures are fairly small confirms this; it's uneconomical for a victim to spend the legal fees required to redeem most things worth less than $10,000. It is, therefore, more economic for the government to target seizures that are not likely to be contested. Prosecutors allege that most seizures are not contested because the victims are guilty and do not want to draw further attention to themselves.

A more realistic reason is the monumental amount of time, energy, and money it takes to do so, and the fact that many just do not know where to start. Seizures are not contested in other cases because the prosecutors appear to intimidate the victim with the threat of criminal prosecution should that happen.

A further problem that will lead to the ruthless implementation of these laws is corruption. Laws that permit large amounts of cash to be seized in secrecy encourage corruption. It is not difficult to see how an agent might get ideas about alternative uses of the cash and goods that pass through his hands. The police in many countries around the world expect to retire wealthy, and the police chief of

Mexico City traditionally becomes a near-billionaire. It is the nature of their legal system that permits—even encourages—this abuse. There is no reason why, as laws in the United States permit financial seizure without due process, corruption will not soar here as well.

WILLIAM BENNETT MEETS DOUG CASEY

One personal experience I had on the issue occurred when William Bennett, the drug czar, spoke before a small group which I attend occasionally. The group serves as a forum for the free exchange of ideas. I believe it is an immoral omission to condone wrongfulness, even if it is widely accepted, through silence. Bennett spent most of his time justifying his failures as secretary of education, but I was interested in his performance as drug czar and the civil rights and due process abuses sanctioned under his guidance. Was he simply uncaring, or unaware of the tragic consequences of his drug laws for many law-abiding Americans caught like dolphins in his tuna net?

It was as if Himmler or Eichmann, both of whom could show great personal charm, had spoken before a luncheon group in the Germany of the early '30s, couching theories in socially acceptable terms. Groups suffer from groupthink even if the individuals composing them are sharp. Few people want to cause embarassment by pointing out the unpleasant implications of a certain belief system, so speakers can often get away with murder, as it were.

Of course, I couldn't help but lay into Bennett. I received no encouragement from the assembled group. But afterward several attendees privately expressed support, as well as surprise that anyone would dare challenge the ex-drug czar; I found their fear of confronting his views openly both symptomatic and disturbing. On leaving I was accosted by a man identifying himself as a DEA agent— remember, this was a nonpublic function—who, while conceding that I was accurate on specific examples, assured me that the incidents of abuse were "not as bad" as they seemed.

A REIGN OF TERROR

As invasive as the current legislation is now, it will almost certainly get worse because of the type of people who tend to be drawn to the DEA and its sister agencies. In every society there are a certain number of criminal or suppressive personalities. Many of them like kids and dogs, live in nice neighborhoods and play weekend softball. They are not psychopaths who froth at the mouth; they are more-or-less ordinary people. However, when they encounter the wrong environment, serious flaws in their character emerge. Education or intelligence levels are irrelevant.

Most Gestapo and KGB operatives were also rather ordinary people, and most of them sincerely felt they were doing necessary and honorable work. Bill Bennett, for instance, is familiar with Hannah Arendt's writing on what the "banality of evil" can lead to, although he doesn't believe it applies to him. I hope he's right.

In any event, a certain small but significant percentage of the population will fill the same type of slots in America they would have occupied had they lived in Germany, the Soviet Union, or the deep South at the relevant time. You wouldn't know they were there unless a particular set of conditions drew them out of the woodwork. And creating such conditions is exactly what the sweeping drug laws are doing. Since the war on drugs is far from victorious, and there is now an enticing prospect for abusive revenue generation; you should anticipate more and harsher laws of a similar kind to be enacted.

The nature of American law and law enforcement has changed radically, and at an accelerating rate, since the '50s. It's quaint, in today's context, to see Broderick Crawford on *Highway Patrol* or even Jack Webb on *Dragnet* dealing with malefactors. The idiom of the '90s is SWAT teams, clad in midnight-blue uniforms (black still carries too many overtones from Germany to be fashionable), kevlar vests and helmets, and nomex masks and gloves, breaking down a door at the crack of dawn. Almost every town of substance in the United States, as well as most federal agencies, have their own SWAT teams. Even the FDA has used exactly this approach in raiding doctors' offices for alleged vitamin violations.*

THE DRUG WAR AS THE PROBLEM

Some Americans simplistically believe an opposition to the war on drugs amounts to an endorsement of drugs and an unwillingness to see their destructive effects on society eliminated. I see drug use as debilitating at best and tend to eschew the company of those who use them. But destroying liberty isn't an even remotely acceptable method to discourage drug addiction. Nor is it effective.

In any event, the drug problem is, in large measure, a creation of the government. A certain portion of the population will always have problems dealing with life and will seek solace in drugs, legal or illegal; some evidence suggests that there is actually a genetic predisposition to addiction. The war on drugs will necessarily fail, if only because the more successful it is at interdicting the supply, the higher it will drive drug prices, creating larger profits. Higher profits will be a greater inducement for new individuals and organizations to get into the business. In fact, some allege that elements of the U.S. government have an active interest in the continued existence of the drug trade.†

Those who are caught in the "drugnet" are not rehabilitated by logging hard time in prison as convicted felons. Their condition is, if anything, exacerbated. The war on drugs is the major reason the United States has the highest percentage of its residents incarcerated (in 1991, approximately 1.25 million at any time, or 0.5 percent of the total population) of any country on earth, including South Africa and

---

Health & Healing Newsletter, July 1992—The Takoma Clinic Incident.

†Lt. Col. James "Bo" Gritz, *Called to Serve* (Sandy Valley, Nev.: Lazarus Publishing, 1991).

the Soviet Union. High drug prices on the street not only encourage supply but force the typical user into crime to get his hands on enough money to support his habit, a significant form of "collateral damage." Just as prohibition in the '20s was the major force leading to the success of the U.S. Mafia, today's prohibition is almost solely responsible for the creation of new, and much more aggressive, organized crime syndicates.

There is no reason to believe that the current drug war is any more effective than was the prohibition on alcohol, from 1920 to 1933. In 1926, six years after alcohol was prohibited, state insane asylums reported the number of persons "demented" due to alcohol had increased by 1,000 percent. In 1929 Metropolitan Life reported that deaths from alcoholism had increased 600 percent.* Drug hysteria is growing and is now starting to impinge on users of alcohol and tobacco, America's two traditional recreational drugs. In their case illegalization is unlikely, although taxes on both will undoubtedly soar, perhaps sufficiently to create black markets in them as well. In brief, the $115 billion that has been spent since the war on drugs was declared has probably served only to make the "problem" worse.

It is unfortunate that those who argue for the legalization of drugs and against the forfeiture laws do so almost entirely on pragmatic grounds: they do not work, or they are inefficient. This begs the far more important question of whether an individual has the right to dispose of his own life and property as he pleases, as long as he doesn't violate the rights of another person—the two tenets of common law discussed earlier.

Where is all of this likely to lead? Few laws are ever struck from the books; the distortions and additional "criminality" they cause tend to be dealt with by yet more laws. Each of these laws, and the regulations it spawns, requires additional funds and personnel for enforcement and produces grounds for more lawyers and more suits between citizens.

Like most broad trends, there is little reason to believe this one will reverse itself, although there will certainly be short-lived reactions against it, like past vogues for "sunset" provisions, "paperwork reduction," "freedom of information," "taxpayer rights," and the like. These reactions are positive, but they inevitably lack the momentum to effect a change. As with trends in the financial markets, the laws will not change until some true crisis makes change imperative or unavoidable.

Civil loss of freedom will exert a persistent and dismal effect on the financial markets. Part of the fallout will be increasing capital flight and relocation of wealthy or talented individuals from the United States. Weak property rights in Third World countries result in depressed prices of hard assets and account for their best people being abroad.

Are there any positive aspects or potential for profit? An investment banker asked Bill Bennett that question at the luncheon I mentioned above. He responded: "Buy prison construction bonds. We're going to be building a lot of them."

*Clifton Daniel, ed., *Chronicle of the Twentieth Century* (Mount Kisco, N.Y.: Chronicle Publications, 1982).

34

The Real Problem

> The most dangerous man, to any government, is the man who is able to think
> things out for himself, without regard to the prevailing superstitions and taboos.
> Almost inevitably he comes to the conclusion that the government he lives
> under is dishonest, insane, and intolerable, and so, if he is romantic, he tries to
> change it. And even if he is not romantic personally he is apt to spread discon-
> tent among those who are.
>
> H. L. Mencken

> Authority has always attracted the lowest elements in the human race. All
> through history mankind has been bullied by scum. Those who lord it over their
> fellows and toss commands in every direction and would boss the grass in the
> meadow about which way to bend in the wind are the most depraved kind of
> prostitutes. They will submit to any indignity, perform any vile act, do anything
> to achieve power. The worst off-sloughings of the planet are the ingredients of
> sovereignty. Every government is a parliament of whores. The trouble is, in a
> democracy the whores are us.
>
> P. J. O'Rourke

I give a good number of speeches each year. For some time I've asked audiences a
question: "What useful purpose does the U.S. government serve?" I do that not to
be challenging or provocative, but to actually find out if anyone else can think of a
useful purpose the government serves. The question at first shocks, then amuses and
then perplexes almost everyone because it is both so obvious and outrageous that no
one ever thinks of asking it. Most people accept the institution of government
because it has always been there; they have always assumed it was essential. People
do not question its existence, much less its right to exist.

But that is exactly what I do in this chapter. Throughout this book I've noted
problems caused by government. Government sponsors untold waste, criminality,
and inequality, in every sphere of life it touches, giving little of value in return. Its
contributions to the commonweal are wars, pogroms, confiscations, persecutions,
taxation, regulation, and inflation. And it's not just some governments of which

that's true, although some are clearly much worse than others. It's an inherent characteristic of all government.

THE NATURE OF THE BEAST

The essence of something is what makes the thing what it is. But surprisingly little study of government has been done by ontologists (who study the first principles of things) or epistemologists (those who study the nature of human knowledge). The study of government almost never concerns itself with *whether* government should be, but only with *how* and *what* it should be. The existence of government is accepted without question.

What is the essence of government? After you cut through the rhetoric, the doublethink and the smokescreen of altruism that surround the subject, you find that the essence of government is force. And the belief it has the right to initiate the use of force whenever expedient. Government is an organization with a monopoly, albeit with some fringe competition, on the use of force within a given territory. As Mao Zedong said, "The power of government comes out of the barrel of a gun." There is no voluntarism about obeying laws. The consent of a majority of the governed may help a government put a nice face on things, but it is not essential and is, in fact, seldom given with any enthusiasm.

A person's attitude about government offers an excellent insight into his character. Political beliefs reflect how a person thinks men should relate to one another; they offer a practical insight into how he views humanity at large and himself in particular.

There are only two ways people can relate in any given situation: voluntarily or coercively. Almost everyone, except overt sociopaths, pays at least lip service to the idea of voluntarism, but government is viewed as somehow exempt. It's widely believed that a group has prerogatives and rights unavailable to individuals. But if that is true, then the Ku Klux Klan (KKK), the Irish Republican Army (IRA), the Palestine Liberation Organization (PLO)—or, for that matter, any group from a lynch mob to a government—all have rights that individuals do not. In fact, all these groups believe they have a right to initiate the use of force when they find it expedient. To the extent that they can get away with it, they all act like governments.

TERRORISTS, MOBS, AND GOVERNMENTS

You might object that the important difference between the KKK, IRA, PLO, or a simple mob and a government is that they aren't "official" or "legal."

Apart from common law concepts discussed in chapter 33, legality is arbitrary. Once you leave the ken of common law, the only distinction between "laws" of governments and the "ad hoc" proceedings of an informal assemblage such as a mob, or of a more formal group like the KKK, boils down to the force the group can muster to impose its will on others. The laws of Nazi Germany and the U.S.S.R. are now widely recognized as criminal fantasies that gained reality on a grand scale. But at the time those regimes had power, they were treated with the respect granted to any legal system. Governments become legal or official by gaining power. The fact that every government was founded on gross illegalities—war or revolt— against its predecessor is rarely an issue.

Force is the essence of government. But the possession of a monopoly on force almost inevitably requires a territory, and maintaining control of territory is considered the test of a "successful" government. Would any "terrorist" organization be more "legitimate" if it had its own country? Absolutely. Would it be any less vicious or predatory by that fact? No, just as most governments today (the ex-Communist countries and the kleptocracies of the Third World being the best examples), demonstrate. Governments can be much more dangerous than the mobs that give them birth. The Jacobin regime of the French Revolution is a prime example.

THE ORIGIN OF GOVERNMENT

Rousseau, whose ideas played some part in that unpleasantness, was perhaps the first to popularize the fiction now taught in civics classes about how government was created. It holds that men sat down together and rationally thought out the concept of government as a solution to problems that confronted them. The government of the United States was, however, the first to be formed in any way remotely like Rousseau's ideal. Even then, it had far from universal support from the three million colonials whom it claimed to represent. The U.S. government, after all, grew out of an illegal conspiracy to overthrow and replace the existing government.

There's no question that the result was, by an order of magnitude, the best blueprint for a government that had yet been conceived. Most of America's Founding Fathers believed the main purpose of government was to protect its subjects from the initiation of violence from any source—government itself prominently included. That made the U.S. government almost unique in history. And it was that concept—not natural resources, the ethnic composition of American immigrants, or luck—that turned America into the paragon it became.

The origin of government itself, however, was nothing like Rousseau's fable or the origin of the United States Constitution. The most realistic scenario for the origin of government is a roving group of bandits deciding that life would be easier if they settled down in a particular locale, and simply taxing the residents for a fixed percentage (rather like "protection money") instead of periodically sweeping through and carrying off all they could get away with. It's no accident that the ruling classes everywhere have martial backgrounds. Royalty are really nothing more than successful marauders, who have buried the origins of their wealth in romance.

Romanticizing government—making it seem like Camelot, populated by brave knights and benevolent kings—painting it as noble and ennobling, helps people to accept its jurisdiction. But, like most things, government is shaped by its origins. Author Rick Maybury may have said it best in *Whatever Happened to Justice?*:

"A castle was not so much a plush palace as the headquarters for a concentration camp. These camps, called feudal kingdoms, were established by conquering barbarians who'd enslaved the local people. When you see one, ask to see not just the stately halls and bedrooms, but the dungeons and torture chambers.

"A castle was a hangout for silk-clad gangsters who were stealing from helpless workers. The king was the 'lord' who had control of the blackjack; he claimed a special 'divine right' to use force on the innocent.

"Fantasies about handsome princes and beautiful princesses are dangerous; they whitewash the truth. They give children the impression political power is wonderful stuff."

If Bill Clinton succeeds through tremendous increases in regulations in creating his new Camelot, it won't be a dream but a nightmare.

IS THE STATE NECESSARY?

The violent and corrupt nature of government is widely acknowledged by almost everyone. That's been true since time immemorial, as have political satire and grousing about politicians. Yet almost everyone turns a blind eye; most not only put up with it, but actively support the charade. That's because although many may believe government to be an evil, they believe it is a necessary evil.*

What (arguably) makes government necessary is the need for protection from other, even more dangerous, governments. I believe a case can be made that modern technology obviates this function.

One of the most perversely misleading myths about government is that it promotes order within its own bailiwick, keeps groups from constantly warring with each other, and somehow creates togetherness and harmony. In fact, that's the exact opposite of the truth. There's no cosmic imperative for different people to rise up against one another—unless they're organized into political groups. The Middle East, now the world's most fertile breeding ground for hatred, provides an excellent example.

Muslims, Christians, and Jews lived together peaceably in Palestine, Lebanon, and North Africa for centuries, until the situation became politicized after World War I. Until then an individual's background and beliefs were just personal attributes, not a *casus belli*. Government was at its most benign, an ineffectual nuisance that concerned itself mostly with extorting taxes. People were busy with that most harmless of activities, making money.

---

*The larger question of whether anything that is evil is necessary, or whether anything that is necessary can be evil, is worth discussing, but this isn't the forum.

But politics does not deal with people as individuals. It scoops them up into parties and nations. And some group inevitably winds up using the power of the state (however "innocently" or "justly" at first) to impose its values and wishes on others, with predictably destructive results. What would otherwise be an interesting kaleidoscope of humanity then sorts itself out according to the lowest common denominator peculiar to the time and place.

Sometimes that means along religious lines, as with the Muslims and Hindus in India, or the Catholics and Protestants in Ireland; or ethnic lines, like the Kurds and Iraqis in the Middle East, or Tamils and Sinhalese in Sri Lanka; sometimes it's mostly racial, as whites and East Indians found throughout Africa in the 1970s, or Asians in California in the 1870s. Sometimes it's purely a matter of politics, as Argentines, Guatemalans, Salvadorans, and other Latins discovered more recently. Sometimes it amounts to no more than personal beliefs, as the McCarthy era in the 1950s and the Salem trials in the 1690s proved.

Throughout history government has served as a vehicle for the organization of hatred and oppression, benefitting no one except those who are ambitious and ruthless enough to gain control of it. That's not to say government hasn't, then and now, performed useful functions. But the useful things it does could and would be done far better by the market.

HOW THE WORLD WOULD WORK WITHOUT GOVERNMENT

Many people who are sympathetic to the notion of minimizing institutionalized coercion are still skeptical about how, or even if, the world would work without government. Who, they ask, would build the roads and run the schools? Who would keep order in society and protect it from predators?

Some of these questions reflect beliefs as quaint and silly as those of inner-city children who believe that milk naturally comes from cartons. But since much of all news concerns the doings of government, and since various levels of government control close to half of the economy, it's understandable how Americans have come to see the state as a permanent fixture in the cosmic firmament, "naturally" and "necessarily" responsible for almost everything. Americans have become almost as myopic as the Soviets were in that regard. Some believe that if the government didn't build the roads, we would still have no industrialization or infrastructure. Similarly, some Soviets had a hard time figuring out who would build cars, if not their government.

Actually, an inability to understand how the world would work without government shows an inability to understand how it works right now. What holds society together isn't the coercive power of the state; it's peer pressure, social opprobrium, moral approbation, and, especially, self-interest. Few people would argue that the reason diners pay their restaurant checks is fear of the police, just as few would argue that the only reason diners do not stand on table tops, disrobe, and create a scene is because of some ordinance prohibiting it. The coercive power of the state has almost no part in forming the glue holding society together.

Does government have any rightful place in society? One argument is that, since the state holds a monopoly on the legal use of force, its logical function is to protect individuals from force. That implies a defensive military to protect you from force originating outside the government's jurisdiction; a police force to protect you from force inside its jurisdiction, and a court system to allow you to adjudicate disputes without resorting to force.

But only a small and decreasing fraction of government resources actually go toward these legitimate goals, and it is spent with pathetic inefficiency. The military is a gigantic pork barrel program; the police harass as much as they protect; and even if you can afford it, it is nearly impossible to get into court and equally difficult to get out, once you are in.

In fact, an excellent case can be made that defense, police, and courts are far too critical to the smooth functioning of society to be left to the type of person predisposed to working for the government. When it comes to the police, I'd prefer a Mike Hammer, or even a Thomas Magnum, trying to solve a crime, than the typical cop, whose main skill is writing his quota of traffic tickets.

Private arbitration agencies, who would have to compete based on the fairness, intelligence, and cost-effectiveness of their decisions, would be a big improvement over often corrupt, glacierlike, and politically motivated courts, who must decide cases based on arbitrary statute law.

How would criminals be tried, in the absence of statute law, and punished without government prisons? For one thing, there would be a lot less illegal activity if victimless crime were abolished. For another, the first concern of a justice system should be making the victim whole, not arbitrarily punishing the miscreant. Sentences should, therefore, be meted out in terms of monetary damages to the victim—plus the costs of apprehension, trial, and supervision on whatever level appropriate. Felons would have an incentive to become productive, in order to regain their freedom. And victims would not be doubly penalized by having to pay tax to incarcerate those who had already harmed them.

In general, government judicial systems are far more concerned about crimes against the state than crimes against the individual. In China, as the Tiananmen Square revolt demonstrated, the gravest crime consists of agitation for democracy; in the United States, it consists of nonsupport of the government by refusing to pay taxes or obey regulations. And in all cases a show of humility, a respectful attitude, and the renunciation of politically incorrect ideas are required.

The sentencing of the Chinese students who incited the Tiananmen riots in 1989 was based mainly on their attitudes. One leader, Ren Wanding, was given the longest sentence because he hung tough, refused to apologize, and showed no regret. Others, guilty of more serious "crimes," received shorter sentences because they played the game of "self and mutual criticism."

Everyone in the United States claimed to be outraged at what happened to the students, especially Ren. But few acknowledged the extent to which punishment disproportionate to the crime committed is routinely imposed here in the United States. Tax protesters regularly get more hard time than violent criminals.

Some would say that a few abuses are a small price to pay for having a national defense. That, too, is questionable. The U.S. government actually created much of the danger the U.S.S.R. once presented. As pathological as it was, the U.S.S.R. would have had no reason to attack North America if it were just a grouping of 250 million individuals, entirely apart from the fact it would have been 1,000 times more costly than their ill-fated adventure in Afghanistan. How could they possibly invade a country where they would have to conquer each citizen as an individual? It is a different matter entirely if they need only force another government to surrender. In any event the Soviets would have collapsed long before they did, had not the U.S. government funneled billions in aid and loans to them.

Although even these "natural monopolies" of government do not really exist, it might be acceptable if government was strictly limited to ensuring national and domestic safety and to adjudicating disputes. Without a legislature, regulatory agencies, and the taxes it takes to enforce their dictates, the economy would blossom. In a decade the United States would be as far ahead of Japan as Japan is ahead of Romania. Anything that needs to be done can and would be done more efficiently by entrepreneurs, at a profit.

In the perverse "real world" of today, however, the police, courts, and the military are among the least significant parts of government; moreover, government fails to produce quality products in any other worthwhile area it pursues, such as education. Indeed, its main products are taxation, regulation, inflation, and wealth redistribution, which all eventually destroy their supposed beneficiaries as surely as they do those who are taxed overtly.

DEMOCRACY

But what about the fact that "the people" apparently like it that way? Isn't that what democracy is all about?

Democracy is vastly overrated. It's not like the consensus of a bunch of friends agreeing to see the same movie. Most often it boils down to a kinder and gentler variety of mob rule, dressed in a coat and tie. The essence of positive values like personal liberty, wealth, opportunity, fraternity, and equality lies not in democracy but in free minds and free markets, where government becomes trivial. Democracy focuses people's thoughts on politics, not production; on the collective, not on their own lives.

Although democracy is just one way to structure a state, the concept has reached cult status, unassailable as political dogma. It is, as economist Joseph Schumpeter observed, "a surrogate faith for intellectuals deprived of religion." Most of the founders of America were more concerned with liberty than democracy. Toqueville saw democracy and liberty as almost polar opposites.

Democracy can work when everyone concerned knows one another, shares the same values and goals, and abhors any form of coercion. It is the natural way of accomplishing things among small groups.

But once belief in democracy becomes a political ideology, it's necessarily transformed into majority rule. And, at that point, the majority (or even a plurality, a minority, or an individual) can enforce their will on everyone else, by claiming to represent the will of the people.

The only form of democracy that suits a free society is economic democracy in the laissez-faire form, where each person votes with his money for what he wants in the marketplace. Only then can every individual obtain what he wants without compromising the interests of any other person. That's the polar opposite of the "economic democracy" of socialist pundits, who have twisted the term to mean the political allocation of wealth.

But many terms in politics wind up with inverted meanings. "Liberal" is certainly one of them.

THE SPECTRUM OF POLITICS

The terms *liberal* (*left*) and *conservative* (*right*) define the conventional political spectrum; the terms are floating abstractions, with meanings that change with every politician.

In the nineteenth century, a liberal was someone who believed in free speech, social mobility, limited government, and strict property rights. The term has since been appropriated by those who, although sometimes still believing in limited free speech, always support strong government and weak property rights and who see everyone as a member of a class or group.

Conservatives have always tended to believe in strong government and nationalism. Bismarck and Metternich were archetypes. Today's conservatives are sometimes seen as defenders of economic liberty and free markets, although that is mostly true only when those concepts are perceived to coincide with the interests of big business and economic nationalism.

Bracketing political beliefs on an illogical scale, running only from left to right, results in constrained thinking. It is as if science were still attempting to define the elements with air, earth, water, and fire.

Politics is the theory and practice of government. It concerns itself with how force should be applied in controlling people, which is to say, in restricting their freedom. It should be analyzed on that basis. Since freedom is indivisible, it makes little sense to compartmentalize it, but there are two basic types of freedom: social and economic. According to the current usage, liberals tend to allow social freedom but restrict economic freedom, while conservatives tend to restrict social freedom and allow economic freedom. An authoritarian (they now sometimes class themselves as "middle-of-the-roaders") is one who believes both types of freedom should be restricted.

But what do you call someone who believes in both types of freedom? Unfortunately, something without a name may get overlooked, or if the name is only known to a few it may be ignored as unimportant. That may explain why so few people know they are libertarians.

A useful chart of the political spectrum would look like this:

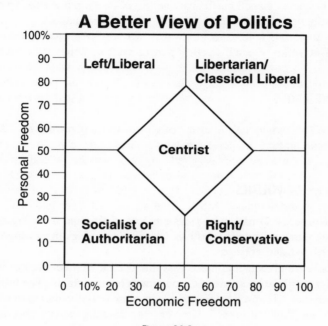

Figure 34-1

A libertarian believes that individuals have a right to do anything that doesn't impinge on the common-law rights of others, namely force or fraud. Libertarians are the human equivalent of the Gamma rat, which bears a little explanation.

Some years ago, scientists experimenting with rats categorized the vast majority of their subjects as Beta rats. These are basically followers, who get the Alpha rats' leftovers. The Alpha rats establish territories, claim the choicest mates, and generally lord it over the Betas. This pretty well corresponded with the way the researchers thought the world worked.

But they were surprised to find a third type of rat as well, the Gamma. This creature staked out a territory and chose the pick of the litter for a mate, like the Alpha, but didn't attempt to dominate the Betas. A go-along-get-along rat. A libertarian rat, if you will.

My guess, mixed with a dollop of hope, is that as society becomes more repressive, more Gamma people will tune in to the problem and drop out as a solution. No, they won't turn into middle-aged hippies practicing basket weaving and bead stringing in remote communes. Rather, they will structure their lives so that the government—which is to say taxes, regulations, and inflation—is a non-factor. Suppose they gave a war and nobody came? Suppose they gave an election and nobody voted; gave a tax and nobody paid; imposed a regulation and nobody obeyed it?

Libertarian beliefs have a strong following among Americans, but the Libertarian party has never gained much prominence, possibly because the type of people who might support it have better things to do with their time than vote. And if they believe in voting, they tend to feel they are "wasting" their vote on someone who can't win. But voting is itself another part of the problem.

NONE OF THE ABOVE

From 1960 to 1992 when the "protest" candidacy of Ross Perot at least temporarily halted the trend, an ever smaller percentage of the electorate voted every four years. Increasingly, the average person is fed up, or views the federal government as irrelevant. Until 1992, when many decided not to run, at least 98 percent of incumbents typically retained office. That is a higher proportion than in the Supreme Soviet of the defunct U.S.S.R., and a lower turnover rate than in Britain's hereditary House of Lords, where people lose their seats only by dying. The political system in the United States has, like all systems which grow old and large, become moribund and corrupt.

The conventional wisdom holds that this decline in voter turnout is a sign of apathy. But it may also be a sign of a renaissance in personal responsibility. It could be people saying: "I won't be fooled again, and I won't lend power to them."

Politics has always been a way of redistributing wealth from those who produce to those who are politically favored. As H. L. Mencken observed, every election amounts to no more than an advance auction on stolen goods, a process few would support if they saw its true nature. Protesters in the '60s had their flaws, but they were quite correct when they said "if you're not part of the solution, you're part of the problem." If politics is the problem what is the solution? I have several answers that may appeal to you.

The first step in solving the problem is to stop actively encouraging it. Many Americans have intuitively recognized that government is the problem and have stopped voting. There are at least five reasons many people do not vote:

1. Voting in a political election is unethical. The political process is one of institutionalized coercion and force; if you disapprove of those things, then you shouldn't participate in them, even indirectly.

2. Voting compromises your privacy. It gets your name in another government computer bank.

3. Voting, as well as registering, entails hanging around government offices and dealing with petty bureaucrats. Most people can find something more enjoyable or productive to do with their time.

4. Voting encourages politicians. A vote against one candidate—a major, and quite understandable, reason why many people vote—is always interpreted as a vote for his opponent. And even though you may be voting for the lesser of two evils, the lesser of two evils is still evil. It amounts to giving the candidate a tacit mandate to impose his will on society.

5. Your vote doesn't count. Politicians like to say it counts because it is to their advantage to get everyone into a busybody mode. But, statistically, one vote in scores of millions makes no more difference than a single grain of sand on a beach. That's entirely apart from the fact that officials manifestly do what they want, not what you want, once they are in office.

Some of these thoughts may impress you as vaguely "unpatriotic"; that is certainly not my intention. But, unfortunately, America isn't the place it once was, either. The United States has evolved from the land of the free and the home of the brave to something more closely resembling the land of entitlements and the home of whining lawsuit filers. The founding ideas of the country, which were highly libertarian, have been thoroughly distorted. What passes for tradition today is something against which the Founding Fathers would have led a second revolution.

This sorry, scary state of affairs is one reason some people emphasize the importance of joining the process, "working within the system" and "making your voice heard," to ensure that "the bad guys" don't get in. They seem to think that increasing the number of voters will improve the quality of their choices. This argument compels many sincere people, who otherwise wouldn't dream of coercing their neighbors, to take part in the political process. But it only feeds power to people in politics and government, validating their existence, and making them more powerful in the process.

Of course, everybody involved gets something out of it, psychologically if not monetarily. Politics gives people a sense of belonging to something bigger than themselves, and so has special appeal for those who cannot find satisfaction within themselves. We cluck in amazement at the enthusiasm shown at Hitler's giant rallies but figure what goes on here, today, is different. Well, it's never quite the same. But the mindless sloganeering, the cult of the personality, and a certainty of the masses that "their" candidate will kiss their personal lives and make them better are identical.

And even if the favored candidate doesn't help them, then at least he'll keep others from getting too much. Politics is the institutionalization of envy, a vice which proclaims: "You've got something I want, and if I can't get one, I'll take yours. And if I can't have yours, I'll destroy it, so you can't have it either." Participating in politics is an act of ethical bankruptcy.

The key to getting "rubes" (i.e., voters) to vote, and "marks" (i.e., contributors) to give is to talk in generalities while sounding specific, and looking sincere and thoughtful, yet decisive. Vapid, venal party hacks can be shaped, like Silly Putty, into saleable candidates. People like to kid themselves that they are voting for either "the man" or "the ideas." But few "ideas" are more than slogans artfully packaged to push the right buttons. Voting "the man" doesn't help much either, since these guys are more diligently programmed, posed, and rehearsed than any actor.

This is probably more true today than it's ever been, since elections are now won on television, and television is not a forum for expressing complex ideas and philosophies. It lends itself to slogans, and glib people who look and talk like game-show hosts. People with really "new ideas" wouldn't dream of introducing them to politics, because they know ideas can't be explained in sixty seconds.

I'm not intimating, incidentally, that people disinvolve themselves from their communities, social groups, or other voluntary organizations; just the opposite, since those relationships are the lifeblood of society. But the political process, or government, are not synonymous with society, or even complementary to it. Government is a dead hand on society.

USING THE "A" WORD

One of the most important books I've ever read, and possibly one of the most profound books ever written, is called *The Market for Liberty* by Morris and Linda Tannehill. The book is a cogent, well-reasoned presentation of how society would work in the absence of government. But nowhere in the book is that system named. What might it be called? I knew one of the authors, Morris Tannehill, and asked him why he never used the word *anarchism* in his text. He allowed that although the concept of society being organized on principles of voluntarism and laissez-faire was acceptable to most people of good will, the name for such a system, anarchism, had been purged from the vocabulary of those who wanted to be taken seriously. George Orwell recognized the force of such purging in his book *1984*, where he had his dystopian state reducing the number of words in the dictionary every year. A concept without a name is hard to grasp.

By definition, *democracy* means "rule of the people," *monarchy* means "rule of one," *oligarchy* means "rule of the few," and so forth. *Anarchism* means only "no rule." It doesn't mean "chaos," "disorder," or "violence." Like so many words, its true meaning has been misappropriated and twisted. The popular perception of an anarchist is a man dressed in a black cape skulking about with a round bomb, fuse lit. And certainly there have been violent anarchists, just as there have been violent Americans, violent Christians, violent parents, and violent doctors. But that's never been an essential or even an accidental characteristic of any of them.

Paradoxically, anarchism is the gentlest of political systems. It is the political manifestation of the ancient Chinese Taoist philosophy, what philosopher Alan Watts called the "watercourse way," where everything flows unrestricted, at its own pace, to its own level. Some have suggested that I abstain from using the word *anarchy* because it carries so much emotional baggage and arouses atavistic fears. But ideas should speak for themselves, and semantics should be used to clarify, not obscure, their meaning.

In many ways, reality is just a creation of widely shared opinions. Nothing should be accepted just because it exists, including the state. Concepts take on lives of their own, unless someone challenges them. And the concept of the state is sorely in need of challenge.

HOW TO GO THERE FROM HERE

Like the weather, everybody complains about politics, but nobody does anything about it. What can and should be done? In my view, a gentle shift to the right or the left has no hope of success. The Reagan administration had many ideological conservatives in its ranks whose battle cry was "If not us, who? If not now, when?" They had some limited success in rolling back the state in a few areas, like firing the striking air traffic controllers and reducing the maximum income tax rates, but were ineffectual overall. In fact, their main success was in expanding state activities favored by conservatives, like the military, the DEA, customs, NSA, and CIA, while leaving most of the liberal establishment intact.

The experience of Third World countries probably gives the best hint of what will happen in the United States. Third World governments have tried every conceivable variation on a socialist theme. Without exception, they ran their societies into the ground. It's rare that a downward trend can be turned around once it is underway, for the same reason it is impossible to stop a boulder once it starts rolling downhill. They only stop when they've hit bottom. There is no reason the United States should be any different. It will just take longer, since the country has so much capital and a more pronounced antiauthoritarian tradition than any other country.

A renaissance in liberty is more likely to occur in some country that's already been devastated by collectivism than in the United States. I've made it an avocation to try putting theory into practice by meeting with Third World leaders and presenting them with a plan to revitalize their bankrupt countries. What's to be done with basket cases?

In essence, I suggest that 100 percent of the government's assets, which typically means almost everything in these countries, be put in a public corporation, with the shares distributed pro rata to every man, woman, and child in the country although extra shares would necessarily be given to those in authority and a percentage would be put in trust for the next generation. A small percentage of the shares would be sold on major world markets to generate capital and establish a market price.

Since the assets of the government theoretically belong to the people, it's only fair to give those assets directly to the owners. This is important, since most "privatization" plans floated today feature auctioning off government assets, which ensures that only the rich, who have the money to bid, and the government, which gets the proceeds, benefit directly.

Distributing shares directly to the people puts the power where it belongs, but it's not enough. It would also be necessary to:

1. Spin off all state industrial and agricultural enterprises to shareholders, while reserving perhaps 30 percent for distribution to current employees, both to encourage loyalty and to act as a golden handshake for the many who will be redundant.

2. Allow the formation of unregulated stock exchanges where the above shares can be traded, and capital raised for new enterprises. Permit the establishment, without regulation, of private and foreign banks.

3. Take 100 percent of government gold and foreign currency reserves and use them to make the national currency completely convertible to all holders. It would soon become the world's most desired currency. Citizens would save it, not look to dump it for any tangibles available.

4. Totally abolish all duties, subsidies, exchange controls, taxes, ministries, bureaus, and regulations, with no exceptions. Ex-government employees could liquidate shares to sustain themselves while they found productive work.

5. The government would serve no function except to protect residents from common-law crimes of force and fraud. But private police forces and courts would be allowed on an equal basis. Schools, and all other useful government functions would be "spun off" like all other assets.

In every case, it's not a matter of "doing something," but simply of getting rid of laws, like a decades-old encrustation of barnacles, that make it impossible for the market to give people what they need. One thing that wouldn't be either needed or wanted is aid from foreign governments. As it always has, such aid only serves to entrench the old power structure. So counterproductive is aid that it's amazing people of good will even consider it. The answer lies in laissez-faire and freedom.

Should any country do something even approaching this proposal, its standard of living would surpass America's in only a few years, and the country would be inundated with foreign capital, labor, and entrepreneurs. What are the chances of it happening? Don't plan your life around it. But stranger things have occurred, and the leadership of several countries I've approached may try it, if only out of desperation. It would make them legitimately rich, domestically loved, and figures of world stature. That certainly beats waiting for the next revolution to put them up against the wall.

A similar plan would work in the United States; I discussed it briefly in *Strategic Investing*, but America has become one of the most conservative countries in the world, with a power structure for whom "change" is no more than an election-year buzzword.

KANSAS?

In my 1976 book, *The International Man*, I speculated about the inevitability of the breakup of many of the world's countries, most of which are arbitrary and artificial constructs of a bygone era. We've already seen the dissolution of the U.S.S.R.,

Yugoslavia, and Czechoslovakia, and that fate seems likely in Canada, China, and India. Most of Africa will eventually be restructured as well. But what about the United States? Few Americans consider the possibility, but it's likely at some point. Nothing lasts forever.

Economics will be at the root of any political upheaval. The federal government's taxes on some products, and subsidies on others, can only serve to antagonize people of different regions who depend on those products in different ways. When the average person's attention is drawn to the matter, he realizes that the federal government no longer serves much of a useful purpose; in a few years 100 percent of his taxes will go just to pay the interest on the national debt, and he gets little but harassment and regulations in return. And someone in the hinterland certainly has little desire to fund the welfare check of someone else in New York or Los Angeles. As times get tougher, more people are going to "just say no." And even start jumping ship, individually or collectively.

One straw in the wind was the 1992 referendum in nine rural counties in western Kansas to, believe it or not, secede from both Kansas and the United States. The referendum, held on presidential primary day in April of that election year, turned out over 50 percent of eligible voters, of whom 85 percent supported independence. More people voted on the referendum than voted in the primary itself. This is heady, radical stuff. In the heart of Middle America, Kansas, the average guy wants to secede.

The issue came to a head when a statewide school levy would have resulted in one county paying $350,000 more and receiving $3.5 million less. That's a big number when all nine counties together have only 36,000 residents. Another smoldering issue was the fact that 93 percent of the tax revenue generated by local gas wells goes to the state, while high state taxes are driving drillers from the area.

I spoke to the leader of the movement, Chris Concannon, an attorney. He always supported the Republicans, but feels they no longer represent his views on the way things ought to be. I told him that with the massive local support he's got, he should get the word out and take the show on the road. There's been a veritable media blackout on what's happening in those nine west Kansas counties, even though nothing like it has occurred since Shays's Rebellion after the War for Independence.

There's bound to be more of this type of thing as time goes on. The proposed separation of northern and southern California is another straw in the wind. It's going to take time to build momentum. But just as big companies are a shrinking force in the market, so are big countries, and that includes the United States.

One relatively new factor that will accelerate the trend is massive Hispanic immigration to Florida, Texas, and California. It doesn't appear that this latest wave of immigrants is being acculturated to nearly the degree of immigrants in the past, with the exception of getting hip to the welfare benefits available and the potential for filing lawsuits. This is no reflection on the new immigrants. It's a natural consequence of the laws encouraging such behavior. The U.S. legal and welfare structure makes it harder, not easier, for new immigrants to prosper.

THE FATE OF GOVERNMENT

Now, at the end of the twentieth century, the main danger to your wealth comes from government. Throughout this book, I've pinpointed opportunities to profit from the distortions government creates, or to at least limit the degree to which you're adversely affected by them. But speculating in self-defense would be unnecessary, were it not for the government.

I don't expect that the world will soon adopt a libertarian philosophy, but I do believe progress in that direction is inevitable, if only because of technological advances. Inventions like gunpowder, the printing press, and the computer have done far more to overpower oppression than every volume of political thought ever written. As technology has advanced, it has empowered the individual and has made the collective, the state, less important.

As progress continues, the state will become irrelevant. Marx will prove right: the state will wither away. But not because of political revolution, which can never be the answer.

There's reason to believe that the entire nature of life itself will be transformed within the next few decades, and the problems we have today—not just with government, but with the environment, poverty, pollution, and the material world at large—will become trivial.

That is the subject of the next chapter.

35

An Unlimited Future

I suspect reality is probably not only stranger than we imagine, but stranger than we can imagine.

J.B.S. Haldane

Any sufficiently advanced technology is indistinguishable from magic.

Arthur C. Clarke

The long upward trend of civilization, the accumulation of knowledge and capital and the rise in the general level of affluence, is likely to continue. It will be a story with a happy ending, notwithstanding the pitfalls along the way. And that's without even factoring in the probable technological breakthroughs to come in everything from space exploration and bioengineering to computer science.

At least one technology now developing, which very few people have heard of, has the potential to change the nature of reality as we know it, within the lifetime of most people now reading this book. That is nanotechnology: the use of machines and computers so small as to be in most cases submicroscopic, and so numerous as to approach the virulence of bacteria. This technology could solve virtually all of the material problems that have confronted man since he first manipulated tools—decisively, massively, and elegantly. The implications of this are enormous.

SOME PERSPECTIVE

I've often said that while the Greater Depression has the potential to be worse than even I think it's going to be, the further future will almost certainly be better than anyone can imagine. The economic turmoil we will see over the next decade will look like a baby step backward compared to the subsequent great leap forward. Of course, all futurism is necessarily only intelligent conjecture. Anticipating the future is a challenge; it's hard enough living in the present, since all our data and perceptions are out of the past.

That's probably why speculative science fiction has long been a better predictor of the future than the calculated projections of scientists: it's less conservative. Futurists can only extend and extrapolate present trends. They can't take into account breakthroughs and new discoveries, like the completely unexpected existence of the tunnel diode effect in transistors, because such events by their very nature are unpredictable.

Consider this nineteenth-century example. As the cities grew and the population grew wealthier, the horse population exploded. As a result, the streets of cities like New York and London were polluted with the noxious emissions of oat-powered "vehicles." If the trend toward more people and more horses had continued, the cities would have become uninhabitable. Not only the ordure gave people pause; it was also the horrible racket created by the clatter of wagon wheels and hooves against cobblestones and the cracking of whips. The storage of horse feed promoted a plague of vermin. The deteriorating situation was made to order for precursors of today's professional hysterics like Rifkin, Erlich, and Nader.

It was technology, in the form of the automobile, not legislation or regulation, that eliminated all those problems and created new ones. Depending on how loosely we define the word *significantly*, there have been at least seven significant technological revolutions since the beginning of human history.

First was probably the discovery that objects lying around the landscape could be employed as tools. Then perhaps a million years later, but only 10,000 years ago, people started cultivating plants and domesticating animals. It became possible to smelt rock and refine it into metal only about 5,500 years ago. For the first time man could alter the nature of raw matter and transform brittle rock into malleable metal. Cities started to arise at about the same time. Next was an energy revolution, starting a bit more than 200 years ago, when men replaced naturally occurring wind, stream, and muscle power with steam and then electricity. About 100 years ago mass production and interchangeable parts resulted in an abundance of manufactured goods. The computer revolution is the most recent of these fundamental revolutions. It allows man to multiply his brainpower by orders of magnitude, and it was the application of brainpower that made all the previous revolutions possible.

The rate of change has been accelerating exponentially and should continue to accelerate. Nanotechnology, already on the horizon, will almost surely be the next revolution. Notwithstanding the fact every improvement brings its own set of problems, life has improved for more and more people since the industrial revolution. Where will it lead? The most radical and most favorable outcome imaginable is also the most likely, and in the very near term. Nanotechnology promises not only to change the way you live but to change the entire nature of life as we perceive it. It's hard to overestimate the degree or quantity of change it holds in store.

ENGINES OF CREATION

At the heart of the technological evolution of the last few decades has been miniaturization. As things become smaller, they necessarily become cheaper, faster, and more flexible. They require less maintenance and less power.

Until very recently, everything that concerned us was on a more-or-less human scale; anything smaller than could be seen by a watchmaker through a loupe and manipulated with tweezers was only a curiosity.

The computer chip demonstrates how something very small can also be very powerful, but it's still a crude object compared to a bacterium or even a mite. A chip is smaller than a fingernail, and its surface is inscribed on the micro scale—patterns from one-tenth to one-hundredth of a millimeter in size. Its workings are invisible to the unaided eye. The future, it is widely believed, lies in further miniaturization. But that's correct only in a manner of speaking, since it views the direction of change from the wrong end of the telescope.

In actuality, the future does not lie in making smaller and smaller scratches and imprints on silicon. The next stage will probably be the building up of computers and machinery out of individual atoms themselves. The problem will not be how to build ever smaller devices, but how to construct bigger ones out of individual molecules. This is the manipulation of matter on the level of atoms and molecules. The scale is that of a nanometer—one-billionth of a meter. The process is nanotechnology.

WHAT COULD NANOTECHNOLOGY DO?

People today tend toward jaded cynicism when the potential of a new technology is described, if only as a reaction against the credulity of people in the '50s, who were convinced they would soon be living in the world of the Jetsons. But the age of nanotechnology is different. Nanomachines would have an almost infinite variety of uses in almost every field.

In medicine, nanotechnology has the potential to cure almost every illness and fraility afflicting the human body, including old age. Nanomachines could be programmed to course through your arteries and clear them of plaque. They could be programmed to knit a shattered bone overnight, or to regrow damaged nerves, or to reconstruct a diseased heart. Nanomachines could be programed to root out and disassemble cancerous cells or alien bacteria and viruses in your body. By replacing aged body parts, molecule by molecule, with total precision, nanotechnology might make a state resembling unending life possible. Several decades hence, we will view today's most-advanced surgical and pharmaceutical techniques the way people today see the medicine of the Civil War era.

Nanotechnology promises to solve most environmental problems. Pollution can be defined as the state of things being out place. There's nothing wrong with lead (unless it's in the atmosphere), and petroleum is very valuable (unless it's in your water supply). Nanomachines could be programmed to seek out offending compounds and segregate them—whereupon they would be transformed from noxious pollutants to valuable resources.

Or they could disassemble dangerous molecules into their basic components—in many instances hydrogen, oxygen, and carbon. Further industrial pollution would cease, since pollution is only a sign of waste, inefficiency, and primitive technology.

Space travel would become safe and cheap as it became possible to create rocket ships and engines from seamless, flawless structures, in a matter of hours, out of carbon transformed into crystalline diamond.

Resource scarcity would be a complete nonproblem, as would manufacturing. The nanomachines could be programmed to retrieve any element from almost any pile of dirt or mountain. Nanomachines could assemble these elements into the molecules of a desired compound, and from there into any product imaginable.

Perhaps inadvertently, science fiction has already anticipated nanotechnology. The obelisks in Arthur C. Clarke's *2001* trilogy can be explained as creations of nanotechnology, basically agglomerations of many trillions of molecule-sized machines with immense computing power. In the trilogy's final book, the obelisks multiply at a geometrically accelerating rate and consume the mass of Jupiter, turning it into a second sun. That trick could be performed by small machines reaching into the Jovian atmosphere, grasping atoms, rearranging them into machines like themselves, which in turn do the same. This illustrates a potential—and not unrealistic—risk of nanotechnology.

Another example is offered by the malevolent T1000 in the movie *Terminator 2*. The machine's ability to transform its appearance and shape instantly could be within the grasp of nanomachines.

HOW WOULD IT WORK?

The possibility of a near-infinite number of microscopic computers, each with the power of one of today's mainframes, directing ever smaller assemblers and robots, is not only realistic, it's almost inevitable. In essence, nanotechnological manufacturing would require two types of devices, computers and assemblers, all small enough that thousands could fit in the space of one human cell. It's possible to determine the ultimate limits of computing power, the cost of which has been dropping (and capabilities increasing) at a compound rate of over 30 percent annually for decades. It is realistic that—even at current rates, not counting breakthroughs—computers with the power of today's mainframes will be microscopic in size by about the year 2025.

The nanocomputers would direct "assemblers," nanomachines that would put individual molecules together into desired forms, including the creation of more assemblers. Depending on the size of the project, many trillions of them would work to create structures small enough to attack an AIDS virus in a cell, or large enough to tunnel through the earth to connect New York and London with a direct link.

The key is the creation of software to instruct the machines. IBM has found, to its loss, that software is much more valuable than hardware. Nanotechnology will take that trend to the *nth* degree.

It's likely that the distinction between computer science, engineering, and various branches of biology will blur in the decades to come. After all, DNA is really just a program that instructs everything from an amoeba and a flower to a human body how to assemble itself. And then, after assembly, how to replicate itself, choosing the raw materials and energy necessary from appropriate "food" molecules. Nanomachines in the form of genes already order the nature of life on earth. It's just going to provide more complexity and diversity when humans control what nanomachines do and create.

WHEN?

In April 1990, two scientists with IBM, at New Almaden, California, used a scanning tunneling microscope (STM) to manipulate 35 individual xenon atoms on a nickel crystal, spelling out the letters IBM. (See Figure 35-1.)

At the end of 1992, chemists at the University of California built an electrical battery one-hundredth the size of a human red blood cell. The battery consisted of copper and silver atoms that were manipulated with a scanning tunneling microscope; the longest dimension of the battery was 70 nanometers—.000,000,7 centimeters. (See Figure 35-2.)

The manipulation of materials on a nano-level is no longer exotic. The bumps that encode information on compact discs (CDs) are roughly 130 by 600 nanometers in size. The lubricating layer on top of a computer's hard disc must currently be about 10 angstroms (10 angstroms equal one nanometer) in thickness, with tolerances of plus or minus only 3–4 angstroms.

The scanning tunneling microscope, which allows the mapping and positioning of atoms with great precision, was invented in 1979. They are now commercially available through the mail and have been used in high school science fairs.

The progress toward nanotechnology could proceed and improve gradually, like that of the automobile since about 1900. Or it could burgeon overnight, as did nuclear technology after the detonation of the first atomic bomb. The odds favor the latter, since nanotechnology is capable of literally changing every aspect of human existence. Abrupt change has occurred frequently in the past. In communication, messages went from the speed of a horse (Pony Express) to near the speed of light (Western Union's telegraph and then Marconi's radio) almost overnight. Figure 35-3 illustrates how people in the future may view the change.

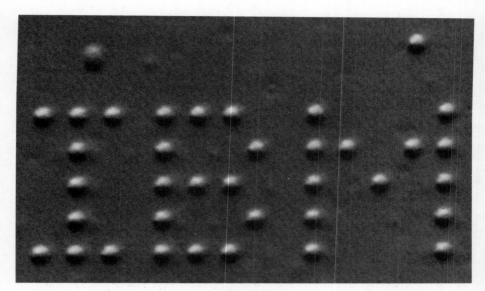

Figure 35-1

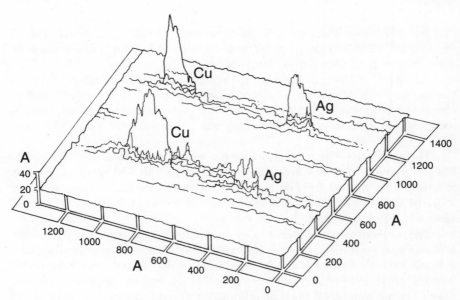

A scanning-tunneling-microscope picture of the world's smallest battery shows pillars of silver and copper atoms on a graphite surface. The numbers along the edges give the dimensions of the device in angstroms (ten-billionths of a meter).

Source: Popular Science

Figure 35-2

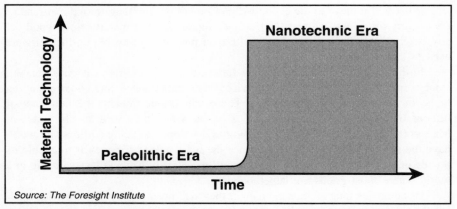

Source: The Foresight Institute

The expected abrupt transition from the paleolithic to nanotechnic eras (a long-term perspective). Stone-age agriculture and Moon landings lie in the transitional zone.

Figure 35-3

Eric Drexler, who is probably the leading theoretician in the field, believes we'll see numerous practical applications of nanotechnology within thirty years. As with most scientists, his projections are probably conservative.

THE IMPLICATIONS

The evolution of nanotechnology is probably inevitable. Its potential is so great that instead of the old scientific dictum "What can be done, will be done," it will be possible to say, "What can be imagined, can be created." It's simply a matter of writing the software to instruct the nanomachines.

The computer revolution was once the exclusive province of the world's top scientists, who needed the resources of the U.S. government to create the ENIAC in the 1940s. That machine filled a room, even though it had much less power than today's cheap calculators. By the '70s it was possible for two young men working in a garage to create the basis for the personal computer industry, giving the average man the power only top government scientists had possessed a few decades earlier. This in turn was a major factor in the collapse of the Soviet empire and in the restructuring of the world's political landscape.

Just as the industrial revolution gave the individual a standard of living superior to that of a king before its start, the nanotechnology revolution will give every individual access to more wealth than any billionaire alive today. Its power today to transform reality makes it plausible for everyone to, in effect, control his local environment as thoroughly as the crew of *Starship Enterprise* controls the environment of the "holodeck."

What will it mean to the economy? For one thing, the long-term downtrend of commodity prices will plunge. Not only commodities, but manufactured goods of any description will be worth little more than the royalty payable on the software used to create them.

In the long-run nanotechnological future, the value of shares is questionable, since corporations exist to provide services and create goods—and goods are going to be in a state of superabundance. There will unquestionably be hundreds of billions of dollars made—and scores of people who do as well as Bill Gates of Microsoft—as various enabling technologies develop. But being a billionaire won't have the significance it does today, since the main value of money is to enable its possessor to manipulate reality. Money will necessarily become less valuable in a world where most goods are superabundant.

Of course as long as men exchange, they will need money. But notwithstanding the arguments I made earlier, that function is unlikely to be served by gold in a nanotechnological era. Its cost of production will drop to trivial levels. The market will find some type of substitute money, probably related to the software that will make the world go round.

One good bet to retain value is raw land in idyllic locations; the trend I described for remote real estate will stay in motion for a long time.

Nanotechnology will not affect your three-to-five-year investment strategy much. I do not expect it to help us avert the Greater Depression. But everyone should have a long-range perspective. I've included this chapter for that reason.

As nanotechnology develops I expect the prices of commodities and manufactured goods to plunge and the value of remote, pristine real estate to soar. I also expect government and some modern-day Luddites to oppose nanotechnology's progress.

Hopefully, as with computers, the field will grow in the hands of private enterprise so that our federal agencies do not withhold the technology from us (as too "strategically important") or use it against us.

We're living on the cusp of the most important times in the history of the world. Everything is important from a point of view rooted in the present, but few things really are important if you look at them from a 100-year perspective. Recognizing how profoundly and totally different our existence will likely be only a few decades hence provides as valid a Zen experience as could be gained from a lifetime sitting in a lotus posture. It certainly inspires a very mellow form of optimism. And it puts the hiccups we'll encounter along the way into perspective, much along the lines Haldane and Clarke intimated with their quotes at the start of this chapter. Nanotechnology offers the prospect of more than just the "End of History." It offers *Childhood's End** for mankind itself.

Keep your mind clear, your powder dry, and the world will turn. The next chapter will give you a few ideas along those lines.

Childhood's End, by Arthur C. Clarke, a science fiction treatment of the next stage of man's evolution.

36

The Bag Can Be Full Enough

No matter what their income, a depressing number of Americans believe that if only they had twice as much, they would inherit the estate of happiness promised them in the Declaration of Independence. The man who receives $15,000 a year is sure that he could relieve his sorrow if only he had $30,000 a year. The man with $1 million a year knows that all would be well if he had $2 million a year. Nobody ever has enough.

Lewis Lapham

He who knows he has enough is rich.

Tao Te Ching

It is better to *live* rich than to *die* rich.

Samuel Johnson

Charlie, my first stockbroker, said, "The bag is never full enough." He made that comment in reference to the amount of money you need to do what you would like. I was twenty-three at the time and, although I implicitly recognized the truth of what he was saying, it really wasn't very relevant at the time. I was just a year out of college, and my requirements were low. I could put all my worldly possessions in my Mustang; and since they about filled it up, I already seemed to have too much junk. In a way the bag was too full, even though there was very little in it. But the phrase stuck with me.

As time went by I acquired books, athletic equipment, furniture, clothes, animals, and "stuff." My overhead constantly rose: larger house, bigger utility bills, more insurance, better cars. It is now easy to see what Charlie was driving at: the more you have, the more you seem to need.

This gives rise to the question of exactly how much you actually *do* need. And that leads to the question of what it takes, at least in the material world, to make you happy. Of course, it is well known that money won't make you happy, but it certainly can soften the condition of unhappiness. We all want more money. And "we" includes everyone from your barber to Fidel Castro, and your kids to Mother

Teresa. The first rule of existence is to survive, and the more material goods you have, the better your chances are. More *is* better.

Of course, there's more to life than material goods. You need time to do the things you have always wanted to do, most of which take little or no money. And people who are obsessed with money almost never have any time. We all know people who drive themselves crazy with work, not because they like it, as Sam Walton did, nor because they need the money. We are back to that word *need* again.

A friend, with whom I'll hop a freight and ride the rails for a week most summers, is a professional hobo. He needs no more than $10 a day, and neither do I when I'm with him. Sam Walton was a multibillionaire, but he apparently needed no more than $100 a day, not counting his comfortable but modest home. But I know some aging yuppies who seem to need $1,000 daily to maintain their lifestyles; as a result they work fifteen-hour days but still have loads of debt and little cash. It's relative, but less can also be more.

A WAY OUT

It is also a question of psychology. A friend, Paul Terhorst, was a partner in a large accounting firm. He made big money, but in order to maintain the image required of a partner, he had to spend big money. He needed a big house in a good area with a big mortgage, a prestigious car (actually two), and expensive suits. He had to entertain and keep up with the Joneses. He worked so hard and long to support the lifestyle necessitated by his success that he had no time for the things he really wanted to do.

Paul sat down and did some arithmetic. He totaled how much he would collect by liquidating all his assets: the cars, the house, the pension, the artwork. It came to $500,000. Was it enough to live the life he and his wife wanted?

Invested at 8 percent it would yield $40,000 a year, only about a third of what he was earning. But he no longer would have to pay Social Security taxes, which are due only on "earned" income. He would not need auto, homeowners', and similar insurance. He would no longer need to maintain his possessions and support gardeners, maids, and mechanics. He would no longer have monstrous house and car payments. He and his wife would no longer have to keep up with the Joneses. And his income would be about twice what the average person made working full-time. So he decided to quit his job. Instead of working for capital he would let his capital work for him.

It was quite a shock. He had been raised with the idea that we are not supposed to do what we want to do before age sixty-two (retirement). And the concept that we are who we are, not what we do, took some getting used to. But he chose wisely.

In the ten years since Paul and his wife, Vicki, have dropped out of the rat race, they have read everything they ever wanted to read, been everywhere they've ever wanted to go, and still do whatever they want to do. In his spare time Paul has written several novels and played a lot of chess and in general has been able to follow his desires.

In fact, Paul has more money now than he did when he retired, he is in better health, and he has had a lifetime of experiences he would never have gained if he had continued as an accountant in Los Angeles. He spends a lot of time in Third World countries where the climate is good, the natives are friendly, and the cost of living is low. When he is in the United States, he usually rents a place near the ocean in the South where there are few jobs and prices reflect that fact. He doesn't need a job but appreciates the low cost of living and the mellow lifestyle that can be found away from the economic mainstream.

Best of all, if he wants to go back to work, he can. But I doubt he will; he is having too much fun and doing too much to want back what he has already given up. More likely he will use a small part of his capital to do deals which interest him when his thoughts turn to money.

I have observed his lifestyle and those of several others who have done much the same thing. There is much to recommend it in the Age of Envy, when ostentatious wealth of the kind people in the '80s were so fond of may bring all kinds of attention you do not want.

The key concept is not working for your possessions, but liquidating them so the capital they represent can work for you. Instead of making a $6,000 monthly mortgage payment on a $700,000 house in which you have $200,000 of equity, you would be better off putting the $6,000 in a money market fund each month and collecting another $15,000 per year in interest from the $200,000 equity that would be available if you sold the house. This is especially true in an environment of falling property prices, as we have had for the last couple of years and are likely to have for at least several more. By the time you add in the car payments, taxes, insurance, and the rest of it, you may find that your possessions own you and you are spending most of your time working for them, not yourself. It's nice to have a lot of stuff, but it may be nicer to have a lot of income and experiences and a lot less stress.

Some people are taking this approach even further and are adopting the lifestyle popularized by writer Harry Shultz, the Permanent Traveler, the Perpetual Tourist, the Prior Taxpayer. Rent a place in southern France in the spring, go skiing in Chile in July and August, go hiking in the Rockies during September, then rent a place on the beach in South Africa for a couple months to catch up on your reading. You get the idea.

You are interested in money or you wouldn't be reading this book. But the purpose of having more money is to get what you want out of life. And you may have more than enough money to do that right now, if you just take stock and reallocate it. Think about it, because the clock is always ticking. Perhaps Paul Terhorst's approach isn't for you, but if you at least see it as an option, it will lead you to consider other options. There are many paths up the mountain.

What you decide to do, if anything, will reflect your views on money itself.

MONEY AS A ZEN EXPERIENCE

Attitudes toward money are a psychological watershed that reflect on every aspect of life. Your attitude toward money reveals your attitude toward life itself. There are two schools among those who take the trouble to formulate their thoughts.

One school, the dominant view of society, sees money itself, or at least the love of money, as the root of all evil. It is viewed as the root of divorces and lawsuits, robberies and murders, lying and fraud. But money, although evil to them, is considered a necessary evil, and that thought helps to rationalize the effort to get more of it.

The other school, to which I belong, sees money as a moral good, representing all the good things in life you want to have, do, and provide for others. Insofar as you spend the days of your life working for it, money represents concentrated life. This view doesn't need to rationalize the quest for wealth.

It is odd that the "money is evil" school is usually seen as morally superior—more detached, spiritual, and concerned about ethereal values. It is odd because when these folks attempt to make money, they are living a lie and being hypocrites. If they do not make money, they are being self-destructive, parasitic, and a burden to others.

Loathing money in principle, but being forced to deal with it in practice, presents what Marx would call an internal contradiction. It calls for constant justification and a constant effort to make reality conform to a belief system, rather than matching the belief system to reality. That is why legislation on economic matters is almost universally disastrous: it amounts to no more than a dramatization of the fantasies and wishful thinking of those who draft it. Such legislation would be a joke, not to be taken seriously, except for the inconvenience and destruction it causes.

Money, wealth, and possessions are a hot button for people in general; they bring up an area of "charge" that's almost tangible. That kind of reaction is predictable in areas of life (sex, politics, and religion are others) fraught with irrational motives and impulses. Because it is so highly charged, many people have trouble confronting money directly. Confronting it doesn't mean studying conventional economics, full of bizarre mathematical formulas describing abstractions that have nothing to do with the real world. Confronting money—growing comfortable with the concept—is a subjective, introspective process; economics, after all, is really a division of philosophy. As with all "charged" areas of life, when you confront it squarely, money is no more intimidating or confusing than a flower or an ice cream cone.

Antagonism toward money goes beyond dollars and bank accounts, however. From an economic viewpoint, money is a medium of exchange and a store of value; its main value is to represent other goods. So, what do money-haters think about the material universe that money represents? The logical conclusion is that they don't like the world at large, or at least they are very uncomfortable with it. That is hardly a formula for spiritual serenity and is doubly strange for people who pretend to being detached, spiritual, and ethereal.

Anticapitalists tend to view money as an artificial and deadly barrier to personal evolution, when it is really an integral stepping-stone to further evolution. People who blame money for the evils of the world suffer from a lack of responsibility at best; assigning blame isn't an optimal way of making evils go away. In fact, readily assigning blame elsewhere has caused most of the poverty, war, and general misery that history catalogues.

Attitudes toward money tend to be ingrained. The philosophical notions underpinning the way one deals with the world cannot be swayed by written arguments and appeals to logic. Where the roots to the problem are psychological or spiritual, an intellectual understanding doesn't really help.

THE BIG PICTURE

I notice that—notwithstanding their philosophical aversion to money—as people get older, they seem to get more, not less, money-oriented. This is somewhat counter-intuitive; you might think that the older you get and the less time you have left, you would focus more on inner values. But instead, once people hit middle age, they seem to become more grasping and to try to clutch the material world to themselves ever more strongly, at the very time they should be trying to let go of it. It is perverse, but humanity is replete with contradictions.

So, despite most people's philosophical aversion to money, they do their best to accumulate more and spend less as they get older. Those who are successful leave an estate that can be distributed to their children or to charity.

Certainly it is nice to have a bequest from a parent or "rich uncle"; sometimes it can be put to good use and generate a great deal of pleasure. As often as not, however, it can lead to indolence, dissipation, and guilt. Receiving the unearned often leads to guilt; compounded with the prevailing views on money, it is not surprising that heirs often suffer from low self-esteem.

That is partially why giving money away to charities is appealing. But most charities turn into vehicles for their organizers; board members and executives travel first class, hire secretaries, pay themselves fat fees, and create bureaucracies whose existence eventually becomes more important than the original objective of the charity. And charities can wind up destroying those they are supposed to help, just as government welfare programs often do. Certainly Ford and Carnegie would have a fit if they could see what the foundations bearing their names have done with their money. I suspect they would have sooner put it in a big pile and burned it.

So, you might ask yourself, what's the real meaning of money? And, for that matter, what's the meaning of life? Once you have enough money, you have the leisure to address the bigger question. People who are barely making ends meet have less time for philosophical reflection.

It is understandable that when you think about how much money you "need," how much time you should spend, and the risk you should take to accumulate the stuff, it puts you in a quandary. The enormity of the task and its seeming futility cause some people to not even try to become wealthy. The attitude toward money they have absorbed from society often persuades them they have chosen wisely in eschewing wealth.

I have had many millions of dollars pass through my hands. But much more valuable than the money are the experiences and knowledge I've gained from the money I no longer have. We come into the world with nothing and we die with nothing. But in between, while we are living in the material world, we try to lay claim to it. That is natural because the first imperative of life is to survive, and the more we have, the easier it is to do so. It leads back to the condition of those who are anti money or anti wealth; by hating these things, they, by implication, hate life.

Even while we are alive, our ownership of things is fleeting. A fire, a flood, a war, or some action of the government could take it all away in an instant. And even though the situation may at that moment seem hopeless, it is not really serious. You finally realize that what you really own are not your possessions, but your experiences, skills, and knowledge. That is all that's really essentially you, and that can never be taken from you. Should you lose your material possessions, as has happened to millions of people throughout the world, throughout history, then it is your essential self that will allow you to regain possessions, if you so choose.

My objective in this book has been to present options and strategies that should prove rewarding over the rest of the decade. I'm using them myself. I have little doubt that although the rest of the '90s will be grim in many ways for most people, they will result in the creation of a whole new class of multimillionaires. I sincerely hope that you are one of them.

Good luck and good hunting.

Further Helps

There's never any "last word" on a subject, and that's certainly true of investment strategies. But you might want to contact the following people, organizations, books, and publications for more information in their respective areas.

Brokers. There are tens of thousands of stockbrokers out there; most just sell what management tells them to, or passively take orders. I've known the following for years, and can vouch for their competence. Each has a different approach and specialty.

IN THE UNITED STATES

Rick Rule, gold, oil, and other resource stocks
   1-800-477-7853, 1-619-943-3939

Bruce Greene, options, commodities and big board stocks
   1-800-322-8740, 1-708-564-5054

Gene Jewett, telecommunications issues
   1-800-488-4485, 1-202-783-8162

Ben Johnson, gold stocks
   1-800-547-4898, 1-503-256-2011

Maggie Carey, NYSE issues
   1-800-777-0210, 1-212-415-7878

Jim Love, McDermid St., Lawrence
   601 West Hastings St., Vancouver, BC V6B 5E2
   1-800-663-8198, 1-604-654-1110

Greg Hall, Canaccord
   2200-609 Granville, Vancouver, BC V7Y 1H2
   1-800-663-8061, 1-604-643-7446

Ron Loewen, Pacific International
   1500-700 W. Georgia St., Vancouver, BC V7Y 1G1
   1-800-663-8450, 1-604-664-2966

For gold and silver coins, the following are solid, competitive and ethical:

Jefferson Coin and Bullion,
   2400 Jefferson Highway #600, Jefferson, CA 70121.
   1-800-593-2585

Bill Bradford, R. W. Bradford Coins.
   1-206-385-5097

Van Simmons, David Hall Coins.
   1-714-261-0509

George Hall, Monex International.
   1-714-752-1400, 1-806-949-4653

Money Management

The best alternative is almost always to manage your own money. But some don't
have the interest, don't care to devote the necessary time, or are just too busy.

   In the area of stocks, I work as a consultant with Adrian Day, of *Investment
Consultants International*. His firm offers gold, hedge, short, and international
accounts, and his record is nothing short of spectacular. 1-410-224-8885, fax
1-410-224-8229.

   In commodities, I've worked with *Darrell Brookstein* for years.
1-805-965-9927.

   The money market fund to which I serve as a consultant is Permanent Portfolio
Fund run by *Terry Coxon*, 625 2nd Street #102, Petaluma, CA 94952.
1-707-778-1000. He can help you with portfolio and tax planning and international
asset protection strategies.

Books

I've made a number of references to the thoughts of Herman Kahn, in chapters 1
and 31. His books are now out of print, but worth finding in used book stores. In
particular, you might enjoy *The Next 200 Years*, *The Coming Boom*, and *World
Economic Development*.

The best short book ever written on economics, and the subjects covered in Part I of this book, is Henry Hazlitt's classic *Economics in One Lesson*. In addition, almost anything written by Harry Browne, John Pugsley, Friedrich von Hayek, Ludwig von Mises, Mark Skousen, and Milton Friedman approach the subject with clarity and intelligence. Skousen's recently published *Economics on Trial* deserves a special mention for its excellent debunking of most current notions taught in schools. Another recent book, which breaks new ground, is Michael Rothschild's *Bionomics*. Harry Figgie's *Bankruptcy 1995* is widely available and particularly topical.

There are thousands of investment books, dealing with the matter covered in Part II. I have a low opinion of most, finding them pedestrian, superficial, conventional, and amateurish. Your best bet is to choose what to read by the author, rather than the subject. Once again, look for works by Harry Browne, Jack Pugsley, and Mark Skousen. Among other books currently in print, you should read Seth Klarman's *Margin of Safety*, Jim Davidson's *The Great Reckoning*, Peter Lynch's *One Up on Wall Street*, and Arthur Lipper's *Venture Capital and Investing in Private Companies*. Gerald Loeb's classic *The Battle for Investment Survival*, and Benjamin Graham's classic *The Intelligent Investor* are essential components of an investment library.

Few data are available on the subject matter discussed in chapter 26. My own *The International Man* is still timely, even though it was written in 1976.

My thoughts on what the baby boomers will be up to had their genesis in William Strauss and Neil Howe's *Generations*, an original study of the cyclical nature of American history, going back to the seventeenth century.

Rick Maybury's *Whatever Happened to Justice?* is a simple, but well-done study of the nature of law and our legal system—the subject of chapter 30.

Morris and Linda Tannahill's classic *Market for Liberty* first drew my attention to how society would work without government, the subject of chapter 31; I consider it one of the most important books ever written. David Friedman's *Machinery of Freedom* is also good. In the way of periodicals along these lines, I suggest *Liberty Magazine*, Box 1181, Port Townsend, WA 98368; *Reason Magazine*, Box 526, Mount Morris, IL 61054, and *Freedom Daily*, Box 9752, Denver, CO 80209

Eric Drexler has, so far, written the only books on the subject of nanotechnology, *Engines of Creation* and *Unbounding the Future*, the subject of chapter 35.

Paul and Vicki Terhorst's *How to Retire at 35* amplifies many of the themes in chapter 36.

Many of these books can still be found in bookstores, but with fifty thousand new volumes published annually it can be tough on even the biggest stores to keep all worthwhile books in stock. There are four mail-order companies that should carry most of them, and many others of interest:

Laissez-Faire Books, 532 Broadway, New York, NY 10012
  1-800-326-0996

Paladin, P.O. Box 1307, Boulder, CO 80306
   1-303-443-7250
Liberty Tree, 134 98th Ave, Oakland, CA 94603

Newsletters

There are hundreds of investment newsletters available, and they vary greatly in approach and quality. I don't always agree with the advice offered by those below, but they are well thought out, and the authors' economics are generally sound.

Analysis & Outlook (Bill Bradford), Box 1167, Port Townsend, WA 98368

Deliberations (Ian MacAvity), $225, Box 43310, Tucson, AZ 85733

Dow Theory Letters (Richard Russell), $225, Box 1759, La Jolla, CA 92037

Early Warning Report (Rick Maybury), $149, Box 1281-Q, Orangevale, CA 95662

Financial Privacy (Mike Ketcher), $156, Box 1277, Burnsville, MN 55337

Forecasts & Strategies (Mark Skousen), $177, 7811 Montrose Rd, Potomac, MD 20854

The Free Market (Lew Rockwell), $25, Ludwig von Mises Institute, Auburn, AL 36849-5301

Gold Mining Stock Report (Bob Bishop), $119, Box 1217, Lafayette, CA 94549

Gold Newsletter (James Blanchard), $79, 2400 Jefferson Highway #600, Jefferson, LA 70121 or 1-800-877-8847 for a free copy.

Growth Stock Outlook (Charles Allmon), $195, 4405 East-West Hy, Chevy Chase, MD 20814

Harry Browne's Special Reports, $250, Box 5847, Austin, TX 78763

Insider's Report (Larry Abraham), $99, Box 467939, Atlanta, GA 30346

International Living, 824 E. Baltimore St., Baltimore, MD 21202

Investment Analyst (Adrian Day), $87, 824 E. Baltimore St., Baltimore, MD 21202

John Pugsley's Journal, $125, 824 E. Baltimore St., Baltimore, MD 21202

Kondratieff Wave Analyst (Donald Hoppe), $125, Box 977, Crystal Lake, IL 60039

Low Profile (Mark Nestmann), $149, Box 84906, Phoenix, AZ 85701

Oil and Gas Analyst (Rick Rule), $95, 7770 El Camino Rd, Carlsbad, CA 92009

The Reaper (R.E. McMaster), $195, Box 84901, Phoenix, AZ 85071

Remnant Review (Gary North), $95, Box 84906, Phoenix, AZ 85071

Ron Paul Investment Letter, $99, 18333 Egret Bay Blvd, #265, Houston, TX 77058

Safe Money (Martin Weiss), Box 2923, West Palm Beach, FL 33402

Smart Investing (Ken Gerbino), $139, 7811 Montrose Rd, Potomac, MD 20854

Strategic Investing (James Davidson), $109, 824 E. Baltimore St., Baltimore, MD 21202

My own monthly newsletter is *Crisis Investing*, $145, Box 5195, Helena, MT 59604. I can be reached at that address (c/o Bruce Meadows, of Assets Management).

Return to: *Crisis Investing* Box 5195 Helena, MT 59604 406-443-0741	The markets will fluctuate radically over the next several years. Doug Casey monitors them, and provides monthly buy and sell advice in his newsletter *Crisis Investing* published since 1979. Return this coupon for a free sample issue.

Name

Street   Apt. #

City   State   Zip Code

Miscellaneous

Network Marketing/Retail: The most knowledgeable and ethical person I know of in the multilevel business is *Toni Reilly*, of Genesis 2000 Biologic Systems, 602-934-9141 or 1-800-448-3479 ext. 500. Their product line is nutritional and health items that are not available elsewhere.

Law: A good lawyer is, unfortunately, of critical importance in today's world. Two excellent men, who are sympathetic with the views in this book and have a national and international clientele are:
Bob Martin, 818-793-8500
Ken Korb, 617-367-9595

Index